*Sexual Orientation
& Human Rights in
American Religious Discourse*

Sexual Orientation
& Human Rights in
American Religious Discourse

Edited by
SAUL M. OLYAN &
MARTHA C. NUSSBAUM

New York   Oxford   •   Oxford University Press 1998

Oxford University Press

Oxford   New York
Athens   Auckland   Bangkok   Bogota   Bombay
Buenos Aires   Calcutta   Cape Town   Dar es Salaam
Dehli   Florence   Hong Kong   Istanbul   Karachi
Kuala Lumpur   Madras   Madrid   Melbourne
Mexico City   Nairobi   Paris   Singapore
Taipei   Tokyo   Toronto   Warsaw

and associated companies in
Berlin   Ibadan

Published by Oxford University Press, Inc.
198 Madison Avenue, New York, New York 10016

Library of Congress Cataloging-in-Publication Data
Sexual orientation and human rights
in American religious discourse/
edited by Saul M. Olyan and Martha C. Nussbaum.
p. cm.
Includes bibliographical references and index.
ISBN 0-19-511942-8
1. Homosexuality—Religious aspects—Christianity. 2. Gay rights—
Religious aspects—Christianity. 3. Homosexuality—Religious
aspects—Judaism. 4. Gay rights—Religious aspects—Judaism.
5. Homosexuality—Government policy—United States. 6. Gay rights—
United States. I. Olyan, Saul M. II. Nussbaum, Martha Craven.
1947-   .
BR115.H6S49 1998
261.8'35766'0973—dc21   97-30759

1   3   5   7   9   6   4   2
Printed in the United States of America
on acid-free paper

Acknowledgments

This book would not have been possible were it not for a number of individuals who contributed time, ideas, and energy at different stages in its development. Without the efforts of Gail Tetreault, Danya Ruttenberg, Andrew Flescher, Jillian Spear, Keith Green, Lydia English, Wendy Schiller, Sumner B. Twiss, Stanley Stowers, Shaye J. D. Cohen, Kathryn Tanner, and Eugene Rogers, the conference out of which this volume grew would not have been nearly the success that it was. A number of units at Brown University contributed money and other forms of support to the conference, and we would like to take this opportunity to thank each of them: Religious Studies, Judaic Studies, Philosophy, American Civilization, Political Science, Afro-American Studies, the Center for the Study of Race and Ethnicity in America, and Classics. We would also like to thank the Dean of the Faculty (Faculty Development Fund), the Office of the President, and the C.V. Starr Foundation Lectureships Fund for significant financial support. The Rhode Island Committee for the Humanities awarded the organizers an early response grant, and Steven A. Freedman, M.D., generously contributed a private donation to support the conference. We are grateful for the consistent support and interest of Cynthia Read at Oxford University Press during the development of the book, especially when things got rocky. Nathaniel Levtow's efforts during the production stage have been indispensable, and Abraham G. Hendin's assistance with computing is much appreciated; our thanks to Brown's Program in Judaic Studies for providing both of them to us as editorial assistants. Saul Olyan would also like to thank Ellen Barth for her assistance tracking down documents during the development of the introductory essay for the Judaism section. Martha Nussbaum thanks Sonia Katyal for assistance at the proofreading stage. Finally, a word of thanks to each of our contributors.

Contents

Part Two: Two Legal Perspectives

Contributors

VICTOR ANDERSON, Assistant Professor of Christian Ethics, Vanderbilt University Divinity School

CHARLES E. CURRAN, Elizabeth Scurlock University Professor of Human Values, Southern Methodist University

MARGARET A. FARLEY, Stark Professor of Christian Ethics, Yale Divinity School

LEWIS R. GORDON, Associate Professor of Afro-American Studies and Religious Studies, Brown University

KEITH GREEN, Adjunct Assistant Professor in the Humanities and Master of Liberal Arts Programs, University of North Carolina at Asheville

JAMES P. HANIGAN, Professor of Moral Theology, Duquesne University

WILLIAM D. HART, Assistant Professor of Religion, Duke University

ANDREW KOPPELMAN, Assistant Professor of Law, Northwestern University

MICHAEL W. MCCONNELL, Presidential Professor, University of Utah College of Law

LOUIS E. NEWMAN, Associate Professor of Religion, Carleton College

DAVID NOVAK, The J. Richard and Dorothy Shiff Chair of Jewish Studies, University of Toronto

MARTHA C. NUSSBAUM, Ernst Freund Professor of Law and Ethics, University of Chicago, with appointments in the Law School, the Divinity School, and the Department of Philosophy

SAUL M. OLYAN, Dorot Associate Professor of Judaic Studies and Associate Professor of Religious Studies, Brown University

JUDITH PLASKOW, Professor of Systematic Theology and Women in Religion, Manhattan College

EUGENE F. ROGERS, JR., Assistant Professor of Religious Studies, University of Virginia

CHERYL J. SANDERS, Professor of Christian Ethics, Howard University School of Divinity

MAX L. STACKHOUSE, Stephen Colwell Professor of Christian Ethics, Princeton Theological Seminary

KATHRYN TANNER, Associate Professor of Christian Thought, University of Chicago Divinity School

SUMNER B. TWISS, Professor of Religious Studies, Brown University

Introduction

Sexual orientation is currently a topic of intense debate within a number of American religious traditions, just as it is throughout American society. Roman Catholics, Jews, and members of major Protestant denominations are presently engaged in vigorous deliberation about the proper place of bisexuals, lesbians, and gay men in religious communities; about how those communities ought to regard same-sex sexual behavior; and about whether those communities and their individual members ought to advocate, oppose, or take no public position on civil rights protections and other proposed legal rights and benefits—including marriage—for gay men, lesbians, and bisexuals. These debates have recently had a significant impact on the formation of public policy in this country. One example is the legal debate surrounding Amendment Two, the Colorado law prohibiting state and local agencies from passing laws protecting lesbians, gay men, and bisexuals from discrimination. At the trial, the state's witnesses included prominent Roman Catholic and Jewish theological scholars, who testified about the relationship of the law to the state's interest in protecting both religious freedom and public morality. In the process, these witnesses presented interpretations of the teachings of their own traditions that are not uncontroversial within those traditions. The State District Court's opinion in the case did recognize that the protection of religious freedom is "a compelling state interest," although that did not lead to a ruling that Amendment Two was constitutional, since the court ruled that it would have been possible simply to exempt religious institutions from local nondiscrimination laws, as two of the existing local ordinances actually had. Therefore, Amendment Two was not "narrowly tailored to achieve that result in the least burdensome manner possible." Upon eventual appeal to the Supreme Court of the United States, Amendment Two was found to be unconstitutional by a majority of 6–3; the majority argued that it violated the Equal Protection clause of the Fourteenth Amendment to the Constitution of the

United States.[1] (When the case was argued before the Supreme Court, it was argued in a way that did not involve debate about whether the state had a "compelling interest" in the amendment, and therefore the issues of religion and public morality that had played a role in the original trial played no role in the Supreme Court's reasoning about the case.)

The Colorado constitutional amendment was in no way an isolated case: in the courts, in political discourse, and within religious communities throughout this country, sexual orientation has become a contested issue of great prominence, *the* issue of the nineties according to some, and Americans of faith as well as religious groups are contributing—often vigorously—to the ongoing debate as it unfolds. As bisexuals, lesbians, and gay men continue to press for legal rights and protections, as they increasingly demand that their presence in various political, social, and religious institutions be fully acknowledged and even accepted, and as their opponents react to their increasing restiveness with state and local referenda opposing civil rights protections for bisexuals, lesbians, and gay men, statutes outlawing same-sex marriage, opposition to the religious ordination of gay men, lesbians, and bisexuals, and any number of other initiatives, how will the rest of American society respond? Will "mainstream" America come increasingly to accept gay men, lesbians, and bisexuals as fully equal citizens, with all the rights, privileges, and obligations accorded to other Americans? Or will lesbians, gay men, and bisexuals be pushed back to the margins, present but not fully acknowledged or accepted as members of society? Without doubt, citizens of faith and religious communities will help to determine the outcome through their contributions to public deliberation.

There are many public contexts in which religious discourse has been brought to bear on this divisive debate. In recent discussion concerning sexual orientation and military service, civil rights protections for lesbians, bisexuals, and gay men, same-sex marriage, parenting and foster parenting, and even benefits for same-sex partners of bisexual, gay, and lesbian employees of major corporations and institutions, individual Americans who locate themselves squarely within a religious tradition, and American religious groups themselves, have articulated positions both pro and con, thereby helping to shape the debate. The Southern Baptist Convention recently called for a boycott of Disney because the company had extended benefits to the partners of gay and lesbian employees; in contrast, Judaism's Reform Movement has advocated military service and civil marriage for lesbians, gay men, and bisexuals, while officially opposing antigay referenda. Within the Roman Catholic Church, cardinals and archbishops have spoken out both for and against state and local civil rights laws aimed at protecting gay men, lesbians, and bisexuals, as Charles Curran points out in his essay in this volume.

Division is also discernible with respect to the way in which American religious groups integrate, ignore, or exclude their gay, lesbian, and bisexual members. Most American religious groups view same-sex sexual behavior negatively, and many accept as members in good standing only those lesbians, gay men, and bisexuals who are celibate or are quiet about their sexuality. In stark contrast, a few American religious groups will ordain openly gay and sexually active clergy and allow all clergy to perform commitment ceremonies for same-sex couples (e.g., the

Unitarian Universalist Association); one religious group—Reconstructionist Judaism—even goes so far as to accord to committed, homosexual partnerships the same religious status it assigns to committed, heterosexual marriages. Clearly, Americans of faith and American religious institutions have made their voices heard on both sides of this societywide controversy.

In light of the recent conflicts both within religious communities and in the public domain, it seems urgent to foster a climate of reasoned dialogue and debate on these controversial issues. The essays in this volume, most of which derive from a conference held at Brown University in the spring of 1995, are intended to promote both academic and public understanding of the different positions that exist on sexual orientation and its public policy dimensions within four major American religious traditions. We believe that a more adequate understanding of the debates as they are actually unfolding will help to promote a more productive approach to the issues, an approach that values argument, scholarship, and mutual respect. The intense emotions many people have about these questions have sometimes prevented them from speaking to others with the regard due to fellow citizens with deeply held convictions. We offer this volume as a contribution to the possibility of an informed, rational public deliberation, where very often there has been little more than dogmatic assertion and a lack of serious intellectual engagement.

The impetus for this project came, in fact, from just such a case of respectful confrontation. In February 1994, Martha Nussbaum was at the University of Virginia delivering a lecture on some of the texts concerning homosexuality from ancient Greek tradition, as they figured in the trial of Amendment Two in Colorado, where she had been a rebuttal witness for the plaintiffs. In the question period, someone asked her whether some of the conservative positions she had failed to find in the Greek texts could not be supported from within the Jewish tradition. Nussbaum replied that, although she is Jewish and indeed a convert to Judaism, she learned only the minimum of Hebrew that is required of converts, and therefore did not feel competent to address the thorny textual and linguistic issues that she knew to be at stake in debates about biblical texts such as Genesis 19 and Leviticus 18:22 and 20:13. But, she said, there was a scholar of Jewish thought who had testified as an expert witness for the state in the Colorado case, a scholar named David Novak. Her questioner commented, "I am David Novak."

Novak and Nussbaum discovered that they could engage in a reasoned debate on a divisive issue, and that each would like to learn more about the other's interpretations and understandings. The idea for the conference at Brown was generated on that very occasion. Nussbaum approached Saul M. Olyan, and together, with the help of Keith Green, Sumner B. Twiss, and several others both at Brown and at other institutions, we formulated a project proposal and raised the money necessary to mount the conference. Essential to the plan for the conference was the decision to invite papers that would develop distinct and conflicting positions on sexual orientation and its public policy dimensions, situating these positions within a major religious tradition. We chose to focus on four American religious traditions—Judaism, Roman Catholicism, mainline Protestantism, and the

African-American churches—and assigned each its own panel. Why these four traditions and not others? Each of them has a history of at least some division and debate on this issue; in contrast, there has been little or no open debate within most Protestant fundamentalist churches, or within Islam, for example. Each panel was to have three papers: a paper defending a "conservative" or "traditionalist" position; a paper defending a "progressive" or "liberal" position; and a response intended to point out the weaknesses and the strengths, the salient points, and the most intriguing arguments of each paper in order to promote discussion and dialogue between the speakers themselves and between participants and the audience. The writers were asked to address the following questions:

> 1. How do you understand the history and tradition of your religious community with respect to same-sex orientation and/or preference and conduct?
> 2. What moral stance do you believe your religious community ought to take on this issue at this time? Do you believe that these moral arguments (1) are, and (2) ought to be arguments that are persuasive independent of issues of revelation?
> 3. What implications for the formation of law and public policy do you find in the traditional position(s) of your religious community and in the current viewpoints advocated there (e.g., regarding such issues as legal protection from discrimination on the basis of sexual orientation, or the legal status of same-sex domestic partnerships)? Should the position of your religious community have a bearing on these public debates?

The format of the first section of this book is much like that of the conference, except that an introductory essay precedes each triad of two essays and response. The introductions are intended to provide the reader with a broader context before the reader attempts to tackle the individual essays in each panel. The second section of the book consists of two essays, one by Michael McConnell of the University of Utah Law School, and one by Andrew Koppelman of Northwestern University School of Law. Each of these addresses the contemporary conflict in American society over the morality and legality of same-sex sexual relations, and each makes reference to the positions of religious people and religious institutions. The focus of each of these essays, however, is on the legal dimensions of this conflict, and each explores how we might find a modus vivendi in a state position of neutrality on the "moral status of homosexuality," as Koppelman puts it. McConnell suggests that a valuable way to approach our deep-seated disagreements about homosexuality is to consider, as a parallel, the history of our constitutional dealings with religion. What would law and public policy be like, he asks, if we were to treat sexual orientation the way we now treat religion, maintaining a public neutrality guided by the ideas of free exercise and nonestablishment? Such a solution, he argues, may offer us a "workable and mutually satisfactory peace." Koppelman too draws his idea of state neutrality from the model of religion's disestablishment. He describes his piece as "tentative and exploratory," placing the option of state neutrality on the table for consideration without actually endorsing it himself. (In his past work, Koppelman has in fact advocated state opposition to the "stigmatization of homosexuality.")

The essays in this volume not only advocate particular positions on the divisive issues under consideration; but also allow readers to gain access to wider areas of deliberation within particular religious communities that may otherwise have remained unknown to them. When one reads these essays as a collection, one is frequently struck by the similar manner in which arguments have been formed and debate developed in very different religious contexts. In her essay in this volume, Judith Plaskow points out how both liberals (or progressives) and conservatives (or traditionalists) in the various religious traditions tend to fashion their arguments similarly with respect to sexual orientation: conservatives frequently cite biblical texts and, in some cases, the postbiblical tradition, to support a negative position on same-sex sexual acts; progressives, in contrast, tend to argue that homosexuality is innate and traditional texts can be reinterpreted or invalidated in the contemporary context. But the essays in this volume demonstrate that the similarities between very different religious communities go well beyond strategy of argument or approach; they are evident also in the way in which some writers perceive the very situation of their own communities. Cheryl Sanders argues that the disintegration of the black family in contemporary urban America demands that monogamous heterosexual marriage be the only acceptable lifestyle model advocated by black churches. This crisis of the black family, in conjunction with the traditional, scripturally based opposition of the black churches to homosexuality, leaves little room for the acceptance of nonmonogamous and nonheterosexual relationships by the churches. Similar arguments are presented by Jewish traditionalists, who oppose the acceptance of homosexuality as a legitimate alternative to heterosexuality. David Novak mentions the slaughter of one-third of the Jewish people in the Holocaust, high rates of intermarriage, and low birth rates among Jews in contemporary America among his reasons for opposing such innovations as same-sex marriage and for advocating a continuation of the traditional prohibition of same-sex sexual relations: "Inasmuch as Jews have always been a small, vulnerable minority among the nations, and even more so today, it should not be surprising that many Jews believe that it is detrimental to the Jewish people to recognize any kind of sexual relationship that does not minimally produce Jewish children." Both Sanders and Novak understand the situation of their respective communities similarly and, to a greater or lesser degree, base important aspects of their arguments on this perception of embattlement or crisis.

Not only are the situations of communities sometimes perceived similarly, as an examination of the essays of Sanders and Novak demonstrates, but the locus of debate and the way in which it plays itself out in different communities may be similar, too. Victor Anderson describes how community opposition to the presence of "The Ad Hoc Committee of Proud Black Lesbians and Gays" in Chicago's annual Bud Bilikin Parade resulted in an attempt to exclude the lesbian and gay group, a tactic that ultimately failed after the group threatened to take legal action. A very similar scenario occurred in 1993, when the largely gay congregation Beth Simchat Torah sought to march under its own banner in the annual "Salute to Israel" parade in New York City. In this instance, negative community reaction, particularly from Orthodox quarters, ultimately prevented the members of the mostly gay, bisexual, and lesbian synagogue from marching as an identifiable group. The annual St. Patrick's Day parades in New York and Boston have experienced similar difficulties. In each case, a self-identified lesbian, gay, and bisexual group—Irish Catholic, black, Jewish—sought to participate openly in a communitywide celebration; in each case, opponents from within the communities in question sought to prevent their participation. Thus, each of these community events became a contested locus, a battleground in the struggle to define who is or is not a part of the community, and under what terms.

Needless to say, along with the similarities noted above, there are serious differences. Some of the religious communities represented in this volume value and embrace the findings of contemporary historical and philological scholarship on the Bible and other sacred texts, while other groups do not; hierarchy plays a larger role in the organization of some communities than it does in others, where individual congregations have a great deal of independence to develop policy on controversial issues; three of the traditions represented here are divided into multiple denominations or movements, while the fourth—the Roman Catholic Church—is not. One can therefore speak of an official Roman Catholic teaching on homosexuality, but one cannot do the same for Judaism or mainline Protestantism, where there is much contemporary variety. Finally, two of the traditions represented in this volume—Judaism and the African-American churches—are associated with particular minority groups in this country, and this fact has certainly affected the shape of debate within those communities. Each gay, lesbian, or bisexual African American or Jew is a member of at least two minority groups at once; many speak of pressure by heterosexuals in their communities to privilege race or religion over sexual orientation in the formation of their identities (see Anderson's essay in this volume for a discussion of the privileging of race over sexuality/gender in what he calls the "cult of black masculinity"). Homosexuality may be viewed by some heterosexual Jews and blacks as a threat to ethno-religious or racial solidarity, or a threat to community survival (as noted above), nonissues in other communities.

The essays in this volume explore and contribute to the debate about sexual orientation and its public policy dimensions from within four major American religious communities and from a legal perspective. Recently, liberal political thinkers such as John Rawls and Thomas Nagel have argued that a liberal democracy such as the United States must rely on arguments that are not sectarian and that can be publicly assessed in terms of conceptions and commitments that all citizens share. Thinkers from major religious traditions have criticized this position from a variety of viewpoints, holding that an insistence on secular reasoning in the public sphere deprives religious citizens of the opportunity to assert their deeply held convictions in a manner consistent with their own integrity. The essays in this volume demonstrate that both traditionalist and progressive religious discourse is shaping debate about divisive issues of contemporary, public interest. They also suggest that it is indeed possible to engage in civil discourse about such issues.

As the distinguished Roman Catholic thinker John Courtney Murray said, "argument ceases to be civil . . . when its vocabulary becomes solipsist, premised on the theory that my insight is mine alone and cannot be shared. . . . When things like this happen, men cannot be locked together in argument. Conversation becomes merely quarrelsome or querulous. Civility dies with the death of the dialogue."[2] On a profoundly divisive issue, these essays offer a basis for dialogue.

Saul M. Olyan
Martha C. Nussbaum
June 1997

Notes

1. *Romer v Evans*, 116 S. Ct. 1620 (1996).
2. John Courtney Murray, S.J. *We Hold These Truths: Catholic Reflections on the American Proposition* (New York: Sheed and Ward, 1960), p. 14.

Part One

RELIGIOUS DISCOURSE

JUDAISM

Introduction: Contemporary Jewish Perspectives on Homosexuality

SAUL M. OLYAN

As in the case of many other major religious groups in the United States, the last fifteen years have witnessed a great deal of conflict and change in the American Jewish community with respect to issues of sexual orientation. Gays, lesbians, and bisexuals, invisible a generation ago in the major institutions of Jewish life, have come out in number in recent years, many demanding a place for themselves in the Jewish mainstream, often with the implicit or explicit support of heterosexual family members, friends, and other community members. Few walks of American Jewish life have been immune to these developments; in certain contexts, divisive struggles and often revolutionary transformations have occurred. Conflict and change can be seen in individual congregations, the national synagogue organizations, and the rabbinate of the major non-Orthodox branches of American Judaism;[1] it is evident in Jewish Centers, youth organizations, Zionist groups, and summer camps. Some Jewish institutions have made radical changes in their positions on homosexuality and homosexuals; others, many with Orthodox affiliations or a strong Orthodox presence, have resisted any such change. Conflict among Jews over how to view homosexuality, and the place of gays and lesbians in the Jewish community, mirrors in many respects the struggles over these issues that currently divide other American religious communities, and American society as a whole.

Individual congregations, and the national synagogue organizations affiliated with the major non-Orthodox branches of American Judaism, have been the locus of considerable policy debate and development over the past two decades. Many Reform and Reconstructionist synagogues, and some in the Conservative movement, have welcomed openly lesbian and gay couples and singles into their congregations, where some individuals have risen to positions of leadership in worship, education, administration, and social action. Yet the national synagogue organizations of the major non-Orthodox branches of American Judaism remain somewhat divided on whether gay and lesbian congregants should have equal access to positions of congregational leadership (as teachers, board members, youth group advisers) and to liturgical honors. On the one hand, the Reform and Reconstructionist movements have official policies of nondiscrimination on the basis of sexual orientation in all aspects of synagogue life.[2] The Conservative movement, on the other hand, has adopted a policy welcoming gay and lesbian Jews (including those who are sexually active) into Conservative congregations, but allowing individual rabbis to decide whether these congregants may teach, hold leadership positions, receive honors in worship, and advise youth groups.[3] The Reform and Reconstructionist movements admit congregations to their synagogue associations that declare themselves to be predominantly gay and lesbian; the Conservative movement does not. Though the Rabbinical Assembly prohibits Conservative rabbis from performing same-sex commitment ceremonies, Reform and Reconstructionist rabbis perform them at their discretion. Since 1993, Reconstructionist policy guidelines have affirmed the "holiness" (*qedushah*) of committed same-sex partnerships, placing them on an equal footing with committed heterosexual relationships. In contrast, in a 1990 policy statement, Reform's Central Conference of American Rabbis reaffirmed without equivocation the centrality of procreative, monogamous heterosexual marriage in Jewish life, "and its special status as holy," while nonetheless recognizing the potential "ethical and spiritual value" of "other human relationships." Thus, even among the non-Orthodox branches of American Judaism, no real consensus has been reached on the issues of homosexuality, the status of gay partnerships, and gay participation in synagogue life, with perhaps one exception: all three non-Orthodox movements welcome all gay and lesbian Jews into their congregations as a matter of policy.

Within the three major non-Orthodox Jewish movements, access of open gays and lesbians to the rabbinate and the cantorate has been a divisive issue. Reconstructionism and Reform have instituted major changes with respect to rabbinic and cantorial training and employment; the Conservative movement, in contrast, has chosen not to innovate in this area. In 1984, the Reconstructionist movement instituted a nondiscriminatory admissions policy for its rabbinical college, and this was followed by resolutions in 1990 banning discrimination in the placement of rabbis in congregations. In June 1990, after a spirited debate, the Central Conference of American Rabbis, the rabbinic arm of the much larger Reform movement, voted to admit sexually active and openly gay, lesbian, and bisexual candidates to rabbinic training at the three branches of the Hebrew Union College-Jewish Institute of Religion, Reform's rabbinical seminary. This was a momentous change both for American Judaism and for American religious life in general. By instituting this new policy, Reform Judaism became the largest American religious denomination (at 1.5 million), and only one of three major religious groups in the United States, to knowingly ordain openly gay, sexually active clergy.[4] The struggle in the Conservative movement to resolve the issue of gay and lesbian ordination has resulted in a very different policy. In March 1992, after some heated debate and a divided (though very lopsided) vote, the Committee on Jewish Law and Standards of the Conservative movement's Rabbinical Assembly affirmed the movement's policy to exclude "avowed homosexuals" from admission to rabbinic and cantorial programs, and from membership in the Conservative rabbinic and cantorial organizations. The reasons for this decision are not given in the policy statement itself, but a number of the ideas motivating committee members to vote to exclude gays and lesbians from the rabbinate may be discerned from a reading of the responsa adopted by committee vote; these texts provide "differing philosophical and legal rationales" for the policy adopted by the committee and movement.[5] Reasons given for excluding "avowed homosexuals" from the rabbinate and the cantorate include the notion that rabbis and cantors, as religious leaders, are religious role models, and gay and lesbian rabbis and cantors make poor religious role models in a religious context that values Halakhah;[6] that sexually active gay and lesbian rabbis violate Torah (Lev. 18:22, 20:13); that the community is not ready for such innovation;[7] that gay and lesbian rabbis could serve as negative role models, influencing the sexual development of "borderline cases" (in other words, influencing others to become gay or lesbian).[8]

Debate and division concerning the role lesbian, gay, and bisexual Jews are to play in mainstream Jewish communal institutions has by no means been restricted to the synagogue and seminary. Other Jewish contexts have witnessed struggle as lesbian, gay, and bisexual Jews have made their presence known and taken steps to participate more fully in mainstream Jewish life. In the spring of 1993, a controversy erupted when members of the largely gay Congregation Beth Simchat Torah sought to march in the "Salute to Israel" parade in New York City under their own banner. Eventually, even after protracted negotiations and a compromise between the congregation and the organizers of the parade had been reached, the gay congregation was still excluded. Various other groups—many Orthodox— had threatened to boycott the parade when they found out about the compromise, which had been revealed by the congregation's rabbi in an article in the *New York Times*. And what was the compromise? The members of Congregation Beth Simchat Torah were to march with the Association of Reform Zionists of America, but not under any banner identifying them as a gay and lesbian group.[9] It is difficult not to notice the similarities between this scenario and the controversies over gay and lesbian marchers in recent St. Patrick's Day parades in New York and Boston. Clearly, contemporary conflict in the Jewish community is not unlike the struggles in other ethno-religious communities with respect to the participation of open gays and lesbians in communal events and institutions.

Beginning with a 1965 resolution of Reform's National Federation of Temple Sisterhoods deploring harassment of homosexuals and urging decriminalization of same sex sexual acts between consenting adults, a number of Jewish communal institutions—including the major non-Orthodox branches—have taken public positions on issues affecting the lives of gay men and lesbians, including issues of public policy. Reform's Union of American Hebrew Congregations and Central Conference of American Rabbis each passed similar resolutions in 1977 advocating antidiscrimination laws in employment and housing[10] and the decriminalization of gay sex acts. The Conservative movement's Rabbinical Assembly (1990) and United Synagogue of America (1991) have each condemned violence against lesbians and gay men in American society, and have urged "full civil equality for gays and lesbians in our national life." In recent years, resolutions have been passed by various institutions in the Reform movement advocating military service for gays and lesbians, opposing antigay civil rights referenda, and, most recently, advocating civil gay marriage.[11] As a result of the 1996 resolution of the Central Conference of American Rabbis supporting "the right of gay and lesbian couples to share fully and equally in the rights of civil marriage and . . . oppos[ing] governmental efforts to ban gay and lesbian marriage," the Union of Orthodox Jewish Congregations of America and the Orthodox Agudat Yisrael took public positions of opposition to civil gay marriage in the United States.[12]

This spirited discussion of sexual orientation and debate about the roles of gay and lesbian Jews in the communities and institutions of mainstream American Judaism over the past twenty years or more is the larger context for the three essays that follow. David Novak, a distinguished scholar of Jewish thought and rabbi, argues for the justice of the prohibitions of Leviticus 18:22 and 20:13, and against the recognition of gay marriages by American society. Procreation is, for Novak, a privileged purpose of sexuality; gay and lesbian unions, he reasons, by their very design, are nonprocreative, in that procreation is not the intention of these unions. Thus, society has no "interest" in recognizing such unions. "Society's interest in traditional family life is so strong," argues Novak, "that to compromise it in any way could seriously weaken it." Novak, who describes himself as a "religious and secular traditionalist," cites mainly texts in the rabbinic tradition to bolster his claims, with some attention to classical philosophers and Christian thinkers as well. Novak argues that the secular penalization of homosexual conduct is "counterproductive," as it represents an invasion of privacy and therefore has the potential to threaten other rights that are, unlike any right to homoerotic sex, accepted by popular opinion and tradition. Judith Plaskow, preeminent Jewish feminist theologian, Professor of Religious Studies at Manhattan College, and an out lesbian, advocates a very different position in her programmatic paper. Plaskow presents a critique of the traditional discourse of both liberals and conservatives concerning homosexuality and the Jewish tradition, urging us to embrace a more sophisticated understanding of gay and lesbian sexuality that goes beyond the "nature versus choice" nexus adopted by so many on both sides in the contemporary debate, both within the Jewish community and in the larger American society. After a critique of the use made by contemporary liberals of biological and historical arguments concerning the etiology of homosexuality, Plaskow argues that the issue of homosexuality must be placed "in the context of a feminist critique of gender roles, compulsory heterosexuality, and traditional sexual ethics." Instead of trying to "normalize" gays and lesbians "within the framework of a heterosexist system that will now be adjusted at its margins," Plaskow advocates a critique of the system itself. Louis Newman, Associate Professor of Religion at Carleton College and noted author in the area of Jewish ethics, offers an assessment and critique of each paper. He points out that though the two papers seem at first blush to be so different, and to address very different constituencies, the two authors do share some basic methodological assumptions. Both, he argues, acknowledge the authority of the tradition in some sense, yet both implicitly recognize that the tradition is evolving and that ethics is a constructive enterprise for its practitioners.

Notes

1. Orthodox communities have not experienced the kind of division, conflict, and change that I describe in other parts of the Jewish community. Even among the modern Orthodox, there has been little open debate about these issues. For a widely cited modern Orthodox perspective, though one that is now two decades old, see Norman Lamm, "Judaism and the Modern Attitude to Homosexuality," in *Contemporary Jewish Ethics*, ed. Menachem Marc Kellner (New York: Sanhedrin, 1978), pp. 375–99. For the dissenting perspective of a closeted gay Orthodox rabbi, see Yaakov Levado (pseudonym), "Gayness and God: Wrestlings of an Orthodox Rabbi," *Tikkun* 8, no. 5 (September/October 1993): 54–60, and his "Family Values: A Response to Reuven Kimelman," *Tikkun* 9, no. 4 (July/August 1994): 57–60.

2. See the series of Reform resolutions reprinted in the volume by the UAHC Task Force on Lesbian and Gay Inclusion, *Kulanu (All of Us): A Program for Congregations Implementing Gay and Lesbian Inclusion. A Handbook for UAHC Congregations* (New York: Union of American Hebrew Congregations Press, 1996), and the similar resolutions of the Reconstructionist movement reproduced in the volume by the Reconstructionist Commission on Homosexuality, *Homosexuality and Judaism: The Reconstructionist Position. A Report of the Reconstructionist Commission on Homosexuality* (Wyncote, PA: Federation of Reconstructionist Congregations and Havurot/Reconstructionist Rabbinical Association, 1993). Other references I make to Reform and Reconstructionist policy are based on documents in these two volumes.

3. See the "Committee on Jewish Law and Standards Consensus Statement of Policy Regarding Homosexual Jews in the Conservative Movement," available with responsa by individual rabbis and previous Rabbinical Assembly and United Synagogue resolutions in the collection, *Papers on Issues Regarding Homosexuality* (The Committee on Jewish Law and Standards, The Rabbinical Assembly, 1992). Other references I make to Conservative movement policy and discussion are based on materials in this collection.

4. The Unitarian Universalist Association and the Reconstructionist movement in Judaism are the two others. See Jeffrey L. Sheler, "Homosexuality Doctrines," *US News & World Report*, 16 July 1990, p. 55.

5. The adopted responsa are "Homosexuality," by Joel Roth; "Jewish Norms for Sexual Behavior," by Elliott Dorff; "Homosexuality and the Policy Decisions of the CJLS," by Reuven Kimelman; and "On Homosexuality," by Mayer Rabinowitz. These are all available in *Papers on Issues Regarding Homosexuality* cited above in n. 3.

6. Roth, "Homosexuality," p. 123: Open gays and lesbians should not be rabbis and cantors "because their lifestyles suggest that homosexuality is halakhically acceptable." Note that Roth's concern is *open* gays and lesbians, not those who keep their orientation private. See also the comments of Rabinowitz, "On Homosexuality," p. 9, who states that leaders (including rabbis, cantors, and educators) "must abide by the halakhic norms that the community accepts and sets. Therefore, those who 'advocate' homosexuality as an acceptable alternate Jewish lifestyle would not and may not be accepted."

7. This seems to be the thrust of Dorff's position, "Jewish Norms," p. 28.

8. I take Kimelman's remarks ("Homosexuality and the Policy Decisions," p. 13) regarding role models to apply to rabbis and presumably other leaders who might be thought of as role models, though he does not state clearly about whom he is speaking. A dissenting paper by Howard Handler, which critiques the views articulated in the adopted responsa, may also be found in *Papers on Issues Regarding Homosexuality*, cited in n. 3.

9. See the *New York Times*, 5 May 1993, sec. C, p. 18; 8 May 1993, sec. A, p. 23; 10 May 1993, sec. B, p. 1.

10. The resolution of the Union of American Hebrew Congregations mentions employment and housing specifically; the resolution of the Central Conference of American Rabbis is formulated more generally, mentioning "discrimination against [homosexuals] as persons." The resolution of the Union of American Hebrew Congregations paraphrases the equal protection clause of the Fourteenth Amendment in its formulation.

11. See the resolutions reprinted in *Kulanu (All of Us)*, pp. 131, 134, 135, 139.

12. "Reform Rabbis Back Same-Sex Unions," *Christian Century* 113, no. 15 (1 May 1996): 478.

Religious Communities, Secular Society, and Sexuality: One Jewish Opinion

DAVID NOVAK

Religious and Social Recognition of Sexuality

Since the pioneering investigations of Freud at the beginning of this century, most of the old conventions concerning human sexuality have been called into question. That has required both those who advocate that these conventions be changed and those who advocate that they remain in force to devise new arguments for their respective positions. The current debate over homosexuality, especially, has called for such new arguments because the case at hand seems so radical when made by those who advocate change and so lacking in rational persuasion when made by those who advocate tradition.

Traditionally, both religious communities and secular society have discriminated against homosexual persons in three ways: (1) they have proscribed homoerotic acts; (2) they have penalized those who engage in homoerotic acts; (3) they have denied the rights and obligations of the institution of marriage to homosexual persons who have wanted to enter it through the innovation of legally sanctioned homosexual unions. With the rise of the gay movement in the past twenty-five years or so, all three of these forms of discrimination have been publicly challenged. This challenge has been made not only by gay people but also by a number of straight people, who believe that these forms of discrimination are unjust and should, therefore, be repealed on moral grounds.

Out of this challenge the following questions seem to emerge: (1) by religious criteria, is the religious proscription of homoerotic acts just? (2) by secular criteria, is the secular proscription of homoerotic acts just? (3) could there be one reason for or against this proscription that would satisfy both religious and secular criteria? (4) although the proscription of homoerotic acts logically entails the denial of the institution of marriage to homosexual couples, does that proscription also logically entail public penalties for these acts? In other words, could a religious community or a secular society proscribe homosexual acts, refuse homosexual unions the status of marriage, and still be consistent in not publicly penalizing those who engage in homoerotic acts?

These are all normative questions, which can be discussed only with normative coherence in the context of a community or society whose normative authority one recognizes as binding on herself or himself. Therefore, anyone discussing these questions cannot hide behind any normative anonymity. Along these lines, let me state at the outset that I am an American Jew or a Jewish American, depending on where the normative emphasis at any time is to be located. As such, I am beholden to two and only two normative orders: Judaism and the United States of America. All other normative orders to which I am beholden (for example, family, municipality, profession) are essentially subsets of one or the other of these larger normative orders. Moreover, I consider my being beholden to the normative order of Judaism, called the *Torah*, to be prior both chronologically and ontologically to my being beholden to the normative order of the United States. In other words, I can accept only secondary secular authority because it has been justified as being in principle (if not always in specific practice) consistent with the primary religious authority for me.[1] That is why I must first discuss the question of the religious discrimination of gay people.

The Jewish Prohibition of Homosexuality

There are few prohibitions that are more unambiguous than the traditional Jewish prohibition of male homosexual acts. Even though one could argue that the original prohibition in Leviticus 18:22 ("With a male you shall not lie as with a female") only applies to an act of anal intercourse between two males, the subsequent tradition saw the prohibition as including all sexual acts between males.[2] Hence the rabbinic term *mishkav zakhur* comes very close to meaning what we mean today by "homosexuality."[3] And even though there is no explicit biblical prohibition of female homosexual acts, there is a rabbinic prohibition of them.[4] Thus it could well be maintained that the prohibition of homoerotic acts, be they male or female, comes under the general rubric of proscribed sexuality called by the Rabbis *giluy arayot*, literally meaning "uncovering of the genitals"—that is, for sexual acts.[5] Furthermore, however different the respective penalties might be for different homoerotic acts, the fact is that in Rabbinic Judaism any prohibited act is considered deserving of divine punishment.[6]

At the level of Jewish religious observance, one could leave the matter here— that is, one could simply state that homoerotic acts are proscribed and that there is no way that this general prohibition could be repealed in a community where the Halakhah has genuine governance and not just arbitrary guidance.[7] Nevertheless, the traditional sources themselves do not end their discussion of the matter here. Instead, they include two other considerations.

The first such consideration is that the general prohibition of illicit sexuality as *giluy arayot* is considered by the Rabbis to be one of the seven Noahide areas of law (*sheva mitsvot benei Noah*), which by definition are taken to be binding on all humankind collectively and on every human being individually.[8] The second such consideration is that the Rabbis also considered the general category of illicit sexuality to be a matter that "even if it had not been written [in the Torah], it should have been written."9 As Nahmanides argued about a similar area of law, even though the Torah recognizes and further specifies it, the prohibition itself is inherently rational and does not require the Torah to initially establish it.10

Now there is a difference between norms that are taken to be universal but *not* rational and norms that are taken to be both universal *and* rational. The former would apply only when the community that recognizes and formulates them has political power over a more general group outside itself. But in the case of norms assumed to be both universal and rational, they are taken to apply whenever rational persons understand their reasons. Persuasion is their more appropriate method of communication. They do not entail the imperialism of one community over a general group of outsiders. Instead, they apply as much to the insiders of the religious community as they do to the outsiders of the more general society.11 Concerning such laws, the Talmudic principle is that nothing prohibited to the gentiles is permitted to the Jews.12

Religious and Secular Reasons

Here we can begin to see how the realms of the religious community and the secular society overlap, so that we may be able to discuss the prohibition of homoerotic acts in both localities in tandem. That overlapping, however, can be seen only when we assume that the difference between religious community and secular society is not that God is necessarily to be present in the former and just as necessarily to be absent in the latter. That is only the case when affirmation of the "secular" is taken to be essentially "secularist." Indeed, when that is the case, one cannot affirm the religious and the secular together with any coherence; one must choose between one *or* the other. Yet one can affirm them both together coherently when the difference between them is that in religious community one *must* affirm both the will and the wisdom of God, but in secular society one must affirm only what she or he thinks is to be socially mandated in a rational manner. One *may* only affirm what is rational as being originally the wisdom of God. For Jews, that means that among ourselves we must affirm the authority of both those commandments that do not have general reasons (like the dietary prohibitions) and those commandments that do have general reasons (like the prohibition of murder). However, in secular society we may affirm the wisdom of only those commandments (like the prohibition of murder) that apply to everyone for good reasons. All we require is that the wisdom of these commandments be capable of discussion; we do not require that the divine source of these wise commandments be affirmed by anyone else.13 The absence of such a requirement makes the affirmation of a secular realm possible without our having to accept secularist foundations for it, however.14

The foundation of secular society, then, is the liberty to speak the name of one's own God in public, the liberty of anyone else to speak the name of her or his own God in public, the liberty of those who do not care to speak the name of their own God in public, and the liberty of those who have no God not to have to affirm anyone else's God. The denial of any of these liberties makes a society either antireligious or a theocracy. The difference between religious persons and nonreligious persons is that the former believe public wisdom has a divine source whereas the latter believe it is either self-sufficient or has sources other than divine. But those who do speak the name of their God in public can do so only in connection with those commandments of their God that apply to everyone for good reasons. Anything else is questionable special pleading.[15]

In that sense, I agree with Richard Rorty, who argues that those who speak of "God's will" are "conversation stoppers" in a democratic society.[16] However, I disagree with Rorty, who seems to think that that is the only possible mode of religious conversation in public. One may also speak of the wisdom of God and that is a different mode of discourse. Furthermore, I agree with Plato that it is better to argue for a practice based on *why* it is to be done (its wisdom) than simply on *who* originally authorized it (its will).[17] However, unlike Plato, being a believer in divine *creatio ex nihilo*, I thereby believe that God is the source of both wisdom and authority, and that the relationship with this God that revelation enables is the highest good.[18] Therefore, although in secular society one need not mention the divine source of wisdom since secular society is not itself concerned with the God-human relationship, the religious person must never forget the divine source of any wisdom.[19] For the religious person comes to secular society out of a prior community in which she or he is forever rooted and to which he or she must ever return. The essential purpose of that community is to proclaim the name of God.[20] As such, one cannot dismiss by means of Occam's razor those who see a divine source of what is rationally evident inasmuch as the affirmation of this divine source is not a superfluous premise in an otherwise self-sufficient argument. For in its original and primary context, that of the religious community, affirmation of the divine source of wisdom and authority is the most necessary premise for anything that is to be said and done. Whereas outside this community one may at best designate God as a possible cause, within the community God is the One who initiates and sustains the covenant.[21]

The Justice of the Prohibition

Let me now argue for the justice of the prohibition of homoerotic acts in terms of its wisdom, a criterion that is both religious and secular. It is secular inasmuch as one does not have to believe in a historical revelation to accept it. And it is religious inasmuch as one who believes in a historical revelation that includes it is not thereby denying the authority of that revelation by affirming the natural wisdom of this prohibition, too.

In order to understand the wisdom of this prohibition, one has to discern what the purpose of human sexuality is. At the prima facie level, there seem to be three purposes of human sexuality: (1) pleasure, (2) personal communion, (3) procreation. Thus human persons engage in sexual activities because they desire (1) the unique enjoyment of bodily union, (2) the transcendence of personal loneliness, (3) full family life. Some theorists have attempted to affirm all three purposes as three separate, albeit related, goods.[22] Others have attempted to emphasize one of them at the expense of the others.[23] However, here I would argue that all three purposes or desires are essentially one, with procreation being *primus inter pares*.

The way to see all of these purposes in unison is to assert that the purpose of sexuality is to initiate and maintain the institution of the family. It is to assert that only within the situation of family life can human persons be fulfilled, and that any situation in which family life is absent, especially when that absence is intended, takes a toll on one's humanity. In the full sense of the term, "family life" means the intended permanent union of a man and a woman, which therewith intends the conception, birth, and parenting of children.[24] As the Bible puts it, "A man shall leave his father and his mother and cleave unto his wife, and they shall become one flesh" (Gen. 2:24). In traditional Jewish exegesis, "one flesh" refers to the heterosexual couple themselves who intend to conceive a child by their union, and the child itself who results from their permanent, sustained union.[25] And from this passage, the Rabbis see all the universal (and rational) sexual prohibitions—that is, from a positive commandment they infer these prohibitions.[26]

Now the argument against this traditional definition of family life is that it is too exclusive. Specifically, it seems to exclude homosexuals, sterile persons, and celibate persons from true human fulfillment. In terms of our present topic of discussion, it can be assumed that the charge of homosexual exclusion is the most serious. (I shall return to the questions of the marriage of sterile persons and celibacy.)

The charge is most serious when made by those homosexuals who want *both* the proscription of homoerotic acts *and* the exclusion of homosexual unions from the status of marriage to be repealed. For those homosexuals, on the other hand, who do not regard the permanence of marriage to be a universal desideratum, the repeal of the proscription of homoerotic acts is sufficient. However, I choose to address myself to the charges of pro-family homosexuals inasmuch as they seem to affirm the traditional proscription of sexual promiscuity that marriage entails. (Hence I assume that their appeal to be included in the social institution of marriage includes their opposition to adultery, even if both marital partners know and approve of it; "open marriage" is an oxymoron.) They request only the widening of the parameters of the traditional institution of marriage, not its elimination or marginalization. These homosexuals, then, present the most formidable challenge to both the religious and secular institution of marriage as traditionally constituted. Indeed, they are often found in all of our religious communities, which is rarely the case with those homosexuals who see permanent sexual unions as being a heterosexual prejudice. Even in secular society, pro-family homosexuals are usually quite conservative in terms of wanting as little social change as is just. In other words, they want a place *within* religious communities and secular society, not the radical revolution of either entity. As such, they are speaking *to* us, not *against* us, who are religious and secular traditionalists. Their stated intention is to be *with* us.

Nevertheless, the reason the definition of family cannot be stretched to include homosexual unions is that by design these unions preclude procreation. Homosexual unions do not produce children, nor do they intend to produce them. Even the insemination of lesbian women, who intend to raise their children with their lesbian partners, is not the intention of the lesbian union itself; their union does not produce the child. That is why the minimal contribution of a male, in the form of his sperm, is still needed in this situation. But I would also argue that such an abstraction of a generative substance from its source in a human person is itself an immoral use of something *personal* (unlike waste fluids) as a means to an end extrinsic to that *person* himself.[27] This is essentially unlike a heterosexual marital union in which two persons conceive and raise children together, and remain their parents forever, however impermanent their own relationship might actually be.

Following this point, I would add that certainly there are many differences between homosexual women and homosexual men, including their thinking on sexuality. In fact, the differences are such that homosexual women usually call themselves "lesbian" and homosexual men usually call themselves "gay." Yet one point in common that I have noted is that both groups of homosexuals seem to regard the institution of fatherhood to be at best instrumental for procreation. Artificial insemination as the preferred method of conception makes the instrumental role as impersonal as possible. Any ongoing role for fathers, working in concert with the mothers of their children, seems to suggest the bête noir of "patriarchy." However, if there is to be a family in the full sense of the term as it is traditionally used—that is, a miniature community including men, women, and children—then it would seem that there has to be some division of authority and responsibility between the parents. Accordingly, there should be at least proportional equality between fatherly authority (patriarchy) and motherly authority (matriarchy).[28]

If there is no intention to produce children, what interest does society have in recognizing any such union? But society does have an interest in the production and raising of children because experience has clearly taught us that society, which fulfills a natural need of human beings, intends its own transmission into the future. So it needs new citizens, and these new citizens are best produced, cared for, and raised to responsible adulthood in a home founded on a permanently intended heterosexual union. In any large-scale absence of such unions, we see major social pathology, a fact clearly evidenced by the social pathology (primarily violence in all forms) we see today in the breakup or absence of two parent (that is, male-female) families in growing segments of our society, but especially among the poor, who are always most vulnerable to any pathology. Society's interest in traditional family life is so strong that to compromise it in any way could only seriously weaken it. That seems to me to be the best argument for the traditional prohibition of homoerotic acts and homosexual marriages.

Now this seems a better argument if we assume that homosexuality is a matter of choice. If so, we can then argue for a familial imperative, as it were.[29] But what if we assume, as most homosexuals insist, that their homosexuality is not a matter of choice? (Of course, all sexual acts performed by nonpsychotic persons, whether homoerotic or heteroerotic, are chosen. That is what gives them moral significance, as we shall soon see.) What if by some determinism, whether natural or historical, sexuality, whether heterosexual or homosexual, is just there within one? Why should what is determined in one group of humans—that is, heterosexuals— be allowed some form of socially acceptable sexual activity (marital intercourse), but what is determined in another group of humans—homosexuals—not be allowed any form of socially acceptable sexual activity? And, following this, what if we assume that attempts to repress homosexuality or even sublimate it are contrary to the *nature* of those persons who have been *made* homosexual one way or another? The answers to these fundamental questions are largely determined by just what we mean by the term *nature*.

Contrary to Nature?

It seems to me that there are four basic meanings of the term *nature*.

One, *nature* can mean what we experience as necessity. Thus everyone would agree that the presence of sexual appetite is such a natural necessity, it is an *inclinatio naturalis*.[30] However, unlike breathing or eating, which are acts without which we could not live, sexuality is something without which we could survive. Most of us, nevertheless, would see such a life as humanly deprived. Such a choice would be seen by most of us as depriving us of a basic human need.[31]

Two, *nature* can mean realities (as opposed to fantasies) that we experience as attracting us—that is, natural ends. To use the words of Aristotle, it is not only what is necessary (*anagkaion*) but what is also advantageous (*sympheronton*).[32] Although one could argue that the perpetuation of the species is a natural necessity in animals, most of us would regard human sexuality to be more a personal matter than a strictly genetic one. As such, for us as humans, at least as an activity, it is a matter of choice, even if our inclinations are not. Our choice intends an end (*telos*) already present by nature, one which we desire to attain.[33] Our sexual acts are not just the push of a need but also the delightful pull of a desire whose good intent we happily confirm.

Based on these two meanings of *nature*, it is difficult to argue that homoerotic acts and homosexual unions are "unnatural."

As for the first meaning of *nature*, even Thomas Aquinas argued that there are cases when one's individual nature—that is, one's biological inclination—is different from that of the majority of other people. If that is the case, then such minority persons, in our case homosexuals, are not by virtue of their inclination acting *contra naturam*.[34] Indeed, one could argue (although Aquinas himself certainly did not) that to frustrate such inclination might very well be an act (of omission, that is) that itself is *contra naturam*. And that is the argument made by what I have termed above "conservative" homosexuals. As Andrew Sullivan, especially, has argued based on this criterion of nature, all that such homosexuals ask for is the recognition of their rights (and for him marriage is such a right, secularly and religiously) as a definite minority.[35] The expansion of minority rights in our religious communities and in our secular society, which has become such a feature of contemporary polity, gives a renewed context to these claims inasmuch as these homosexuals are only arguing that they are *a* minority among others, not the only one.

As for the second meaning of *nature*—namely, what is desirable even if not necessary in the strictly biological sense—it is clear that there is a plurality of such goods of human nature. Just as biological needs have to be attended to in harmony with each other, so do human desires. Most of us would agree, I think, that a rational ordering of one's whole life requires that no single desire predominate to the extent of causing neglect of all others. As such, I think most of us would agree that, however desirable sexual acts are, they cannot be allowed to overrule our other human desires. A sexually obsessive life would be a disordered, unhappy human life. So, whether sexual desire is our most characteristic human desire, as Freud argued with his theory of libido, or not, most of us would agree that sexuality is an inherent part of human nature. It is not just instrumental.

Now some have argued that homosexuality per se is obsessive and, therefore, is inherently disordered.[36] Among male homosexuals, especially, there seem to be far higher rates of promiscuous, compulsive sexual activity. Even if this is true (although the data have been challenged on empirical grounds), however, it is not conclusive. For some homosexuals, especially of the conservative variety, have argued that promiscuity among homosexuals is to be taken as personally unhealthy, but that it would decrease if they were allowed to participate in the stabilizing social institution of marriage, whether secularly or religiously or secularly and religiously. (Actually there are already some religious communities that do recognize and even celebrate gay marriages.[37])

This is also important to note in terms of marriage being a form of personal communion. Not only is marriage certainly not the only form of personal communion, most of us would agree that it is unhealthy for a person to confine all her or his personal communion to one's sexual partner, even if that partner is one's own spouse. Friends with whom one is related in nonsexual ways are for most of us an indispensable part of living well.[38] Furthermore, most of us would regard as unhealthy a spousal relationship of personal communion that was confined to sexual activity. In all of these senses of personal communion, it must be admitted that there is nothing that privileges heterosexuality.

It is only when we get to the third meaning of *nature* that we do find that heterosexuality is privileged. I take that third meaning to be the original meaning of our word *nature*, which comes from the Latin *natura*, which is itself derived from the Latin word for being born, *natus*. What is natural, then, is what is connected to birth and whose intent includes the desire to procreate in the original way—that is, by an act of heterosexual intercourse. Natality is our connection with the chain of life. Our nature is vital.

Procreation not only is the act that conceives human life, but also includes the joint rearing of children and remaining the parents of these children, minimally for as long as both parents live.[39] What is intended here is not only the present good of family life when children are physically and emotionally dependent on their parents, but also the good of family life as a continuum. That continuum includes more than just the two generations most immediately present in most homes; it also includes the previous generations in the person or memory of grandparents and before, and the future generations in the person or anticipation of grandchildren and beyond.[40] Most of us want our families to remain intact, even transgenerationally. That is why the divorce of parents is so often deeply upsetting to the children, whatever their age. For the children of divorced persons often feel as though a vital connection with the living community has been broken, even when they no longer need their parents for physical support.[41]

In this view of nature, only heterosexual, marital intercourse is natural inasmuch as it intends the same relationship that minimally gave us life; maximally, it gave us our family, our first human community, in which to live; optimally, it gave us a community in which to live well. All valid intercourse, then, reconfirms the origin and value of our own lives.[42]

Finally, there is the fourth meaning of *nature*, which is nature as an inherent limit (*peras*) on activity in the world—in our case, human activity.[43] Not only is nature immanent but also specific. Each area of human activity in the world has its own inherent limits, which experience discovers and reason orders. Certainly, human sexual activity is no exception in its specifics. Here too, I think, heterosexuality and the procreative union it intends enjoy an exclusive privilege.

Procreation is necessary for the continuity of humankind. The vast majority of humans have always desired not only life but also to pass life on. Since that transmission of life is done heterosexually, one could not very well morally disapprove of heterosexual intercourse per se. Hence those few radical feminists who argue that all heterosexual intercourse is *ipso facto* rape cannot be taken seriously. For to follow their reasoning, the vast majority of human beings, women and men, would be required to permanently repress their sexual inclination.[44] So, it would seem that even homosexuals would have to approve of heterosexuality—that is, if they value their own lives, which were conceived by the heterosexual acts of their parents. As we have seen, the best they could do is argue that because of the involuntary condition of their sexual inclination, they are exempt from any heterosexual imperative. As such, they argue that they may substitute what is sexually possible and desirable for them. Nevertheless, heterosexuals can argue against homosexuality in a way that homosexuals cannot argue against heterosexuality—that is, when they both agree that the continuity of human life is an essential end of human action. For homosexuals need heterosexuals, minimally as their parents, in a way that heterosexuals do not need homosexuals for the sake of human survival.

In order to allow that dispensation from what even homosexuals must recognize as a rational norm, homosexual theorists must argue for sexuality as an area of human activity that itself contains no limiting norms. For if sexual activity is chosen primarily on the basis of one's involuntary inclination, what possible moral limits could one inherently impose upon it? However, doesn't our moral experience begin when we learn to internalize limits on what we may do with our genitals and what we may not do with them? Isn't repression a necessary part of our introduction to social reality, only being harmful when taught in a cruel, irrational manner? Wouldn't any parent raising a child, who sent a message either explicitly or implicitly that what the child does with her or his genitals is a matter of moral indifference, be failing in his or her moral education of that child? For aren't the parents supposed to be the intermediaries between elementary narcissism and human community and society?[45] Could there be human community or society where there is unrestrained sexual activity? Isn't that why family morality begins with the prohibition of incest, from which all other sexual restrictions follow?[46]

All of these questions suggest that only heterosexuals who are committed to a permanent procreative relationship are able to argue for the inherent natural limits on sexual activity, limits that no stable community or society can afford to ignore. Even though sexual activity itself is to be done in private, its public significance is evident.

However, aren't most homosexuals like most heterosexuals in being morally opposed to rape and the seduction of children? Aren't these prohibitions limits on sexual activity?

The fact that most homosexuals are opposed to rape and the seduction of children is good, but that does not mean that homosexual theorists are thereby capable of arguing for inherent natural limits on sexual activity per se because of that opposition. For as we have been learning of late, often from feminist teachers, rape itself is not an act whose intentionality is erotic; rather, it is an assault on another person, using one's genitals as a weapon. Accordingly, its rational prohibition is a subset of our disapproval of violence, most of which is conducted with weapons other than the genitals. And as for the seduction of children, most of us would also regard that as either an assault on victims by those who have emotional power over them, or the robbery of their innocence and their subsequent ability to develop into adults who will have satisfying personal (including sexual) relationships.

The most that homosexual theorists can argue for, as far as I can see, is that sexual activity is an essentially private matter between consenting adults. That, however, is a necessary but not sufficient condition of human sexual acts that are morally justified.[47] It is not sufficient because, as I have argued above, it does not delve deeply enough into the public significance of sexual acts between these consenting adults.[48] For the only criterion of this minimal condition is that each party intend her or his pleasure in a way approved by the other party with whom he or she is sexually engaged at present.

However, in the Jewish tradition, pleasure itself is a desirable accompaniment to sexual activity; it is not its essential purpose. Indeed, Jewish tradition asserts that pleasure is never an end in and of itself, but its value is dependent on whether or not it accompanies acts that are either good or bad.[49] Along these lines, let it be said that all acts are transitive—that is, they intend objects outside their actors. For Judaism it can be maintained, I think, that all acts ultimately intend personal objects.[50] Even nonpersonal objects have to be included in a valid personal relationship in order that their use be justified. The world is to be enjoyed, but that enjoyment is always for the sake of enhancing relationships that are themselves considered good.[51] Thus I am to enjoy the produce of the earth, but that enjoyment is considered to be a form of theft unless I include it in my relationship with God by using that enjoyment as an occasion to thank God.[52] So also is my sexual pleasure, which is acceptable when it contributes to my intimate relationship with my wife.[53] And that intimate relationship involves her being the mother of the children we have either already brought into the world or whom we intend to bring into the world.[54] Since pleasure can only be experienced by a self, to make pleasure an end in and of itself is to make myself the ultimate object of my acts. Hedonism, which is pleasure for its own sake, can only be narcissism. Once pleasure is shared by two persons, it is no longer just a physical sensation. It acquires interhuman meaning.[55]

So, in the end, we are left with family life, which includes (but does not subsume) personal communion and which is to be accompanied by sexual pleasure (and other pleasures as well). Homosexual unions, even if including the good of personal communion and accompanied by sexual pleasure that is not compulsive, still do not intend the core of the good of family life, which is to procreate in both the narrowest and widest senses of that term. And Judaism makes the severe demand on those who by inclination cannot and do not intend this overall good minimally to refrain from sexual activities that contradict it.[56]

Within the parameters of normative Jewish tradition, homosexuals have, it seems to me, two legitimate options. One, they may remain celibate, based on the assumption that inability to perform a positive precept (marriage) does not thereby dispense one from a negative precept (the prohibitions of homoerotic acts). Or, two, they may at least explore the possibility of therapeutic intervention in order to change their sexual orientation with those psychotherapists who believe (in the face of much opposition from many, but not all, of their professional colleagues) that such change is possible and beneficial. However, I would strongly suggest that homosexual persons not enter heterosexual marriage or be encouraged to do so. Such marriages can only cause misery to both the homosexual partner (even if physically capable of heterosexual intercourse) and the heterosexual partner, who is often unaware of the true sexual orientation of her or his spouse. Because of such deceit, any such marriage is an immoral farce.[57]

Heterosexual Jews should become much more sympathetic to the plight of their homosexual brothers and sisters and not encourage them to seek deceitful and harmful "solutions" to their real predicament.

Exceptions to the Norm of Procreation

We are still left with the problem of the marriage of sterile persons and those who choose to be celibate.

As for sterile persons, there are actually restrictions in Jewish law prohibiting some individuals with certain genital deformities from marrying.[58] Nevertheless, as regards most sterile persons, they are unaware of their sterility until they have long been in a marriage. Here again, Jewish law does regard the commandment to procreate to be so important that one may obtain a divorce from a sterile spouse if he or she is determined to fulfill this commandment with a new spouse.[59] However, it seems that the tradition is so respectful of the integrity of the marital unit that where sterility is not intended, many authorities do not make such a divorce a mandate.[60] In fact, such persons are encouraged to adopt children whose parents cannot raise them or do not want to do so.[61] These children are seen as being required to practice the commandment of filial honor and respect for these adoptive parents.[62]

The hardest case is, of course, the marriage of persons who know they are sterile, usually persons who are clearly beyond the age of childbearing. But here I would say, following Wittgenstein's theory of family resemblances, that there are enough similarities to most marriages to allow such marriages.[63] Indeed, to distinguish between fertile and infertile couples *ab initio* would require a judgment to allow or not to allow marriage to be made in the case of each and every couple. However, in the Jewish legal tradition there is ample precedence for simply assuming that *most* heterosexual couples are fertile and, therefore *all* heterosexual couples are to be considered as such.[64] At the *prima facie* level, there is no generally evident difference between fertile and infertile couples. That is quite unlike the very evident difference between most heterosexual couples who are fertile and all homosexual couples who are infertile. Most men and most women are capable of conceiving a child, whereas no two men and no two women are so capable. Law is made for what is usual (*de minimis non curat lex*).[65]

Furthermore, in a homosexual union *ipso facto* sterility is intended, which is not the case in a heterosexual union. Unlike a homosexual union, it is not meant to be a substitute for a normal heterosexual union. Indeed, most persons in this category are those who earlier in life did procreate, or they were persons who without intention could not marry any earlier in life. Indeed, in many such cases, the new spouses figuratively "adopt" the children of their new spouses. For the spouse of one's parent is functioning in many ways like one's other parent (especially the spouse of one's widowed parent).

As for celibacy, Judaism obviously recognizes that there are persons who for a variety of physical and emotional reasons are incapable of initiating or sustaining a marriage. Like any disability, this is regarded to be an unfortunate state of affairs, and persons who suffer from this disability are not to be made to feel any worse than they often already do, especially in a community where natality is so highly regarded and desired. However, voluntary celibacy of heterosexuals physically and psychologically capable of marriage is another matter. Jewish tradition does not regard this as an acceptable state of human life and the sources are replete with statements of disapproval.[66] Nevertheless, although there are social pressures for single persons to marry, those pressures are never so severe as to exclude celibate persons from participation in the religious and social life of the community. There are even unmarried (and therefore presumed to be celibate) rabbis in these communities.[67] My experience in traditional Jewish communities has been that most people compassionately assume that when a person is celibate, it is ultimately due to some disability rather than being the result of a real choice. The same assumption is usually made about childless couples in the community.

As for the clergy of other religions who are required to be celibate, and here one thinks of Roman Catholic clergy, a Jew need not have an opinion; indeed, she or he should not have one. Fortunately, all the Noahide laws (with the exception of the positive precept that a gentile society have a system to administer the due process of law) are negative precepts. Therefore, all violations of them are sins of commission rather than sins of omission.[68] That is why Jews are to have an opinion about homoerotic acts wherever they obtain and, conversely, that is why non-Jewish celibacy is none of our business.

Nevertheless, I must add that the Jewish prohibition of homoerotic acts is stronger than the Christian prohibition of them precisely because Judaism does not approve of celibacy, let alone regard it as a higher form of human holiness. For if the commandment to procreate (in its full and narrow sense) is considered to be exceptionless, then any avoidance of it is considered to be wrong.[69] Avoidance by the substitution of some nonfamilial sexuality, which is a positive act, is the most severe wrong. Avoidance by, as the Rabbis put it, "sitting and doing nothing," is a lesser wrong.[70] It is also a lesser wrong because inactivity is usually pursued with much less passion than activity, especially activity accompanied by intense pleasure. This creates a problem for Roman Catholics (and to a slightly lesser extent for Orthodox Christians, who do require celibacy of some of their clergy), who must be prepared to argue why one nonheterosexual form of life is holy and another sinful. Although they can do so, their argument is necessarily more theologically arcane than the Jewish one. And even those Protestant Christians, who do not require or even advocate clerical celibacy, are still like all other Christians who worship a God who chose to become incarnate in a male celibate body. I mention this because some traditional Jews have made common cause with some traditional Christians of late over the issue of homosexuality.[71] Yet both sides should be aware that they are approaching it from different theologies at least on some points, even if their norms are practically identical.

The Penalization of Homosexual Persons

Homosexual persons have been traditionally penalized in two ways. One, their homoerotic acts have been the occasion for leveling criminal sanctions against them. Two, they have been denied the right of marrying each other.

We have already seen the reasons that the right of marriage has been denied homosexual unions. For Jews, especially, the secular rationale of that refusal can be supplemented by a religious rationale. That is, the commandment to procreate, which is regarded as universal, is for Jews the commandment to reproduce new members of the covenanted people of Israel.[72] The primacy of birth is so important in Judaism that even though converts are accepted, their entry into Judaism is conceived under the legal fiction of being "born again."[73] One must also add to that the especially contemporary poignancy of the fact that even fifty years after the Nazis exterminated one-third of the Jewish people, the Jewish people, owing to assimilation, intermarriage, and a low birth rate, have not even recovered their pre-1939 population. Inasmuch as Jews have always been a small, vulnerable minority among the nations, and even more so today, it should not be surprising that many Jews believe it is detrimental to the Jewish people to recognize any kind of sexual relationship that does not minimally produce Jewish children.

For those reasons and more, there still are social (if not criminal) penalties for homoerotic acts. Thus in a traditional Jewish community, it is most unlikely that a openly practicing homosexual would be elected to a position of religious leadership. In some ways, the reaction to homosexual persons might be compared to the reaction to Jews who are married to non-Jews. While many traditional Jewish communities would include such persons in a variety of religious and social activities, they would do nothing that in any way indicated approval of the intermarriage in which such persons are living. Although there are numerous other transgressions that are being openly practiced by Jews, even those who live in traditional communities, intermarriage and homosexuality have in common the fact that by design they do not produce Jewish children. That is why they are the subject of such particularly religious opprobrium.[74]

As for secular penalties against those who engage in homoerotic acts, I think there is some consensus even among those who otherwise disapprove of homosexuality that such penalties are socially counterproductive. For better or for worse, unlike religious communities which really do not have any notion of a "right to privacy" (even though privacy is protected in many situations by Jewish law[75]), our secular society has more and more assumed that there is such a right. To effectively penalize homoerotic acts between consenting adults would entail such massive invasions of privacy that many other rights would be threatened. And these rights, which unlike the right to engage in any sexual act with whoever agrees to do so with one, are accepted by popular opinion and tradition (for example, the right to privileged communication). Furthermore, sexual acts are the result of notions of human virtue that are better taught in subsidiary social settings than by becoming the subject of statutes of the state that are largely unenforceable. As the Talmud points out, just as there is no point in legislating to no avail, so is there no point in morally admonishing those who are clearly unprepared to listen.[76]

Notes

Works frequently cited have been identified by the following abbreviations:

B. = *Babylonian Talmud (Bavli)*
Y. = *Palestinian Talmud (Yerushalmi)*
M. = *Mishnah*
T. = *Tosefta*
Tos. = *Tosafot*
MT = Maimonides, *Mishneh Torah*

1. See D. Novak, *Jewish Social Ethics* (New York: Oxford University Press, 1992), pp. 67–83. Cf. John Courtney Murray, *We Hold These Truths: Catholic Reflections on the American Proposition* (New York: Sheed and Ward, 1960), pp. ix–x.

2. For the literal definition of *mishkav zakhur* as anal intercourse between two males, see *Sifra*: Qedoshim, ed. Weiss, 92a re: Lev. 18:22 and Deut. 23:18; M. Sanhedrin 7.4; B. Sanhedrin 54a–b; Y. Sanhedrin 7.7/24d–25a. For a discussion of modern Bible scholarship on the subject, see S. M. Olyan, "'And With a Male You Shall Not Lie the Lying Down of a Woman': On the Meaning and Significance of Leviticus 18:22 and 20:13," *Journal of the History of Sexuality* 5 (1994): 179–206.

3. For the clearest use of this more general meaning of the term, see B. Shabbat 17b, where *mishkav zakhur* includes even sex play among very young children (*tinoq*), which is most unlikely to involve penile penetration of the anus of another. For the general prohibition of any sexual contact between males, see M. Kiddushin 4.14; B. Pesahim 51a; B. Berakhot 43b; Maimonides, *Commentary on the Mishnah*: Sanhedrin 7.4, ed. Kafih, p. 122, and MT: Isurei Bi'ah, 22.2; *Sefer ha-Hinukh*, no. 209; *Tur*: Even Ha`Ezer, 24, and Karo, *Bet Yosef* and Sirkes, *Bayit Hadash* thereon; Karo, *Shulhan Arukh*: Even Ha`Ezer, 24.1, and Phoebus, *Bet Shmu'el* thereon. Also see D. Novak, *The Image of the Non-Jew in Judaism* (New York: E. Mellen, 1983), pp. 211–16, and idem, *Jewish Social Ethics*, pp. 86–98, 109–110.

4. See B. Yevamot 76a and Tos., s.v. "mesolelot"; B. Shabbat 65a; MT: Isurei Bi'ah,

21.8 re: Lev. 18:3. Cf. B. Niddah 61a, Tos., s.v. "amar R. Ami." Also cf. M. L. Satlow, 'And They Abused Him Like a Woman': Homoeroticism, Gender Blurring, and the Rabbis in Late Antiquity," *Journal of the History of Sexuality* 5 (1994): 15–17.

5. See B. Shabbat 13a and Rashi, s.v. "giluy arayot," and Tos., s.v. "u-fliga."

6. See B. Berakhot 6b; B. Eruvin 21b re: Eccles. 12:12.

7. Re: the permanent impossibility of the repeal of scriptural law that is perpetually binding (*d'oraita*), see B. Kiddushin 29a re: Num. 15:23 and B. H. Epstein, *Torah Temimah* (Vilna: Romm, 1904): Num. 15:23, n. 61. Re: the present impossiblity of the direct repeal of rabbinic law (*de-rabbanan*), see M. Eduyot 1.5; B. Avodah Zarah 36a; MT: Mamrim, 2.2-4.

8. T. Avodah Zarah 8.4; B. Sanhedrin 56a–b; MT: Melakhim, 9.5.

9. *Sifra*: Aharei-Mot, ed. Weiss, 86a re: Lev. 18:5; B. Yoma 67b.

10. Nahmanides, *Commentary on the Torah*: Gen. 6:2, 13.

11. Throughout this paper I use the term *community* in the sense of *Gemeinschaft* and *society* in the sense of *Gesellschaft*, following the often used distinction between the two made by Ferdinand Tönnies in his seminal work, *Community and Society*, trans. C. P. Loomis (East Lansing: Michigan State University, 1957).

12. B. Sanhedrin 59a.

13. See MT: Melakhim, 8.11, which only eliminates from the world-to-come those gentiles who do not acknowledge the divine source of universal Noahide law. Their affirmation of its rationality, nevertheless, is sufficient to ensure that they be regarded as "wise" in the sense of having practical wisdom. For the dispute regarding the correct text in Maimonides on this point, see Novak, *The Image of the Non-Jew in Judaism*, pp. 288–94.

14. See Hermann Cohen, *Religion of Reason Out of the Sources of Judaism*, trans. S. Kaplan (New York: F. Ungar, 1972), pp. 123–30.

15. This does not mean that religious persons may not request exemptions from certain civic duties—e.g., work on the Sabbath—based on their own religious laws. What they may not do is to even suggest that their own religious laws have secular authority for everyone in the society. That is why the religious opponents of elective abortion, for example, have to argue on natural law grounds. Their adversaries, however, often attempt to expose their natural law arguments as being in truth nothing but rationalizations for their specifically religious position. The same seems to be the case for the public argument over homosexuality, *mutatis mutandis*.

16. See his "Religion As Conversation-Stopper," *Common Knowledge* 3 (1994): 1–6.

17. See Plato *Euthyphro* 10A–E.

18. See Ps. 73:28; also, D. Novak, *Jewish-Christian Dialogue: A Jewish Justification* (New York: Oxford University Press, 1989), pp. 152–54.

19. See B. Hagigah 3b re: Eccles. 12:11.

20. See Isa. 43:21; M. Avot 2.12.

21. For the plausibility, but not the rational necessity, of affirming God's causality in a secular context, see Kant, *Critique of Pure Reason*, B655. Cf. Exod. 33:14-15.

22. See John M. Finnis, "Law, Morality, and 'Sexual Orientation,'" *Notre Dame Journal of Law, Ethics and Public Policy* 9 (1995): 27–39.

23. See Augustine, *De Bono Coniugali* 9.9.

24. In the Jewish tradition that does not mean, though, that couples may not time the birth of their children and limit their number. See D. M. Feldman, *Birth Control in Jewish Law* (New York: New York University Press, 1968), pp. 46–59.

25. See B. Sanhedrin 58a, Rashi, s.v. "ve-davaq;" Rashi, *Commentary on the*

Torah: Gen. 2:24; Nahmanides, *Commentary on the Torah*: Gen. 2:24; also, Y. Kiddushin 1.1/58c.

26. B. Sanhedrin 58a.

27. See B. Hagigah 15a and Rashi, s.v. "b'ambati," where the situation of artificial insemination from a nonspouse is considered to be a grotesque accident. For the rabbinic notion that sexuality, unlike one's possessions, is personal and, therefore, may not be separated from the person as the subject of any sale or gift, see B. Kiddushin 19b and Rashi, s.v. "be-davar she-be-mammon." In the discussion following the original reading of this paper at Brown University on 7 April 1995, Prof. Andrew Koppelman of Northwestern University raised the counterexample of blood donation. My answer was that the saving of human life overrides this concern for human dignity in the case of blood donation in a way that would not be the same in the case of semen donation (see B. Ketubot 19a and parallels). Furthermore, semen donation entails more of human personhood than blood donation (see B. Niddah 31a). For the question of the extent to which one may donate a body part to save another human life, see R. David ibn Abi Zimra, *Teshuvot Radbaz* 3, no. 1052.

28. For the notion of proportional equality, see Aristotle *Nicomachean Ethics* 1131a10., even though I am applying it here differently than Aristotle would, viz., assigning more authority to a wife and mother than he would. Cf. ibid., 1138b7–10. See D. Novak, *Law and Theology in Judaism* (New York: KTAV, 1976), 2: 47–86.

29. See *Sefer ha-Hinukh*, no. 1 re: Gen. 1:28; Isa. 45:18; also, Reuven Kimelman, "Homosexuality and Family-Centered Judaism," *Tikkun* 9, no. 4 (July/August 1994): 53–57.

30. For the primary *inclinatio naturalis* being the drive to live, see Aquinas, *Summa Theologiae*, 2/2, q. 64, a. 5; also, D. Novak, *Suicide and Morality* (New York: Scholars Studies, 1975), p. 44.

31. For the notion of natural necessity (*to anagkaion*), see Aristotle *Metaphysics* 1015a20ff.

32. See Aristotle *Politics* 1254a20.

33. See Aristotle *Nicomachean Ethics* 1112b12ff.; idem, *Metaphysics* 1072b10.

34. Aquinas, *Summa Theologiae*, part 2/1, question 46, article 5.

35. See his "Here Comes the Groom: A (Conservative) Case for Gay Marriage," *New Republic*, August 1989, p. 22; also, see his fullest and most theological statement on the subject, "Alone Again Naturally: The Catholic Church and the Homosexual," *New Republic*, 28 November 1994, pp. 47–55.

36. See Germain Grisez, *The Way of the Lord Jesus: Living A Christian Life* (Quincy, IL: Franciscan Press, 1993), 2: 653–54.

37. For the rabbinic notion that social recognition of homosexual marriages *de jure* is worse than the presence of homoerotic activity *de facto*, see B. Hullin 92a–b and Rashi, s.v. "ein kotvin;" *Vayiqra Rabbah* 23.9.

38. See Aristotle *Nicomachean Ethics* 1155a5. Aristotle here is speaking of *philia*, which is a nonerotic relationship.

39. Although Judaism permits divorce, it regards it as a tragedy. See B. Gittin 90b re: Mal. 2:13; also, D. Novak, *Law and Theology in Judaism* (New York: KTAV, 1974), 1: 6–9.

40. See Ps. 128:6; B. Kiddushin 30a re: Deut. 4:9.

41. Hence they cannot observe the commandment "honor your father and your mother" (Exod. 20:12) with both objects in tandem. See B. Kiddushin 31a.

42. In the discussion following the original reading of this paper at Brown University on 7 April 1995, Prof. Andrew Koppelman of Northwestern University questioned

whether this point would be valid in the case of a child conceived through rape. In response, I pointed out that even though rape or any other illicit act of parents is to be repudiated by their children (see B. Berakhot 7a re Exod. 34:7 and Deut. 24:16), nevertheless, even a child born of an illicit union, who is socially stigmatized because of that union (*mamzer*), is still required according to Maimonides to honor his or her parents (MT: Mamrim, 6.11; see B. Yevamot 22a, and *Tur*: Yoreh De`ah, 240 and Karo, *Bet Yosef*, s.v. "katav ha-Rambam"). That minimally means recognition of their role in his or her coming to be. For more on the importance of parenthood as a natural institution, see Novak, *Law and Theology in Judaism* 1:72–79, 2:47–55.

43. See Aristotle, *Metaphysics* 1022a14.

44. See Andrea Dworkin, *Intercourse* (New York: Free Press, 1987), esp. pp. 126–43. For a somewhat more nuanced presentation of a similar view, see Susan Brownmiller, *Against Our Will* (New York: Simon and Schuster, 1975).

45. See Hegel, *Phenomenology of Spirit*, trans. A. V. Miller (Oxford: Clarendon Press, 1977), nos. 450, 268. Note, also, the suggestion of Martha Nussbaum in *The Fragility of Goodness: Luck and Ethics in Greek Tragedy and Philosophy* (Cambridge and New York: Cambridge University Press, 1986), pp. 370–71, that Aristotle's emphasis of the political necessity of the family (*Politics* 1262a5ff.; contra Plato *Republic* 463Dff.) is related to his heterosexuality.

46. See Freud, "The Most Prevalent Form of Degradation in Erotic Life" (1912) in *Collected Papers*, trans. J. Strachey (London: Hogarth Press, 1952), 4: 205–206.

47. For the condition of consent in mutual sexual matters, see B. Kiddushin 2b; Meiri, *Bet Ha-Behirah*: Kiddushin, ed. Sofer, 8; MT: Ishut, 14.8. Also, see B. Baba Batra 48b; MT: De`ot, 5.4.

48. See B. Kiddushin 12b; MT: Ishut, 1.1, 4.

49. Cf. Plato *Philebus* 60Dff; Aristotle *Nicomachean Ethics* 1173b30ff.

50. That is why the pleasures of eating are to be included in interhuman fellowship. See M. Berakhot 7.1; B. Berakhot 45a re: Ps. 34:4, and B. Berakhot 59b and Tos., s.v. "ve-Rabbi Yohanan"; B. Kiddushin 31a–b.

51. Hence the nihilistic enjoyment of destruction per se is prohibited (*bal tash'hit*). See Deut. 20:19–20; Maimonides, *Sefer ha-Mitsvot*, neg. no. 57; Novak, *Jewish Social Ethics*, pp. 118–32.

52. See B. Berakhot 35a–b and Y. Berakhot 6.1/9d re: Ps. 24:1.

53. See B. Nedarim 20b; MT: Isurei Bi'ah, 21.12.

54. For the notion that the character of the sexual relationship of parents influences the character of their children, see B. Nedarim 20a–b.

55. Thus the initiation of marriage is an occasion of communal celebration. See B. Ketubot 7a–b; Meiri, *Bet ha-Behirah*: Ketubot, ed. Sofer, 73.

56. See B. Sanhderin 75a; MT: Yesodei Ha-Torah, 5.9.

57. Along these lines, note how deceit can be grounds for annulment of a marriage. See M. Kiddushin 2.2; T. Kiddushin 2.4; MT: Ishut, 8.1

58. See Deut. 23:2; M. Yevamot 6.5; B. Yevamot 61a–b and 76a–b; Y. Yevamot 6.5/7c and 8.2/9a–b.

59. M. Yevamot 6.6; B. Yevamot 64a; Y. Yevamot 6.6/7c.

60. See B. Yevamot 64a, Tos., s.v. "yotsee"; B. Ketubot 77a, Tos., s.v. "leetnei"; *Hagahot Maimoniyot* on MT: Ishut, 15.7, n. 4; R. Isaac bar Sheshet Parfat, *Teshuvot Rivash*, no. 15; Isserles, note on *Shulhan Arukh*: Even Ha`Ezer, 1.3 and 154.10 (and Eisenstadt, *Pit'hei Teshuvah* thereon, n. 27).

61. See B. Sanhedrin 19b.

62. Usually, these adoptive parents are their adopted children's teachers; hence they

are to be honored as parents since the honor due both teachers and parents is virtually identical. See R. Moses Schreiber, *Teshuvot Hatam Sofer*: Orah Hayyim, no. 164.

63. See Wittgenstein, *Philosophical Investigations*, trans. G. E. M. Anscombe (New York: Macmillan, 1958), sec. 67, 32.

64. See M. Yevamot 4.10; B. Yevamot 42b; MT: Gerushin, 11.20.

65. See, e.g., B. Shabbat 35b and parallels; B. Eruvin 63b and parallels; B. Hullin 11a; Maimonides, *Guide of the Perplexed*, 3.34.

66. See M. Yevamot 6.6 and *Bavli* and *Yerushalmi* thereon; also, Novak, *Jewish Social Ethics*, p. 98 n. 9.

67. For some restrictions on celibate rabbis, see T. Sanhedrin 7.5; B. Sanhedrin 36b, and Rashi, s.v. "zaqen"; MT: Sanhedrin, 2.3.

68. See B. Sanhedrin 58b–59b and Tos., s.v. "ve-ha."

69. For this distinction between an avoidable norm (*mitsvah*) and an unavoidable one (*hovah*), see MT: Berakhot, 11.2.

70. See B. Yevamot 90a–b.

71. See "The Homosexual Movement: A Response by the Ramsey Colloquium," *First Things* 41 (March 1994): 15–20.

72. See B. Yevamot 62a; MT: Ishut, 15.6 and R. Vidal of Tolosa, *Magid Mishneh* thereon.

73. B. Yevamot 22a and parallels.

74. It is true that in the case of a Jewish woman married to a gentile, her children are Jews. However, the likelihood of their living a traditional Jewish life is slim. See B. Kiddushin 68b re: Deut. 7:4 and Rashi, s.v. "ki yasir"; Rashi, *Commentary on the Torah*: Deut. 7:4.

75. See, e.g., M. Baba Batra 1.1, 3.7; B. Baba Batra 2a–b, 60a re: Num. 24:5.

76. See B. Avodah Zarah 36a and parallels; B. Yevamot 65b re: Prov. 9:8; and Rashi, s.v. "lomar" re: Lev. 19:17 (cf. B. Arakhin 16b).

Sexual Orientation and Human Rights:
A Progressive Jewish Perspective

JUDITH PLASKOW

This essay begins from the premise that the religious and public policy dimensions of sexual orientation are so thoroughly intertwined that it is almost impossible to disentangle them. Religious injunctions against homosexuality have shaped negative public attitudes toward bisexuals, gays, and lesbians and have been used to justify repressive civil legislation. The contemporary gay rights movement emerged in reaction to the pervasive homophobia of American culture, a homophobia formed and fueled by religion.[1] As the movement encouraged the visibility and activism of lesbians, gay men, and bisexuals, including those religiously involved, many religious denominations have found themselves deep in debate about both the legitimacy of homosexuality and gay religious participation and leadership. The parallel civil debate about gay and lesbian rights has been charged with religious emotion, and similar types of arguments have been advanced in secular and religious contexts. The question, then, is not so much *whether* religious arguments should have a bearing on public discussion as what the content of those arguments should be.

For progressives, serious discussion of this question must start, I believe, from a curious and important contradiction between theory and politics around gay, lesbian, and bisexual rights. At the same time that various social constructionist understandings of sexuality have become widely accepted in academic circles, providing the foundations for both important new historical research and discussions of sexual identity, the gay, lesbian, and bisexual movement has tended to depict sexual identity as inherent and unalterable.[2] Particularly as the New Right has made homosexuality an important battleground in its struggle to enshrine in law traditional sexual and "family" values, lesbians, gays, bisexuals, and our allies have argued strongly that some people are just born with an attraction to their own sex that is at once ineradicable and a fundamental part of identity. It is my contention in this paper that, while biological arguments may be strategically use-

ful, it is ultimately a mistake to ground support for gay and lesbian rights on biologically based understandings of sexual orientation. A progressive position, I will
argue, must use the insights of social constructionism to place the issue of homosexuality in the larger context of the feminist critique of gender roles, compulsory
heterosexuality, and traditional sexual ethics. I will lay out such a position within
a Jewish framework, with an eye toward the larger public discussion of human
rights and sexual orientation.[3]

The Liberal Jewish Discussion

The emergence of the gay rights movement has precipitated an ethical crisis within
many U.S. religious denominations. The existence of increasingly visible and vocal
lesbians, gay men, and bisexuals within every religious group has forced denomi-
national bodies to take stands on a host of issues related to homosexuality. Task
forces and the debates attending them have often generated anger, bitterness, and
deep division between those who would protect what they see as the integrity of
tradition and those who would defend the rights and integrity of gay and lesbian
members.[4] One of the more striking aspects of the current debates about homosexuality and religious tradition is the similarity of arguments across denomina-
tional lines. Within Jewish, Catholic, and Protestant contexts, conservatives point
to the supposedly unrelieved condemnation of homosexuality in both the Bible
and religious tradition, while many liberals appeal to the supposed innateness of
homosexuality to reinterpret or question the contemporary validity of the same
limited number of texts.

In the Jewish discussion, Leviticus 18:22 and 20:13 are taken as the key biblical
passages condemning homosexuality and defining it as an abomination. Exegeses
of other texts—the Sodom story, for example, or the rape of the Levite's concubine
in Judges—simply confirm the Levitical prohibitions.[5] While lesbianism is not
mentioned explicitly in the Tanakh, the rabbis find a reference to it in Leviticus
18:3, "You shall not copy the practices of the land of Egypt . . . or the land of
Canaan." The Sifra interprets the practices in question as a man marrying a man
and a woman marrying a woman, a position that is codified by Maimonides.[6] The
rabbis also explore the meanings of the term *to'evah* (abomination) and elaborate
on the Levitical injunction against male homosexuality, arguing that it applies to
both the active and passive partners.[7] All in all, traditional references to homosexuality are very sparse, a fact that many conservatives interpret as signaling the
rarity of homosexuality among Jews.[8]

I agree with conservatives that the weight of Jewish tradition is against homosexual relations. Indeed, what strikes me as far more compelling than the small
number of sources actually addressing the issue is the pervasive assumption that
heterosexual marriage is the norm for adult life. To my mind, the central issue for
the contemporary debate is not the meaning of this or that particular passage—
though I certainly recognize the strategic importance of new interpretations in enabling Halakhic (Jewish legal) change—but the meta-Halakhic question of the authority of traditional teachings on sexuality. This question can be further broken
down into at least two others. First, since Halakha (Jewish law) is an evolving sys-

tem, always responding to new social, economic, and political conditions, are there grounds for Halakhic change on the issue of homosexuality? And second, how should gay rights advocates within Judaism understand their relationship to Halakha?

In response to the first question about the grounds for Halakhic change, Halakhic liberals have adopted the same argument used by much of the gay rights movement in the public arena. They have highlighted new data on the fundamental and ineradicable nature of sexual identity, claiming that it undermines the Torah's prohibitions. Hershel Matt (z'l), for example, who was the first rabbi to call for change in Jewish attitudes toward homosexuality, argued that "the clear and consistent assumption behind all of the Torah's commands and prohibitions is . . . that human beings have freedom to obey or disobey them."[9] Where such freedom does not exist, violations of Jewish norms are judged more leniently. Matt pointed out that, while the Torah and tradition clearly presuppose that homosexual acts are freely chosen, contemporary evidence suggests that homosexuality is a "basic psychic orientation, involving the deepest levels of personality," and that, most important, it is almost impossible to change.[10] On the basis of this evidence, he argued for full acceptance and respect for constitutional homosexuals who otherwise live faithfully by Jewish law.[11]

When the law committee of the Conservative movement debated the legal status of homosexuality in 1991–92, the whole issue of choice was very much to the fore. Elliot Dorff, for example, in calling for a broad reconsideration of Jewish sexual values, emphasized the centrality of choice in his evaluation of homosexuality. He argued that it is *the* critical factor pressing the movement to rethink its Halakhic position. All Jewish traditional sources, he said, assume that homosexuality is a violation of the law because it is a matter of choice. We now know, however, on the basis of both scientific research and the testimony of gay and lesbian Jews, that this is not true. Yet while the new data convinces Dorff that it is inappropriate to see homosexuality as a moral abomination, he does not yet find it sufficiently conclusive to justify fully overturning traditional Jewish norms.[12]

Bradley Artson, who wrote the brief on behalf of full acceptance that precipitated the Conservative movement's discussion, based his argument on historical, rather than empirical, evidence. His understanding of the fixed and fundamental nature of homosexual identity was rooted in recent studies of the emergence of that identity toward the end of the nineteenth century. The fact that, until then, the label *homosexual* referred to acts rather than persons allowed Artson to argue that the homosexual behavior prohibited by the Torah was very different from what we mean by homosexuality today. "The Torah was not speaking about the constitutional homosexual," he says, "because it had no awareness of the possibility of such a person. . . . The Torah did not prohibit what it did not know."[13]

Matt, Dorff, and Artson put forward two versions of a widely promulgated argument that can be very powerful in both the religious and the civil spheres. Since there is no point in legislating against or punishing people for what cannot be changed, it seems that, could researchers only pinpoint the mechanism through which homosexual identity is acquired or transmitted, not only would Halakha have to accommodate this new knowledge but also sodomy statutes and discrimination against gays and lesbians would have to disappear. Such arguments do not simply take the teeth out of traditional prohibitions, moreover. They do so in a way that performs three important functions: (1) they allow for formal acknowledgment of traditional sources of authority; (2) they cause minimal disarray to traditional sexual values; and (3) they provide reassurance that accepting homosexuals will not increase their numbers.

Perhaps the central appeal of empirical studies pointing to the inborn nature of homosexual identity is that they allow proponents to support social change from within the framework of Halakha or commitment to the authority of Scripture. Thus, a number of the religious thinkers who draw on biological arguments distinguish between "true" or "obligatory" homosexuals and those who *could* lead heterosexual lives.[14] Hershel Matt, for example, argued that while a truly Jewish approach would counsel compassion for the constitutional homosexual, homosexuals or bisexuals who deliberately violate the Torah for their own pleasure or who could change with some effort still remain bound by the Torah's standards.[15] Since Matt never actually placed anyone in the category of gays who deliberately reject tradition, it appears that the concept of "situational" homosexuality functioned in his thought as a formal marker that allowed him to affirm tradition even while changing it. If constraint is the criterion for gay legitimacy, in other words, then Halakha or traditional social norms can still be affirmed as applying to those who have choice—should any such people exist. In this way, biological arguments provide a ready means of responding to social change without having to question tradition at a fundamental level.

Second, precisely because such arguments remain within the framework of tradition, they allow for acceptance of gays and lesbians with minimal disruption of sexual norms. As Hershel Matt expressed it, Torah norms apply to all who are capable of living by them. Obligatory homosexuals are "God's exceptions," who can live fully and faithfully by Torah's standards "except for the sexual identity of their mate[s]."[16] This formulation, like much of the recent rhetoric of the gay rights movement, assumes an assimilationist model of homosexual identity in which gays and lesbians are normalized through acceptance of dominant values. Bradley Artson, for example, argues for full and equal acceptance of monogamous gay and lesbian relationships—including the development of commitment and separation ceremonies—precisely on the grounds that ceremonial recognition would bring homosexual relationships into the framework of Halakha.[17] The fact that many gays and lesbians have adopted dominant family patterns, forming committed monogamous relationships and rearing children together, provides further grounds for this argument.

Third, constitutional constraint as the measure of homosexual acceptability also serves to define a certain discrete minority of the population as gay or lesbian while assuming that everyone else is naturally heterosexual. This construction does two things. It allows gay and lesbian activists and their allies to organize on the basis of a readily available and widely understood vocabulary of minority rights that fits with U.S. political rhetoric and sensitivities.[18] And it also helps to allay anxieties about the potentially deleterious effects of accepting gays and lesbians, particularly on the formation of young people's sexual identities. Again

Hershel Matt illustrates a line of argument that has been used repeatedly in both the religious and civil arenas. After considering whether gays and lesbians ought to be ordained, and thus allowed to function as guides and role models, he concludes that since "one does not choose to *be* homosexual, a homosexual rabbi could not influence a person to *become* homosexual."[19]

Problems with the Liberal Position

Since, in the inflamed and often anxious context of religious and public debate, the limits of the liberal position are also its strengths in terms of gaining allies, criticizing these arguments feels a bit like the proverbial "biting the hand that feeds." The notion of a fixed homosexual identity has provided a firm foundation for gay and lesbian organizing. It has furnished the basis for a civil rights argument in the religious and larger communities. And it has convinced some skeptics and turned them into friends. Despite these achievements, however, I would argue that the liberal position is riddled with contradictions that ultimately undermine its effectiveness and point in the direction of a more far-reaching analysis. Rather than seeking to establish gay, lesbian, and bisexual rights on the narrowest possible grounds, bisexuals, lesbians, gays, and our allies need to confront the evidence pointing to the complexity of sexual orientation, and then situate the issue in the larger context of a reexamination of sexual identity and sexual ethics.

As I can indicate only briefly here, claims about the "givenness" of gay identity are often based on faulty research and misrepresent or ignore evidence that undermines their premises. First, the great majority of studies—biological, psychological, and sociological—on which arguments for a fundamental and irrevocable sexual orientation are based ignore the experience of lesbians. The same androcentrism that has affected every other area of human knowledge, entering into the creation of fundamental paradigms and shaping the formulation of basic questions, also has informed sexological research.[20] This fact has skewed the data in several significant ways: (1) Although researchers often speak of "homosexuality" as if it were a unified phenomenon both within and across sex lines, in fact a number of the biological mechanisms that have been proposed to explain homosexuality in men cannot be generalized to lesbians.[21] (2) Studies of lesbian communities have yielded understandings of sexual identity that are far more complicated than the better known gay male accounts of an early and irresistible same-sex attraction. There seem to be several distinct trajectories of lesbian identity development, only one of which supports the idea of sexual orientation as a fundamental constitutional element outside of conscious control.[22] (3) These same studies suggest that the relationship between identity and behavior is also complex and contradictory. Not only are identity labels not terribly reliable predictors of actual sexual practices, but they are also fluid over time.[23] (4) Perhaps most significant, the experience of many lesbians challenges the opposition between nature and choice that grounds so many arguments about homosexuality. Many lesbians see their sexuality both as consciously chosen *and* as reflecting who they truly are.[24] Their lesbianism is a choice, but an erotic choice, not a purely political one, and certainly not arbitrary.

Second, if studies of lesbian lives challenge the notion of clear sexual categories, the existence of bisexuality is even more disruptive. Indeed, bisexuality is so problematic for both heterosexual and gay and lesbian self-understandings that, in virtually all arguments about sexual orientation, it is formally acknowledged and then substantively ignored. All the religious liberals, Jewish and non-Jewish, pay their respects to the Kinsey scale and the supposed bisexual potentialities of all human beings—and then proceed to argue on the basis of a binary understanding of sexual orientation as if these did not exist. Moreover, large numbers of bisexuals—including married men who engage in homosexual activity—are labeled as gay in studies of homosexuality, a fact that thoroughly confuses neat categories of any kind.[25] Indeed, the presence of bisexuals in homosexual research samples points to the fundamental methodological absurdity of biological research on homosexuality. By superimposing binary categories on complex data and then taking for granted the question of whose brains or glands will be dissected, such research presupposes what it seeks to explain.

Third, much of the historical research that grounds Artson's second version of the liberal argument similarly confounds clear sexual categories. The claim that the concept of sexual orientation was unknown before the modern period, and that therefore "true" homosexuals cannot be condemned by the Bible, is borrowed from a new gay history that is as concerned to dislodge the narrow sexual categories of the present as it is to recover the past. When Foucault and others argue that prior to the nineteenth century, the term *homosexual* was never a noun indicating a type of person but rather an adjective describing behavior, they are *criticizing* the notion of *any* stable sexual constitution.[26] While there is ample room for disagreement about whether this new history necessitates the radical conclusions some of its authors would draw, it certainly leaves open the question of whether current sexual classifications refer to anything real in human nature or are simply categories imposed on the flux of human sexuality—if there is any "sexuality" at all.[27] It is rather disingenuous, then, to use this research as if it proclaimed the discovery of a new scientific or historical truth unavailable to the Torah.

The reason that Matt, Dorff, Artson, and others ignore this large body of evidence pointing to the complexity and malleability of human sexual identity is connected to the strengths of their arguments that I outlined before. It is precisely the point of this perspective to leave untapped the potential of gays and lesbians to raise far-reaching questions about the sex-gender system. It is the restrictedness of the arguments that makes them acceptable. Assuming that gays and lesbians are "just like everyone else" except for the quirk of their sexual orientation, the liberal position attempts to normalize them within the framework of a heterosexist system that will now be adjusted at its margins.

This argument ignores the fact, however, that from the perspective of the same heterosexist system, gays and lesbians are *not* like everyone else. Within both the Jewish and U.S. contexts, primary emotional and sexual bonds between women are invisible and unthinkable.[28] Judaism does not condemn sex between women to the same degree as it condemns sex between men because "nothing happens" between women; it is the presence of a man/penis that defines the possibility of sexual relations.[29] Gay men, while acknowledged to exist, are profoundly threatening, for they expose the erotic underpinnings of the homosocial social order. They challenge the dominant understandings of masculinity and male sexuality, standing in an ambiguous relationship to male privilege.[30] To take gay and lesbian experience seriously, then, rather than incorporating it at the margins of the dominant system, would necessitate raising fundamental questions about a heterosexist, patriarchal social order, about gender roles, and about the fluidity and nature of human sexuality. This larger project, which was initially what the gay liberation movement saw itself as about, is far more threatening to traditional religious values. Yet it also has the potential to begin a conversation that addresses the complexity of people's lives, and that might lead to a new understanding of the nature of eroticism and its relationship to the holy.

Toward a New Perspective

Let me be clear, before I move on, about the limits and intent of my critique of the liberal position. I am quite aware that the danger of the evidence I have cited is that it can be interpreted to mean that all sexuality is fluid on an individual level, and that anyone can at any time choose or be taught to conform to religious norms. This would increase the pressure on gays and lesbians to undergo psychotherapy or other programs for change to bring them into conformity with religious injunctions. But historical and sociological studies that may be quite important and useful on the social level do not explain how individuals come to define themselves in relation to particular sexual categories; nor do they indicate that such categories can be changed according to whim.[31] Thus, I do not want to dispute or diminish the claims of those gays and lesbians who "always knew" that they were gay or lesbian and/or who feel themselves such from birth. My point is to make room for the variety of human sexual experience, to shift the burden of proof from the individual, who must now fit her or his life into a restricted set of sexual narratives, to the categories of sexual self-understanding themselves. The question then is not, Is this person truly gay or lesbian and thus deserving of acceptance by his/her religious community? but, Where do we get our sexual categories, and what religious, social, political, and economic functions do they serve?

This is the crucial shift in starting point: from seeking to justify the existence of gays and lesbians within a particular religious framework to seeking to understand—and dismantle—the categories that create the need for such a justification;[32] from seeking to enlarge the umbrella of our sexual categories so that they cover minorities at the margins, to assuming the diversity of human sexuality along many axes and proceeding from there. Lesbians and gay men are not a "them" whose presence needs to be justified; *we* are part of every religious community. We are members and leaders of congregations, parents, children, clergy, laity, active and engaged, bored, angry, and alienated. Just as Pogo declared, "We have met the enemy and he is us," so gays and lesbians are already part of that "we" that imagines itself as extending (or denying) rights to those "others."[33]

Having said early on that I agree with conservatives that the weight of tradition is against homosexual expression, I am now suggesting that it is the tradition's boundaries and categories that require justification. This shift in perspective is in many respects an extension of feminist arguments I have made throughout my work, and I can only briefly indicate some grounds for it here. First, I would contend that Jewish sexual norms are rooted in concerns about purity, status, and control of women's sexuality that serve the interests of male elites and that have long ceased to reflect the ethical insights or values of contemporary Jews. In this context, the current crisis in traditional sexual standards, of which debates about sexual orientation are only a part, provides an excellent opportunity to expand the range of voices participating in the development of Jewish sexual values, and thus the range of experiential and ethical insight on which the tradition can draw.[34] Second, and I will develop this point further, what we take to be full and authentic tradition is itself shaped from the perspective of the same elites. If we place at the center those the dominant tradition has marginalized or condemned, we broaden our sense of Jewish historical possibilities in which current arguments and judgments are grounded. Third, drawing on a wider range of texts and appealing to other Jewish values than those used to condemn homosexuality, I would argue that starting with the experience of the marginalized is itself thoroughly authorized by Jewish tradition. As Lisa Edwards argued in a sermon on *Ahare Mot* and *Kedoshim* (the Torah portions that contain Lev. 18 and 20):

> We are your gay and lesbian children: "You must not seek vengeance, nor bear a grudge against the children of your people" (Lev. 19:18); we are your lesbian mothers and gay fathers: "Revere your mother and your father, each of you" (19:3) . . . ; we are the stranger: "You must not oppress the stranger. You shall love the stranger as yourself for you were strangers in the land of Egypt" (19:34) . . . ; we are lesbian and gay victims of gay-bashing and murder: "You may not stand by idly when your neighbor's blood is being shed" (19:16); we are your gay and lesbian neighbors: "You must not oppress your neighbor (19:13). You must judge your neighbor justly (19:15). You shall love your neighbor as yourself" (19:18).[35]

Criticizing Compulsory Heterosexuality

This shift from a "gay as other" to a gay-centered perspective does not mark the end of encounter with tradition, however, but rather the beginning. I would argue that such an encounter has at least three dimensions, each of which is just in its earliest stages of development. The first is a critical examination and analysis of the ways in which Judaism helps to create and enforce a system of "compulsory heterosexuality."[36] This phrase refers to the complex political and social processes through which a polymorphous human sexuality comes to be channeled and expressed in certain narrow and definite ways. It names the complex web of ideologies and institutions through which people learn and are made to be heterosexual. Over the course of the last twenty-five years, feminists have shown how gender roles are communicated from birth and enforced by social and ideological structures as diverse as family, peer group, school, medicine, religion, and workplace. Still much less visible are the ways in which expectations of heterosexuality are imparted and maintained through all the same mechanisms. The romantic fairy tales told to children; the grade school readers, even in their multicultural versions; the obsessions of the media; the constant questions, "Do you have a boyfriend/girlfriend yet?" all convey the assumption of heterosexuality, at the same time that social ostracism, beatings, military discharges, psychiatric incarceration, job firing, and the like enforce the boundaries of acceptable behavior, punishing those who fail to get the message and trying to force them back into line. So pervasive is this network of stories, expectations, rewards, and punishments that it is as invisible and taken for granted as the air we breathe.

The analogy between compulsory heterosexuality and gender roles as political and social institutions is not accidental. Gender roles are a mainstay of compulsory heterosexuality and are, in turn, sustained by it. Part of the task of a gay critique of Jewish tradition is to examine the confluence of these themes in Jewish life and sources. Genesis 3:16, for example—"Your desire shall be for your husband and he shall rule over you"—offers a succinct condensation and coupling of compulsory heterosexuality and women's subordination. In these words of God punishing Eve for her role in eating the fruit of the tree of knowledge, her (heterosexual) desire for her husband is clearly linked to her subservience to him.[37] This connection, sanctified in narrative, is enforced and regulated by the legal portions of the Torah. As I have argued in the context of a feminist critique, biblical law is deeply concerned with delineating and protecting male rights to a woman's sexuality, guarding against the violation of these rights with the severest possible penalties. Women's sexuality, both as fecundity and source of licit intercourse, is perceived as their main contribution to the family and is to be channeled to serve the interests of its male head. One can see in the strict laws concerning virginity and adultery modes of constructing and policing relationships between gender roles, obligatory heterosexuality, and the constraint of female sexuality.[38] These relationships require a great deal of further exploration.

The few biblical passages dealing directly with homosexuality need to be read in the context of this same critique of compulsory heterosexuality. In a situation in which intense political debate over the scanty references to homosexuality has shaped the framework for their interpretation, we need to ask whether these texts represent important moments in the construction of heterosexuality or, in their historical contexts, reflect different concerns. The fact that biblical injunctions against homosexual behavior are directed entirely at men seems to indicate the importance of male sexuality, too, being directed toward procreativity and the heterosexual family. Or rather, since the Tanakh accepts the existence of prostitution,[39] a man lying with a man after "the lying down of a woman" (Lev. 18:22) seems to pose a more profound boundary violation than a man having heterosexual sex with someone other than his wife. Although it is tempting to read the Levitical prohibitions as seeking to maintain heterosexuality, procreativity, and appropriate gender roles, the fact that Leviticus 18:22 seems to refer only to the insertive—that is, more "masculine"—partner, makes such a straightforward reading questionable.[40]

It may be, as Saul Olyan argues, that the prohibitions against male anal intercourse in Leviticus have a somewhat different purpose than the surrounding sexual legislation. The fact that the laws about sex between men—unlike the injunctions against incest, adultery, and bestiality—are found only in this context indicates that they cannot be separated from Leviticus's purity-related concerns. Olyan suggests that the violation involved in male anal sex may be that of mixing defiling fluids—in this case, semen and excrement.[41] Writing in a more theological vein, Gary Comstock places the Levitical injunctions in the context of a broader program of social control carried on by the priesthood after the exile. Allowed to return to Judah only as dependents on Persian rule, Israel's ruling elites could hope to exercise power only in the religious sphere. Comstock suggests that the whole range of Levitical rules tightly regulating personal behavior and emphasizing divine threats and punishments may have represented an effort on the part of these elites to hold onto power in the one area where they still had some influence.[42] While such a reading does not address the specific import of the prohibition of sex between men, it does draw attention to the relationship between cultural change and anxiety and the effort to maintain boundaries in the sexual arena.

Whatever the original purpose of the biblical condemnations of homosexual behavior, appeals to these passages constitute a major strategy in *contemporary* efforts to enforce compulsory heterosexuality. The whole controversy over the proper interpretation and use of these biblical texts serves to reinforce gay and lesbian marginality and to increase the pressure toward heterosexual dating and marriage. Some conservative interpreters have expressed concern about the impact of religious debates on wider antigay attitudes. They have sought to restrict the applicability of biblical prohibitions, arguing that religious injunctions are relevant to decision making only in the religious sphere.[43] But such attempts to draw a line between the religious and secular realms are disingenuous. Given the historical importance of religious attitudes in shaping public reactions to homosexuality, religious appeals to traditional prohibitions cannot help but validate and contribute to negative and discriminatory attitudes and behaviors in the larger society.

Broadening the Sources

The second dimension of a gay-centered encounter with tradition involves broadening the sources considered in relation to homosexuality so that the existence of homosexual activity in Jewish history begins to become visible.[44] The purpose of such an approach is not to deny the weight of tradition against homosexuality, but to begin to uncover the more complex reality the official opprobrium masks. It is striking that, until now, those on both sides of the religious debate on homosexuality have generally been satisfied with arguing over a limited number of texts. Even those who seek to show that biblical prohibitions no longer apply rarely consider the possibility of a positive witness to homoeroticism in the stories about David and Jonathan or Naomi and Ruth.[45] It is as if the desire to extend rights to contemporary gays and lesbians does not confer the ability to imagine heroes of the past engaging in same-sex relationships. The tradition is still read through the lenses of presumed heterosexuality, and the mutually exclusive categories of our own society—either homosexual or heterosexual; if homosexual, then not married—make it very difficult to imagine a different past.

The narrowness of the view of Jewish practices that flows from this perspective becomes very clear in relation to later materials. A number of prominent medieval poets, thinkers, and liturgists wrote, among their other works, love poems to young boys. Not only is this material simply unknown to most Jews but also many interpreters have gone to great lengths to deny that the poems are based on actual experience. But even if some of the homoerotic imagery does simply reflect literary convention, the willingness of prominent teachers and poets to use such tropes indicates a greater elasticity in the Jewish sexual ethos than is generally acknowledged.[46] Moreover, the existence of man-boy relationships among Jews is attested in a range of medieval sources, Jewish and non-Jewish. They suggest that in a number of cases in which Jewish men were accused of having sex with boys, the rabbis responded leniently or turned their backs on the evidence.[47] Perhaps, then, the sparseness of Halakhic condemnations of homosexuality testifies not so much to the absence of such behavior as to the fact that it was not viewed with much severity. In this case, the Talmudic dictum that the rarity of male-male relationships among Jews makes preventive legislation unnecessary may be taken in the same spirit as the words of the chief rabbi of Haifa, who announced that there are no bastards in that city.[48] Such recovery of the complexities and contradictions of Jewish sexual attitudes and behaviors is linked to the critique of compulsory heterosexuality, in that naming heterosexuality as an institution is crucial to perceiving the data that might challenge or undermine it.

Creating a New Ethic

The third dimension of encounter with tradition is the creation of a new Jewish sexual ethic. A narrow focus on the issue of homosexual rights, by singling out the behavior of a vulnerable minority, serves to distract attention from the larger crisis in Jewish sexual ethics and the need for a fundamental rethinking of Jewish sexual values. Shifting attention from the acceptability of homosexuality to the constraints and deformations of the traditional ethical system makes it possible and necessary to open up thinking about sexual ethics in at least two ways. First, it becomes possible to articulate a sexual ethic that applies across differences in sexual orientation without advocating some version of heterosexual marriage as a universal norm. And second, it becomes necessary to place sexual values in the context of a larger ethical system. Although those involved in the debate about the appropriate interpretation of normative texts often seem to imply that an adequate sexual ethic must be sought only in those sources that deal directly with sexuality, I maintain that sexual ethics does not constitute a discrete realm.[49] The norms that guide our sexual behavior ought simply to be an extension of those we seek to realize in all relationships with others. The values that might guide our thinking about an inclusive sexual ethic are drawn partly from Jewish tradition, but also represent a counter to tradition and its ethic of domination. These values include justice, mutuality, an expanded notion of generativity, and the value of integrity in sexual expression.

Justice is a central Jewish value, and one that must be reinterpreted and extended in the context of sexual ethics. The importance of justice as a norm is that it pertains not simply to the quality of interpersonal relationships but also to the social system in which they are embedded. As I have argued elsewhere, what takes place in the bedroom can never be separated from the larger social setting of which the bedroom is part.[50] Patterns of domination and injustice in the larger society are both taught and repeated in the family and in intimate relationships, which are often the first schoolhouses for learning domination. While the interdependence of the so-called public and private spheres has ramifications for many dimensions of sexual interaction, it affects gays and lesbians in particular ways. Religious and social condemnation serve to keep people closeted to themselves and to others. They induce people to marry who never should marry. They generate self-doubt and self-contempt that can make healthy relationships difficult or impossible. A common argument against the acceptance of gays and lesbians is that they have difficulty forming enduring relationships. To the distinctly limited extent that this criticism is valid, it does not take account of the complete absence of social supports for gay and lesbian partnerships, and thus the connection of interpersonal difficulties to larger structures of injustice. Insofar as emotional and sexual intimacy are basic human goods, the demands of justice require that the social preconditions for achieving and sustaining intimacy are available to all persons.

Mutuality as a value is connected to justice in that it seeks the equalization of power in relationships, serving as a counter to the ethic of domination that characterizes compulsory heterosexuality. Privileging marriage as the only legitimate avenue of sexual expression makes it difficult to see the extent to which it is bound up with gendered inequalities in power or to evaluate the quality of sexual interactions within the institution of marriage. When two people marry, it is as if a curtain falls on their relationship behind which all behavior is assumed to be unobjectionable. Rising rates of sexual and domestic violence are seldom mentioned in discussions of the sanctity of marriage, nor are religious understandings of marriage examined in terms of their role in the origins of abuse.[51] Gay and lesbian relationships, lacking social and religious legitimacy, less easily fall into preestablished patterns; they must continually invent and reinvent themselves. While this certainly does not mean that all such relationships are models of mutuality, still mutuality is more possible in gay and lesbian relationships than in those that are rooted in socially sanctioned unequal roles. In breaking the links between marriage, gender roles, and the constraint of women's sexuality, gay and lesbian relationships point in the direction of greater mutuality in our intimacy constellations.

Generativity and intergenerational continuity are important Jewish values that are often invoked in condemning homosexuality. A central argument against accepting gay and lesbian relationships is that they are not procreative and thus cannot contribute to ensuring the Jewish future. Since this claim is empirically false, in that many lesbians and gay men do have or seek to have children, a Jewish community worried about the next generation should want to support *all* adults concerned with raising Jewish children. At the same time, however, the growing number of actively involved Jews not living in traditional family constellations argues for a broadening of the concept of generativity.[52] As the tradition has often acknowledged, Jews can contribute in many ways to nurturing the next generation. In fact, a persistent theme in rabbinic texts is the tension between commitment to procreation and family and a total engagement with Torah. The fact that the rabbis were vitally concerned with the reproduction of Torah learning and the raising up of disciples points to the diversity of ways in which Jews have expressed their concern for the future.[53] However generativity is understood, loving sexual relationships can enhance and foster it. By contributing to individual creativity and a general sense of well-being, they strengthen the capacity to make commitments to the next generation, whether these take the form of engaging in larger communal projects or bearing and raising children.[54]

A final value, integrity, may serve to integrate the personal and communal dimensions of sexual ethics. Many years ago, I suggested "integrity" to Hershel Matt as a key third term between his poles of arbitrary choice and constitutional determinism. In using the word, I was groping toward a way of describing gay and lesbian identity that sidestepped the question of causes and origins in favor of the significance and appropriateness of sexual decision making. Mary Hunt has recently advocated the same term as a way beyond the fruitless debates about whether homosexuality is chosen. "Does it make an *ethical* difference," she asks, "if . . . good things flow from the relationship—people are nurtured, the world is a safer, happier place, energies for justice are harnessed?"[55] Her understanding of integrity is important because, in providing criteria for recognizing ethical sexual choices, it situates the individual firmly in community. Integrity includes both what is synchronous for the individual—"I had to do it for myself"—*and* what spills over into creative involvement in the larger collectivity. I suggest that it is precisely the recognition of this integrity in many Jewishly active and involved gays and lesbians that has precipitated the crisis over homosexuality in the Jewish community and led to the current debates. Perhaps if we focused less on the justification of gay and lesbian existence in relation to certain texts and more on the fruits of sexual relationships for self and community, we would be better able to address the real problems of domination and abuse that characterize all too many sexual relationships, and at the same time encourage the intimacy and mutuality that distinguish holy sexuality.

Conclusion

As I suggested at the beginning of this essay, I believe that religious debates about sexual orientation intersect at many points with debates in the public arena. Although it is not appropriate in the U.S. context that particular religious prohibitions or claims be directly translated into policy, religious values do shape civil discourse insofar as they inform both public discussion and the consciences of individuals. More specifically, in a social and political situation in which anti-gay-rights forces constantly appeal to biblical attitudes as a warrant for discriminatory legislation, liberal arguments for rejecting their relevance continue to be important and necessary because they engage the basic framework of biblical authority on which such appeals are grounded. I believe, however, that lesbians, gay men, bisexuals, and our allies must continually look beyond particular battles to the larger task of creating just gender and sexual relations in our society and religious traditions. What are the conditions that will allow every individual to grow in sexual integrity, free from domination? In laying out some issues central to this larger question, I have tried to connect critically and constructively with the values of my own tradition, at the same time addressing the values that underlie public discourse about sexual orientation.

Notes

1. I move back and forth in this essay between using the term *gay* as a generic for gay, lesbian, and bisexual and using all three terms. Since the liberal religious discussion within Judaism (and Christianity) has deliberately not addressed the issue of bisexuality, however, I use only the terms *gay* and *lesbian* when referring to that discussion.

2. Steven Epstein makes this same point in "Gay Politics, Ethnic Identity: The Limits of Social Constructionism," in *Forms of Desire: Sexual Orientation and the Social Constructionist Controversy*, ed. Edward Stein (New York and London: Routledge, 1992), p. 243. While some bisexuals see bisexuality as fundamentally challenging assumptions about the immutability of sexual identity, others define bisexuality as a third inherent category. See the various essays in Loraine Hutchins and Lani Kaahumanu, *Bi Any Other Name: Bisexual People Speak Out* (Boston: Alyson Publications, 1991); also Elizabeth Daumer, "Queer Ethics, or the Challenge of Bisexuality to Lesbian Ethics," *Hypatia* 7, no. 4 (Fall 1992): 91–105.

3. For an earlier synopsis of my argument, see "Lesbian and Gay Rights: Asking the Right Questions," *Tikkun* 9, no. 2 (March/April 1994): 31–32.

4. For an excellent discussion of the issues from a gay perspective, see Gary David Comstock's book, *Unrepentant, Self-Affirming, Practicing: Lesbian/Bisexual/Gay People Within Organized Religion* (New York: Continuum, 1996).

5. Maurice Lamm, *The Jewish Way in Love and Marriage* (San Francisco: Harper & Row, 1980), pp. 65–66; Joel Roth, "Homosexuality," in *Papers on Issues Regarding Homosexuality* (The Committee on Jewish Law and Standards, The Rabbinical Assembly, 1992), pp. 4, 8–9.

6. Rachel Biale, *Women and Jewish Law: An Exploration of Women's Issues in Halakhic Sources* (New York: Schocken Books, 1984), p. 195; Roth, "Homosexuality," pp. 10–12.

7. Roth, "Homosexuality," pp. 12–15, 25–35.

8. Lamm, *The Jewish Way*, pp. 65, 66, citing B. Kiddushin 82a.

9. Hershel Matt, "Sin, Crime, Sickness, or Alternative Life Style? A Jewish Approach to Homosexuality," in *Walking Humbly with God: The Life and Writings of Rabbi Hershel Matt*, ed. Daniel Matt (Hoboken, NJ: KTAV, 1993), p. 226. This article first appeared in *Judaism* in 1978.

10. Matt, "Sin, Crime, Sickness," p. 227.

11. Hershel Matt, "A Call for Compassion," in *Walking Humbly With God*, p. 237. This article originally appeared in *Judaism* in 1983.

12. Elliot Dorff, "Jewish Norms for Sexual Behavior: A Responsum Embodying a Proposal," in *Papers on Issues Regarding Homosexuality*," pp. 7–15.

13. Bradley Artson, "Gay and Lesbian Jews: An Innovative Jewish Legal Position," *Jewish Spectator* (Winter 1990–91): 6–14, quotation, p. 11.

14. This is a standard distinction within the traditional psychoanalytic position. See, e.g., Charles Socarides, "The Homosexualities: A Psychoanalytic Classification," in *The Homosexualities: Reality, Fantasy, and the Arts*, ed. Charles Socarides and Vamik Volkan (Madison, CT.: International Universities Press, 1990), p. 11.

15. Matt, "Sin, Crime, Sickness," p. 228.

16. Matt, "A Call for Compassion," pp. 237, 238; Hershel Matt, "Homosexual

Rabbis?" in *Walking Humbly With God*, p. 241. The latter article initially appeared in *Conservative Judaism* in 1987.

17. Bradley Artson, "Enfranchising the Monogamous Homosexual: A Legal Possibility, A Moral Imperative," *S'vara: A Journal of Philosophy, Law, and Judaism* 3, no.1 (1993): 15–26.

18. Epstein, "Gay Politics," p. 239.

19. Matt, "Homosexual Rabbis?" p. 232.

20. Annabel Faraday, "Liberating Lesbian Research," in *The Making of the Modern Homosexual*, ed. Kenneth Plummer (Totowa, NJ: Barnes and Noble Books, 1981), 114–15.

21. William Byne, "The Biological Evidence Challenged," *Scientific American*, May 1994, p. 50.

22. Barbara Ponse, *Identities in the Lesbian World: The Social Construction of Self* (Westport, CT: Greenwood Press, 1978), pp. 140, 159–61; Carla Golden, "Diversity and Variability in Women's Sexual Identities," in *Lesbian Psychologies: Explorations and Challenges*, ed. the Boston Lesbian Psychologies Collective (Urbana and Chicago: University of Illinois Press), pp. 25–26.

23. Ponse, *Identities in the Lesbian World*, pp. 173–92; Golden, "Diversity and Variability," pp. 27–29, 31.

24. Golden, "Diversity and Variability," p. 32.

25. A. P. McDonald, "Some Comments on Research and Theory," *Journal of Homosexuality* 6, no. 3 (Spring 1981): 21.

26. See, e.g., Michel Foucault, *The History of Sexuality. Volume I: An Introduction* (New York: Vintage Books, 1980); David Halperin, "Is There a History of Sexuality?" in *The Lesbian and Gay Studies Reader*, ed. Henry Abelove, Michele Aina Barale, and David Halperin (New York and London: Routledge, 1993), pp. 416–31; Jeffrey Weeks, *Coming Out: Homosexual Politics in Britain, from the 19th Century to the Present* (London: Quartet Books, 1977).

27. John P. DeCecco and John P. Elia, "A Critique and Synthesis of Biological Essentialism and Social Constructionist Views of Sexuality and Gender," in *If You Seduce a Straight Person, Can You Make Them Gay?: Issues in Biological Essentialism Versus Social Constructionism in Gay and Lesbian Identities*, ed. John P. DeCecco and John P. Elia (Binghamton, NY: Haworth Press, 1993), pp. 1–26; David F. Greenberg, *The Construction of Homosexuality* (Chicago: University of Chicago Press, 1988), pp. 488–94; John Boswell, "Revolutions, Universals, and Sexual Categories," in *Hidden from History: Reclaiming the Gay and Lesbian Past*, ed. Martin Duberman, Martha Vicinus, and George Chauncey, Jr. (New York: Meridian Books, 1990), pp. 17–36; David Halperin, "Sex Before Sexuality: Pederasty, Politics, and Power in Classical Athens," in *Hidden from History*, pp. 37–53.

28. Marilyn Frye, *The Politics of Reality: Essays in Feminist Theory* (Trumansburg, NY: Crossing Press, 1983), pp. 152–73.

29. Biale, *Women and Jewish Law*, pp. 194–95; cf. Frye, *The Politics of Reality*.

30. Diana Fuss, *Essentially Speaking: Feminism, Nature and Difference* (New York and London: Routledge, 1989), pp. 45–49.

31. Dececco and Elia, "A Critique and Synthesis," p. 13; Epstein, "Gay Politics," p. 260; Eve Kosofsky Sedgwick, *Epistemology of the Closet* (Berkeley and Los Angeles: University of California Press, 1990), pp. 40–41; Carole Vance, "Social Construction Theory: Problems in the History of Sexuality," in *Homosexuality, Which Homosexuality?* ed. Dennis Altman, Carole Vance, Martha Vicinus, Jeffrey Weeks, et al. (Amsterdam: Schorer and London: GMP, 1989), pp. 16–17.

32. Shane Phelan, "(Be) Coming Out: Lesbian Identity and Politics," *Signs: Journal of Women in Culture and Society* 18, no. 4 (Summer 1993): 771.

33. I think, for example, of the battle over a gay rights ordinance in Wichita, Kansas, in 1977–78, during which it turned out that the organist in the largest Baptist church in the city—a church firmly against the ordinance—was a gay man who had been a life-long member of the church.

34. Judith Plaskow, *Standing Again at Sinai: Judaism from a Feminist Perspective* (San Francisco: Harper San Francisco, 1990), chap. 5.

35. Lisa Edwards, "A Simple Matter of Justice" (Unpublished sermon, April 29, 1993), pp. 8–9.

36. Adrienne Rich, "Compulsory Heterosexuality and Lesbian Existence," in *Powers of Desire: The Politics of Sexuality*, ed. Christine Stansell and Sharon Thompson (New York: Monthly Review Press, 1983), pp. 177–205; Gayle Rubin, "The Traffic in Women: Notes on the 'Political Economy of Sex'," in *Toward an Anthropology of Women*, ed. Rayna Reiter (New York: Monthly Review Press, 1975), pp. 171–80; Jonathan Ned Katz, *The Invention of Hetersexuality* (New York: A Dutton Book, 1995).

37. It is interesting that, while feminist scholars have noted that women's subordination is a punishment for sin, they have not speculated on the relationship between this subordination and heterosexuality. See, e.g., Phyllis Trible, *God and the Rhetoric of Sexuality* (Philadelphia: Fortress, 1978), pp. 115–39.

38. Plaskow, *Standing Again at Sinai*, pp. 171–75.

39. See, e.g., Genesis 38:15–18; Proverbs 5:15–23.

40. Saul M. Olyan, "'And With a Male You Shall Not Lie the Lying Down of a Woman': On the Meaning and Significance of Leviticus 18:22 and 20:13," *Journal of the History of Sexuality* 5, no. 2 (1994): 186, 189, 199.

41. Ibid., pp. 202–203, 205.

42. Gary David Comstock, *Gay Theology Without Apology* (Cleveland, OH: Pilgrim Press, 1993), pp. 63–68; cf. David Greenberg, *The Construction of Homosexuality*, pp. 193–95.

43. At a conference on Sexual Orientation and Human Rights in American Religious Discourse, held at Brown University in April 1994, a number of the conservative panelists made this argument.

44. See, e.g., Arthur Waskow, *Down-to-Earth Judaism: Food, Money, Sex, and the Rest of Life* (New York: William Morrow, 1995), pp. 296–300.

45. But gay and lesbian writers have explored this possibility. See, e.g., Rebecca Alpert, *Like Bread on the Seder Plate: Jewish Lesbians and the Transformation of Tradition* (New York: Columbia University Press, 1997), chap. 3; Faith Rogow, "Speaking the Unspeakable: Gays, Jews and Historical Inquiry," in *Twice Blessed: On Being Lesbian or Gay and Jewish*, ed. Christie Balka and Andy Rose (Boston: Beacon Press, 1989), pp. 75–76; Tom Horner, *Jonathan Loved David: Homosexuality in Biblical Times* (Philadelphia: Fortress Press, 1978), esp. chaps. 2, 3.

46. Raymond Scheindlin, *Wine, Women, and Death: Medieval Hebrew Poems on the Good life* (Philadelphia: The Jewish Publication Society, 1986), pp. 82, 86–88.

47. Norman Roth, "'Fawn of my Delights': Boy~Love in Hebrew and Arabic Verse," in *Sex in the Middle Ages*, ed. Joyce E. Salisbury (N.Y. and London: Garland, 1991), pp. 162–16; and idem, "'Deal Gently With the Young Man': Love of Boys in Medieval Hebrew Poetry in Spain," *Speculum* 57 (1982): 22–23.

48. I am unable to trace the source of this ruling.

49. Margaret Farley, "An Ethic for Same-Sex Relations," in *A Challenge to Love:*

Gay and Lesbian Catholics in the Church, ed. Robert Nugent (New York: Crossroad, 1983), pp. 100–106.

50. Plaskow, *Standing Again at Sinai*, 198.

51. On the latter issue, see Renita Weems, *Battered Love: Marriage, Sex, and Violence in the Hebrew Prophets* (Minneapolis: Fortress Press, 1995).

52. Martha Ackelsberg, "Families and the Jewish Community: A Feminist Perspective," *Response* 14 (Spring 1985): 15–16; and idem, "Redefining Family: Models for the Jewish Future," in *Twice Blessed*, p. 115.

53. Howard Eilberg-Schwartz, *The Savage in Judaism: An Anthropology of Israelite Religion and Ancient Judaism* (Bloomington and Indianapolis: Indiana University Press, 1990), pp. 229–34; and Daniel Boyarin, *Carnal Israel: Reading Sex in Talmudic Culture* (Berkeley and Los Angeles: University of California Press, 1993), chap. 5.

54. Plaskow, *Standing Again at Sinai*, pp. 209–10.

55. Mary E. Hunt, "Sexual Integrity," *Waterwheel* 7, no. 3 (Fall 1994): 3.

Constructing a Jewish Sexual Ethic: A Rejoinder to David Novak and Judith Plaskow

LOUIS E. NEWMAN

Introduction

The essays of Professors Novak and Plaskow address themselves to two basic questions: (1) what is, or should be, the Jewish teaching with respect to homosexuality? and (2) how and why is that teaching relevant to moral and legal discussions regarding homosexuality in our democratic and pluralistic society? It is evident that these two distinguished scholars have quite different responses to these questions, but before turning to the details of their views, I wish to attend briefly to questions of a methodological nature. Specifically, what does it mean to offer a Jewish position on homosexuality? What do we understand ourselves to be doing when we offer such a view and how do we proceed, as a practical matter, in constructing it?

Professors Novak and Plaskow share more in the way of common methodological assumptions than might at first be apparent. They agree that, in considering the ethics of homosexuality (or, presumably, any other issue), the teachings of Jewish tradition are, in some significant sense, authoritative. This does not mean that they understand the nature and source of that authority in similar ways. Indeed, they do not. But, as contrasted with secular philosophers who are free to draw upon the views of earlier thinkers and/or construct their own as they please, Novak and Plaskow understand their task as constructing a *Jewish* view, meaning one in consonance with the values expressed in this religious tradition as they understand it. Further, they implicitly agree that this tradition is not static, but evolving. Constructing a Jewish ethical position on homosexuality is not simply a matter of consulting the appropriate authoritative text(s), as if the tradition did not offer a multiplicity of resources, coming to us from many different times and places.

While these initial observations may seem self-evident, they have important implications for how Novak and Plaskow address the issues before us. The fact that neither is (1) secular nor (2) fundamentalist means that they understand Jewish ethics as a *constructive* enterprise. They each, in their own ways, construct a Jewish view of homosexuality, to borrow a phrase from Hermann Cohen, "out of the sources of Judaism." Thus, as their modest subtitles imply, they concede that others, using similar sources, could construct a different Jewish ethic.

But my point here is not only to draw attention to the fact that Novak and Plaskow are both Jewish thinkers, or that both are modern. Rather, I wish to emphasize two important but seldom appreciated implications of these shared assumptions. From the commitment to Judaism as a source of values, it follows that no traditional Jewish value or principle can be dismissed simply on the grounds that it conflicts with contemporary liberal values or principles, however cherished. Many modern Jewish ethicists of a liberal persuasion have tended too quickly to dismiss any element of their tradition at odds with widely shared contemporary values, especially autonomy and personal freedom. In short, to engage meaningfully in constructing a Jewish ethic of homosexuality means to leave open the real possibility that Judaism may challenge us to reevaluate and even reject liberal views that we typically place beyond scrutiny. This is the challenge of modern Jewish ethics to liberal-minded thinkers such as Plaskow.

By the same token, to do Jewish ethics in a modern context is to reject a simple "traditionalism." The views of traditional authorities cannot be taken simply at face value. They must, at the very least, be subjected to historical-critical analysis to determine if they are based on metaphysical assumptions that we do not share, or if they assume a social reality that no longer exists, or if they rely upon scientific knowledge that we now know to be incomplete or faulty. In short, the fact that the vast majority of traditional Jewish authorities rejected homosexuality as morally unacceptable does not, in and of itself, settle the question at hand. We are required to make judgments about how and when we appropriate the teachings that have been handed down to us. This is the challenge of modern Jewish ethics to traditionally inclined thinkers such as Novak.

In their discussions of Judaism and homosexuality, both Plaskow and Novak have given us much that we can affirm. Yet both positions can be critiqued for the ways in which they do (and do not) respond to the aforementioned challenges. I turn, then, to an examination of the ways in which each constructs a Jewish position on homosexuality.

Response to David Novak

David Novak notes that biblical law categorically prohibits homosexual acts between men and that subsequent rabbinic interpretation extends this prohibition to women. The reasoning behind this prohibition becomes clear, Novak thinks, when we take account of the fact that rabbinic authorities understood these prohibitions as universal and rational laws, not merely as special restrictions governing the Jewish people alone. The bulk of Novak's argument, then, consists of illuminating the "logic" of this prohibition that, like the rabbis, he regards as universally applicable. This is precisely why he believes strongly that Jewish teaching on homosexuality can and should be introduced into public discourse on the subject.

The Jewish objection to homosexuality, as Novak understands it, is that it contravenes the natural and ultimate purpose of sexuality, namely procreation. Moreover, the purpose of procreation is the preservation of family, understood as a man and a woman in permanent union together with their offspring. Since the entire raison d'être of family, then, is to serve as the context—the only natural context—in which to create and raise children, it follows that there can be no family with two persons of the same gender as they are obviously incapable of producing children. Marriages between heterosexuals who are infertile by reason of their age or other disability are permissible, Novak argues, because their infertility is unintended. Such marriages, in other words, do not in themselves violate the natural purpose of family, which is to create male-female unions capable, in principle, of producing children. For homosexuals, by contrast, their sexual orientation (whether innate or learned) precludes their producing children; hence, they cannot create families. Because their sex is nonprocreative, it cannot be the basis for a family, which Novak sees as the only situation in which "human persons [can] be fulfilled," and so it is forbidden.

First it must be noted that Novak's presentation is, as I suggested earlier, a "construction" out of the Jewish sources he cites. Nowhere does the tradition explicitly articulate the theory of human sexuality that he presents. The persuasiveness of his theory, then, depends upon the extent to which it explains all that the tradition does say about human sexuality, and homosexuality in particular. And, notwithstanding the impressive array of evidence he cites in support of his view, there are reasons to doubt that traditional Jewish views of sexuality are exactly as Novak suggests.

The cornerstone of Novak's analysis is his insistence that in Judaism the primary purpose of sex is procreation and the only natural context for procreation is the traditional marriage. Yet Judaism appears to acknowledge multiple purposes to human sexuality and marital union, as evidenced by one of the seven traditional marriage blessings: "Praised are you, Adonai . . . who created joy and gladness, bride and groom, pleasure, song, delight, and happiness, love and harmony, peace and companionship. . . ." Clearly the tradition recognizes that there is more to the union of man and woman than preparing the stage for procreation. By the same token, if procreation were truly the ultimate purpose of marriage, we would expect the tradition to prohibit divorce for any reason other than infertility. But, again, the tradition recognizes the legitimacy of divorce, not only in cases of infertility but also when there is no longer love or commitment, joy, or stability in the relationship. The same reasoning explains (better than Novak's, I believe) why Judaism recognizes the legitimacy of marriages between those who are too old to have children. The point is not that all heterosexuals are presumed capable of procreation (or analogized to those who are), but rather that their marriages are fulfilling in other ways that make them sacred quite apart from the possibility of procreation.

In addition, Novak's linkage of sex, marriage, and procreation may be in tension with several other aspects of Jewish law regarding sexuality. Even the most traditional rabbinic authorities recognize the legitimacy of at least certain types of contraception. Thus, it is clear that we can intentionally eliminate (or minimize) the possibility of procreation and yet engage in sexual intercourse. Yet on Novak's reading of the tradition, intentional nonprocreative intercourse seems to violate the very purpose of heterosexual union. In addition, the tradition permits heterosexuals to engage in sexual acts other than intercourse—oral sex, for example—which by their nature are not procreative. There is more to sexual relationships, it seems, than intercourse for the purpose of procreation in the context of a family designed to raise offspring.

But even if Novak's presentation is defensible vis-à-vis the Jewish sources he cites, there appear to be logical flaws in this argument from "nature." First, it is not at all apparent that procreation is the primary and natural purpose of sexuality. Novak himself notes two others—pleasure and personal communion—but then quickly asserts (on what basis?) that these are subsumed under procreation. And even if we were to concede that procreation *is* the primary purpose of sexuality, it would not follow that sex for the purpose of pleasure or personal communion is illegitimate. By analogy, even if the primary purpose of eating is to receive the nutrition necessary for physical survival, it does not follow that eating for the sheer delight of the taste is either immoral or unnatural. If it were, we would be forced to condemn both eating when we aren't hungry and eating triple chocolate cake and other delicacies even when we are. What holds for our physical appetite applies *mutatis mutandis* for our sexual appetites as well.

Moreover, Novak's claim that children "are best produced, cared for, and raised to responsible adulthood in a home founded on a permanently intended heterosexual union" is unsubstantiated. Do we have any evidence that children raised by two parents married to one another are better adjusted people or grow up to be more responsible citizens than those raised by single parents or, for that matter, by homosexual couples? What is clear is that society has an interest in the welfare of all its citizens, especially children. In order to ensure their welfare, states have clearly demonstrated their readiness to place children in foster homes, orphanages, and group homes; to legitimize adoption of children by single parents; and (in extreme cases) to terminate parental rights entirely. All of this suggests that, in this country at least, society acknowledges that children's welfare can be protected and their development nurtured in a variety of familial settings, not only (or even primarily) in the family headed by a heterosexual married couple.

Finally, it is hard to know how to assess Novak's discussion of the role heterosexuals play in the quest for human survival. He appears to believe that heterosexuals enjoy some kind of moral advantage insofar as "homosexuals need heterosexuals . . . in a way that heterosexuals do not need homosexuals for the sake of human survival." But even if this is true biologically, it is unclear what sort of moral weight this carries. Arguably, our survival as a species is more dependent on farmers than it is on actuaries or used car salesmen, more on MD's than on PhD's (certainly in religious studies!). What is not clear is whether there are any moral implications to these facts and, if so, what they are.

In all, Novak's interpretation of Jewish sexual ethics needs a fuller defense than it receives here, for there is much in Judaism that does not square with the "natural law" argument he offers. And, as I have suggested, some of the logical turns in his argument are questionable. Yet he must be commended for his clear affirmation that in Judaism sexuality is invested with social and communal significance. The contemporary notion that sexuality, or at least sexual behavior between consenting adults, is a strictly private matter and hence not within the purview of the state finds no support within traditional Jewish sources. That, in itself, represents a potentially very significant contribution that Jewish sexual ethics can make to public debate. In a society arguably obsessed with personal freedom and self-expression in all areas of life, Judaism challenges us to acknowledge that sexuality cannot be severed from social institutions of varying sorts (including, but not limited to, marriage, family, and parenting) that both channel and nurture our sexual natures. From my perspective, Judaism has a role to play in the public debate over homosexuality, not because its values are based on arguments from nature which are ostensibly "universal" but simply because it offers us ways of understanding sexuality, society, and the relationship between them that may well speak to those outside of the religious community that generated them.

Response to Judith Plaskow

Judith Plaskow's concern is to construct a Jewish view of homosexuality that does not rely on the premise, assumed by most liberals, that sexual orientation is biologically determined. From her perspective, this "standard" liberal view focuses too narrowly on homosexuals and so too on reinterpreting the Jewish textual sources that prohibit their sexual conduct. As a result, homosexuals are treated as a marginal group, while the dominant assumptions of Jewish sexual ethics remain unchanged. Instead, she argues, we must thoroughly reassess the traditional categories in this area, for at their core lie mistaken beliefs about human sexuality, as well as sexist views of gender roles and of compulsory heterosexuality. Two important conclusions emerge from her more radical critique of the Jewish tradition: first, a Jewish ethic that affirms the legitimacy of homosexuality as a matter of choice (and not only for those who "have no choice"); and second, a revisioning of the Jewish past in which models of sexual intimacy are expanded to include homosexuality as well as heterosexuality. From her perspective, Judaism has a role to play in contemporary debates about homosexuality precisely because historically, religions, Judaism included, have fostered homophobia. As she puts it, the question is "not so much *whether* religious arguments should have a bearing on public discussion as what the content of those arguments should be."

It is important to note first that Plaskow's position is not constructed within a *Halakhic* framework. In the tradition of Reform Judaism and along with many other contemporary feminists, she is not interested in reinterpreting the established legal norms, but in reassessing the value of the entire body of traditional teaching on sexuality. In this respect, she and Novak speak from and to very different communities of Jews. Her concern is with the meta-Halakhic questions regarding the authority of traditional teachings. This emerges most clearly when she notes the shift in her starting point "from seeking to justify the existence of gays and lesbians within a particular religious framework to seeking to understand—and dismantle—the categories that create the need for such a justification." In short, it is human sexuality as we understand it that is a given and the tradition's categories that must be challenged. But this approach raises serious questions, including not only "how gay rights activists within Judaism should understand their relationship to Halakha" but more fundamentally whether Plaskow's project is feasible altogether and, if so, on what basis.

Once we call into question the central categories that a religious tradition has utilized for many centuries, we are arguably no longer working within that tradition. What sort of authority, legal or otherwise, can one vest in a religious tradition that one believes to be corrupt at its very core? And having freed ourselves from Judaism's inherited teachings on sexuality, in what sense is the newly constructed ethic "Jewish?" Consider, for example, Jewish ethical teaching with respect to another issue: adultery. Given Plaskow's assertion that Jewish sexual ethics as a whole is tainted by sexism and so must be subjected to a radical critique, it is not far-fetched to imagine someone who argues that traditional Jewish prohibitions about married persons having multiple sexual partners similarly need to be questioned. Imagine an adulterous relationship—call it an "open marriage"—when no deceit is practiced and all parties concerned recognize the value of the relationship. Could we construct an argument "out of the sources of Judaism" that validates such a relationship, which even calls upon us to recognize the sexism inherent in a system that sanctions monogamous relationships in which men dominate women? I suspect that we could. I also question whether such a view would be recognizably Jewish. Returning to the question of homosexuality, if, as Plaskow suggests, a new sexual ethic is Jewish on the grounds that "starting with the experience of the marginalized is itself thoroughly authorized by Jewish tradition," then it appears that there is virtually no result that, in theory, could not be sanctioned by Judaism, however much it deviated from traditional teachings.

More specifically, if we claim to be doing "Jewish sexual ethics," we must be willing to vest Jewish tradition with some authority. This, in turn, means that we must be willing to allow that the teachings of this tradition, at some point and to some degree, limit what we regard as right and wrong, permissible and prohibited. But if Plaskow regards the tradition as a whole as flawed in its understanding of human sexuality, then it is not clear how we can draw upon it at all in constructing a usable sexual ethic for our time. My central question for her essay, then, is how we can challenge the most basic assumptions of traditional Jewish ethics and yet claim that we are constructing a Jewish ethic. At one point Plaskow indicates that the shift to a "gay-centered" perspective marks not "the end of encounter with tradition . . . but rather the beginning." In essence, the question is what the scope and quality of such an encounter can be given the radical departure from the tradition that she insists is necessary.

In the latter part of her essay, Plaskow takes up this challenge, but in ways that I find less than satisfying. In contrast to Judaism's "ethic of domination," she sketches an ethic based on "justice, mutuality, an expanded notion of generativity, and the value of integrity in sexual expression." All of these are values worthy of consideration in a new sexual ethic, but it is what Plaskow fails to consider that concerns me most: holiness. More than any other concept, it is holiness, (Hebrew, *kedusha*) that is held to characterize intimate relations between men and women. Indeed, marriage is *kedushin*, a holy bond between husband and wife. One wonders whether Plaskow affirms any ongoing value for holiness as the foundation of and standard for intimate sexual relationships. And, if she does, would traditional understandings of holiness need to change in any way to accommodate same-sex relationships? To appropriate this traditional category into a new Jewish sexual ethic would entail considering a set of questions that Plaskow has not raised: Can we order our lives as sexual beings in ways that facilitate and enhance (or, conversely, preclude or inhibit) a relationship with God? Can we assume that God has ordered the sexual dimension of human existence for some purpose and, if so, what restrictions might this imply for the ways in which we express our sexuality? Is more required to sustain a holy sexual relationship than just conforming to general moral standards of justice, mutuality, and integrity? A truly Jewish view of sexuality, I am suggesting, ought to encompass not only moral considerations but specifically religious ones as well. The tradition affirms that God's presence is manifested, among other places, in the relationship of husband and wife. The intriguing and important question that Plaskow and others need to address is what this demand would mean in the context of same-sex relationships.

This leads directly to another question: whether Jewish ethics as Plaskow understands it has anything distinctive to contribute to public debate on this question. Her analysis of the issue focuses primarily on the ways in which Judaism could be made more inclusive, partly by embracing and elaborating upon those aspects of the tradition that point toward homoerotic relationships. This has the potential to be enormously valuable for Jews concerned to understand their own sexuality in relationship to that of David and Jonathan, or of Ruth and Naomi, or as consonant with a medieval tradition of love poetry. But once gay rights is understood as a question of human rights, the underlying principles involved will necessarily be universal. Of course, there could still be a specifically Jewish justification for extending human rights to gays and lesbians, and developing such a justification could lend support to gay rights activists in our society. But does Judaism have anything new or distinctive to add to the legal dimensions of the current debate? Insofar as the new sexual ethic that Plaskow offers relies primarily on general moral considerations rather than specifically Jewish ones, it would appear that it does not.

Finally, at one point in her essay, Plaskow comes dangerously close to committing the genetic fallacy. She writes that "Jewish sexual norms are rooted in concerns about purity, status, and control of women's sexuality that serve the interests of male elites and that have long ceased to reflect the ethical insights or values of contemporary Jews." Even if her statement is correct (and arguably, Jewish sexual norms are based on other principles as well), we must not confuse the origins of a practice or principle with its value. Many current Jewish practices are rooted in beliefs that we no longer consider valid, and yet those practices continue to be meaningful (and observed) precisely because we have succeeded in reinterpreting the forms and institutions that already exist. In theory, at least, Jewish sexual norms are no exception. If Plaskow believes that they are, she needs to explain why.

By the same token, it is important not to judge the morality of any activity only by its results. At one point Plaskow approvingly quotes Mary Hunt's view that if "good things flow from the relationship" the origin of homosexuality is no longer of much significance. But there are many instances in which behavior is morally unacceptable, even though some moral goods may result. It is not at all apparent, then, that moral questions about the origin of homosexuality, especially the extent to which it is chosen, can be set aside, even if we could all agree that homosexual relationships often have positive, morally praiseworthy qualities.

In all, Plaskow's call for a radical reassessment of Jewish sexual norms raises complex questions about the nature of authority and continuity in Judaism. Fuller answers to these questions must be offered for her position to be persuasive. Moreover, she needs to attend more closely to the ways in which creating a more inclusive Jewish sexual ethic will contribute both to an understanding of the religious dimensions of sexual relationships generally and to the public discourse on gay rights.

At the same time, Plaskow makes an extremely important contribution to this debate in her recognition that the issue of homosexuality must not be discussed in "we–they" terms. Whatever else modern research on human sexuality has taught us, it is clear that people do not divide neatly into groups of "homosexuals" and "heterosexuals." Once we acknowledge the complexity of human sexual orientation, we cannot isolate homosexuality as an "aberration." This, in turn, means that the Jewish religious understanding of sexuality and its relationship to concepts of covenant, holiness, and other moral norms must be considered as a whole. Plaskow's quotation of Lisa Edwards's exegesis of Leviticus brings this point home powerfully and can serve as a reminder to Jews and non-Jews alike that gays and lesbians are parents and children and neighbors, as we all are.

Conclusion

Novak and Plaskow offer two sharply different readings of Jewish tradition on sexuality. While I have found much in their essays to challenge, I see them as in many ways complementary. Together they enable us to appreciate how difficult it can be to construct a position on homosexuality that is both consonant with traditional teachings and responsive to contemporary scientific knowledge and social reality. In the end, it is the clash of their voices that may be most instructive. For this religious tradition, at least, everything depends upon how we utilize the multifaceted resources that have come down to us, what intellectual constructs we bring to them, and especially how we understand the tradition's authority in our lives. In that sense, Novak and Plaskow remind us that we do not turn to religious traditions for answers to issues of sexual ethics—the "answers," in the end, are of our own making. What they offer us instead is a vast repertoire of values and institutions, symbols and texts, that can both challenge and enrich our understanding of humanity, sexuality, and society.

ROMAN CATHOLICISM

Introduction to Roman Catholic Perspectives on Sexual Orientation, Human Rights, and Public Policy

SUMNER B. TWISS

As with the other religious traditions represented in this volume, the Roman Catholic tradition and community incorporate a variety of views on same-sex behavior and relationships. Unlike those other traditions, however, the moral teachings of the Catholic Church hierarchy are presumed to be normative for all Catholics, laypersons and theologians alike. This is not to say that moral theologians do not dissent from the hierarchy's official teachings, for they do dissent even in the face of possible official censure. In the case of same-sex behavior, the hierarchy promulgates the teaching that although homosexual orientation is not itself morally evil, all such behavior is morally wrong and to be avoided (e.g., by abstinence or celibacy).[1] Although this position is defended by many moral theologians, others dissent from it, maintaining that even while heterosexual marriage is normative for all sexual acts and relationships, nonetheless committed same-sex relationships can be seen variously (for example, as morally preferable to other homosexual behavior that is more wrong; or as not morally wrong when considering that the entire relationship is oriented to permanent mutual love; or even as morally good [though still short of the heterosexual ideal]).[2] These moral positions are often correlated with public policy positions on, for example, the legal recognition of same-sex domestic partnerships, ranging from strong opposition to such recognition (the official view) to varying degrees of support for legal recognition (dissenting views).

The authors of the three papers in this section are all prominent moral theologians who express particular interest in the relationship between morality and law, as well as specific public policy implications when considering, from a Catholic perspective, the realities of same-sex orientation, behavior, and lifestyles and social discrimination against these. Despite the fact that our authors work within the same tradition, employ similar moral methodologies, appeal to many of the same sources, and acknowledge the human rights of gays and lesbians, they articulate different perspectives on a number of issues (for example, the morality of same-sex acts and relationships; how exactly morality bears on law and public policy; and what ought to be appropriate public policy regarding domestic partnerships among gays and lesbians). It is important to be aware of our authors' positional similarities and differences, for these may be instructive in discerning significant new possibilities for, as well as constraints on, how the tradition can or ought to respond to such issues in the future. What follows here is a very brief sketch of each author's position that attempts to highlight certain controversial issues both intrinsic to each position and among the three considered comparatively.

Working within a natural law approach coordinated with and informed by Scripture and traditional sources of Catholic moral theology, James Hanigan develops and defends the hierarchy's moral position on same-sex orientation and behavior. He argues for the normativity of the procreative purpose of human sexuality and male/female complementarity in the unitive meaning of marriage, subsequently using these norms to assess homosexual activity as intrinsically wrong and homosexual orientation as ontically disordered (though not itself immoral, since not voluntarily chosen) because of its strong tendency to immoral acts. Hanigan is quite candid about the fact that this position on the morality of homosexual behavior constitutes the "contextual horizon" for his subsequent consideration of law and public policy; that is, for Hanigan, moral views are not independent of public policy, although they are not determinative, either.

Moral views are not determinative because traditional as well as contemporary Roman Catholic thought has considered carefully the relationship that ought to exist between morality and law, especially regarding human sexual behavior. Although, as Hanigan notes, the tradition on moral grounds regards the state as having the duty to protect and encourage the institutions of (heterosexual) marriage and the family and to discourage behaviors that might threaten their well-being, it is also to develop specific policies and laws mediated by consideration of the common good and a corollary principle of toleration of some immoral acts if the social cost of preventing them would be disproportionate to the good achieved by prevention. Furthermore (and this is the contemporary move), Hanigan argues that constitutive to the common good are the recognition and protection of human dignity and the human rights of all persons to the fullest extent possible, subject only to prudential judgments about encouraging or discouraging certain kinds of behavior on behalf of the common good. On this basis, then, Hanigan proposes that state involvement in laws and policies regarding the personal lives of its citizens must always be justified on one of the two related grounds—the protection of the human rights of persons (and classes of persons) and the promotion of the common good (subject to the principle of toleration).

Applying this position to gays and lesbians results, according to Hanigan, in a set of discriminate public policy judgments. First, as persons with human dignity, gays and lesbians have protectable human rights that may under particular historical and social conditions (for example, economic discrimination or interpersonal violence on the basis of sexual orientation) require special public legislation (for example, nondiscrimination laws). Second, on the basis of other than "the being of humanity," the state may discriminate between persons and classes of persons in a just way by encouraging certain kinds of behavior (for example, traditional marriage) and discouraging others (for example, same-sex partnerships) for the common good. That is to say, while the state may tolerate same-sex behavior and relationships (informally, so to speak), it is under no obligation to promote actively such relationships by legitimizing them under the law as officially recognized domestic partnerships with benefits akin to those associated with marrying and raising a family. Here Hanigan's contextual horizon becomes quite dominant, since he himself recognizes—in order to dismiss—the claim that gays and lesbians have "a right in social justice to conditions under which their lives and relationships can most readily flourish." The reason for such dismissal is "the natural and social significance of human sexuality"—namely, the normative priority of heterosexual marriage and family predicated on procreative purpose and male/female complementarity and union.

At this point, certain questions arise. Given the fact that Hanigan acknowledges that sexual orientation is not chosen, that sexuality is a constitutive element of personality and personal being in the world (thus shaping us profoundly), that the full range of human rights to the fullest extent possible arguably includes the right of self-development in intimate relationships in order to have a meaningful and fulfilling existence (he does not specifically cite this latter right),[3] are there really no grounds from a Catholic perspective for supporting the legal recognition of domestic partnerships for gays and lesbians? Are the norms of heterosexual relationship in marriage solely determinative here? With these questions in hand, let us turn to Charles Curran.

Curran's strategy of argument bears important similarities to and differences from Hanigan's. To begin with, Curran eschews developing and defending in this essay a moral position on homosexual behavior, though he briefly reports for the record that he has elsewhere argued for the view that "committed homosexual unions are morally good but lacking something found in heterosexual marriages" and a correlative public policy position supportive of nondiscrimination laws as well as same-sex domestic partnerships with legal and social ramifications somewhat short of favoring gay marriage as just another form of marriage. Curran takes this tack in part because he holds that morality has an important but not decisive influence on law and public policy, and he wishes to demonstrate this for the sake of realistic argument by beginning with "the moral position of the hierarchical magisterium," which in his judgment is technically "authoritative" for the church and not likely to change anytime soon. This means, of course, that Curran chooses for strategic reasons to work within Hanigan's moral orientation, though he is also challenging thereby the prescriptive strength of Hanigan's contextual horizon.

While he acknowledges the Thomistically based elements of Hanigan's approach to the relationship between morality and law—for example, appeal to the common good and the principle of toleration—Curran himself prefers to develop and apply more strongly than Hanigan the human rights approach associated with Vatican II and the moral and political thought of John Courtney Murray—namely, the strong constitutional and democratic presumption of freedom as a constitutive part of the common good, and the duty of the state to protect and promote that freedom so long as the public order (that is, justice and human rights, public peace, and public morality) is not disproportionately hurt. Public order, according to Curran, is less expansive than the common good, thereby imposing a relatively high threshold for justifying state interference with the freedom of individuals to act in accordance with their conscience. Moreover, freedom is quickly related by Curran to freedom from social discrimination on any grounds other than disproportionate harm to the public order.

Similar to Hanigan, Curran is thus enabled to argue that legally protecting gays and lesbians against discrimination (that is, protecting their human rights) is a demand of justice. And meeting this demand in no way undermines or disproportionately hurts the public order, according to Curran, because doing so (1) fulfills a claim of justice, (2) does not disrupt the public peace, and (3) does not hurt public morality since, for example, nondiscrimination laws hardly weaken marriage and the family (that is, "gays do not choose to be gay so as to avoid marriage").

Although he agrees with Hanigan that domestic partnership laws do not touch on the fundamental human right not to be discriminated against (since such laws do not involve immunities or freedoms but rather a positive entitlement), Curran nonetheless disagrees with Hanigan that a case for such laws cannot be supported by a traditional Catholic framework. The elements of the case are these: One, such laws will not discourage heterosexuals from getting married. Two, adopting such laws counsels—from the traditional view—the lesser of two moral evils, since faithful homosexual unions have less evil effects than promiscuous homosexual behavior (for example, AIDS). Three, divorce laws, which the hierarchy tolerates, have greater negative effects on marriage and the family and are more opposed to the traditional Catholic understanding of marriage than domestic partnership laws, precisely because people choose to divorce and marry. That is, if the principle of toleration applies in the former more egregious case (divorce), then it ought to apply to the less egregious (domestic partnership); both are entitlements of sorts.

Again, one needs to realize that Curran has chosen to work within the framework of Hanigan's general perspective, and from within that perspective, he challenges Hanigan's contention that the state has no grounds for legitimizing gay and lesbian domestic partnerships. He is able to do this by showing that the state itself may have an interest in promoting "faithful" vs. promiscuous homosexual behavior (two, above); that Hanigan's position is internally inconsistent in denying legal domestic partnerships while allowing legal divorces (three, above); and that this position's assumption that domestic partnerships will weaken marriage and the family is not empirically well founded (one, above). All of this is on Hanigan's own terms and does not in itself challenge his framework beyond perhaps adjusting Hanigan's own human rights approach so as to take into account Vatican II's presumption of freedom and the distinction between public order vs. common good. Now that we have seen some grounds even within the traditional perspective for (grudgingly?) supporting the legal recognition of gay and lesbian partnerships, the question now arises as to whether there are other grounds within the tradition for supporting more robustly and possibly even valuing these partnerships. With this question in mind, let us now turn to Margaret Farley's position.

Farley's contribution is cast in the role of a response to Hanigan's and Curran's, and so we must be prepared for a less than complete development of her position. Nonetheless, she raises a number of criticisms of the traditional perspective that appear to point in a somewhat new direction. To begin with, she contends that a strong negative evaluation of same-sex acts and relationships constitutes in itself a social and political force of considerable influence, thus challenging Hanigan's and Curran's views of only moderate or minimal influence on public policy—for example, an important and decisive influence (contra Curran), more than just a contextual influence (contra Hanigan), indeed having the "power of an unreasoned taboo reinforcing unreflective repulsion." From Farley's perspective, it is insufficient to leave the traditional Catholic position unchallenged, and so she starts by deconstructing traditional Catholic norms of human sexuality and the way they have been applied differentially to same-sex orientation, behavior, and relationships (as contrasted to their application to heterosexual orientation, behavior, and relationships). Moreover, she revisions (historicizes) how the natural law approach within the tradition might be more properly construed as "morality should make sense to most people," which requires taking into account new insights, information, and perspectives, especially when it comes to the heavily socially constructed area of human sexuality (that is, the recognition that sexual roles, gender identities, norms for sexual behavior, and the like are significantly shaped by contingent cultural categories and social forces).[4] Specifically, with respect to gays and lesbians, she suggests that in addition to empirical data and theories, it is important to take serious and careful account of the experientially based testimony of gays and lesbians about the normative structure of their lives, especially when they evince integrity, justice, and love. Such testimony, she suggests, ought to be a significant source for critical moral (re)evaluation of homosexual lifestyles and relationships.

While she lacks the space (and the editorial charge) to develop a full counterposition to the traditional negative evaluation of homosexuality, Farley's remarks clearly suggest the need for reflective scrutiny and possible revision based on new perspectives and hitherto largely ignored sources. She drives this point home by identifying the relevance of recent Catholic positional documents that speak not only of "negative" human rights (for example, civil-political liberties) but also "positive" human rights (for example, regarding the provision of socioeconomic goods). Applying the latter rights to domestic partnership laws, her insight here is that such laws do not simply respond to adventitious human wants but address basic human needs for psychic security, economic security, and physical safety. In her view, such legislation is an instrumentally necessary step in transforming antigay attitudes and behavior so as to make the lives of gays and lesbians more safe and secure physically, spiritually, and economically. Indeed, Farley regards antigay attitudes and behavior as a greater danger to the commonweal than approval and encouragement of homosexual lifestyles. Thus does she link support for domestic partnership legislation to a fundamental aspect of the common good—namely, the fulfillment of human dignity and "positive" human rights. This is a suggestive development presumably made on the basis of informed insight and reasoning that conjoins the testimony of gay experience and contemporary Catholic support for human rights.

At the same time, though, we need to press questions for Farley's position: Is gay and lesbian self-fulfillment in domestic partnership only to be approved as instrumentally necessary to transforming society so that gays and lesbians are safer and more secure materially and psychologically? Is it possible to find grounds within this tradition to approve such partnerships as intrinsically good in themselves because, for example, they are sources and expressions of love between persons and repositories of proper self-love and fulfillment? This is a voice and position of which we have not yet heard enough from our authors, though theirs is a moral tradition very much oriented to the importance of love, human and divine, for all persons.

Notes

1. See, for example, Congregation for the Doctrine of the Faith, "Declaration on Certain Problems of Sexual Ethics" (1975) and "The Pastoral Care of Homosexual Persons" (1986), reprinted in *Medical Ethics: Sources of Catholic Teachings*, 2d ed., eds. Kevin D. O'Rourke and Philip Boyle (Washington, DC: Georgetown University Press, 1993), chap. 21.

2. See, for example, the excellent discussion of Richard A. McCormick, "Homosexuality as a Moral and Pastoral Problem," reprinted in his *The Critical Calling: Reflections on Moral Dilemmas Since Vatican II* (Washington, DC: Georgetown University Press, 1989), chap. 17.

3. For the identification and justification of this right in the context of heterosexual relationships, see Ferdinand Shoeman, "Rights of Children, Rights of Parents, and the Moral Basis of the Family," *Ethics* 91 (October 1980): 6–19.

4. For excellent overviews of the literature regarding the social construction of human sexuality and sexual ethics, see the many articles on this subject in Warren Thomas Reich, ed., *Encyclopedia of Bioethics*, rev. ed. (New York: Simon & Schuster Macmillan, 1995).

Sexual Orientation and Human Rights: A Roman Catholic View

JAMES P. HANIGAN

The Roman Catholic community has a long and complex tradition of thought in regard to sexual morality.[1] The Bible, the primary narrative and fundamental normative source for the church's own self-understanding, as well as for its comprehension of the larger society, has considerable material for reflection and appropriation on the subject of human sexual behavior. The church's saints, its theologians, its pastors and official teachers, as well as its members, have continued over the many years of the church's life to reflect upon the meaning and value of human sexuality in light of both the community's ongoing engagement with the biblical witness and new knowledge about the human person and the changing social conditions in which people live out their sexual desires and relationships.[2]

The Roman Catholic community also has a long and complex tradition of thought in regard to the place and function of the state in human affairs.[3] Again, the Bible and the theological tradition speak to this question of the role of the state, and the community's reflections on governmental authority and activity have continued to the present day in the face of ever-changing political and social circumstances. As with the church's reflections on sexuality, its reflections on the role of the state have undergone significant development over time.[4] Positions once held with considerable tenacity have been abandoned; positions once rejected have been embraced, not just by particular theologians or subcommunities within the larger church, but even by the official teaching office of the church. The two most notable examples of such changes in official positions relevant to the present topic are the contemporary church's acceptance of the duty of responsible parenthood[5] and the right of religious freedom.[6]

This documented fact of development[7]—or, at the very least, change—in the church's moral teaching suggests that the present discussion of the morality of same-sex relations and behaviors and the human and civil rights of gay, lesbian, and bisexual persons is not a completely settled question in Roman Catholic thought. This seems to be especially the case when it is recognized that the Roman Catholic Church, like everyone else, has no long and well-established tradition of thought about sexual orientation, nor does Roman Catholicism have a long tradition of thought about human rights.[8]

Talk about sexual orientation is, of course, an altogether modern phenomenon and we are all still struggling to understand its nature and implications. Rights language is considerably older but no less debated, and is something that Catholic thinkers have widely adopted only in the second half of the twentieth century,[9] though, to be sure, the reality that rights language attempts to address was certainly not unknown to the tradition. For any number of reasons Roman Catholic moral thought developed predominantly in terms of obligations and sins; in its positive emphasis the cultivation of the virtues was emphasized.[10] Freedom was understood to be an important value for Catholic life, but it was almost always tied closely to the value of truth and construed in a positive sense as freedom to be able to do what one ought to do; in effect, as holiness. This notion of freedom included, but was not restricted to, immunity from both internal and external coercion, with the primary form of coercion being understood as slavery to sin.[11] Religious freedom in Catholic thought had, and still has, as its central focus the freedom of the church to be the church;[12] hence the long church-state struggle that has marked so much of western history.

Consequently, when the topic of sexual orientation and human rights arises, the Catholic theologian is treading on soil that has been only lightly cultivated. One struggles not so much to find answers as to frame the right questions.[13] As I wrestle with the issue of sexual orientation and human rights in our contemporary setting, it seems to me that the central point at issue has to do generally with the role of the state in human affairs. The specific questions are: When if ever, in what ways, and on what grounds does the government have warrant[14] to intrude into the sexual lives of its citizens? So the major burden of this essay will be to indicate how the Roman Catholic religious tradition might be helpful in answering these questions.

Given the above formulation of the issue, it would seem that we are dealing primarily with the concerns of political ethics and social justice, not sexual ethics. It is not, I would suggest, the morality or immorality of specific sexual activities that justifies any government's intervention into the lives of its citizens. That justification must be found elsewhere.[15] In Catholic language, not every moral obligation is or ought to be a legal obligation, just as not every legal right is also a moral right.[16] Not every sin is or ought to be also a crime, just as every crime may not be a sin.[17]

In approaching the topic in this way, it is perhaps helpful to the reader if the author acknowledges at the outset his own political orientation. I can recognize in myself neither an antecedent interest in extending the power and authority of the state to achieve some overt or hidden purpose, nor any prior interest in limiting the power and authority of the state to preserve some established practice or set of power relationships. If it is a difference in attitude toward state power and governmental activism that marks the difference in our contemporary politics between the labels liberal and conservative, I acknowledge my personal bias to be against entrusting more power to governments: when in doubt, limit the power of the state. Or, if I may express that bias in a more colloquial fashion, when in doubt, there ought not to be a law.

Still, one cannot address the issue of sexual orientation and human rights in complete independence of one's moral views about human sexual behavior, and certainly the Catholic tradition has not done so. I will, therefore, proceed in this essay in three stages. First, I will indicate how I understand the history and the tradition of my religious community, the Roman Catholic Church, with respect to sexual orientation and/or preference and sexual conduct. Second, I will indicate what moral stance I think my religious community ought to take on this issue of homosexual orientation and conduct at this time in history, and say a word about the degree to which the moral arguments that support this position are or may be persuasive independent of issues of revelation. I will ask whether such a position and the arguments that support it are accessible to the wider public and so have a role in the public discussion. Finally, I will explore the implications for the formulation of law and public policy in the traditional position of my religious community and in the current viewpoints advocated there to see if that position has any intelligible bearing on these public debates.

Since for most of recorded history nothing seems to have been known about what today we call sexual orientation,[18] it is only in the present century that we can expect to find anything relevant in church teaching about the orientation itself. Historically, of course, same-sex conduct between both males and females was known. It was assumed, as far as we can tell, to be a choice of the individuals who engaged in such behavior, though in giving their consent to it, they may well have been seen to be yielding to the prompting of good or evil spirits.[19] In the Catholic religious tradition in which I stand, but certainly not only there, same-sex behavior was judged to be unnatural and so, when voluntarily chosen, sinful, and the grounds for that judgment were thought to be quite clear from both revelation and reason.

None of that is or should be surprising, coming, as it does, from a tradition that understood the primary purpose of human sexuality as created by God to be for the procreation and development of the human species.[20] Sexuality was regarded in the first instance as a biological and social reality, and the good of human sexuality was understood to be, first and foremost, a social good—the establishment of a stable family for the procreation and education of children. Thomas Aquinas, to offer but one instance from the tradition, put forth, as his primary rational argument for sexual monogamy and for the indissolubility of marriage, the consideration that such conditions were essential to marriage in order to promote that social good. Sex required marriage and marriage required monogamy and indissolubility to ensure the appropriate environment, the stable family, for the proper birthing and rearing of children.[21] The interest of the body politic, the state, in the natural and social institutions of marriage and the family, and so indirectly in the sexual practices of its citizens, arose precisely out of its interest in and responsibility for the proper social ordering of family life to serve the well-being of its next generation of citizens.[22]

All uses of sexuality, then, that contravened the procreative purpose or that sought other goods of sexuality to the exclusion of the social good were, on the face of it,[23] in contradiction to the divine purpose for sex because they were in violation of the obvious social nature of sexuality and the natural end of sexual intercourse. Hence they were judged to be unreasonable, to be motivated in part at least by lust, to be harmful to the stability and well-being of the family, and so to be objectively sinful.

Since the social good of sexual activity was of great moment to human life—it had, after all, to do with the very existence and continued well-being of one's family, one's tribe or clan, one's nation, and, indeed, the entire human species—to use one's sexual powers in contradiction to the divine purpose, in ways that would exclude, frustrate, or hurt the social good, was always a serious matter; to do so knowingly and deliberately was, therefore, judged to be a grave or mortal sin.

This narrative-based account of human sexual morality had, in the first place, nothing to do with perceptions of sexual behavior as animalistic, as dirty or shameful; nothing to do with judgments that sex was unworthy of God and of creatures made in God's image and likeness, or of sexual pleasure as somehow base and beneath human dignity. The Genesis creation stories did not allow such a view of what God had created. Such perceptions of and judgments about human sexual desire, of sexual pleasure and sexual conduct (and I do not deny that such perceptions and judgments are to be found too frequently in the tradition of which I speak[24]), followed upon and were subsequent to prior understandings of the highest purpose of human life and the divinely intended purpose of sex. Given the demand for holiness of life, when taken in conjunction with the daily experience of the difficulty of disciplining human sexuality to serve this noble and lofty end, it is not surprising that sexual desire and lust became confused and often identified.[25]

This tradition of which I speak is, after all, a tradition that steadfastly insisted on the goodness of marriage as an embodied, sexual relationship in the face of many, severe attacks by those who claimed a higher wisdom, a higher spirituality.[26] It is a tradition that insisted, and continues to insist, that the right to marry is a natural human right not subject to arbitrary limitation by family, state, or church;[27] a tradition that fought vigorously to establish the free, mutual consent of the partners in the marriage as the very essence and heart of the marital covenant;[28] a tradition that came to regard marriage as a privileged vehicle of grace, a sacrament, than which no higher accolade could be paid;[29] and a tradition that could defend the practice of deliberately chosen consecrated celibacy and virginity only as a supernatural calling or gift.[30] It was a tradition continually informed by St. Paul who had advised married couples to abstain from sexual relations only to foster directly their relationship with God,[31] and then only for a time and by mutual consent, and that regarded marriage as a remedy for concupiscence, not an indulgence of or a license for lust. It was also a tradition, let it be said, that found the primary social location of women to be in the home and their primary social purpose to be largely exhausted by the role of mother or as a consecrated virgin.[32]

Nor was the manifest intractability of the human sexual drive to reasoned argument, moral persuasion, and virtuous control especially dismaying or regarded as possible evidence against this understanding of sexuality and the consequent judgments about proper sexual behavior. In the first place, there were conspicuous examples of men and women, both celibate and married, who by the grace of God had overcome the disorder of their sexual desires and had learned to live chaste lives and to love wisely and well. In the second place, it was taken for granted that the sexual drive and human sexual desires, like all other human drives and desires, had been disordered by sin. Lust, one of the seven deadly sins, was all too real. Human beings were in a constant, daily struggle with themselves; they had to labor to learn to control, shape, and direct all their natural drives and desires in ways that accorded with the divine purpose. They had to learn with the help of God's grace to live lives of virtue in order to love one another. That was what the moral life was all about. Human beings, apart from the grace of God, were enslaved to sin. And the enslavement of human beings to the disordered power of their own sexuality, to lust, was but one sign—albeit a rather common, widespread, and evident sign—of that enslavement to sin and of the continuing power of concupiscence even in the lives of the baptized. The power of concupiscence,[33] to be sure, had many other and more destructive manifestations than improper sexual conduct. But given the operative understanding of sexuality and the divine purpose for it, homosexual behavior was simply one of the more unusual and serious of these manifestations.

Within this narrative account of the meaning and purpose of human sexuality and the importance to social well-being of the institutions of marriage and family, what was seen as the role of the state in regard to sexuality? In general terms, and in light of the principle of subsidiarity,[34] the institutions of marriage and the family were judged to have both a natural priority to and an independence from the state, which gave marriage and the family as social institutions certain rights over against the state.[35] At the same time, marriage as a social institution was naturally ordered to family, and the family had a need for the state in order to be able to fulfill its own function as family. Hence there existed a natural basis for the moral duty of the state to legally recognize, encourage, regulate, and protect the institutions of marriage and family. There was also the more negative responsibility of the state to discourage illegitimacy, divorce, and other forms of immorality such as adultery and homosexual behavior, which might threaten the well-being of marriage and the family.

The move from these more formal obligations of promotion and protection to specific policies and laws was mediated in part by the principle of toleration.[36] Briefly expressed, the principle recognizes that not all sins should be crimes and have legal sanctions attached to them. Some immoral acts are rightly tolerated if the social cost of trying to prevent them would be disproportionate morally to the good that could be achieved by efforts at prevention. So, for instance, both Augustine and Aquinas judged that the social cost in their times of governmental efforts to abolish prostitution would be excessively high and so the practice should be tolerated by the state but not blessed.[37]

It seems essential in unfolding this tradition of thought, however, to emphasize the very significant developments in the Roman Catholic understanding of sexuality and sexual behavior that have occurred in the twentieth century.[38] Along with many other fellow human beings, Roman Catholic theologians have come to recognize, with little or no thanks to theology, that there is a reality that is appropriately called a sexual orientation,[39] and to understand that one's sexual orientation, whatever it may be and however it comes to be,[40] is fundamentally not a matter of conscious free choice or preference. Nor is a change in one's sexual orientation, if it is possible at all, a simple matter of repenting for one's past sins and making a firm purpose of amendment, nor of developing a more fervent prayer life, nor of growing in virtue, nor, in our more contemporary style, of undergoing therapy or finding a support group.[41] Hence sexual orientation itself is not a matter for moral evaluation, not a condition itself meriting either moral praise or blame, not a basis for excluding some people from or including other people within the human family or even the ecclesial community. A heterosexual orientation is no more a basis on which human rights may be claimed than is a homosexual orientation a basis on which human rights may be denied.[42]

We have also come to understand that sexuality is not an accidental feature of human nature and human personality, but a constitutive element, a mode of being in the world. To quote a Vatican document on the subject, "the human person is so profoundly affected by sexuality that it must be considered as one of the factors which give to each individual's life the principal traits that distinguish it."[43] Sexuality is, therefore, something that shapes and influences all our relationships and activities, though we certainly do not always know how it does this or in what precise ways this influence is manifested.

This recognition of the importance of sexuality to human personhood, along with the modern mentality that attempts to think things out from the viewpoint of the individual person rather than from the viewpoint of society, has also enabled Roman Catholic theologians to understand more deeply the personal and interpersonal significance of human sexual relating and activity—what in Catholic language is referred to as the unitive meaning of sex, along with its already achieved understanding of the social, procreative meaning. There are few knowledgeable Roman Catholics today who would simply affirm that the primary and overriding purpose of human sexuality is procreation, or who would deny the profound relational and unitive significance of sexual intercourse. Indeed, so basic has the unitive meaning of sex become in Roman Catholic thought, as both an expression of and an effective cause of relational unity, that the major problematic in Roman Catholic sexual ethics for the past thirty years has been how to understand and explain the connection between the so-called unitive meaning of sexuality and the procreative meaning.[44] It is precisely the shift in understanding I have just described that accounts both for the extensive theological dissent within Roman Catholicism about contraceptive practices in marriage and for the need to reconsider the established teaching about many other sexual practices, including most especially same-sex relationships and acts.[45]

The official teaching of the Roman Catholic Church on the relationship between the unitive and procreative meanings of sex is lucidly clear. Pope Paul VI expressed it bluntly in his encyclical letter, "Humanae Vitae": "the church . . . teaches that each and every marriage act . . . must remain open to the transmission of life."[46] "That teaching . . . is founded upon the inseparable connection, willed by God and unable to be broken by man on his own initiative, between the two meanings of the conjugal act: the unitive meaning and the procreative meaning."[47]

What is not so clear is the basis for affirming this connection to be inseparable in every single act of sexual intercourse and so normative for human sexual behavior. The teaching has been called, by more than one Catholic theologian, a position in search of an argument,[48] though the present Pope, John Paul II, among others, has expended quite a lot of ink trying to make the argument.[49] Oddly enough, and for reasons that escape me, Catholic theologians have, for the most part, paid but slight attention to the substance of the Pope's arguments. For our purposes here, however, the above sketch enables us to see why, despite the new appreciation for sexuality as a constitutive aspect of human identity and the positive evaluation of the interpersonal significance of human sexual activity, the Roman Catholic Church, at least in its official teaching, remains convinced of the immorality of homosexual conduct, and why as a consequence it continues to understand and describe the homosexual orientation not as sinful, but as ontically disordered.[50]

In light of the current debate within the Roman Catholic community about sexual ethics and the perceived unpersuasiveness of many of the arguments advanced to defend the traditional and official teaching of the church, what stance do I advocate for my religious community on the issue of homosexual orientation and conduct? And are the moral arguments that would support my position persuasive independently of issues of revelation? Before answering those two questions, however, I would insist again that it is the second question that is most crucial. For I remain convinced that one's answer to the first question has only marginal relevance to practical questions of law and public policy.[51]

In the eight years since the book I wrote on this subject appeared,[52] I have heard, read, and seen nothing to convince me that the teaching of my religious community about homosexual behavior is manifestly false and so should be challenged.[53] There is much the church, both in its official capacity and in the persons of its members, might do differently or more aggressively in terms of pastoral care and to welcome gay and lesbian Catholics into the church community, in the support it offers to those who seek to minister to the various homosexual communities, in the language it employs to speak about sexual morality, and in defense of human rights. But I have found no substantive grounds in Scripture, in reason, in experience, for disputing the truth of its teaching on the status of the homosexual orientation or the morality of homosexual acts. I continue to think that the procreative dimension of human sexuality is more than accidental to the human person and so to the moral meaning of human sexual behavior, and that the biological and anatomical complementarity of male and female bodies is of more than descriptive interest to questions of human sexual behavior.[54]

Within the parameters of my religious community itself, it makes little sense to talk about moral arguments that are persuasive independently of issues of revelation. Even those moral issues in Catholic moral teaching that are thought about and resolved through appeals to the natural law, which is most of them, are not thought to be cleanly answered in independence of what the community believes about God's self-communication, about the nature and destiny of the human person as revealed in the person and mission of Jesus, and about the continuing work of the Holy Spirit in the life of the community.[55]

If the question of the public availability of religiously inspired and informed moral arguments seeks to know whether the moral stance one holds in regard to same-sex sexual acts and relationships can be made persuasively, apart from any appeal to the Bible, to the theological tradition, or to church authorities and without using the language specific to one's religious tradition, I must confess that I do not know, but I doubt it.[56] I can certainly make the argument in language that does not embody any such appeals, but, of course, the background, the contextual horizon[57] in which I use the more secular language remains my religious understanding of reality. So I might find the argument persuasive whereas one who does not share or who explicitly repudiates my horizon would not.

Still, I do believe it incumbent upon theologians in the Roman Catholic tradition, for reasons intrinsic to their faith, to make as intelligible and persuasive as possible the ethical positions they advocate, especially those that are liable to have an affect upon the laws, policies, and behavior of the political and social communities in which they live. This obligation becomes all the more pressing the more pluralistic a society becomes and the more that political and social freedom are valued.

To be concrete about answering this question, I was asked some few years ago by an auxiliary bishop of the Catholic diocese of Pittsburgh to testify before the Pittsburgh City Council about a proposed ordinance that had to do with explicitly extending certain civil protections to openly gay and lesbian persons. While waiting for the call to testify, I listened on the radio to much of the testimony being given. Many of the people who testified before the council invoked specific biblical passages to condemn both homosexual acts and homosexual persons, or simply claimed God's authority to oppose the ordinance. Other people, far fewer in number, invoked other biblical passages or a generic form of the Golden Rule in support of the ordinance. All such appeals seemed to me then and now to be quite out of place, theologically, constitutionally, and politically.

Theologically, appeals to isolated biblical texts apart from the narrative structure of the biblical faith turns the Bible against itself in a war of texts, and has the ultimate and unfortunate consequence of asking the state to become the final arbiter of the proper exegesis of the church's own book.[58] Constitutionally, such appeals are a fundamental violation of the First Amendment, in as much as they ask the state to enshrine a particular religion's sacred texts as law simply on the reputed authority of the text itself. Politically, such appeals are both inappropriate and harmful inasmuch as they leave no room for the resolution of differences beyond the sheer exercise of power. As events turned out, the ordinance was withdrawn for rewriting before I was called to testify so I cannot repeat here what I said then, since I never said it. Nor did I ever see the specific language of the ordinance before or after it was rewritten, since it was tabled and disappeared from public view.

It does seem, however, to be both practically reasonable and fully consonant with the Catholic theological tradition to say that even religiously inspired and informed arguments made publicly to effect public policy must appeal to widely shared public beliefs and values that are at least consonant with one's religious beliefs and be based on something other than appeals to specific religious authorities, including direct appeals to God's Will. Indeed, the failure to do this by direct invocation of religious beliefs or claims deeply confuses the function of the state and the church. In Christian terms, politics does not have an eschatological goal as the church does. The state can only and rightly seek a limited human justice, a limited, relative public order and peace. Hence, I emphasize once more the importance of some form of the principle of toleration and the kinds of arguments it requires to mediate the move from religious convictions to public policy and law.

So we arrive at the third step in the present essay, the implications for the formulation of law and public policy in the official teaching of the Catholic tradition on both sexual morality and social ethics and in the current viewpoints advocated from within that tradition. How might the theological views of this religious community have a bearing on the public debate?

I propose to try to answer these questions, in keeping with the long tradition of Catholic moral thought, from the perspective of what fidelity to the Roman Catholic faith requires of its members in relation to their fellow citizens,[59] not in terms of what non-Catholics either owe or should allow Catholics to say or do in the public forum. That is to say, I am focusing here on what Catholics owe to themselves as Catholics and to their neighbors as fellow human beings and citizens as they try to live out the truth of their faith and enflesh the virtues of love, justice, compassion, fortitude, and prudence in their personal and public conduct.[60] How should Catholics exercise their public responsibilities to and their public participation in the life of the social and political community in regard to human rights and sexual orientation? I will frame my attempt at an answer in three propositions.

First, the Roman Catholic Church, in its official statements, in its ways of organizing itself, in its public activities, and, more important, in the daily life and activities of its members, must affirm, protect, and defend the human dignity of all persons, and so champion the full range of human rights of every human being, to the fullest extent possible.[61] Violations of human dignity in the form of the denial or abuse of human rights must be frankly and publicly acknowledged as such and be vigorously and unambiguously condemned. Above all, in the present context, it must be made clear in both word and deed that sexual orientation is irrelevant to the possession of human dignity and human rights, in the same way that those historically favored bases of unjust discrimination—race, color, gender, class, ethnic origin, and religious identity—are irrelevant. A denial or violation of the human rights of anyone on the basis of sexual orientation is simply wrong; in theological language it is sinful. If that denial of rights is systematic and institutionalized, it becomes a matter of social sin, in the face of which the imperatives of social justice and personal morality require every human being, to the extent and in the way possible, to refuse cooperation with such a systemic evil.[62] And I would both hope and urge my religious community to preach and practice this truth, first within its own house and then in the public forum.

But human dignity and its corollary, human rights, can all too easily become slogans devoid of meaning.[63] In American society, the interminable public debate over abortion and the growing debate about euthanasia and assisted suicide are clear examples of how easily rights language fails as a vehicle of communication and turns into a rhetorical weapon to be hurled at others in an effort to gain political advantage by occupying the moral high ground of an argument. All too swiftly human rights, legal rights, customary privileges, social needs, and personal wants become lumped together under the label of rights. In the process our understanding of human rights becomes privatized and absolutized, thus turning rights into entitlements to act as one wishes. The noble American vision and experiment of a people adventuring upon self-rule, for which inalienable human rights was an essential foundation, becomes individualized to mean doing one's own thing.

These are, perhaps, harsh words embodying a harsh judgment. But examples abound. Many of the students in my undergraduate classes think that their opinions, as baseless and fanciful as many of them are and are at times acknowledged to be, should be respected simply because they are their opinions. To criticize their opinions, to which they proudly proclaim they have a right, is somehow to demean their human dignity, to fail to respect them as persons. Or again, we are beginning to hear claims advanced today about the preposterous idea of smokers' rights. In such a claim the personal respect and the social space due to persons in virtue of their being human is altogether confused with demands for a social entitlement to a specific form of individually chosen behavior. In the process, the social dimension of human rights and the ethical dimension of public life, what Catholic thought has historically meant by the common good is lost sight of or simply denied in the squabbling of special-interest groups. Human dignity is thus sacrificed to political expediency; claims about human rights are reduced to the quest for power.

The Roman Catholic tradition has struggled, both intellectually and spiritually, with this problem of being and doing, of personhood and action, of what is due everyone in virtue of being human and what is due to particular individuals in virtue of their more particular circumstances and achievements. It has tried to establish an analytic distinction between being and doing, between what the human person is as human and what he or she does and/or has been made to become through the circumstances of human history and personal choice. The classic formulation of this distinction was captured in the expression "Love the sinner and hate the sin"—something a great deal easier to say than to do. But, of course, the distinction has much wider application than to a sinner and sin. It touches upon the difference between our humanness and our specific racial, gender, class, ethnic, religious, or sexual identities. In our present case the distinction pertains to the difference both between human identity and sexual identity and between sexual orientation and sexual behavior.

Human dignity and human rights are rooted in and related to human being. They are not qualified or limited by our more particular biological, social, and historical identities, though the manner and the fullness of their realization certainly are. Human dignity and the rights that are the essential conditions for the protection and realization of that dignity are neither earned nor lost by human behavior, though they can be violated or honored by human behavior, either by one's own behavior or the behavior of others. As human, both dignity and rights are thoroughly social, relational realities rooted in human community, and so their real content and actual extent are defined by the common good.[64] So, for example, the very meaning of one's right to life is defined by both the human dignity and the right to life of one's fellow human beings, as well as by biological and social necessity.[65] The religious language of human dignity and human rights as God given, as being a result of our creation in the image and likeness of God and our ultimate destiny of union with God, has its cultural counterpart for citizens of the United States in the language of our Declaration of Independence, which speaks of inalienable rights, and its constitutional counterpart in the Bill of Rights, which details a list of rights possessed by human beings independent of the authority of the state.[66] All three of these ways of expression acknowledge two important points, which brings me to the second proposition I would advance.

The Roman Catholic community must continue to urge in public debate the important implications of the rootedness of human dignity and human rights in a religious vision of the human person,[67] in the created givenness and goodness of human nature, as it were. For what is of practical and political moment in this vision is a recognition of the transcendent worth and the moral priority of the human person in relation to society. The corollary of such a vision of the human person is the consequent moral responsibility that each person bears as the active subject of his or her own moral choices and moral behavior that is implied in the affirmation of human dignity. For human dignity manifests itself precisely in the capacity of human beings for moral agency, or in what might loosely be termed conscience.[68] There is no higher moral obligation, no more fundamental way to respect the dignity of our fellow human beings than to respect their capacity for moral agency and so to honor the inviolability of their consciences. Such respect and honor are the essential conditions of and the necessary motivation for respectful and vigorous public argument.

To argue for respect for the moral capacity of our fellow human beings may seem to be a noncontroversial and abstract claim, but it is no trivial or rhetorical matter. It is rather a moral claim made upon both oneself and others to speak one's moral views publicly and intelligibly; it is also a reciprocal demand placed on the self and others to listen attentively, albeit critically, to those views. In practical terms relevant to our present topic such respect argues for a positive evaluation of the sheer factual existence of the growing public voice of gay and lesbian individuals, couples, and groups in public discussion. This voice, these voices have a right to be heard. It certainly suggests, for one practical instance, that the "don't ask, don't tell" policy pertaining to homosexual people in the military, as recently implemented in the armed services of the United States, is only half right.[69] For a second instance, the Vatican directives that seem to enjoin silence on homosexual men and women about their sexual orientation are fundamentally mistaken if they are taken as anything more than temporary prudential directives for a particular moment in time.[70]

Respect for the moral capacity of our fellow human beings also suggests, it seems to me, that gay and lesbian groups that have publicly identified themselves as such not only have a right to the space needed for social existence in, for example, our churches, our universities and colleges,[71] and so forth, but that such groups serve a necessary public function: they can contribute to the common good. How will we ever know what particular insights or sensitivities being homosexual might enable gay and lesbian persons to contribute to the human community if there is no social space for them together to explore and publicly to express these contributions? Even if one insists, as my religious tradition has done and continues to do, that a homosexual orientation is a disordered inclination to immoral actions, surely that description is not exhaustive of its significance, any more than a heterosexual inclination, which can also incline heterosexuals to immoral actions, is only that. There are, then, I would suggest, serious practical implications in regard to human rights to the demand to respect the moral capacities of our fellow citizens.

My third proposition is that the Roman Catholic community must continue to bring to the public forum its traditional sense of the embodied social nature of the human person and the subsequent social aspect or social good of all human capacities and activities. While I do not subscribe to the current slogan that the personal is the political, I would embrace the idea that the personal always has a social dimension. What this means in practice, of course, is that there is an essential place for social bodies, including the political body, in our personal affairs, including our sexual ones, but that place is and must be carefully defined. The case for state involvement, for laws and public policies that touch upon the personal lives of citizens, must always be justified on one of two related grounds: either such involvement is needed to protect specific human rights or it clearly serves to promote the common good.[72]

The reader will note that I have used strong words here. Government involvement in the lives of citizens must be needed to do something that ought to be done and that cannot reasonably be done by any lesser body. It must be justifiable as such, and it must clearly serve to promote the common good. Such a claim may not on the surface sound like a religiously informed argument, but it is, once again, deeply rooted in a religious vision of the sacredness of the human person before God, and, hence, an understanding of all natural and human institutions as having no purpose other than to serve the human person in the course of his or her journey to God.[73] Even for those who count themselves atheistic or agnostic in religious questions, the human moral capacity for truth and goodness forbids according an ultimate significance either to any temporal, social arrangement of human affairs (the state) or to their own personal, temporal lives (one's subjective wants).

It is, of course, true that our understanding of what human dignity and human rights mean or require of us is something that emerges only slowly in history under the press of particular circumstances and in the light of newly acquired and assimilated knowledge and the new possibilities and requirements for human life such knowledge affords. Therefore, the common good is not a static reality, nor is the concept of the common good ahistorical and absolutist.[74] We are coming to see today, for example, that respect for human dignity and the right to life of human persons properly and necessarily requires social and legal limits on the uses we make of our environment and the way we treat other forms of life. So, for instance, placing restrictions on smoking in public areas in order to provide people with a healthful, smoke-free environment is both a necessary and proper government intervention to promote the common good and in no way is a restriction of anyone's human rights. Whether respect for human dignity also obliges individuals morally not to smoke at all is not yet entirely clear. Nor would anyone with any sense want to make the government the arbiter of that moral question. What is clear is that governmental action is essential to provide people with the smoke-free environment their health may need.

Similarly, particular historical circumstances may make it clear that there is a need for special public legislation to protect the human rights of a particular class of people. We as a nation have experienced the need and enacted laws to protect the human and civil rights of citizens who were and are presently being denied those rights because of overt racial discrimination in the past and the present. I can see no reason why, in principle at least, similar legislation protecting the human and civil rights of persons denied those rights because of discrimination on the basis of sexual orientation might not be necessary and so proper. Whether there is, in fact, a need for such legislation for gay and lesbian persons in our present circumstances, whether such legislation would be effective in protecting their rights, and what such legislation should specifically say requires prudential judgments for which religious persons have no special insight or unique competence. I would be inclined to listen most closely and give the greatest weight in making such judgments to the views of those claiming to experience such discrimination.

Discrimination, therefore, in both personal and public life on the basis of factors other than the very being of our humanity is not only possible but also necessary, and can certainly be just. We do, we must, and we can fairly discriminate on the basis of more particular identities[75] and on the basis of behavior or performance in our personal and social lives. There is a need for the state to do so as well. The state has, as I have claimed, only two related warrants or grounds for making such discriminations. One is to protect the human and the civil rights of its citizens. Large numbers of our criminal laws that forbid various kinds of behavior like murder, rape, and robbery do exactly this. The state may also seek to encourage or discourage certain kinds of behavior to promote the common good. Laws that require school attendance and the payment of taxes are illustrations of encouragement; laws that put heavy taxes on alcohol and tobacco are illustrations of discouragement.

It is, then, in this area of protecting human rights and promoting the common good that the state has a legitimate and necessary interest in the sexual lives and activities of its citizens. That interest arises precisely because of the natural, given connection between sex and children and the consequences of that connection for the common good. The state has an interest in and an obligation to promote and protect healthy, stable, and free families, and so to acknowledge and regulate the relationship and the institution out of which families grow—the male human and the female human united in marriage. This view of things accounts for the abiding, and to some self-contradictory, Catholic interest in and advocacy for government action to protect and promote the social institutions of marriage and family, as well as its insistence on limiting governmental authority in significant ways in regard to these same institutions.

It might be argued that, if children or the possibility of children account for the state's interest in marriage, then the state should withhold the legal recognition of marriage from the relationship of those couples incapable of conceiving children, as it presently does to homosexual couples. Aside from the enormous practical difficulties of doing this and the massive invasion of personal privacy it would require, there is a more fundamental reason for objecting to such an argument. That reason is precisely the autonomy of the marital relationship in relation to the state. The state rightly recognizes and regulates the institution of marriage. It does not, or it ought not, directly regulate marriages. The decisions whether to marry, whom to marry and when, whether to have children, when, and how many belong not to the state but to the couple. The state has even less a right than the church to tell couples they must have children.[76] To allow—worse still, to encourage—the state to intervene in the marital relationship beyond the legal recognition of generalized natural possibility is to give the state an authority beyond both its right and competence. It is to deny human dignity and the rights that dignity requires.

On the other hand, it is very hard to understand on what grounds the state should acknowledge and legally sanction other kinds of interpersonal relationships or treat them in any way as comparable to marriage. We can and we do, I believe, readily understand and agree on the need for the state to discriminate in regard to certain kinds of sexual behavior and sexual relationships, and so legally prohibit these behaviors and relationships. We urge the state, for example, to enact and enforce prohibitions against rape, incest, pedophilia, and child pornography. We accept with little hesitation the state's prohibition of the marriage of children, its refusal to recognize marriages that were effected by force or the threat of violence, or marriages that are bigamous. Behind these prohibitions are concerns for the human dignity and rights of individual persons and concerns for the good of marriage and the family and so the common good.

When homosexual persons claim a right to public recognition and legal sanction of their relationships, as well as to the benefits attendant upon such status, a fundamental question must be asked. Where is the legitimate interest of the state in such relationships? Is such recognition necessary to protect anyone's human rights? Is it necessary to promote the common good? I am more than willing to listen to reasons why the answer to these questions might be yes. I find myself, however, unable to supply these reasons or imagine what they might be. Two possible lines of reasoning, however, from within the Catholic tradition, do suggest themselves and are worth brief notice by way of conclusion to this essay.[77]

One approach would be to invoke the principle of toleration and to argue that the common good would be less ill-served by legal recognition than it is by the present state of affairs in society. Presumably, legal recognition of homosexual relationships would eliminate some or most of the homophobic behaviors and violent treatment currently experienced by openly gay and lesbian individuals and groups. It would, therefore, both provide a less violent and conflictual social situation for all citizens and at the same time afford a greater degree of protection of the rights of gay and lesbian citizens. Such an argument rather extends the principle of toleration beyond its usual limits inasmuch as it does not ask us to tolerate a behavior by removing or not enacting legal prohibitions and sanctions against it.[78]

It rather urges the state to cooperate positively in legitimizing such relationships. It is comparable to governmental approval of the now common, almost routine practice of divorce and remarriage, which has been less than a rousing success in promoting happy, stable marriages and family well-being.[79]

A second line of reasoning would invoke the protection of human rights and service to the common good in a more positive sense by claiming that individuals have a right to the conditions under which their lives and relationships can most readily flourish. Legal recognition of homosexual relationships would arguably eliminate the social conditions that have caused so much promiscuity and self-hatred and even suicides among homosexual youth and provide the social structures and support that would enable homosexual relationships to flourish in more stable, human, and healthy ways.

Both of these lines of argument, despite resting on presumptions that can be seriously challenged, are not without some merit, but they both seem to me to overlook, and even reject, the evident natural and social significance of human sexuality. Because they do that, they both allow, indeed encourage, the state to become the arbiter of personal morality and to have a decisive say in human sexual affairs that exceeds any warrant or justification I can find for its intervention. At the same time, they excuse the state from doing the things it does have quite legitimate grounds to do. They are arguments comparable to those that approve, legitimate, and insist on the use of public funds to establish the structures that facilitate the practice of abortion, rather than requiring of government the kinds of actions that might make the practice of abortion less thinkable as a necessary or desirable option for pregnant women, despite the public rhetoric that repeatedly claims the latter course of action as its purpose.

I do not see, therefore, any grounds upon which the state can be encouraged to legally sanction same-sex relationships and thus give them equal status with marriage. I do not see how one can encourage government action in this direction without adopting an altogether cynical view of social ethics as nothing but a power struggle between equally unprincipled parties, without rejecting the social nature and meaning of human dignity and human rights, and without accepting the state as the ultimate arbiter of our personal morality in our sexual lives. Those moves are ones, I am convinced, that Roman Catholics are conscience-bound to resist, and that all American citizens would be wise to oppose, in the name of human dignity and human rights and the great experiment of a free and self-governing nation.

Notes

1. Useful and comprehensive sources for this tradition are John T. Noonan, Jr., *Contraception: A History of Its Treatment by the Catholic Theologians and Canonists* (Cambridge, MA: Harvard University Press, 1963); Theodore Mackin, S.J., *Marriage in the Catholic Church: What Is Marriage?* (New York: Paulist Press, 1982); idem, *Divorce and Remarriage* (New York: Paulist Press, 1984); idem, *The Marital Sacrament* (New York: Paulist Press, 1989); Odile M. Liebard, ed., *Love and Sexuality: Official Catholic Teaching* (Wilmington, NC: McGrath Publishing Company, 1978); Lisa

Sowle Cahill, *Between the Sexes: Foundations for a Christian Ethics of Sexuality* (Philadelphia: Fortress Press, 1985).

2. See "Gaudium et Spes" (The Church in the Modern World), in *The Documents of Vatican II*, ed. Walter M. Abbott, S.J. (New York: Crossroad, 1989), pp. 249–58, nos. 47–52.

3. Hugo Rahner, S.J., *Church and State in Early Christianity*, trans. Leo Donald Davis, S.J. (San Francisco: Ignatius Press, 1992); Heinrich A. Rommen, *The State in Catholic Thought: A Treatise in Political Philosophy* (London: B. Herder Book Company, 1945); John A. Coleman, S.J., ed., *One Hundred Years of Catholic Social Thought: Celebration and Challenge* (Maryknoll, NY: Orbis Books, 1991); "Gaudium et Spes," in Abbott, *The Documents of Vatican II*, pp. 259–308, nos. 53–93. For the American context from different political perspectives, see John Courtney Murray, S.J., *We Hold These Truths: Catholic Reflections on the American Proposition* (New York: Sheed and Ward, 1960); Richard P. McBrien, *Caesar's Coin: Religion and Politics in America* (New York and London: Macmillan, 1987); Michael Novak, *The Catholic Ethic and the Spirit of Capitalism* (New York: The Free Press, 1993).

4. The Second Vatican Council's Declaration on Religious Freedom, "Dignitatis Humanae," in Abbott, *The Documents of Vatican II*, 677, no. 1, consciously undertook such development: "in taking up the matter of religious freedom this Sacred Synod intends to develop the doctrine of recent Popes on the inviolable rights of the human person and on the constitutional order of society."

5. Contrast the 1968 letter of Pope Paul VI, "Humanae Vitae" (On the Regulation of Birth), in Joseph Gremillion, *The Gospel of Peace and Justice: Catholic Social Teaching Since Pope John* (Maryknoll, NY: Orbis Books, 1976), p. 432, no. 10, with the 1880 letter of Pope Leo XIII, "Arcanum Divinae Sapientiae" (On Christian Marriage), in Liebard, *Love and Sexuality*, pp. 1–22. The 1930 letter of Pope Pius XI, "Casti Connubii" (On Christian Marriage), in Liebard, *Love and Sexuality*, pp. 23–70, is something of a transition document. See also James P. Hanigan, *What Are They Saying About Sexual Morality?* (New York: Paulist Press, 1982), pp. 26–43.

6. See John Courtney Murray, S.J., "The Problem of Religious Freedom," *Theological Studies* 25, no. 3 (September 1964): 503–75.

7. See John T. Noonan, Jr., "Development in Moral Doctrine," *Theological Studies* 54, no. 4 (December 1993): 662–77.

8. See David Hollenbach, S.J., *Claims in Conflict: Renewing and Retrieving the Roman Catholic Rights Tradition* (New York: Paulist Press, 1979).

9. Pope John XXIII, "Pacem in Terris," in Gremillion, *The Gospel of Peace and Justice*, pp. 203–209, nos. 8–38, provided a major impetus to this acceptance of rights language in Catholic theology.

10. John Mahoney, *The Making of Moral Theology: A Study of the Roman Catholic Tradition* (Oxford: Clarendon Press, 1987), pp. 1–36; Romanus Cessario, O.P., *The Moral Virtues and Theological Ethics* (Notre Dame, IN, and London: University of Notre Dame Press, 1991).

11. The classic Catholic text is Pope Leo XIII, "Libertas Praestantissimum" (On Human Liberty), in *The Church Speaks to the Modern World: The Social Teachings of Leo XIII*, ed. Etienne Gilson (Garden City, NY: Image Books, 1954), pp. 57–85; Pope John Paul II has reemphasized the theme in his 10th encyclical letter, "Veritatis Splendor," which can be found in *Origins* 23 (1993): 297–336.

12. "Dignitatis Humanae" in Abbott, *The Documents of Vatican II*, p. 693, no. 13: "The freedom of the Church is the fundamental principle in what concerns the relations between the Church and governments and the whole civil order."

13. For the significance of how one frames the question, see the exchange of views between David R. Carlin, "The Gay Movement and Aggressive Secularism," and David S. Toolan, "In Defense of Gay Politics: Confessions of a Pastoralist," in *America* 173, no. 8 (23 September 1995): 12–21.

14. In Roman Catholic understanding a warrant for action means both a right and an obligation to act. Justice requires action by the state to preserve public order, or to promote the common good; hence the state has the right to act—i.e., it is right for the state to act. Of course, what the specific action ought to be is a matter of prudential judgment in particular circumstances.

15. Richard Peddicord, O.P., *Gay & Lesbian Rights: A Question—Sexual Ethics or Social Justice?* (Kansas City: Sheed & Ward, 1996), advances the same type of argument.

16. Examples may be helpful here. Catholic thought would generally construe the civil right to vote as a moral obligation of the citizen, but one that surely ought not to be made a legal obligation. There is and needs to be a legal right to divorce in certain marital situations that Catholic theology has recognized, but Catholic thought has typically not seen any moral right to such behavior, only sad practical necessity. After divorce, there is a legal right to marry again, but in Catholic thought and practice there is no moral right to do so and the church does not recognize such marriages as valid.

17. Again examples can be helpful. Catholic thought understands fornication to be a sin but few Catholic thinkers would wish to see it criminalized. Civil disobedience for a just cause is a crime but not a sin. See John F. Tuohey, "The Principle of Toleration and the Civil Rights of Gay and Lesbian Persons," *New Theology Review* 7, no. 3 (August 1994): 35–46.

18. Patricia Beattie Jung and Ralph F. Smith, *Heterosexism: An Ethical Challenge* (Albany: State University of New York Press, 1993), pp. 207–8, n. 2.

19. This certainly seems to be St. Paul's view of the matter in Romans 1:18–32, the classic New Testament text condemning same-sex behavior. For an exegetical discussion of this passage, see Robin Scroggs, *The New Testament and Homosexuality* (Philadelphia: Fortress Press, 1983), pp. 109–29; and Richard B. Hays, "Relations Natural and Unnatural: A Response to John Boswell's Exegesis of Romans 1," *The Journal of Religious Ethics* 14, no. 1 (Spring 1986): 184–215.

20. Noonan, *Contraception*, 30–383.

21. Thomas Aquinas, *Commentarium in IV Libros Sententiarum Petri Lombardi,* Distinction 26, question 1, article 1; see Mackin, *What is Marriage?* p. 179.

22. It would be hard to overemphasize the central place of the family in Catholic social teaching or the repeated insistence that the state has the responsibility to protect and promote family well-being without ever interfering with or overriding the rights of the family. For one conspicuous example, Pope John Paul II, "Familiaris Consortio" (The Apostolic Exhortation on the Family), *Origins* 11 (1981): 437–68, nos. 28–29; also Coleman, *One Hundred Years of Catholic Social Thought,* pp. 103–88. When I speak in the text of the proper social ordering of the family, I intend to include such matters as legitimacy, economic continuity through inheritance and ownership of property, and so forth. I would have no quarrel with the notion that economic considerations were a major motivation for the state's interest in regulating family life, just as they continue to be a major concern for any one today with an interest in family well-being.

23. I say on the face of it for the matter was more complex than the text allows. Questions about intercourse during pregnancy, after menopause, or between partners, one of whom was known to be sterile, all remained to be settled.

24. Peter Brown, *The Body and Society: Men, Women, and Sexual Renunciation in Early Christianity* (New York: Columbia University Press, 1988), makes the most adequate sense out of early Christian asceticism in regard to sex and the resulting ambivalence about sex. He shows clearly how it was that beliefs about the new life and freedom in Christ shaped attitudes and practices in regard to human sexuality. Where the narrative about the larger meaning and purpose of human life is forgotten or ignored, the asceticism and ambivalence take on a wholly different meaning and flavor.

25. David F. Kelly, "Sexuality and Concupiscence in Augustine," *Annual of the Society of Christian Ethics* (1983), pp. 81–116; Elaine Pagels, *Adam, Eve, and the Serpent* (New York: Random House, 1988), pp. 98–126.

26. Mackin, *What Is Marriage*, pp. 127–29.

27. Canon 1058 of the new Code of Canon Law reads: "All persons who are not prohibited by law can contract marriage." For an explanation of the canon, see James A. Coriden, Thomas J. Green, and Donald E. Heintschel, eds., *The Code of Canon Law: A Text and Commentary* (New York and Mahwah: Paulist Press, 1985), p. 743.

28. Mackin, *What Is Marriage?* 168–72.

29. Ibid., pp. 5–7.

30. Heinz-J. Vogels, *Celibacy—Gift or Law?: A Critical Investigation* (Kansas City: Sheed & Ward, 1993).

31. 1 Corinthians 7:5.

32. The degree to which this is still true in the Roman Catholic tradition is clearly reflected in Pope John Paul II's encyclical letter, "Mulieris Dignitatem" (On the Dignity and Vocation of Women), *Origins* 18 (1988), pp. 261–83. See also Lisa Sowle Cahill, "Accent on the Masculine," in *Considering Veritatis Splendor*, ed. John Wilkins (Cleveland: The Pilgrim Press, 1994), pp. 53–60.

33. Karl Rahner, "The Theological Concept of Concupiscentia," in *Theological Investigations I: God, Christ, Mary and Grace*, trans. Cornelius Ernst, O.P. (Baltimore: Helicon Press, 1961), pp. 347–82.

34. The principle of subsidiarity was formally articulated only in 1931 by Pope Pius XI in his encyclical letter "Quadragesimo Anno." But the idea behind the articulation was much older. For the principle and my brief commentary on it, see James P. Hanigan, *As I Have Loved You: The Challenge of Christian Ethics* (New York and Mahwah: Paulist Press, 1986), pp. 82–83.

35. To this day Catholic teaching insists on the rights of the family to be the primary educators of children, of the spouses to be the judge of whether or not to bring children into the world, and so forth. The whole issue of school choice and the government's obligation to support parental choice with tax dollars is rooted in this claim. See "Dignitatis Humanae" in Abbott, *The Documents of Vatican II*, p. 683, no. 5.

36. See Tuohey, "The Principle of Toleration," pp. 38–40.

37. Ibid., p. 39.

38. Noonan, *Contraception*, pp. 387–533; Hanigan, *What Are They Saying About Sexual Morality?* pp. 7–24.

39. Congregation for the Doctrine of the Faith, "Declaration on Certain Questions Concerning Sexual Ethics," in Anthony Kosnik et al., *Human Sexuality: New Directions in American Catholic Thought* (New York and Paramus: Paulist Press, 1977), pp. 304–305, no. 8; and idem, "The Pastoral Care of Homosexual Persons," *Origins* 16 (1986): 379, 381, nos. 3, 11.

40. Robert Nugent, "The Civil Rights of Homosexual People: Vatican Perspectives," *New Theology Review* 7, no. 4 (November 1994): 74–75, n. 8, points out that most mainline Christian churches, including the Catholic Church, have accepted as a

working hypothesis an essentialist understanding of sexual orientation as opposed to a social constructionist understanding. For a fuller discussion of the two theories he refers the reader to E. Stein, ed., *Forms of Desire: Sexual Orientation and the Social Constructionist Controversy* (New York and London: Garland Press, 1990).

41. All these practices are recommended by the church as pastoral care practices to be recommended to people struggling with their sexual desires, but with no claim or expectation that they will change or eliminate a homosexual orientation. Congregation for the Doctrine of the Faith, "The Pastoral Care of Homosexual Persons," pp. 381–82, nos. 12–18.

42. Ibid., p. 11; "What is essential is that the fundamental liberty which characterizes the human person and gives him his dignity be recognized as belonging to the homosexual person as well." No. 10 affirms, "The intrinsic dignity of each person must always be respected in word, in action and in law."

43. Congregation for the Doctrine of the Faith, "Declaration on Certain Questions Concerning Sexual Ethics," in Kosnik, *Human Sexuality,* p. 299, no. 1.

44. Hanigan, *What Are they Saying About Sexual Morality?* pp. 107–19.

45. James P. Hanigan, *Homosexuality: The Test Case for Christian Sexual Ethics* (New York and Mahwah: Paulist Press, 1988), pp. 43–58.

46. Paul VI, "Humanae Vitae," cited from Gremillion, *The Gospel of Peace and Justice,* p. 433, no. 11.

47. Ibid., p. 433, no. 12

48. Richard A. McCormick, S.J., "A Response," *America* 169, no. 8 (25 September 1993): 14, where he is agreeing with Bernard Haring.

49. John Paul II, *Original Unity of Man and Woman: Catechesis on the Book of Genesis* (Boston: St. Paul Books and Media, 1981); idem, *Reflections on Humanae Vitae: Conjugal Morality and Spirituality* (Boston: St. Paul Books and Media, 1984); idem, *The Theology of Marriage and Celibacy* (Boston: St. Paul Editions, 1986). See also Janet E. Smith, *Humanae Vitae: A Generation Later* (Washington, DC: The Catholic University of America Press, 1991).

50. Congregation for the Doctrine of the Faith, "The Pastoral Care of Homosexual Persons," p. 379, no. 3: "Although the particular inclination of the homosexual person is not a sin, it is a more or less strong tendency ordered toward an intrinsic moral evil and thus the inclination itself must be seen as an objective disorder."

51. In saying this I am somewhat at odds with the Vatican Congregation for the Doctrine of the Faith, "Observations Regarding Legislative Proposals Concerned with Discrimination Toward Homosexual Persons," *Origins* 22 (1992): 173–77, especially nos. 13–15.

52. Hanigan, *Homosexuality.*

53. I would change some ways of expressing my views in light of some criticisms the book has received. Among the most challenging works in this regard are the book cited above by Jung and Smith, *Heterosexism*; Robert Nugent and Jeannine Gramick, *Building Bridges: Gay and Lesbian Reality and the Catholic Church* (Mystic, CT: Twenty-Third Publications, 1992), which criticizes my work on pp. 172–183; and Xavier John Seubert, "The Sacramentality of Metaphors: Reflections on Homosexuality," *Cross Currents* 41, no. 1 (Spring 1991): 52–68. Also of interest are Christine E. Gudorf, *Body, Sex, and Pleasure: Reconstructing Christian Sexual Ethics* (Cleveland: The Pilgrim Press, 1994); Mary E. Hunt, *Fierce Tenderness: A Feminist Theology of Friendship* (New York: Crossroad, 1992); James B. Nelson, *Body Theology* (Louisville: Westminster, John Knox Press, 1992); Carter Heyward, *Touching Our Strength: The Erotic as Power and the Love of God* (San Francisco: Harper & Row, 1989); Gareth

Moore, O.P., *The Body in Context: Sex and Catholicism* (London: SCM Press LTD, 1992).

54. For a fuller description of this sort of argument and its theological consequences, see Hanigan, *Homosexuality*, pp. 97–104.

55. Pope John Paul II has been at pains to stress the also revealed character of Catholic morality. See especially "Veritatis Splendor." For my view of the relevance of that letter to Catholic sexual ethics, see James P. Hanigan, "'Veritatis Splendor' and Sexual Ethics," in *Veritatis Splendor: American Responses*, eds. Michael E. Allsopp and John J. O'Keefe (Kansas City: Sheed and Ward, 1995), pp. 208–23.

56. I find altogether persuasive Alasdair MacIntyre's view that all moral argument is tradition-based. See his *After Virtue: A Study in Moral Theory*, 2d ed. (Notre Dame, Ind.: University of Notre Dame Press, 1984); and his *Whose Justice? Which Rationality?* (Notre Dame, IN: University of Notre Dame Press, 1988), pp. 349–69. I also find persuasive his suggestions about the possibility of communication and agreement across traditions: *Whose Justice?* pp. 370–403.

57. I borrow the idea of horizon from Bernard J. F. Lonergan, *Method in Theology* (New York: The Seabury Press, 1979), pp. 235–66.

58. Mackin, *Divorce and Remarriage*, p. 379, points out that Luther, after denying the church's authority over marriage, unwittingly entrusted the exegesis of the scriptural texts on divorce and remarriage to the authority of the state.

59. "Gaudium et Spes," in Abbott, *The Documents of Vatican II*, p. 214, no. 16; "In fidelity to conscience, Christians are joined with the rest of men in the search for the truth, and for the genuine solution to the numerous problems which arise in the life of individuals and from social relationships."

60. This way of proceeding betrays a certain theological position or bias on my part. It is that moral fidelity to the Gospel is not dependent upon what nonbelievers do or allow believers to do, that Christians are called to be faithful but not necessarily successful, nor does it require that believers use their political power to ensure that nonbelievers act as believers think they should.

61. This is the mandate Pope John Paul II laid down as the charter of his pontificate in his first encyclical letter, "Redemptor hominis" (The Redeemer of the Human Person): "the human person's dignity itself becomes part of the content of [the Church's] proclamation," with the consequence that "the Church, because of her divine mission, becomes all the more the guardian of [human] freedom, which is the condition and basis for the human person's true dignity." Pope John Paul II, *The Redeemer of Man* 12 (Washington, DC: United States Catholic Conference, 1979), p. 36.

62. This is not unlike the argument of the work by Jung and Smith in *Heterosexism*. However, since they define heterosexism as "a reasoned system of bias regarding sexual orientation," p. 13, they call only for a change in thinking, not for an active non-cooperation with a system. But one does not do other persons an injustice simply by thinking, or even by saying, that certain of their behaviors are wrong. Indeed, if one is fully convinced of the wrongness of such behaviors, it would be an injustice not to share with others in a rational way the reasons why one thinks so. For we owe one another the truth in love. For the idea of a sinful system in Catholic theology, see Patrick Kerans, *Sinful Social Structures* (New York and Paramus: Paulist Press, 1974), and Mark O'Keefe, O.S.B., *What Are They Saying About Social Sin?* (New York and Mahwah: Paulist Press, 1990).

63. Mary Ann Glendon, *Rights Talk: The Impoverishment of Political Discourse* (New York: The Free Press, 1991; Kieran Cronin, *Rights and Christian Ethics* (New York: Cambridge University Press, 1993).

64. I use the notion that rights are defined rather than limited to connote that beyond the definition there is no reality to rights. For example, in being required to pay my fair share of taxes, my right to use my own money as I see fit is not being limited; it is being defined. Possibly my desires are being limited. My right to life is not an absolute claim to existence, for it requires the choice of two people to first conceive me and so gift me with an existence as the foundation of any claim to rights.

65. Biological necessity most strictly refers to death, but also to disease. I have no right not to die or to become ill in the face of biological necessity. Social necessity refers, among other things, to capital punishment, to war, and in more general terms to the power of the sword wielded by the state. The growing Catholic opposition to the death penalty, for instance, is precisely because there is no longer, in most societies, a social necessity for it. See Pope John Paul II's most recent encyclical letter, "Evangelium Vitae" (The Gospel of Life), *Origins* 24 (1995), p. 709, nos. 56–57.

66. The Bill of Rights, of course, is confusing in as much as some of the rights there articulated are human rights, e.g., the rights to freedom of religion, speech, press, assembly, and some are civil rights, e.g., the right to own and bear arms, or to a trial by a jury of one's peers.

67. It seems clear that the present arguments about sexual orientation and human rights have at their center a debate about the understanding of what it is to be human.

68. The Catholic view of conscience in both its profound personal and social dimensions is spelled out briefly and somewhat poetically in "Gaudium et Spes," in Abbott, *The Documents of Vatican II,* pp. 213–14, no. 16. See also "Dignitatis Humanae," in ibid., pp. 679–83, nos. 2–4. A less poetic, more systematic account of the Catholic understanding of conscience can be found in Hanigan, *As I Have Loved You,* pp. 119–44.

69. The half-right part is don't ask. I find it inconceivable that there is any circumstance in which a government agency, an employer, or any public institution has the right or the need to ask about any individual's sexual orientation.

70. Congregation for the Doctrine of the Faith, "Observations Regarding Legislative Proposals," p. 175. I take this to mean that there are occasions in which such silence might be prudent to avoid unhelpful pain or avoidable scandal. Others take it to mean more than that, and if it does mean more, than I suggest it is wrong. See also John F. Tuohey, "The C.D.F. and Homosexuals: Rewriting the Moral Tradition," *America* 167, no. 6 (12 September 1992), pp. 136–38.

71. The right to social space does not mean institutional approval of all the social group might advocate, nor is the group morally entitled publicly to advocate and behave in ways contrary to the college or church's public commitments or to its founding agreement. Honesty and respect for human dignity in such cases calls for advocacy from without.

72. This is my interpretation and application of a traditional principle of Catholic social thought, the principle of subsidiarity. See Hanigan, *As I Have Loved You,* pp. 82–83. For the meaning of the common good in Roman Catholic thought, see Michael Novak, *Free Persons and the Common Good* (Lanham, MD: Madison Books, 1989), and David Hollenbach, S.J., "The Common Good Revisited," *Theological Studies* 50, no. 1 (March 1989): 70–94. I am working throughout the text with the definition of the common good proposed by Pope John XXIII in "Mater et Magistra," no. 65—namely, that the common good "embraces the sum total of those conditions of social living, whereby men are enabled more fully and more readily to achieve their own perfection." Gremillion, *The Gospel of Peace and Justice,* p. 157.

73. The principle of subsidiarity expresses it this way: "Inasmuch as every social

activity should, by its very nature, prove a help to members of the body social, it should never destroy or absorb them."

74. Hollenbach, 'The Common Good Revisited," and idem, *Justice, Peace & Human Rights: American Catholic Social Ethics in a Pluralistic Context* (New York: Crossroad, 1988), pp. 3–33.

75. What else are affirmative action programs in regard to race than discrimination on the basis of particular historical identities, or similar programs in regard to sex than discrimination on the basis of particular biological identities? *Discrimination* is not a pejorative word. It is the basis of discrimination that is crucial to moral judgment.

76. The Catholic Church requires that couples intending marriage as the church understands marriage must be open to the gift of children in their relationship, and it requires this of all who intend marriage, despite their age or physical condition. Without such an openness, the marriage is not valid. It does not require any couple to actually have children nor does it think the decision about children belongs to anyone else other than to the couple.

77. Andrew Sullivan, *Virtually Normal: An Argument About Homosexuality* (New York, Alfred A. Knopf, 1995).

78. So, for example, the state would be wise to eliminate antisodomy laws, for the social cost of trying to enforce them is entirely too great. But that is quite different than giving explicit legal recognition to the practice of sodomy.

79. Catholic thought has not been happy about this development and still resists it in countries such as Ireland. American Catholics have forgotten by and large how severe a moral dilemma granting divorces and presiding at remarriages used to be for Catholic judges in the American legal system. The evidence that easy divorce and remarriage does not serve families or children is overwhelming.

Sexual Orientation and Human Rights in American Religious Discourse: A Roman Catholic Perspective

CHARLES E. CURRAN

This essay addresses the issue of sexual orientation and human rights in American religious discourse from the perspective of Roman Catholicism.

This complex question has a number of different facets: the moral teaching about homosexuality, whether the teaching is proposed for all humankind and should be found convincing by those who do not share Catholic faith, the way in which religion should engage in public discourse, the relationship between morality and law, and finally the different aspects of law (the legality or illegality of homosexual acts, the rights of homosexual persons not to be discriminated against in our society, the provision of certain benefits to same-sex couples, the legal acceptance of gay marriages).

Focusing the Issue

From a logical perspective an important connection, although not necessarily an absolute agreement, exists between one's moral and one's legal position. If one believes that taking the life of a convicted criminal is morally wrong, one opposes capital punishment and vice versa. However, the connection is not absolute. One could be morally opposed to drinking alcoholic beverages but willing to respect the freedom of others to do so within American civil society. With regard to homosexuality, those who morally approve committed same-sex relations invariably favor lesbian and gay rights, ranging from nondiscrimination to the according of legal benefits to a committed couple in a same-sex relationship. Those who view homosexual genital relations as immoral are more reluctant to support gay legal rights in their many dimensions. Thus one's position about the morality of homosexual genital behavior has a very important but not decisive influence on one's approach to the legality of same-sex sexual relations and the civil rights of gay and lesbian persons.

At the present time the Roman Catholic Church, like society in general and other religious bodies, experiences much ferment and discussion in the area of sexuality in general and homosexuality in particular. The official hierarchical teaching of the Roman Catholic Church condemns homosexual genital behavior since its criterion for the moral use of genital sexuality is within a heterosexual marriage.[1] However, many contemporary Catholic moral theologians have disagreed and called for a change in the existing hierarchical teaching. These disagreeing theologians come from two different positions. The one sees committed homosexual unions as morally good but lacking something that is found in heterosexual marriage. The second position sees the quality of the relationship as the moral criterion for both heterosexual and homosexual unions.[2]

Those who like myself disagree with the hierarchical teaching (I have adopted the first of the two positions mentioned above)[3] would be supportive of protecting gay and lesbian persons from discrimination in civil society and also approving same-sex domestic partnerships with legal and social ramifications. I would not favor gay marriage as just another form of marriage. Thus the great importance of one's position on the morality of homosexual genital relationships and the need to give significant consideration to that question in any discussion about the civil rights of gay and lesbian people. But for three reasons this essay is not going to develop the question of the morality of homosexuality from the Roman Catholic perspective.

First, such a discussion would be repetitive. I and many others have written extensively on the issue and further discussion would add little or nothing to what has already been done. Second, the very nature of the Roman Catholic Church with its hierarchical teaching office makes its position privileged and in the technical sense of the word, "authoritative." I personally defend the rights of Catholics to dissent in theory and in practice from the hierarchical teaching on homosexuality. Many theologians do dissent from this teaching and many committed gay couples continue to practice their Catholic faith. But the pope and bishops are the hierarchical teachers and the spokespersons for the positions of the church. Other Catholic individuals and groups are free to speak out on the issues and even propose positions contrary to the hierarchical teaching office, but they are not themselves and are not looked upon as authoritative spokespersons for the Roman Catholic Church. Third, from a realistic perspective, the hierarchical magisterium is not going to change its teaching on homosexuality in the near future. It has even refused to change its teaching on artificial contraception within marriage. In American civil society, the hierarchical magisterium with its present moral teaching will continue to be the authoritative spokesperson for the Catholic Church even though there are other dissenting voices. As a result this essay will focus on the Catholic understanding of the relationship between morality and law in general and how it bears on civil rights for gays and lesbians when one begins with the moral position of the hierarchical magisterium.

Some preliminary questions already mentioned in the introduction need to be addressed. Most, if not all in the Catholic tradition, whatever their position on the issue of homosexuality, hold that the moral teaching is proposed for all humankind and not just for Roman Catholics. Historically, Catholic moral teaching was based on the natural law, which claimed to be common to and binding on all human beings. Appeals were not made primarily to revelation but to reason. More recently, Catholic theology and teaching have incorporated more specifically theological and scriptural aspects into their approaches to morality but still claim that such teaching is applicable to all and can be convincing to all humankind.[4] Think of the modern papal encyclicals that are addressed to all people of goodwill. The U.S. bishops believe their position on nuclear disarmament, the economy, and abortion apply to all in society and should be convincing to those who do not share Catholic faith.[5]

Religion in general and Catholicism in particular have a right to try to influence and persuade society about what they believe to be for the public good. Roman Catholicism more than any other Christian church has appealed to reason and common human warrants in its approach to social morality thus making it somewhat easier to dialogue with and attempt to persuade all other citizens. Personally, I do not think specifically religious language should be excluded from the public square. If you believe that the Christian Bible calls for justice for all, you have a right to argue and work for such a position in the public sphere. However, to be convincing to others, one cannot simply appeal to authority as such, be it biblical or church or whatever. However, biblical stories such as the Prodigal Son or the Good Samaritan can appeal to many people who do not share the same faith. Religious perspectives should not automatically be excluded from public discourse, but not everything that religions claim to be morally wrong should be prohibited by law or public policy. Law must have a truly political or civil purpose. What is a truly political purpose? Most would recognize the public or common good as the criterion of a truly political purpose. Many differences arise about what constitutes this public good.[6] This essay will discuss the thorny and fundamental question of the relationship between morality and law.

Two Different Theories

What is the understanding of the relationship between morality and law in the Roman Catholic tradition? In this regard some significant development has occurred in recent Roman Catholic understanding at the Second Vatican Council (1962–1965).

As in other matters, the Catholic tradition has given special attention to Thomas Aquinas (d. 1274). Aquinas in his *Summa Theologiae* understood morality to be based on the natural law, which is the participation of the eternal law in the rational creature. Human law is derived from natural law. In fact, human law is truly a law and obliges only to the extent that it is derived from natural law. If something is not in accord with natural law it will not be law but a corruption of law. The human law either directly promulgates the conclusions of the natural law (e.g., murder is a crime) or specifies what the natural law leaves undetermined (e.g., driving on the right side of the street).[7]

Aquinas, however, emphasizes that morality and law are not identical. He answers in the negative the question of whether it belongs to human law to prohibit all the vices. Human law is imposed on the multitude of human beings, the greater number of whom are not perfect in virtue. Human law should prohibit only the more grievous vices from which the greater number of people can abstain and especially those that are harmful to others and threaten the fabric of human society, such as murder and theft.[8] Elsewhere Aquinas approves of Augustine's toleration and regulation of prostitution. His discussion of Augustine occurs in the context of his consideration of tolerating the rights of infidels. Human rule is derived from divine rule and should imitate it. The omnipotent and perfect God permits some evils to occur in this world lest greater goods be taken away or more evils occur. Human legislators can follow the same principle of tolerating evil lest certain goods are impeded or greater evils follow.[9] The principle of tolerating evil becomes very significant in subsequent debates.

Thomas also explicitly holds that the law should not command all the acts of all the virtues but only those that are ordered to the common good.[10] The Thomistic approach thus recognizes two important differences between morality and law. Human law looks only to the common good and human law can and at times should tolerate evil. Both of these characteristics of human law are open to wide interpretation.

Two comments made in the pre-Vatican II Roman Catholic Church show the different approaches to toleration. William J. Kenealy in 1948 argued in favor of the Massachusetts law that forbade the sale, manufacture, exhibition, and advertising of contraceptives. He maintained that the majesty of our civil law should not sanction a perversion of God's natural law. No concern here is given to the possibility of toleration.[11]

John Courtney Murray, writing in the 1950s about morality and law, points to the differences at times between the strictness of Catholic morality in sexual matters that appalls libertarians and the laxness of Catholic government that equally appalls puritans. Murray points out that in 1517 the number of prostitutes in the city of Rome (governed by the pope) considerably surpassed the number of married women. With a realistic shrug of the shoulders, Murray laconically remarks that the figures are not edifying but they are interesting.[12] Here one gets quite a bit of toleration. Thus, prudential judgments bear great weight with regard to both the principle of toleration and what might be harmful to the common good. Here, too, one sees how the disposition of people, history, and so many other factors might enter into whether or not and to what degree one accepts toleration.

The Second Vatican Council (1962–1965) proposed a different understanding of the relationship between morality and law. The council did not deal explicitly with the question of morality and law, but it did discuss the role and function of government and law in a democratic society in its Declaration on Religious Freedom. The document in this case is following the approach of the American Jesuit, John Courtney Murray. One should point out that the final document of the Council on Religious Freedom does not follow Murray's viewpoint totally, but it does accept Murray's understanding of the role and function of law in a pluralistic, democratic society.[13]

Some wanted to see the issue of religious freedom treated primarily as a theological question based on the freedom of the act of faith or a moral question based on the freedom of conscience. Murray, on the other hand, frames the issue as formally a juridical or constitutional issue that has foundations in theology, ethics, and political philosophy. The understanding of constitutional government and its proper role grounds Murray's approach to religious freedom.[14]

The Declaration on Religious Freedom deals with the jurisprudential and constitutional question in its discussion of the limits of religious freedom. When can and should government intervene in the exercise of religious freedom? In so doing the council proposes what Murray himself called the basic principle of the free society and what he thinks secular experts consider the most significant sentence in the declaration—"For the rest, the usages of society are to be the usages of freedom in their full range. These require that the freedom of man [sic] be respected as far as possible and curtailed only when and insofar as necessary."[15] In the use of all freedoms the moral principle of personal and social responsibility is to be observed. But society has the right to defend itself against abuses committed under the pretext of freedom. Here juridical norms in conformity with the objective moral order are to determine when the coercive force of law can intervene. Law can and should intervene to protect public order, which constitutes the basic component of the common good. The public order involves an order of justice and rights, public peace, and public morality.[16]

In his own writings Murray develops somewhat the meaning of these concepts. Murray sees an important distinction between the common good and the public order based on the distinction between society and the state. In the constitutional tradition the state plays only a limited role within society. The purposes of the state are not coextensive with the purposes of society. There are many other groups and institutions within society besides the state. The state as a part of society uses its coercive power for the benefit of society.

On the basis of the distinction between society and the state, Murray makes the distinction between the common good and the public order. The pursuit of the common good devolves upon society as a whole—all its members and all its institutions in accord with the principle of subsidiarity, legal justice, and distributive justice. The public order is a narrower concept indicating where the coercive power of the state may be used. The public order involves an order of justice, of public morality, and of public peace. Murray does not develop these but only mentions, for instance, that public morality comprises certain minimal common standards accepted among the people.[17]

Murray properly recognizes significant shifts represented by this teaching. The Catholic Church has now accepted the theory and practice of a limited, free, constitutional, democratic state.[18] Yes, there is no doubt that the Catholic Church has learned much from the Enlightenment and its understanding of the political order, which at one time it strongly opposed. Catholicism has traditionally seen the individual as a part or member of the broader society and political community. In the language of the contemporary debate, Roman Catholicism has strongly favored a communitarian understanding of humankind. In the words of Aquinas and Aristotle, the human being is social and political by nature. From this perspective Roman Catholicism has been very slow to recognize the legitimate freedom and rights of individuals in political societies, to say nothing about freedom and rights within the church itself. The Declaration on Religious Freedom shows that the

Catholic Church has finally accepted the notion of the limited, democratic, constitutional state. However, Catholicism is not accepting an individualistic anthropology and the absoluteness of free choice. Although the church has now given more importance to freedom than it did in the past, freedom still cannot be absolutized and must exist together with justice, truth, and charity.[19] To make sure that the communitarian dimension remains, I emphasize that the state's promotion and protection of justice also includes social justice.

The differences between these two understandings of the relationship between morality and law are significant but not complete. First, the Thomistic approach begins with the moral law and then brings in common good and toleration to show that the legal can legitimately differ from the moral at times. The second approach begins with the freedom of the person; the coercive force of law must be justified by the requirements of the public order. The first position begins with the moral law and thus seems to give a presumption to the moral law, whereas the second position begins with the freedom of the person and gives the presumption to this freedom. This difference is very significant because it shapes the way the whole issue is looked at. The first position begins with the moral law and then sees if one can tolerate an evil. The second approach sees the issue as the right of the individual to act in accord with the individual's own conscience, provided that the public order is not disproportionately hurt.

Second, the Thomistic and older approach makes the common good the purpose of law, whereas the Second Vatican Council approach makes the public order the criterion for a proper use of the law. The public order is less expansive and inclusive than the common good and by definition forms just a part of the common good. The Declaration on Religious Freedom calls public order the basic element of the common good.[20]

Third, the older Thomistic understanding does not explicitly mention the role of freedom in the common good and in reality downplays the role of freedom. The Vatican II position emphasizes the role of freedom as a constitutive part of the common good of society, and the need of the state to promote and protect that freedom. Thus, one can readily see that the second approach, as found in the Second Vatican Council, would make it easier to justify and defend the basic rights of lesbian and gay persons against discrimination in work, housing, public accommodations, and other areas.

Before applying this understanding to the rights of lesbian and gay persons, a possible objection arises. Is this theory on religious liberty really applicable to the question of morality and law in general and to the particular question of lesbian and gay rights? Murray's explanation underscores the religious freedom issue as being primarily a juridical and constitutional question that has broad implications and is not limited only to the issue of religious freedom. Murray's approach begins by recognizing the complex basis of religious freedom: the free human person under a government of limited powers. Religious liberty is not primarily a theological or ethical issue but a legal and jurisprudential one.[21] The Declaration on Religious Freedom begins by recognizing the growing sense of the dignity of the human person and the increasing demand that human actions should be based on individual, responsible freedom and should not be driven by coercion. This requires that constitutional limits be placed on the power of government so there be no encroachments on the rightful freedom of the person and of associations. This demand for freedom in human society especially concerns the quest for values proper to the human spirit—above all the free exercise of religion in society.[22] Thus there can be no doubt that the Declaration is providing criteria for the proper role of government not only in matters of religious freedom but also in all matters involving the responsible use of human freedom and its legitimate limitations through the coercive power of the state.

In addition, the right to religious freedom is comparable to the human right not to be discriminated against. Both are ultimately based on the dignity of the human person. The right not to be discriminated against is a fundamental human right and not just a remote or secondary human right. All free societies accept such an understanding of the right not to be discriminated against. However, just as there are limits on the right to religious freedom, so too can and should there be limits on the right not to be discriminated against. The same basic principles are to be followed in both cases.

The Rationale in Favor of Nondiscrimination

The argument in favor of the rights of gays and lesbians not to be discriminated against begins with the principle that freedom from discrimination be respected as far as possible and curtailed only when and insofar as necessary. The presumption favors such a right to nondiscrimination or freedom from discrimination. Such a right can only be limited by the demands of the public order. In terms of the rights of others being violated, one possible limitation will be mentioned here. Can religious groups opposed to homosexual acts be forced to hire and employ people who are sexually active homosexuals? One could argue that their freedom to practice their own religion will thus be compromised by the state. I note this limitation here but will not delve any further into the issue.

The protection of gays and lesbians against discrimination, like protection based on race or gender, does not seem to be opposed to justice and social justice, but rather is a demand of justice. Such nondiscrimination does not harm the rights of others. Obviously having sex with a minor should be a criminal offense for both heterosexuals and homosexuals.

The criterion of public peace does not seem to raise any question for preventing discrimination against gays and lesbians, but the criterion of public morality has at times been invoked. The criterion of public morality at the minimum is contrasted with private morality. The very fact that one believes a certain action is morally wrong does not justify discriminating against people who do that action. The prior question concerns making illegal what one considers immoral. I know of no one in the Catholic tradition today who argues that homosexual acts between consenting adults in private should be illegal. Public morality is somewhat difficult to determine and to apply in a pluralistic society. One reason frequently invoked to justify some restrictions on the rights of gays and lesbians is the deleterious influence on marriage and the family that would come from the recognition of such rights. The Catholic tradition has always given great importance to the family as one of the three natural societies (family, state, and church) and has seen the need to protect and promote the institutions of marriage and the family.[23] Will laws prohibiting discrimination against gays and lesbians apparently weaken marriage and the family?

Most authorities today recognize that no one chooses her or his sexual orientation. The *Catechism of the Catholic Church* accepts this understanding.[24] Thus individuals are not going to choose to be lesbian or gay so they can avoid marriage. In a certain sense one could argue that people who choose to be single are a greater threat to marriage and the family. However, no one has proposed any discrimination against single people. But there is a much more pertinent comparison. The Catholic approach to marriage sees divorce and remarriage as morally wrong. From this perspective divorce and remarriage constitute a threat to the institution of marriage with its characteristic of indissolubility. The sanctioning of divorce by law negatively affects marriage and the family more than does protecting gays and lesbians against discrimination. Catholics today are not even bothering to oppose or change the civil law on divorce, let alone calling for discrimination against divorced and remarried people.[25]

Thus the human right of gays and lesbians not to be discriminated against cannot be overturned by the demands of the public order. Such discrimination would be wrong. In the light of the methodology and conclusions proposed above, this essay will now examine other approaches to the question.

Summary and Critique of Other Positions

Roman Catholic bishops in the United States have been divided in their positions about laws preventing discrimination against gays. Cardinals O'Connor of New York, Bernardin of Chicago, and Law of Boston (through the Massachusetts bishops) have opposed legislation outlawing discrimination against gays. However, Archbishops Quinn of San Francisco, Roach of St. Paul, Whealon of Hartford, and Weakland of Milwaukee have all supported nondiscrimination legislation.[26] The bishops of Florida and Oregon have opposed state proposals that would prohibit laws protecting the rights of homosexuals.[27]

A very curious document came from the Congregation for the Doctrine of the Faith in 1992 concerning legislative proposals on discrimination against homosexuals. The document was originally sent privately only to the bishops in the United States, was made public by an unofficial Catholic group, and subsequently was published with a few changes by the Vatican. According to this document a homosexual orientation is not comparable to race, ethnic background, sex, or age with regard to nondiscrimination because it is an objective disorder and is essentially private and unknown unless the person chooses to publicly so identify him or herself. Homosexuals have the same rights as all human persons, but these rights are not absolute and can be limited, for example, in the placement of children for adoption or foster care, the employment of teachers or athletic coaches, and military recruiting. In releasing the document for publication the Vatican spokesperson also released an explanation of the document. These considerations were originally given to the bishops of the United States as a background resource for whatever help they might provide the bishops and were not intended as an official and public instruction of the congregation. These observations also do not pass judgment on any responses already made by bishops or state conferences in the United States.[28] Archbishop Quinn of San Francisco pointed out that he and the bishops of California had opposed discrimination against gay and lesbian persons and their policy would continue even after the Vatican document.[29]

As might be expected, the position accepting discrimination or some limitation of the human rights of lesbian and gay persons often follows the Thomistic approach and begins with the moral teaching of the church. Cardinal Joseph Bernardin of Chicago, a well-respected, moderate prelate, opposed a proposed gay rights ordinance that came before the Chicago City Council in 1986. In defending his position Bernardin explained that, in the case of gay rights legislation, he seeks to balance two values: first, that no person should be discriminated against because of sexual orientation; and second, that heterosexual marital intimacy is normative for genital relations.[30] Bernardin insists of course that he is speaking about public morality—those areas where the state can legitimately legislate. "As a teacher of morality and a citizen, I want to protect the rights of all citizens but I cannot support public protection or sanctioning of sexual activity or a way of life which compromises the normativeness of heterosexual marital intimacy."[31] My purpose is not to refute in depth the Bernardin position but simply to note the underlying theory on which it is based. One begins with a moral teaching regarding the normativeness of heterosexual marital intimacy and moves from there to public policy or legislation. Here Bernardin apparently sees no reason to prevent the move from morality to legislation or to tolerate the evil he sees. By invoking public morality and in the light of other approaches one would expect Bernardin to claim that such nondiscrimination would have a negative effect on marriage and the family. But the Chicago cardinal moves from morality to legality without any other moral considerations.

One scholar, John M. Finnis, rejects the Thomistic view of the relationship between law and morality and appeals to the Vatican II understanding to support his position advocating some restrictions on gay and lesbian civil rights. Finnis describes the standard, modern European position according to which the state is not authorized to make adult homosexual acts in private a punishable offense, but can discourage homosexual conduct and orientation.[32] Finnis, a Catholic philosopher, uses the moral theory associated with Germain Grisez and himself to argue for the immorality of homosexual genital relations. The moral acceptance of homosexual relations is an active threat to the stability of existing and future marriages. A political community that judges that the family and family life are of paramount importance for the community can rightly judge that it has a compelling interest to deny that homosexual conduct or a gay lifestyle is a humanly acceptable choice and form of life, and is thereby doing what it properly can as a community to discourage such conduct.[33]

In conjunction with his basic thesis that the state cannot criminalize consensual adult homosexual acts in private but can discourage homosexual orientation and lifestyle for the good of society, Finnis develops and defends what he calls an instrumental, not a basic, intrinsic, or constitutive, understanding of the common good.[34] A basic, intrinsic, or constitutive notion of the common good denies the subsidiary function of the state and authorizes the state to direct people to virtue and to deter people from vice by making even private and consensual adult acts of vice a punishable crime.

Finnis identifies such an intrinsic, basic, and constitutive notion of the common good with Aristotle and the principle laid down by Thomas Aquinas in his *Treatise on Princely Government,* according to which government should command whatever leads people toward their ultimate heavenly end, forbid whatever deflects them from that end, and coercively deter people from doing evil, and induce them to morally decent conduct. In a footnote, Finnis claims that in two places in the *Summa* (which we mentioned above) Aquinas qualifies but does not abandon this approach.[35]

Finnis proposes an instrumental notion of the common good as found in the Vatican II teaching on religious liberty. This teaching on religious freedom first insists that everyone has the right not to be coerced in religious matters because religious acts transcend the sphere of government. Second, the council puts limits on religious freedom, and here Finnis quotes the passages about public order including the protection of the rights of all citizens, public peace, and public morality. However, the common good, in order to protect the institution of marriage, justifies restricting the rights of homosexuals.[36] Thus Finnis claims to be following what I have called the Vatican II approach to the relationship between law and morality and comes to a conclusion diametrically opposed to mine.

However, I do not think Finnis appreciates and follows the full approach to the role of morality and law found in the Declaration on Religious Freedom and in the work of John Courtney Murray. He never cites what Murray called the basic principle of the free society and the most significant passage from the perspective of secular experts—that freedom is to be respected as far as possible and curtailed only when and insofar as necessary.[37]

Nowhere in his discussion of law and morality does Finnis mention freedom, let alone the presumption in its favor. He fails to point out that freedom is a very important component of the common good. Finnis's article also nowhere explicitly recognizes the reality of pluralism on the issue of homosexuality in our society. The logic of his argument seems to rest on the assumption that all human beings not only accept the conclusion of his moral analysis of homosexual acts but also the moral theory on which it is based. In reality, as already pointed out, gay rights would not disproportionately harm marriage and family precisely because one's sexual orientation is not a matter of free choice. In addition, Finnis always uses the broader term "common good" rather than the narrower term "public order," although he does cite the Declaration's understanding of public order as the fundamental part of the common good. By its nature, public order is less inclusive than the common good.

Finnis uses the Declaration on Religious Freedom to prove his point that the common good of society is instrumental and not basic or constitutive, but he ignores and apparently does not accept the broader jurisprudential and constitutional framework within which this teaching on religious liberty is set.

In general, most of the defenders of some possible discrimination against gay and lesbian persons not only do not use the Vatican II approach to the proper understanding of the relationship between morality and law, but also do not accept its basic principles. In opposing a homosexual rights bill for their state, the bishops of Massachusetts maintained that the passage of legislation of this type would be seen by many as a step toward legal approval of the homosexual lifestyle. This concern is heightened by a common perception in our country that whatever is declared legal by that very fact becomes morally right. The tragic experience about abortion in this country in the last ten years shows the need for great caution in this area.[38] This understanding thus fails to recognize the distinction between morality and law found in the Declaration on Religious Freedom. As bishops, their role is to propose the teaching of the church, in this case the proper role of the coercive force of government and law and the presumption in favor of freedom. Likewise, they fail to recognize that the civil law allows divorce and remarriage and does not discriminate against divorced people, but the Catholic Church still maintains its moral teaching on divorce. Catholic bishops have not made any attempt to change divorce legislation. It seems the Massachusetts bishops are looking at the question of gay and lesbian rights only through the narrow prism of their experience with abortion and they thereby fail to appreciate both the theory proposed in the Declaration on Religious Freedom and the experience gained from other issues such as divorce.

I think that the statement of the Massachusetts bishops helps to explain why those who hold the immorality of homosexual genital relations do not understand the relationship between morality and law in the light of Vatican II's teaching on the role of the state as found in its Declaration on Religious Freedom. First, in their own mind there exists a more direct relationship between morality and law than the conciliar understanding. They were probably trained in the older approach and have never really seen the issue in the light of the theory of the role of the state behind the teaching on religious liberty. It is easier to accept this theory when it safeguards the freedom of what they hold to be morally right (religious liberty) than when it might promote what they hold to be morally wrong (homosexual genital behavior).

The recent opposition of the Roman Catholic bishops of the United States to abortion as a matter of public policy has become the all-important analogy in their minds. These bishops have closely linked morality and law on this issue. (I have argued against changing the existing permissive law on abortion on the basis of the conciliar view of the relationship between morality and law. However, I recognize that with such an understanding of law, one who sees the fetus as a truly individual human being could justify restrictive abortion legislation.) To separate morality and law on the gay and lesbian rights issue might open the door to some relaxation in their struggle against legal abortion. It seems that abortion has become so significant an issue in their approach that the American Catholic bishops will do nothing that will in any way weaken their legal approach to abortion. As noted earlier, the legal aspects of divorce are a closer analogue to the legal aspects of homosexuality.

I think something else is also at work today in the mentality of the Catholic bishops in the United States. There is a moral rigorism present that too readily identifies the moral and the legal. In the language of the older approach there is less willingness to tolerate evil now than there was in the past. Think, for example, of the opposition of the American Catholic bishops to using condoms to prevent the spread of AIDS.[39] If there ever was a clear case of counseling the lesser of two moral evils or tolerating an evil (from their perspective) to avoid a greater one, this would be the case. I will leave it to people more expert than I to say where this rigorism comes from—an Anglo-Saxon mentality, Irish and French rigorist Jansenism, the all-controlling influence of the abortion debate. One thing is sure—there is a rigorism showing itself today in the American Catholic bishops' reaction to questions of morality and public policy.

One might expect those arguing in favor of nondiscrimination laws for lesbian and gay persons, especially when writing from a more scholarly perspective, to appeal to the Vatican II understanding of the role of the state and the relationship between morality and law. But as a matter of fact I have not found such approaches. John Touhey argues against the document of the Congregation for Doctrine of the Faith and in support of the civil rights of gay and lesbian persons on the basis of the principle of toleration—the older approach. He cites Augustine, Aquinas, and the Catholic response in England to the Wolfenden Report in justifying the invocation of toleration here. He buttresses his argument by showing that such rights will not undermine the social fabric, especially with regard to marriage and the family.[40]

Robert Nugent, who has written extensively on the issues of homosexuality and who has exercised a very significant pastoral ministry to lesbians and gays, also argues against the 1992 Document of the Congregation for the Doctrine of the Faith calling for restrictions on the rights of homosexual persons. Nugent takes up the arguments of the congregation and explicitly refutes them without developing a positive rationale of his own on the relationship between morality and law. He maintains, for example, that sexual orientation is comparable to age, sex, gender, and race as a basis for nondiscrimination in the civil forum. Nugent insists that the Vatican respect its own distinction between sexual orientation and action, and also shows that gay rights would not be harmful to marriage, the family, and the common good.[41]

Richard A. Peddicord, in a 1993 doctoral dissertation, also argues that the Catholic teaching should accept and promote the civil rights of gay and lesbian persons with no restrictions or discrimination. Peddicord understands the issue as a conflict between the justice tradition of the church, with its heavy contemporary emphasis on human rights, and the church's sexual teaching. He thus argues for the primacy of the justice aspect, especially in light of the fact that the civil rights of gays and lesbians will not harm marriage, family, and the common good. Peddicord presents the issue in this way precisely because many of the proposals made by bishops—for example, Cardinal Bernardin's approach—use such an understanding and see the issue in terms of the tension between the church's teaching on justice and its teaching on sexuality.[42]

In my judgment it is surprising that Catholic defenders of gay and lesbian civil rights do not employ the Vatican II understanding of the role of government. Nugent's and Peddicord's arguments would be even stronger within that context.

However, both of them have chosen to respond to the issue on the same basis that others have used to argue for some limitation of civil rights.

Domestic Partnership Laws

What about domestic partnership laws? At the very minimum, logic recognizes that on the basis of the Vatican II approach described above, it will be much harder to justify domestic partnership laws for gays than to justify nondiscrimination laws. The right not to be discriminated against is a very basic and fundamental human right, whereas domestic partnership laws do not touch on such a fundamental human right. Perhaps even more significant is the fact that rights against discrimination are basically an immunity—a freedom from unjust discrimination. The Vatican II theory proposed above recognizes that freedom must be promoted as much as possible and curtailed only when necessary. However, domestic partnership laws do not involve an immunity but rather an entitlement—a positive giving of some benefit. The Vatican II approach is much more open to justifying immunities than entitlements.

The factual situation also bears out the contention that it is more difficult, given the hierarchical Catholic teaching on homosexuality and especially homosexual genital relations, to justify domestic partnership laws than nondiscriminating human rights laws for gays and lesbians. I have found no one holding the hierarchical moral teaching who argues in favor of domestic partnership laws. Archbishop John Quinn of San Francisco, who has been a strong supporter of nondiscrimination and the rights of gays and lesbians, has opposed across-the-board domestic partnership laws.[43]

Domestic partnership laws recognize and encourage homosexual unions by providing legal recognition and certain benefits for the couple involved. This is much more than just respecting the basic human rights of all, including homosexuals. Those who are morally opposed to a position can more readily grant civil rights to those they accuse of being morally wrong than positively support a same-sex union they consider to be morally wrong. By recognizing unions other than the union of marriage, society at the very minimum detracts somewhat from its protection and promotion of marriage.

An argument can be made for domestic partnership laws, but I admit it is not nearly as convincing as the argument for nondiscrimination against gay and lesbian persons. At the very minimum such partnership laws are not going to discourage heterosexual people from getting married. Even the *Catechism of the Catholic Church* recognizes that people do not choose their sexual orientation. Consequently, domestic partnership laws are not going to entice some people into a homosexual union who otherwise would have become married. In reality it seems that such provisions for domestic partnerships will not denigrate or harm the institutions of marriage and the family.

To justify support for such partnership laws the Catholic tradition could appeal to the general principle of counseling the lesser of two moral evils.[44] This principle is somewhat related to the general toleration principle—one can tolerate evil to ensure that greater good or lesser evil will occur. On an individual basis one could counsel a person who is determined to be homosexually active to live in a stable and faithful homosexual relationship as a lesser evil than engaging in promiscuous homosexual genital encounters. In an analogous way, one can argue in favor of domestic partnership laws as a way of avoiding the greater evil of promiscuous sexual liaisons. By promoting stable relationships, one avoids a greater evil.

Again, the comparison with divorce is most apropos. The civil law not only allows divorce but also provides civil recognition and benefits to divorced and remarried people. Catholic leaders are not engaging in any activities to change the present divorce law. In both cases the civil law is protecting and promoting to some degree a union that Roman Catholic teaching opposes. But giving legal provision and benefits to divorced and remarried people is more opposed to the Catholic understanding of marriage than domestic partnership laws precisely because people freely choose to divorce and remarry, but people ordinarily do not freely choose their sexual orientation. Thus one could maintain that the provision of domestic partnership laws does less harm to marriage and the family than do the existing laws about divorced and remarried people. However, in the present rigoristic environment, I do not think American Catholic bishops would make or accept this argument for domestic partnership laws.

In conclusion, this essay has focused on the morality and law relationship in the Roman Catholic tradition to see how the official hierarchical moral teaching on homosexuality, especially homosexual genital relations, relates to the legal issues of civil rights for gay and lesbian persons. The approach to the morality-law relationship found in the Second Vatican Council has not been explicitly employed very often in this discussion, but such an approach offers a very firm foundation for laws protecting gays and lesbians against discrimination. On the other hand, such an approach at best provides a less firm foundation for supporting domestic partnership legislation.

Notes

A slightly different version of this essay appeared in Charles E. Curran, *History and Contemporary Issues: Studies in Moral Theology* (New York: Continuum, 1996). Reprinted with permission.

1. Congregation for the Doctrine of the Faith, "The Pastoral Care of Homosexual Persons," *Origins* 16 (1986): 377–82.

2. For an overview of the positions of the many American Catholic moral theologians calling for a change in the present hierarchical teaching on homosexuality, see Robert Nugent and Jeannine Gramick, *Building Bridges: Gay and Lesbian Reality in the Catholic Church* (Mystic, CT: Twenty-Third Publications, 1992), pp. 146–56.

3. See Charles E. Curran, *Catholic Moral Theology in Dialogue* (Notre Dame, IN: Fides Publishers, 1972), pp. 184–219; idem, *Transition and Tradition in Moral Theology* (Notre Dame, IN: University of Notre Dame Press, 1979), pp. 59–80; idem, *Critical Concerns in Moral Theology* (Notre Dame, IN.: University of Notre Dame Press, 1984), pp. 73–98.

4. Charles E. Curran and Richard A. McCormick, eds., *Readings in Moral Theology No. 7: Natural Law and Theology* (New York: Paulist Press, 1991).

5. J. Bryan Hehir, "The Church and the Political Order: The Role of the Catholic

Bishops in the United States," in *The Church's Public Role,* ed. Dieter T. Hessel (Grand Rapids, MI: Wm. B. Eerdmans, 1993), pp. 176–97.

6. For a further development of my thinking on these issues see Charles E. Curran, *The Church and Morality: An Ecumenical and Catholic Approach* (Minneapolis, MN: Fortress, 1993), pp. 65–91.

7. Thomas Aquinas, *Summa Theologiae* (Rome: Marietti, 1952), part 1a 2a, question 95, article 2.

8. Aquinas, *Summa,* 1a 2a, q. 96, a. 2.

9. Aquinas, *Summa,* 2a 2ae, q. 10, a. 11.

10. Aquinas, *Summa,* 1a 2ae, q. 96, a. 3.

11. William J. Kenealy, "Contraception: A Violation of God's Law," *Catholic Mind* 46 (1948): 552–64.

12. John Courtney Murray, *We Hold These Truths: Catholic Reflections on the American Proposition* (New York: Sheed and Ward, 1960), p. 163.

13. For the development of the Declaration itself and Murray's role in it, see Richard Regan, *Conflict and Consensus: Religious Freedom and the Second Vatican Council* (New York: Macmillan, 1967).

14. John Courtney Murray, *The Problem of Religious Freedom* (Westminster, MD: Newman, 1965), pp. 19–22.

15. "Declaration on Religious Freedom," in *The Documents of Vatican II,* ed. Walter M. Abbott (New York: Guild Press, 1966), p. 687, no. 7. Murray's comments are found on p. 687, n. 21. In this edition the footnotes in italics are the official footnotes of the documents, while those in regular type are unofficial footnotes added by Murray himself.

16. "Declaration on Religious Freedom," in Abbott, *The Documents of Vatican II,* pp. 685–87, no. 7.

17. John Courtney Murray, *Problem of Religious Freedom,* pp. 28–31; "Declaration on Religious Freedom," in Abbott, *The Documents of Vatican II,* p. 686, n. 20.

18. "Declaration on Religious Freedom," in Abbott, *The Documents of Vatican II,* p. 687, n. 21.

19. For a fuller discussion, see R. Bruce Douglass and David Hollenbach, eds., *Catholicism and Liberalism: Contributions to American Public Philosophy* (Cambridge: Cambridge University Press, 1994).

20. "Declaration on Religious Freedom," in Abbott, *The Documents of Vatican II,* p. 687, no. 7.

21. Murray, *Problem of Religious Freedom,* p. 26.

22. "Declaration on Religious Freedom," in Abbott, *The Documents of Vatican II,* p. 675, no. 1.

23. Margaret A. Farley, "Family," in *The New Dictionary of Catholic Social Thought,* ed. Judith A. Dwyer (Collegeville, MN: Liturgical Press, 1994), pp. 371–81.

24. *Catechism of the Catholic Church* (Vatican City: Editrice Vaticana, 1994), no. 2358, p. 566.

25. For Catholic approaches, both historical and contemporary, to divorce laws, see Philip J. Grib, *Divorce Laws and Morality: A New Catholic Jurisprudence* (Lanham, MD: University Press of America, 1985).

26. Richard A. Peddicord, "A Studied Ambiguity: Catholic Moral Teaching on the Question of Gay and Lesbian Rights Legislation" (S.T.D. diss., St. Paul University, Ottawa, Canada, 1993), pp. 112–70.

27. Florida Bishops, "On Discrimination Against Homosexual Persons," *Origins* 23 (1993): 395–96; idem, "On File," *Origins* 24 (1994): 388.

28. Congregation for the Doctrine of the Faith, "Observations Regarding Legislative Proposals Concerned With Discrimination Toward Homosexual Persons," *Origins* 22 (1992): 173–77.

29. John R. Quinn, "Civil Rights of Gay and Lesbian Persons," *Origins* 22 (1992): 204.

30. Joseph L. Bernardin, "I Too Struggle," *Commonweal* 113 (1986): 682–84.

31. Ibid., p. 684.

32. John M. Finnis, "Law, Morality, and 'Sexual Orientation'," *Notre Dame Law Review* 69, no. 5 (1994): 1049–55.

33. Ibid., pp. 1055–70.

34. Ibid., pp. 1070–76.

35. Ibid., p. 1073. In my judgment, Thomas Aquinas in the *Summa* does modify such an approach by invoking the common good as the criterion grounding the purpose of human law. However, Thomas Aquinas holds a very inclusive concept of the common good.

36. Ibid., pp. 1072–73.

37. "Declaration on Religious Freedom," in Abbott, *The Documents of Vatican II*, p. 687, no. 7 and n. 21.

38. "Bishops Oppose Homosexual Rights Bill," *Origins* 14 (1984): 73–74.

39. United States Catholic Bishops, "Called to Compassion and Responsibility: A Response to the HIV/AIDS Crisis," *Origins* 19 (1989): 429.

40. John F. Touhey, "The Principle of Toleration and the Civil Rights of Gay and Lesbian Persons," *New Theology Review* 7 (August 1994): 35–46.

41. Robert Nugent, "The Civil Rights of Homosexual People: Vatican Perspectives," *New Theology Review* 7 (November 1994): 72–86.

42. Peddicord, "A Studied Ambiguity."

43. John R. Quinn, "Letter to Mayor Art Agnos," *Origins* 19 (1989): 50.

44. For the classical treatment of the principle in the manuals of moral theology, see I. Aertnys and C. Damen, *Theologia Moralis*, 17th ed. (Rome: Marietti, 1956), I: 366, no. 379.

Response to James Hanigan
and Charles Curran

MARGARET A. FARLEY

The presentations of James Hanigan and Charles Curran together represent the best of the possibilities for dialogue among quite different positions in the Roman Catholic tradition on the moral status of same-sex relationships. I applaud their careful and thoughtful analyses of the issues and their irenic yet forceful arguments for the positions they support. Moreover, the move that both of them make to shift a great deal of the debate from the realm of sexual ethics to political ethics is a helpful one, and it may be that strategically it is the best one if the Roman Catholic community is to come to terms with the pluralism within itself as well as the pluralism in American society on this issue. It may also be the case that for concrete persons whose lives (and not just moral and political theories) are at stake in these debates, the issues of law and public policy are now the most pressing.

Having acknowledged the importance of this move (from the sexual to the political), I find myself nonetheless reluctant to let it pass too quickly without some more attention being given to the raging disagreements within the Roman Catholic tradition on the moral questions surrounding gay and lesbian activity and identity. Though these are to some extent in-house debates, they have implications for, and parallels in, the struggles that all of the Christian churches are now experiencing over these same questions. Their resolution, or at least more respectful accommodation in an acknowledged pluralism, will have an overwhelming influence on whether and how we shall solve questions of social policy. I want, therefore, in my response to these presentations, not to ignore the sexual ethical positions outlined or at least pointed to within them. These positions are, as I understand them, the following: on the one hand, James Hanigan agrees with the official Catholic leadership's judgment of the immorality of gay and lesbian sexual activity; and on the other hand, Charles Curran disagrees with this position, though he judges that while same-sex relationships are not immoral, they are less good than heterosexual marital relationships. Let me address the implications of both of these positions.

The Morality of Same-Sex Relations

The maintenance of a strong negative evaluation of homosexual activities and relationships constitutes in itself a social and political force. This is why it will ultimately be insufficient to leave this moral position unchallenged and hope to enact nondiscrimination laws in spite of it. Though it is true (as Charles Curran points out) that some leaders of the Catholic community, as well as many of its members, have been persuaded at least not to oppose legislation that secures the basic civil rights of lesbians and gays, the continuing massive societal resistance to this legislation is lodged, I believe, in the vehemence of the negative judgment that continues to be made regarding homosexual activity and relationships. This judgment, at least when it is put forward by church leaders and moral theologians, is frequently a carefully reasoned one. But its power as a social force is the power of an unreasoned taboo, lodged in and reinforcing a kind of unreflective repulsion that must be addressed if we are to move forward politically on these issues.

Relevant to this, it seems to me misleading to suggest, as James Hanigan does in his contribution to this volume, that the traditional Catholic view of human sexual morality as a social good primarily in service of the species had (or has) "nothing to do with perceptions of sexual behavior as animalistic, as dirty or shameful, nothing to do with judgments that sex was unworthy of God and of creatures made in God's image and likeness, or of sexual pleasure as somehow base and beneath human dignity." His point is that though such negative perceptions are in the tradition, they are subsequent to insights into the purpose of sex, but do not contribute to its formulation. While it is true, as Professor Hanigan maintains, that the tradition has always affirmed that sex is good because it is part of creation, and that its goodness is in service of the human community as a whole, the doctrine of sin has nonetheless qualified this evaluation from the time that Christianity first emerged.

I do not need to repeat here what we all know of past and present Christian writers' deep suspicions of the power of sex to overwhelm the mind and to introduce disorder into the attitudes and actions of the individual person.[1] The disorder that characterizes sexual desire as a consequence of sin can be corrected, many have thought, only by bringing it under the rule of reason that identifies for it the rational purpose of procreation. It was thereby always easy to extol the virtues of marriage, but equally easy to excoriate the vices of sex. Today, though we have become long on explications of the meaning of sex, the glory of its creation, and the wonders of the spousal nature of human embodiment, we are even longer on the paradigmatic burdens it bears from the damage of original sin.[2]

Paul Ricoeur's conclusions regarding the connection from time immemorial between symbols of evil as "defilement" and our perceptions of sexuality are still relevant.[3] What remains of this in the collective psyche, or in the symbol structure of western culture as a whole, is (I would argue) in many respects alive and well in the power of the sexual injunctions put forward in the Roman Catholic tradition. And it finds particular force in judgments of homosexuality.

It is true that despite appearances to the contrary (and as pointed out by both of my colleagues in their presentations), major developments have taken place in Roman Catholic sexual ethics in the twentieth century. This tradition, like every other, has been dramatically influenced by new interpretations of human sexuality, changing patterns of relationships between women and men, and increased technological control of human fertility and reproduction. The two dominant motifs of the tradition—procreation as the fundamental purpose of sexual intercourse, and male/female complementarity as the essential basis and framework for sexual activity—have undergone significant changes. In much of Roman Catholic moral theology and ethics, the procreative norm as the sole or even primary justification of sexual activity is gone. Procreation is still extremely important as a goal of heterosexual intercourse, and as giving meaning to sexual relations, but new understandings of the totality of the person support a radically new concern for sexuality as an expression and a cause of love.

The view of sexuality as fundamentally disordered (except when it is in the service of procreation) is therefore also gone from a great deal of Catholic thought. Though moral theologians still underline the potential that sex has for evil (as in sexual abuse, rape, harassment, exploitation, domination, betrayal, etc.), the almost total suspicion of its destructive power has been seriously qualified. Moreover, rigid views of male/female complementarity have been softened; equality and mutuality, shared possibilities and responsibilities, now appear, for example, in Catholic theologies of marriage and family. Still, of course, the motifs of a procreative norm and gender complementarity appear in official Catholic teaching on the use of contraceptives, the procedures of tubal ligation and vasectomy, and the unchanged negative assessment of homosexual acts. A kind of cosmic struggle is now engaged on these issues between many moral theologians and church leaders. Yet even in official church teaching there have come important changes. Vatican II undid the pride of place of procreation as the purpose of marriage and sex. Despite the overall argument of *Humanae Vitae*, acceptance of the rhythm method opened room for responsible choices regarding reproduction. Pope John Paul II has carried a personalistic interpretation of sex to new heights. Homosexual acts are still declared evil, but homosexuals as such (that is, individuals whose sexual orientation is toward those of the same sex) are not evil—and even homosexual acts may be good subjectively if not objectively.[4]

Despite these important shifts, has either moral theology or the church's official magisterium changed that much regarding homosexuality? The procreative norm is relativized for heterosexual relations, but it returns when homosexual relations are at issue. The view of sexuality as fundamentally disordered is gone for heterosexual sex, but it reappears as strong as ever in judgments about gay and lesbian sex. Rigid stereotypes of male/female complementarity are softened for general social roles, but the importance of gender complementarity becomes the final strike against the acceptance of same-sex relations.

All of this is eminently clear in the official documents on homosexuality in recent years. While a homosexual *orientation* in persons is not condemned (it is even accepted), homosexual *activity* is judged "intrinsically disordered," hence objectively immoral.[5] The reasons for this include: (1) homosexual acts "close the sexual act to the gift of life [offspring]";[6] (2) they "annul the rich symbolism and meaning, not to mention goals, of the Creator's sexual design"[7] because they "do not proceed from a genuine affective and sexual complementarity [male-female]";[8] and (3) though it may not be in some instances subjectively culpable, homosexual activity "thwarts the call to a life of that form of self-giving which the Gospel says is the essence of Christian living."[9]

These kinds of arguments and assessments appear also in the positions of some Catholic moral theologians. Among them, not a few theologians still judge homosexual activity as simply morally evil. James Hanigan, for example, maintains in his previous work and in his present essay: "I continue to think that the procreative dimension of human sexuality is more than accidental to the human person and so to the moral meaning of human sexual behavior, and that the biological and anatomical complementarity of male and female bodies is of more than descriptive interest to questions of human sexual behavior." Hence, sexual activity between individuals of the same sex is wrong. Hanigan's conclusions are offered without hostility and without the inflammatory language sometimes adopted by other moral theologians. Still, they contribute to the overall milieu in which gay and lesbian individuals, insofar as they are sexually active, are judged to be at least objectively immoral.

The force of this position, and its relevance to the political and social climate, is perhaps more obvious in the discourse of moral theologians such as John Finnis. Finnis, following Germain Grisez, writes, for example:

> Sexual acts are not unitive in their significance unless they are marital . . . and . . . [they] are not marital unless they have not only the generosity of acts of friendship but also the procreative significance, not necessarily being intended to generate or capable in the circumstances of generating but at least of being, as human conduct, acts of the reproductive kind—actualizations, so far as the spouses then and there can, of the reproductive function in which they are biologically and thus personally one.[10]

He correspondingly notes with approval what he takes to be a Greek assessment of homosexual acts as having a "special similarity to solitary masturbation, and both types of radically nonmarital act are manifestly unworthy of the human being and immoral."[11] Like copulation of humans with animals, genital coupling between humans with the same sexual organs must be repudiated as not only offensive but also destructive of human character and relationships. Fearful, therefore, of the social influence of any seeming approval or even toleration of these kinds of activities, Finnis opposes any nondiscrimination legislation beyond the decriminalization of totally private actions, such as sodomy, between consenting adults. Even laws designed to remedy discrimination on the basis of homosexual "orientation" are suspect, since "orientation" can mean "the deliberate willingness to promote and engage in homosexual acts," constituting thereby an "active threat to the stability of existing and future marriages."[12] This means, for Finnis, that no laws are justified that would in any way "require the prompt abandonment of all attempts by the political community to discourage homosexual conduct."[13] In Finnis's view, the state can have a compelling interest that justifies limiting and stigmatizing the evils of homosexuality.

But let me turn now to the position of Charles Curran on the morality of same-sex activity and relationships. Like some other Catholic theologians, Curran thinks that homosexual activity may not be morally evil, but only a form of brokenness, or an incapacity to achieve the human ideal. He tends to agree, for example, with Richard McCormick that heterosexual marriage is "normative" as the context for sexual activity.[14] By this McCormick means that everyone *ought to try* to conform their sexual activity to that norm (though pastoral adaptations are possible). They ought to try to do this because this context is most conducive to the full humanization of human sexuality. Why? Because it offers a procreative potential, and it is grounded in male/female complementarity.

Those who take this "middle" position often attach to it other assertions not unlike the ones given in support of a more negative evaluation of same-sex relations—assertions, for example, that all sex not open to procreation is inherently selfish; or that same-sex relations are essentially narcissistic (not open to the "other"); or that there is an element of the "eternal feminine" that is needed by and that needs a masculine counterpart. These are not the arguments put forward by either Curran or McCormick, but their fortunate refusal to appeal to such reasons makes it all the more clear that procreative potential and gender complementarity are assumed as the basis of their position.

In the Roman Catholic tradition as in any other religious tradition, however, the question must be asked: How do we know, how can we know, whether these and other assertions are true, or whether they simply perpetuate ungrounded myths and serve only to prevent our questioning of irrational taboos? This question, when it is taken seriously, reveals both a contradiction in the traditional views of the Catholic Church regarding homosexuality and the potential strengths of the tradition for self-criticism and change. For deep in this tradition is the conviction that morality ought to "make sense" to most people. Morality is not a matter of legal precedent, or sheer consistency in official teaching, or historical uniformity of practice, or a "divine command" theory of ethics. That morality should "make sense" is what is at the heart of the Roman Catholic commitment to a natural law perspective. It assumes, on the one hand, something in reality to be understood, something about creation that is revelatory of God's will, and, on the other hand, the capability of human reason (aided and healed by revelation and grace) to understand it.

It is, however, generally recognized today by Catholic theologians that natural law is not a "package deal," such that we get it whole, without having to acknowledge the partiality of every perspective and the provisionality of specific moral norms. Rather, it is widely agreed that a natural law approach, in continuity with the Catholic tradition of moral thinking, requires that we take account of the possibility of new insights, new information, new perspectives. Especially in the area of human sexuality we have learned (or many have) how far the social construction of our understandings goes, how conventional are many of our presuppositions regarding gender, parenthood, heterosexuality, and family structure. But for those who still subscribe to a natural law theory, recognition of the large role that social construction plays in the development of moral knowledge does not preclude a remaining need to explore the concrete reality given in our experience. Natural law as a theory today tells us where it is important still to look.

A tradition committed to a natural law approach (that is, to some form of ethical realism, however moderated) should more than any other tradition take account of empirical findings, plausible psychological theories, and human experience across cultures. There are ambiguities in what we learn about sexuality from all of our traditional sources of access to concrete reality—whether Scripture, tradition, the sciences, philosophy, or contemporary experience. All of the sources need interpreting, and all need mutual correcting. But when the last word is not yet (and may never be) in regarding human sexuality, experience as a source becomes particularly important, and particularly important to a natural law tradition.[15]

In our present context, contemporary experience as a source for ethical insight is primarily to be found in the testimony of women and men whose sexual experience is with others of the same sex. Like other sources, experience requires interpretation and discernment regarding its significance for the faith community; like other sources it is a necessary but not sufficient illuminator of reality and its ethical demands. By itself, experience does not provide an incontestable, foundational deposit of insight in a fund of moral wisdom. It does not explain everything else without needing to be explained itself; it cannot be used to establish an "anything goes" conclusion based on any and all experience. Interpretations of sexual experience can yield illusion and falsehood on a par with some interpretations of the Bible and of the Christian tradition. Yet there are some questions for which it is an essential and even determinative source. I would argue that same-sex relations today present one of those questions.

The interpretation offered by individuals who experience same-sex relations will be significant insofar as it represents the word of persons whose whole lives evince integrity, and whose actions cohere with the general ethical norms of justice in human relationships. Since we do have the testimony of such persons, it should be taken into serious account, and the Catholic tradition (with its epistemological commitments) should be the first to consider it. Indeed, we have not only the first-person testimony of individuals faithful in their search for and living out of same-sex love; we also have second- and third-person experience of the witness that the lives of individuals called to same-sex love offer to the Christian community and to wider human societies. The fact that the tradition has not in large part taken these experiences seriously (just as it has not taken into account the experience of persons regarding the use of contraceptives in heterosexual marriages) represents a contradiction internal to the tradition itself. But the demands of methodological consistency lead precisely to this until now largely untapped source; in the consideration of it lies an inestimable strength for the tradition's development.

Political Theory and the Protection of Gay Men and Lesbians

Let me return now to the issues of political ethics that have been so helpfully formulated by both James Hanigan and Charles Curran. Though their interpretations of the morality of homosexuality differ sharply, their proposals for public policy are much closer together. Both subscribe to a political theology that requires respect for individual freedom, though not without some limits. Both are reluctant to legislate sexual morality, but favor governmental protection for homosexuals as well as heterosexuals. Both support laws and policies that secure nondiscrimination against gay men and lesbians regarding basic human and civil rights. They differ on the justification of domestic partnership laws. Hanigan is opposed to them, provisionally, because of what he considers a state interest in discouraging lifestyles that are hostile to marriage and the traditional family. Curran favors domestic partnership laws and argues that they can be acceptable to Roman Catholics if only as a lesser of two evils.

In general, Charles Curran's position is that a Vatican II theory of government will allow Roman Catholics to support (or at least not oppose) nondiscrimination legislation without the need to compromise or change a negative moral evaluation of homosexual activity. Both he and James Hanigan believe that this kind of legislation can be a demand of justice and should be responded to as such. Hence, Curran's concern is to clarify the political ethic that will facilitate this response.

This seems to me to be an important strategy, though the point I have been making is that perceptions of sexual morality are less separable from questions of law on this issue in practice than they may be in theory. I have already claimed that the massive opposition that continues to rise against even nondiscrimination legislation is motivated by moral convictions and attitudes, the vehemence of which suggests that they are not always subjected to rational tests or to considerations such as respect for true moral pluralism among persons of goodwill.

The disagreement between Professors Hanigan and Curran regarding domestic partnership legislation turns on the empirical question of whether or not legally sanctioned domestic partnerships constitute a threat to the common good because they are a threat to marriage and family. Curran's rejection of this argument is, I think, helpful. That is, his counter to the prediction of dire consequences for marriage and family if domestic partnership laws are enacted is illuminating and, at least as far as it goes, persuasive. Moreover, Curran's provision of a way out for Catholics who on some grounds want to approve domestic partnership legislation even though they continue to disapprove of same-sex relations is both creative and useful. Nonetheless, it seems to me that precisely in the light of post-Vatican II political ethics, something stronger may be said in favor of domestic partnership laws than that they offer the lesser of two evils.

Here I want to question whether Charles Curran's distinction between a Thomistic and a Vatican II theory of the state is not drawn too sharply. Concepts of public order, public peace, and justice in Roman Catholic political ethics since Vatican II do not add up to a theory of government that provides only for the restraint of disorder and the protection of negative rights. Rather, while contemporary theories do not incorporate notions of state responsibility for the common good in the sense of providing all that is needed for human flourishing, they do incorporate notions of positive rights as well as negative. Here the adequate model may be found not only in the *Declaration on Religious Liberty* but also in other documents that address, in particular, economic rights (such as the National Conference of Catholic Bishops' *Economic Justice for All*). Given this opening, it may be argued that domestic partnership laws respond to demands of justice in a sense alignable with nondiscrimination laws.

In other words, legislation for domestic partnerships does not simply respond to human wants but to basic human needs—needs for psychic security, economic security, and sometimes physical safety. Even when the value of such laws is primarily symbolic (as it is in some proposed city ordinances), this is not just a boon to gay pride; it is a necessary step in the direction of transforming the hatred, rejection, and stigmatization of gays and lesbians that is presently still being reinforced by teachings of "unnatural" sex, disordered desire, and threatening love. Gay bashing, as both church leaders and moral theologians agree, is not a trivial matter; nor does it exist alone without attachment to multiple forms of avoidance, as well as multiple forms of violence. Lodged in taboos and in myths, the physical and verbal bashing of homosexuals is a greater danger to society (as both a violation of individuals' deep-seated human rights and a threat to human decency and the common good) than any so-called approval or encouragement of homosexual lifestyles. A community's process, therefore, toward a willingness to legislate regarding domestic partnerships begins with, is premised on, and becomes the gradual extension of a stance against violence toward gays. Its goal is the rendering of justice, a protection that is hardly separable from the provision of basic needs.

These considerations, I would argue, belong with the extremely useful ones offered by James Hanigan and Charles Curran. They expand and may help to join the issues already identified, and they are equally rooted in the Roman Catholic tradition. It is through a dialogue such as the one begun here by my two colleagues that our tradition can forge faithful continuity in a concern for the dignity and integrity, the holiness and vocation, of gay and lesbian persons along with all others.

Notes

1. Augustine set strong lines for the development of this perspective. See, e.g., his *On the Goodness of Marriage, On Holy Virginity, Marriage and Concupiscence, Literal Commentary on Genesis.*

2. See, e.g., John Paul II, *Original Unity of Man and Woman: Catechesis on the Book of Genesis* (Boston: Daughters of St. Paul, 1981); Congregation for the Doctrine of the Faith, "The Pastoral Care of Homosexual Persons," *Origins* 16 (1986): 377–82.

3. See Paul Ricoeur, *The Symbolism of Evil*, trans. E. Buchanan (New York: Harper & Row, 1967), pp. 25–46.

4. See, e.g., Congregation for the Doctrine of the Faith, "Declaration on Certain Questions Concerning Sexual Ethics (1975)," in *Readings in Moral Theology No. 8: Dialogue About Catholic Sexual Teaching*, eds. C. Curran & R. McCormick (New York: Paulist Press, 1993), pp. 375–91; idem, "The Pastoral Care of Homosexual Persons."

5. See Congregation for the Doctrine of the Faith, "Declaration on Certain Questions," pp. 380–81, no. 8; idem, "The Pastoral Care of Homosexual Persons," p. 379, no. 3; "Observations Regarding Legislative Proposals Concerned with Discrimination Toward Homosexual Persons," revised text, *Origins* 22 (1992): 173–77; *Catechism of the Catholic Church* (Liberia Editrice Vaticana, 1994), no. 2357.

6. *Catechism*, no. 2357.

7. Congregation for the Doctrine of the Faith, "The Pastoral Care of Homosexual Persons," p. 380, no. 7.

8. *Catechism*, no. 2357.

9. Congregation for the Doctrine of the Faith, "The Pastoral Care of Homosexual Persons," p. 380, no. 7.

10. John M. Finnis, "Law, Morality, and 'Sexual Orientation,'" *Notre Dame Journal of Law, Ethics, and Public Policy* 9 (1995): 30.

11. Ibid., p. 25.

12. Ibid., p. 32.

13. Ibid., pp. 16, 39.

14. See Richard A. McCormick, *The Critical Calling* (Washington, DC: Georgetown University Press, 1989), pp. 305–306.

15. It should be noted here that at least in one respect the Catholic tradition, along with others, has indeed taken account of new information available through various human sciences and reports of human experience. That is, the contemporary understanding of homosexual orientation, along with the move to distinguish this from homosexual activity, represents a fundamentally new insight. (Even theologians such as John Finnis recognize this, though he argues that the meaning of "orientation" is equivocal, and hence refuses to go as far as even some official church documents in making the concept a basis for respect for homosexual persons and nondiscriminatory policies in their regard.) This new insight, however, also needs further clarification in the light of varied experiences—in much the same way that I go on to argue the need for experience generally as a significant source for our understanding of same-sex relations. That is, a homosexual orientation has been assumed to undergird acceptance of gay and lesbian individuals and to justify nondiscrimination policies in their regard precisely insofar as it is understood to be unchangeable, not subject to choice, etc. This kind of "essentialism" (or even "strategic essentialism") does accord with many persons' experience, but not all (the givenness of a homosexual disposition not subject to choice may be, for example, more readily generalizable for gay males than for lesbians, whose experience seems to be less either/or heterosexual/homosexual and more on a possible continuum). The whole issue of just how "given" homosexual orientation is in the experience of gay men and women is too complex to pursue here, however, since it involves a whole set of questions—not only anthropological but ethical and political as well. Insofar as this remains an issue, of course, it reinforces the need to take account of human experience in expanding our knowledge of the moral possibilities for same-sex relationships.

MAINLINE PROTESTANT CHURCHES

Introduction to Essays Representing
Mainline Protestant Churches

KEITH GREEN

Gays and lesbians challenge not only contemporary Christian sexual ethics but also political ethics and ecclesial politics. Ecumenical Protestants interminably debate the moral status of sexual relations of gay men and lesbians, and draw from their positions a variety of implications for political ethics and ecclesial politics. Evangelical Protestants exhibit more consensus in their view that same-gender sexual relations are morally wrong, but like their kin in the ecumenical churches, they debate the implications of this belief for policy and legal issues regarding gays and lesbians. These issues include legal protection from discrimination based upon sexual orientation, the decriminalization of sodomy, the legal status of lesbian and gay relationships, and the adoption of children by gays and lesbians. The essays in this section of the volume represent different ways that ecumenical Protestants relate sexual ethics and political ethics, with particular attention to the question of the ecclesiastical celebration of same-gender unions.

It is important to see that conflicting positions on political issues concerning lesbians and gay men among Protestants reflect much more than their positions on questions of sexual ethics. As Kathryn Tanner points out in her response to the essays by Max Stackhouse and Eugene Rogers, positions on these questions reflect broader views about the orders of creation and the place of humans within it, the nature of covenant, the character of sanctification, the relation between nature and grace, and conceptions of the inspiration and authority of Scripture. Diverse understandings of these theological issues are reflected in deep ambivalence about the nature and appropriate function of political order or, more particularly, the appropriate function of the state as the institutional embodiment of "law" in relation to the function of the church as the institutional embodiment of "gospel." The sixteenth-century Protestant reformers and their successors bring to the surface tensions between the demands of citizenship in these two "cities" or "kingdoms." Since not everyone who is a citizen of the earthly city is a citizen of the heavenly city, what demands does citizenship in the latter make of the exercise of citizenship in the former?

Among the early reformers, it is safe to say that there is only consensus in the notion that the state's function is soteriologically inferior and incomplete. The state is the institutional embodiment of "law" in human communities and its function is to manage some of the symptoms of fallenness. The church is the institutional embodiment of "gospel"; its presence in the world reflects God's forgiveness for, and anticipates God's final healing of, fallenness. They represent different movements in God's own reconciliation with fallen humans. The state performs its role through the threat, and sometimes the application, of violent coercion with the aim of preventing harm to the order of creation and humans in their individual and common lives, and by enjoining covenanted relations. But this conception can be turned into meaningful normative prescriptions for political life only if there is consensus about the symptoms of fallenness and an appreciation of the inevitable limits of politics as a remedy for fallenness.

I believe we can identify three forms that this "Protestant" conception of political authority has taken, and see that each has different implications for the meaning that positions about the moral status of same-gender sexual relations should have for matters of law and policy in the earthly city.

1. When sixteenth-century Protestant reformers urged the political authorities under which they lived to take up reform of the church even without the support of its longstanding authorities, they implied that the state's rightful exercise of power involves (among other things) eliminating the dangers of false religion. Some of their contemporary successors likewise demand that the state protect everyone, whether they think they need it or not, from the dangers of "false" sexuality and family, of which lesbian and gay relations are undoubtedly the most outstanding (or "flagrant") example. The practical norm implicit in this view is that the moral wrongfulness of lesbian and gay sexual relations (if indeed they are morally wrong) must translate into legal prohibition (for example, sodomy laws), and the state must not "recognize" these relations, or force others to tolerate them, by proscribing sexual orientation-based discrimination. The very existence of lesbian and gay relations is perceived as a positive affront, if not an active threat, to the orders of creation presumably revealed in the divine commands embodied in the "old" law. The demand of revealed law on this matter is typically regarded as sufficiently perspicuous to be beyond serious debate. We can see behind this sort of view notions that God's intentions for human sexuality are clearly enough revealed in God's creation of humans as male and female (with the command to be fruitful and multiply); that these intentions are further reflected by unambiguous prohibitions of same-gender sexual relations and the reendorsement of these prohibitions by New Testament authors; and that the 'power of the sword' is appropriately exercised to enjoin conformity to these orders of creation, any departure from which constitutes harm to human dignity and society.

2. By contrast, John Locke is more impressed by the notion that the role of the state is to prevent citizens of the earthly city from injuring each other as they go along their individual earthly journeys to whatever inscrutable final destiny awaits them. We can see that Locke's view reflects the reformers' Augustinian "two king-

doms" model of the state-law/church-gospel relation in a different way. According to the "liberal" conceptions of the role of the state that emerge from this idea, the state's function within its society is the same as it is with respect to relations between states. It is to wage a just war against the injustices that actively diminish the earthly peace. The state must limit itself to preventing uninvited and destructive intervention in the life journey of one individual by another, or to "avenging" the "right" of any individual to pursue his or her journey unmolested. In contrast to the sorts of positions identified in (1), such latitudinarian views do not believe that it is the state's proper function to enjoin a full conformity of one's life to God's revealed orders of creation—even if we happen to agree about what this is—because such conformity is meaningful only if it is voluntary. And it is voluntary only in the absence of any form of coercion that would give an individual any other reason to conform to this order beyond his or her apprehension of it as true. The attraction that this sort of view has held in societies deeply shaped by Protestant traditions quite certainly reflects the typically Protestant notion that a moral argument about any issue must be accepted or rejected by reasoning individuals on the strength of the argument alone, and not because it is the official teaching of an authoritative magisterium.

This view has different implications for reconciling the norms of sexual ethics with the proper function of the state. Since, to modify a phrase that Thomas Jefferson used with respect to irreligious neighbors, the sexual doings of my lesbian and gay neighbors do not exactly break my leg, the state has no more business criminalizing same-gender sexual relations than it does criminalizing religious practices. And this remains true, even if these relations morally fail to realize God's intentions in creation for differently but complementarily gendered persons in ways that heterosexual marriage doesn't. The practical norms are at least that sodomy should not be criminalized even if it is not morally licit, since perhaps the state must avenge even a right to do wrong if the wrong does not interfere nonconsensually in the life journey of another. Discriminating against lesbians and gays in hiring, housing, and so on arguably constitutes the sort of harm from which the state must protect any citizen. It interferes in the work and public living of persons—basic constituents of their life journeys—in ways that have no relation to a fair estimation of merit. It also constitutes an instance of persons applying, through their arbitrarily discriminatory actions, reasons to accept a particular conception of God's orders of creation other than the degree of plausibility it has for another rationally autonomous person. Discrimination, exposure to the constant threat of arbitrary violence, and failure to have one's covenanted intimate relations recognized all represent attempts to usurp full participation in public and political life and use it as a reward for accepting the discriminator's conception of the human good. Vulnerability to such exclusions violates the dignity of rationally autonomous persons by evading the necessity of appealing to their eminently rational understanding to garner their consent and conformity to one particular ideal of human good in creation.

3. Other progeny of the sixteenth-century reformers believe that we must go as far as humanly possible by political means to bring about social conditions in human history that fulfill God's creative intentions for humans. Inequitable distri-

butions of material goods and social power seem the inevitable outcome of fallen but autonomous individuals living in uncoerced pursuit of their various perceptions of human good. And the counsel that we must live patiently with these inequities seems an evasion of calling and mission to realize God's creative intentions in history. Representatives of positions (1) and (2) described above have tended to agree that none matters less in the sight of God or stinks any higher in heaven's nostrils than any other. Representatives of (3) go beyond partisans of the first or second in the idea that systematically disenfranchising any citizens of the earthly city politically, economically, or socially is treating them as if these two important truths were not true. They share with representatives of (1) a rejection of the minimal conception of the state as the avenger of injured right that is central to (2). But conceptions of the orders of creation typical of (1) are rejected because they conflict with considered moral beliefs about human equality, justice, and perhaps the integrity of autonomy in matters of religious belief and conceptions of human flourishing. Partisans of (1) appeal to the presumed clarity of God's revealed intentions in Scripture and counsel us to live patiently with the inequities that paradoxically emerge when God's presumed creative intentions are put into political practice. The injustices, they say, can only be apparent, seeing, as we do in this life, through a glass darkly. Partisans of (3), by contrast, notice that such conceptions of God's orders in creation suspiciously appear to legitimate those whom these inequities happen to privilege, and conclude that finding them in the text of Scripture is not a matter of the presence of a perspicuous and static meaning but of the ideologically loaded conceptions of alienated communities of readers. No conception of God's intentions can, therefore, precede liberatory practice; and God's intentions become known only as they are practically realized in human history as we actively live out love of neighbor.

On this view, disempowering lesbians and gays in political and social life reflects a failure to be "converted to the neighbor," to use an expression of Gustavo Gutierrez. If we genuinely love our lesbian sisters and gay brothers as we are commanded, then we will always treat them as if what they are—children of God, precious in God's sight, made in God's image—matters more than who they happen to be as a matter of identity. And it is significant that we are fundamentally the same thing, having the same value in God's sight. According to this view, the state must actively redress the inequalities that gays and lesbians, among others, suffer as the undisputed objects of much social discrimination and often relentless violence. And if a failure to recognize the formal covenanting of lesbian and gay relations constitutes the arbitrary and systematic disempowerment of a group, the state must also recognize such relationships.

No essay in this collection exemplifies the first position. Rogers notices that versions of it have legitimated such practices as the ecclesial exclusion of the gentiles, slavery, the subordination of women, the politics of apartheid, and the political disenfranchisement of Jews. Versions of it are still typically marshaled in opposition to the ordination of women, the occupation by women of other positions of familial and political leadership, recognizing covenanted lesbian and gay relationships, and sometimes the decriminalization of sodomy. As such, forms of the first position treat some groups as if some characteristic they possess is more the mark of original sin or of primordial idolatry than features that humans possess universally. If sexual desire for a person of the same-gender is already "disordered" morally, then it is a mark of fallenness (like womanness, or being the offspring of Ham) that persons in general do not bear. This characteristic is then assumed to expose its possessor to a particular risk of sin, or predestine him or her to a special vocation—that of motherhood along with pain in childbirth for women, slavery or political exclusion for the African, or celibacy for the gay or lesbian.

Stackhouse defends a version of the second position identified above. Sexual relations are to be faithful to the values of fidelity, fecundity, and family, and any social arrangement in which the realization of any one of these values is systematically excluded is an "adjustment, exception, compromise, or relative approximation" only. These norms transcend the history of any particular human community and its traditions and practices. They function, therefore, as a more universal set of norms in reference to which the social and political arrangements of any particular community may be evaluated. Any human community must engender covenanted forms of human cooperation that "give shape to life in ways that approximate, under conditions of sin, the patterns and purposes of holy living that God intends." Stackhouse, therefore, regards even covenanted same-gender sexual relations as an irreconcilable departure from this normative sense of human flourishing. He suggests that even though such relations should not be criminalized, they must not be entered into by those who are ordained to ministry. Nor, presumably, should they be recognized legally or celebrated ecclesially. As such, he appears to embrace the more minimal and even skeptical conception of the state typical of (2); but he does not believe that ecclesial exclusion from ordination or the celebration of relations constitutes palpable injustice. And since these are matters of ecclesial polity and not of positive law in the larger political community, they fall beyond the competence of the state in the grand scheme of God's dealings with inevitably fallen humans.

Rogers's essay, which focuses on the ecclesial recognition and celebration of covenanted gay and lesbian relations, exemplifies some elements of the second and third positions above. It marshals the conceptual resources of a broad range of theological and liturgical traditions to argue that a failure to honor the covenanted relationships of lesbians and gays is incompatible with the character of the free redemptive movement of God's spirit in grafting all humans—even beyond nature—into the trunk of salvation. And this truth is a cornerstone of the Protestant understanding of God's reconciliation with fallen human beings that no argument about matters of sexual or political morality or ecclesial practice can contravene. Rogers emphasizes that God's relation with humans is imaged metaphorically by marriage, not because it is potentially procreative but because it is ideally a faithful, permanent friendship. Covenanted relations between gay men and lesbians are concrete social embodiments of this theologically meaningful friendship no less that heterosexual marriage. But Rogers asserts that God "goes beyond nature" in grafting, for example, the gentiles into the trunk of God's people (appealing to Romans 11:24). The notion that God's saving grace is offered equally to every human being—the sheer grace of God's creation and redemption to necessarily bodily human beings—demands as a matter of consistency not only acknowledging the potential moral integrity of lesbian and gay relations but also celebrating the fact of their covenanting. Gay and lesbian relations can be one more bodily concrete and theologically meaningful and revealing way in which God catches human beings up into the community of love that God is by nature.

In her assessment of these two essays, Kathryn Tanner points out that the arguments of both Stackhouse and Rogers exemplify the strongly theological character of Protestant ethical reflection. Freed from institutional constraints of an authoritative and tradition-defining magisterium, both seek to ground their arguments upon "concepts and principles that are biblically based." Both proceed as if an argument is to be accepted on the grounds of its theological-intellectual merits alone. There is positive scope for self-criticism and change on this understanding of moral insight, even though the theological foundations to which a valid theological argument must appeal are often hard to reconcile with the demands of other socially current intellectual commitments. The validity of such arguments, according to Tanner, is a matter of coherence with and extension of other more fundamental and less ambiguous theological truths. Acknowledging that she more nearly shares Rogers's understanding of "wider theological issues about how to understand nature and creation in relation to grace and redemption," she argues that Rogers's view about lesbian and gay relations "fits" more coherently with these understandings. Tanner would appear to reject the starting point for moral reflection that marks (3) above—the notion that socially current considered moral beliefs can legitimately function as a *starting point* for a theological argument. Her view, like that of Rogers, is that constitutive theological truths about the value of all humans as God's creation and the free offering of grace to all humans demand, as a matter of consistency, a frank acknowledgment that lesbians and gays are unjustly oppressed by ecclesial and political exclusions. And the fact of this oppression is particularly poignant considering that the church is that community of God's people for whom these truths are morally fundamental. Fidelity to the prophetic witness of the church to these truths at least demands, therefore, a renewed and transformed practice of covenanting relations that includes those of lesbians and gays.

All three essays initiate and exemplify engagement in a conversation that must go on about the meaning of lesbians, gays, and their relations as significant social realities. Every major ecumenical Protestant church body has, at some point in the last two decades, supported the decriminalization of sodomy and the legal protection of lesbians and gay men from violence and discrimination in employment and housing. All these churches, with the notable exception of the Southern Baptist Convention, have consistently seen this as the legitimate demand of justice. As early as 1963, a body of clergy largely from these churches and the Anglican Church, actively opposed the casual brutality of the police in San Francisco to which gay men and lesbians were constantly exposed. Yet none of them sanctions covenanted lesbian and gay relationships or their celebration; and only the United Church of Christ has officially supported in any way the ordination of gays or lesbians actually involved in a sexually expressed relationship. Stackhouse defends this overall position, where Rogers finds in it profoundly flawed inconsistencies that demand the recognition of covenanted gay and lesbian relations.

The Prophetic Stand of the Ecumenical Churches on Homosexuality

MAX L. STACKHOUSE

Over the last quarter-century, a debate has raged in the ecumenical Protestant churches belonging to the National and World Councils of Churches. It is about sexuality, particularly homosexuality. The discussion has been intense. In fact, more church documents, statements, background papers, study books, and proposals have been written on human sexuality in this period than in any comparable period of church history. More than one hundred and fifty of the most important documents from Catholic, evangelical, and ecumenical Protestant sources have been collected in a recent set of volumes, and it is likely that the results can already be discerned, although some advocates argue that debates are just getting started.[1]

What seems to be clear is that significant modifications have taken place among Protestants and that these modifications have taken place within a reaffirmation of the classic tradition, much in the way that the ancient prophets recalled the ancient covenants of God and adapted them to changing situations. It is certainly so that these stances both reflect and will have a substantive influence on the raging cultural and political debates over "family values" generally and homosexuality particularly in the years to come. Disagreements, of course, continue, but the results are rather clear:

1. The churches affirm that genital activity should be confined to a heterosexual marriage, and all intimate relationships should approximate the ideals of that rite.
2. Most churches support the human and civil rights of homosexual persons, but resist giving religious approval to homosexual behavior or same-sex marriage.
3. Most churches (some ambiguously) deny ordination to advocates of or those involved in homosexual practice, which is not viewed as equal to heterosexual marriage.

4. Most churches have adopted feminist theories of justice in regard to equality of dignity, opportunity, status, and pay, but resist attempts to turn all questions into gender issues.
5. Pastoral care for adults who are single, gay, unable to procreate, or divorced is seen as morally and spiritually required, even if their situations are not approved.

In brief, the overall results of a quarter-century of debate reflect a rejection of a radical effort to overturn the classical position, and they are remarkably consistent. The official statements are also consistent with the classical traditions, even if each is stamped by its tradition's distinctive concepts. The inclusion of "justice feminism," as an aspect of normative theology that is likely to increase, has significantly modified the classical uses of traditional symbolism, but not the basic teachings about the normative character of the heterosexual family.

The debates, however, have been so multifaceted, so laden with cross-cutting arguments and sensibilities, ideologies, and conceptions, that the case for these decisions taken as a whole has nowhere been made. Because I largely agree with them, it is the purpose of this essay to set forth an understanding of the logic by which they make sense. This is all the more necessary in view of recent efforts to grant co-equal moral status and economic benefits to same-sex companionate relationships.[2]

The Deeper Background of the Controversy

It is an enduring, reasonable, and coherent conviction of those religions born out of biblical traditions that the authors of the Adam and Eve stories of Genesis were inspired to see the human situation with a degree of revealing accuracy. God created humanity and gave to this earthy creature a dignity that was nearly godlike, enabling a communion with God as well as a capacity to exercise freedom and to recognize the laws and purposes of God, thus also to choose against them. This most precious of creatures was also distinguished into male and female, a differentiation that both makes possible an interaction between them that is similar to a relationship with the Creator and makes them potential partners in the processes of creation.

It is also against the distortions of the patterns implied in this story that the prophets protest. They take the breaking of the basic patterns of the moral stage of life as an indicator that the dramatic judgments and renewal of salvation history are necessary, as we see in Ezekiel and Hosea. And it is to this story that Jesus turned (Mark 10:2–12; Matt. 19:3–6) when the issue of responsible relationship was debated in his day. Something of the right order of life, the good ends of existence, and the engaged participation in the sustaining contexts of life, and their relation, are implicit in it. It is thick with meaning.

As to the basic normative structure stated in these texts for human sexuality, three elements are primary. First, the fundamental relationship that humans are to have with God and with each other is to be one of fidelity in communion (Gen. 1:27–28). One is not to live only by or for oneself. Persons, in the biblical tradition, are to be respected and honored. Each is made "in the image of God" (Gen. 1:26). Here is the deepest root of what became, later, spoken of as the "soul," the seat of human "dignity," the source of "conscience," and thus the center of all rights and duties and the core of that freedom and knowledge that allows personal responsibility.

And yet, individualism is not the chief implication of this insight. Persons are not only rooted in a relationship to God but also intended for human relationship. "It is not good that one should be alone" (Gen. 2:18). The question is whether there is a normative character to the relationship. We are given the freedom and power to name the realities Adam and Eve discovered under God's care and to till the garden and to keep it, but we are not to decide matters opportunistically, to use the creation only to satisfy felt needs, or to deny the integrity of the primal relationship that brought all that is into being (Gen. 2:15–17). It is right to be faithful; it is wrong to violate limits: "Of this tree you shall not eat." Personal and relational existence, morally and spiritually considered, is rooted in a God-given right order of things that, in some measure, everyone knows.

Moreover, we are to use the resources of creation—the world, the mind, and the body—to see that life flourishes. The command "be fruitful and multiply" is one of the earliest and most repeated of the commands. That which defies or stultifies life is contrary to that purpose. The capacity to reproduce is a gift; generativity is a mark of how God invites creatures to participate in the blessing of ongoing creativity. This means, among other things, that humans are to see their sex as a part of the ongoing flow of life, as a blessed link in the generations, becoming fathers and mothers to the generations of tomorrow in a way that can be honored, and then honoring the fathers and the mothers who went before.

To be sure, the mere proliferation of progeny is not the sufficient mark of human responsibility to the future. The serving of God and of fellow humanity may call some to stand beyond the ordinary functions of life, as saints and sages in many traditions testify. Further, the formation of affectional bonds that knit together lives in mutual affirmation may itself be generative of social relationships that are to be even more honored than mere parenting, as we see in the life of Jesus. This motif is present throughout the Bible, not only in stories such as those of Abraham and Sarah, or of Jacob and Leah, but also of David and Jonathan and of Ruth and Naomi, and among the first disciples of Jesus (Mark 10:28–30). It may even be that greater moral integrity will be recognized by God in some same-sex affections than is found in many opposite-sex relationships. Thus, we dare not prematurely attempt to separate the "wheat from the tares" in this life. Nevertheless, these affections are not something that can and should displace the common expectation that we should seek to approximate the primary structures and purposes of human sexuality given in creation.

Not only are fidelity within a framework of created order, and fruitful generativity within a framework of honorable affectional relationships, part of the moral fabric established in the deepest structures of human life, but humans are called by the biblical tradition to form and sustain social institutions where both fidelity and fruitful generativity become part of the common life. When a man and a woman in their differentiation and their complementarity see each other as truly other, yet the same as the self ("flesh of my flesh" [Gen. 2:20–23]), they are no longer bound only to previous kin relationships. They are invited to form new intimate bonds without guilt: "Therefore a man leaves his father and his mother and cleaves to his wife, and they become one flesh. And the man and his wife were both naked and were not ashamed" (Gen. 2:24–25).[3]

Thus, to fidelity and fecundity is added family, a social and institutional matter that is always found amid various other structures of society that give it a specific stamp. Real families, of course, almost never are formed within an idyllic setting of plentiful goodness, although falling in love echoes that primal sensibility. Real families are almost always found in situations of temptation and distortion. Love inevitably occurs in the context of social history where betrayal, scarcity, and pain are well known. At times the family shape has been patriarchal, sometimes matri-archal, always at least a little tribal or clannish, historically often feudal or mano-rial, recently bourgeois or suburban, and increasingly "dual-career." Each pattern suggests that the actual shape of family life and thus the operating definitions of fi-delity and of fecundity are worked out in the context of a civil society at large. Therefore, even if the demand to embody "one flesh" remains, precisely how it is to be related to a fidelity to the right order of things, or to generative fecundity, be-comes also partly an issue of the whole fabric of society. The conflicts over these are already known in the hostilities of Cain and Abel, and in the establishment of the arts and crafts by which the larger structures of civilization are created and sustained (Genesis 4).

Yet, while the existential integration of these three aspects of morality is ever fraught with conflict, the primal biblical witness tells us that from the beginning life entails both the dignity of each person and, in regard to the secondary issue of sexuality, a calling to live in a normed relationship under God—a heterosexual and monogamous relationship marked by fidelity, fecundity, and family as a criti-cal structure in the fabric of civilization. This has been seen as valid within and beyond the tradition wherever it has been encountered and all who approxi-mate these patterns, from whatever culture or religion, are recognized as married. All other options are seen as adjustments, exceptions, compromises, or relative approximations.

Although parts of the tradition would accent aspects of this heritage with dif-ferent emphases, this is the triadic standard by which sexuality is classically per-ceived. Sometimes in history one or another of these three aspects of a full moral vision has been under attack and has to be defended by prophetic outcries, but all are necessary to the whole. It would be an error, one which parts of the tradition have made from time to time, to take one or another of these and to make it the whole in the assessment of human sexuality. Thus, a view that accents only the right order of things can become legalistic; one that accents only fecundity can ig-nore affection; and one that accents only "traditional family values" can fail to see the changing place of family life in the fabric of social history. The parts belong to a basic pattern that repeatedly has to be reaffirmed by being reformed in a chang-ing context.[4]

It must be emphasized that this pattern stands within a larger vision, one that suggests that marriage is not in itself an ultimate matter. God, in this tradition, has no consort and is neither sexed nor gendered, even if human images of or language about God is. Further, Jesus instructed us that "there is no giving or taking in marriage in heaven," and the ultimate vision of the New Jerusalem has no mention of marriage.[5] When we speak of sexuality and the moral forms it is to take, therefore, we are speaking within the confines of history, not of the most ultimate aspects of redemption. That is a matter that must be left to God.

Still, historical matters are not to be decided by historical experience alone. It would also be an error, in this view, to begin with an understanding of this or that person's sexual inclinations or desires, and then to construct a moral vision or a spirituality that would support whatever is the case. That would subordinate a normative ethical vision to individual feelings and deny that historical experience itself is experienced under norms that history neither contains nor exhausts. For one thing, the image of God that gives each person moral integrity is no more sexed or gendered than is God, and it is on this basis that persons can claim rights or know duties that this or that particular social history denies. For another, the prophetic tradition appears in the biblical heritage when Nathan called even the priest-king David to account for violating these norms to meet his own desires (2 Sam. 11, 12). So also, when the priests of Baal tried to install a fertility cult in the land, Elijah was raised up to stop it (1 Kings 18, 19).

Christians inherited this prophetic tradition (Mark 10:11–12; Matt. 19:9–12) and later used it also to restrain excesses on the other side of the sexual spectrum when some argued that reproduction only trapped more souls in the evils of the world. Against various Gnostic, Montanist, and Cathar movements, which held that male and female were interchangeable or that spirituality opposed materiality so that the earthly fertility of procreation was immoral, Christian theology called marriage a "holy estate."

Christians generally believe that this prophetic tradition was most fully revealed in a messiah whom it anticipated. In this presence of God in human flesh, the love of God is made concrete. Jesus Christ reveals in life, more than any other historical event, the integrating order, purpose, and context of life, and thus this love is to be appropriately manifest in each area of life.[6] This is what gives the basic patterns of life, more or less obvious to all, their inner conviction and personal coherence for Christians. Love, like the possibilities given in creation, has in it both freedom and order that take on both existential intensity and transcendental significance. Without freedom it is only instinct; without order, it is mere emotion. Authentic love integrates these and links them to both faith and hope. Without fidelity, it loses logic; without hope, it loses purpose.

To be sure, distinctive expressions of freedom and structure are proper to different relationships in life. Honoring the right order of things as a sign of faith and enacting generative fertility as a sign of hope, both proper to the formation of family life, can be organized within this general normative framework in a number of ways. Indeed, it is not unlike every other area of life that is to be lived as a context in which the grace of God's love can be made manifest. There is no single blueprint for politics, economics, culture, law, or education any more than there is for sexuality. But that some patterns lack or threaten or deny or exclude these qualities must be acknowledged.

In fact, most Christians believe that everyone knows something of these normative standards and qualities, for what is revealed in Scripture and in Christ accords with how God formed all humans at their deepest levels. These religious themes are not something imposed on people, or distinctive to one religious group, but reveal how life is really constituted. That is why many believe that all morally honest people know that something is wrong with relationships that are driven only by instinct or emotion or that do not sustain fidelity or hope. And that is why people feel violated by the infidelity of those they love, lament the prospect of infertility, resent social policies that weaken families, and turn to extreme ideological or lifestyle strategies to overcome these difficulties.

For this reason, the Christian tradition has held that it is proper for the church to guide the formation of public thought and the institutions in which sexuality is most directly expressed—especially the family, but also education, law, and economics—as they influence or inhibit the formation of the social channels in which sexuality can find expression. The earliest Christians began to advise believers on how to live their sexual lives, as we can see in both the Pauline and Pastoral letters and early books of moral instruction. Further, whenever Christians had a chance to shape civilization, they formed patterns for the expression of sexuality that sustained fidelity, fecundity, and family, all infused with love, and developed critical stances toward attitudes and policies that distorted these, even when these distortions came from sources within the faith.[7]

Distinctive Protestant Perspectives

The biblical view represents the deepest context within which current approaches to sexuality are debated in Christian circles; but we must note also a secondary context, the theological tradition, and turn, later, to a tertiary context: the current gay-advocacy suspicions of the biblical and the theological traditions. It may be that Protestant views are especially problematic in this regard, for Protestants are often suspicious of natural law arguments that developed in other parts of Christian thought.

In most Protestant views the focus is more on creation and grace than on nature and law, a distinction that manifests itself in, for example, the moral priority of fidelity in relationship over the role of fertility in procreation. Often, in fact, Protestants are doubtful of the view that grace simply completes or perfects nature. Grace is held to be constitutive of creation in most Protestant views, which often hold that what we call "nature" is "fallen"—the purposes intended by God are contorted, garbled, or made ambiguous in the actual operation of things. What we examine when we study what is "natural" is what is distorted, incomplete, or contingent, even if it bears traces of God's grace in the capacity to be reformed toward order, purpose, and reliable relationship.[8] Thus, in most Protestant traditions, humans may alter, or even have a duty to alter, "natural" patterns of life to limit its defects and to use technology to alter what is out of accord with God's intent so that it may more nearly approximate grace-full principles, purposes, and relationships. This tradition, for example, has come to advocate (sometimes slowly, but actually in concert with these accents) social reform, a right to divorce or abortion under certain conditions, the equality of women (including in church offices), technological innovation, and birth control as moral obligations.

Further, ecumenical Protestantism feels a compelling responsibility both to interpret and to shape the common life on theological grounds. This perspective tends to reject the view that theology and theologically grounded ethics are private matters, pertinent only to believing selves or particular religious groups, and to insist that it is a decisive mode of public discourse, pertinent to all members of society and necessary to the framing of policies that govern all. Those who wish to relegate theology to the margins of political debate and reduce the moral influence of religion on the common life on the grounds that we live in a morally and religiously pluralistic society, or that only secular rationality ought to be the basis of public policy, will find their most persistent opponents less among those who want the state to accept their particular dogma than among those who hold that "ecumenical" theology rooted in grace is more rational and universal than secular or sectarian positions.

The contemporary debates in the ecumenical churches about homosexuality are, thus, neither new nor only about the inner life of churches. They echo convictions that touch the nerves of the civilization's heritage. It is unlikely that we can grasp the profound bases of reservation about homosexuality in our society if we do not understand that this reservation is rooted in a fundamental theological conception about the nature of human identity under God and of how human life therefore ought to be lived in society. On the whole, this public theological tradition has held that what is found in symbolic and mythic form in the Genesis stories and reinforced by Christ is, in fact, the most public and universal truth that humanity knows about the basic normative structure for sexuality. It is how God wants us to live.

These deeper convictions have been challenged in recent years, and that has caused much controversy that bears on this issue. It may well be that we can identify some of the deeper issues in the debates by pointing to certain developments in our history that demanded a rereading of Scripture and a reconstruction of our theological ethics in view of various challenges. Each one is a marker of a larger transition from earlier practices and perspectives to present debates.

One involves the conviction by Martin Luther that the Roman Church had misinterpreted the Scriptures by presuming a sharp contrast between spiritual and material reality, and thus falsely giving a privileged status both to celibacy and the capacity of the priesthood to confer grace through sacramental performance.[9] Marriage was an order of creation graciously given by God to sustain life and constrain lustful tendencies in society, but it was not the actions of the church that conferred the grace, even if it continued to be celebrated in and registered with the church as a part of the church's proper, public role. Implicit in this challenge is a repudiation of the synthesis of "lower" nature and "higher" grace that had been worked out in medieval theology. Grace and nature are woven together in a more subtle mix.

The other was the recovery of the biblical theme of covenant, especially by the Calvinistic wing of the Reformation. The covenant was the forming of a new institution under God that would allow the orders of creation to sustain and bless life,

even when they are distorted by sin. All people are to form covenants of commitment that give shape to life in ways that approximate, under conditions of sin, the
patterns and purposes of holy living that God intends.[10] This is true in regard to
power and politics, to culture and learning, and to wealth and economics. States,
universities, and corporations are potential centers of covenantal responsibility. It
is even more true in regard to sexuality and family life, for these are the most
widespread and most directly personal of covenantal spheres. Marriage, understood as covenant rather than as sacrament or as contract,[11] is the primary theo-
logical-social relationship by which the defects of the fall, known in broken nature
and manifest in lustful desires, find their evils constrained and their residual
graces, effaced but not obliterated by the fall, enabled to approximate holy living.
Each of these areas or "orders" of life (e.g., religion, politics, economics, culture,
law, education, and family) are distinct; but properly structured by a theologically
grounded covenantal ethic, they strengthen both the whole fabric of civil society
and the soul of each person.

This covenant was to take place in accord with the laws and purposes of God,
as discerned and made manifest in the mutual pledges of "troth"—enduring faithfulness under God—between a man and a woman, as confirmed by the community of witnesses to be in accord with the first principles of righteousness and the
well-being of society. The wedding, thus, is a public declaration before God and
the people; it is society's public honoring of a valid covenant of marriage that will
actually have been made privately in pledges of love.

Puritan Contributions; Puritan Conflicts

There were many variations on these themes in the several Protestant traditions,
but the adoption of the covenantal model in the rites of marriage that soon followed stands as a symbol of a shift from sacrament to covenant as the primary
way of understanding not only human sexuality but also the social and ethical
context in which sexuality was to be understood in much of modern theology and
society.

Because of frequent confusions, we must note the difference between the views
of the Puritans, who first mediated this covenantal view to the Anglo-American
world, and the Victorians, who reasserted an older tradition that spirituality and
materiality, grace and nature were contraries, and thus that the more religious or
moral one was, the less concerned with the physical side of life one would be. This
view not only fed moralistic protests against the rising influence of the biological
sciences and of economics but also issued in a prudery in regard to human sexuality, to which the term "puritan" is sometimes applied. However, like most
Protestant traditions, this heritage did not think that sex was evil or bad, an indicator of inferiority, or a brutish necessity that had to be endured. While undoubtedly laden with residues of patriarchy, the Protestants thought God created not
only sex but also marriage *before* the Fall for our companionship, increase, and
well-being, even if, after the Fall, sex was sufficiently distorted that the covenant
became all the more necessary as a decisive way of limiting sin and of providing a
means whereby we could, by the grace of God, sense the joys of heaven.[12] At the

same time, it must be admitted that in many Protestant sermons and households, this larger tradition became temporarily wedded to Victorian presumptions (as later generations were to Romanticism, Existentialism, or Freudianism), and the notion was lost that the ecstasies of sex both echo the bliss of creation and anticipate the joys of the kingdom yet to come, even if they are not redemptive per se.[13]

Sex in marriage, thus, was designed not only to regenerate the species, thereby connecting us ethically, biologically, and socially to the nurture of the future, but also to regenerate the spirit, remind us of the divine life, and empower the spirit to rightly order life so that the paired complementarity of God's design of humankind could be concretely manifest in ways that would also overcome the terrors of loneliness and egocentrism to which humans are prone. Sinful humans would be drawn into structured bonds of interdependence that link the interpersonal unit of the family to the institutional composition of civil society and tie the affections of the soul to godly living. Fidelity to and in this covenantal relationship was an emblem of our fidelity to God's covenantal design for life as it was to be actualized in all areas, even if it sometimes led to the sufferings of the cross. The attention given to familial covenants thus becomes a manifestation of a very high estimate of sexuality, not of its low estate. In this context, humans had a "duty to desire."[14]

This tradition never advocated celibacy, disengagement from politics, or vows of poverty as marks of faith. Nor did it speak of the "right to privacy" as an individual right, although it often sought the independence of the church, the press, the school, and business, as well as the home, from too much state intervention. Covenanted "societies" had a sacred inviolability and were the primary units in which persons worked out their gifts and callings.[15] It cannot be said that all moral difficulties were overcome by these developments or that those who lived according to this view were fully righteous, any more than it can be said that every Hebrew after Sinai refrained from idolatry, adultery, and covetousness, or every Catholic, after receiving the sacraments, lived a holy, pure, and sanctified life in accord with the highest possibilities of human nature. But these developments can be said to offer a prophetic interpretation of the previous biblical and theological traditions that is both faithful to their deepest structures of reason and revelation and conducive to modern, complex civilizations in a way that brings greater possibilities of free will guided by and toward just order.

Decisive in this development for our questions was the growing sense of distinction between sin and crime. In accord with the larger heritage, the Protestant churches argued, compellingly, that not everything that has been treated as sinful (such as some abortions) should be criminalized and not all that is criminal (such as some civil disobedience) should be treated as sinful. Indeed, each of them could be, like just revolutions, the least evil option that one may be called upon to undertake with a humble courage, while holding with confidence to the promise of forgiveness offered to those who seek to discern how God wants us to live in this world. We should be tolerant, especially legally, but we should not engage in or approve behavior that increases the likelihood of abortion or war, even if some people genuinely feel desires that could lead to those results. Similarly with homosexuality.

The distinction of sin and crime augmented the tendency to see marriage as a voluntary act, not a sacramental one, and thus aided the growth of contractual views of marriage in the culture. Yet these distinctions did not exempt sexual feelings and behaviors from moral and theological guidance; indeed, all human life in these areas is subject to theological discernment, ethical evaluation, and social judgment, and the standard remains the enduring, faithful, equitable, monogamous, heterosexual, covenantal model. Preferably, they are also to be fecund, but should use proper means of birth control, which the state must allow, to make sure that children are wanted, well spaced, and cared for.

Those who live in other kinds of relationships—separated, divorced, unfaithful, abusive, homosexual—may well be accepted as members of churches and recognized as persons under God's care; but their inclinations and their behaviors, whether intended or not, are among those that are not affirmed as ideal. It is indeed likely that, in this view, few or even no marriages fulfill all aspects of the kind of covenant such as God established with Israel or Christ with the church, and thus every human approximation to the marriage covenant has elements that are deficient or problematic. That is what most ecumenical Protestants affirm when they are alert to the tradition's deepest roots, and that is why the Old and New Testaments, which witness to these covenants, are deemed revelation and are taken as the standards for our relative covenants.

That is also the basis for the Protestant view that "all are sinners in need of the grace of God." Sin, in this view, is less the intentional betrayal of some principle or norm than a basic condition that makes saving grace necessary whatever our intentions, and even in spite of our best intentions. In addition to this "state of sin" that we call "original," there are of course particular "sins"—specific acts that we do, duties we neglect, attitudes that we take, feelings that we savor, egoisms that we indulge, either willfully or without moral or spiritual protest—that are contrary to what we know to be right and good and fitting. Even more distorting are the rationalized forms of denial of our sin or of justifications for our sins, which compound the fault. The resistance to the ordination of gay clergy is, at its deepest levels, rooted as much in this issue as it is in certain behaviors. Protestant pastors are not inclined to argue that separated, divorced, unfaithful, or abusive relationships are fully compatible with the ideal, and in most of theological history homosexual pastors did not claim that their situation was normative, either. It is suspected that under contemporary ideological confusions, they are likely to distort the normative message, thereby morally and spiritually legitimating sin or sins with the authority of their office.

Temptations to rationalize a particular bias attend us all, not only gay clergy. Yet, in spite of the general condition of sin and our particular list of sins of omission or commission, ecumenical Protestants hold that we can make some relative discernment as to the marks of a properly covenantal relation, just as we can, with a relative degree of confidence, tell the difference between better or worse political regimes, better or worse corporate behaviors, and better or worse academic institutions. And in this area, ecumenical Protestants throughout their history and still today are doubtful whether homosexual relationships are or can be as nearly approximate to the ideal as heterosexual ones. Congregations thus are suspicious of nonmarried clergy, even if the distinction between sin and crime and their own awareness of their own defects leads Protestants to believe that "it takes all kinds to make a world," and that Christians ought to "live and let live" in terms of legal policy.[16] In accord with this emphasis, a number of the ecumenical churches have increasingly advocated the decriminalization of homosexuality, even if they have not moved toward approving it.[17]

More Recent Protestant Disputes

Among the intriguing issues surrounding the debates about these teachings is the fact that those who oppose this general consensus frequently link their objections to economistic interpretations of the origins and function of classical moral concepts and thereby undercut, perhaps unintentionally, the theological tradition. This can easily be seen in a recent article by Walter C. Righter. As the Episcopal bishop accused of heresy for ordaining a priest who has been living with a United Church of Christ clergyman, he puzzles about the possible reasons for such charges, now that they have been dropped. He notes that some studies show a link between homophobia and misogyny, and he speaks of pent-up anxiety about change in moral standards to which many are "accustomed." Such irrational motivations are presumed to be behind the opposition to his actions, not theology or morality. When he does speak of these, he says that the Ten Commandments "long thought to be a moral code for all ages" are now held to be "a property code" designed "to preserve property rights that no longer exist." Indeed, the entire debate about the family, he claims, is primarily about a "fault line between the past and the future" in regard to property and society, and "we are privileged with the necessity of forming a new social contract." He ends with a text from *Star Trek*: "Boldly go where no person has gone before."[18]

Although many find the whole idea of heresy quaint, even offensive, it is doubtful that the perspectives offered by the bishop will be persuasive to believers, even if most agree that misogyny, homophobia, reactive anxiety about change, and the applications of property issues to persons are frightful. The view he advocates undercuts the very prospect of a normative theology and an enduring morality able to assess and guide changing experience in changing societies. However, his perspective has wide currency in parts of academia and numerous advocacy movements in the ecumenical churches, many of which already practice some form of pastoral blessing of same-sex marriage.

Nevertheless, as we can see in recent decisions by the United Methodist, Reformed, Presbyterian, and Lutheran Churches, all of which repudiate such views in favor of the classical, covenantal tradition, Protestant Christians are unlikely to adopt such views, even if they do not want to condemn individuals and are seeking to reconstruct the wisdom and insight present in the Bible and the Reformation. They are nevertheless more likely to hold fast to the prophetic tradition that was willing to judge distortions of God's covenantal laws and purposes. In this, they recognize the indispensable place of theology and ethics in social analysis, both to understand why people do what they do and to offer guidance as to how we ought to live. Because religions vary and religious conflicts are sometimes the most intense of conflicts, many seek nonreligious concepts to interpret social realities. Some things about humans are, in fact, rather constant: Most people want and need companionship and basically like sex, peace, and plenty. They avoid loneliness, conflict, and sexual and economic poverty. But sexual activity, material plenty, personal companionship, and social solidarity tend to be more reliably present when a stable way of linking them is found, and the only durable way of linking them has been the family. But the family, it turns out, is rather fragile on its own under conditions of a sinful and broken world. It requires an embodied sense of sacredness to stabilize it, and that sacredness must be graced by a divine righteousness and purpose.

"Religion," and the critical reflection on it by means of systematic theology and theological ethics that seek to work out its moral implications for all the aspects of society, are the distinctive human activities that distinguish humanity from other creatures of the earth. It will not do to see all human motivations in terms of psychodynamic impulses or economic interests. Our most profound, determinative nature is not only "natural" in the biophysical sense, but also spiritual, intellectual, and moral. Insofar as these structure the social realities of life, they cannot be ignored in the analysis of the fabric of society. In fact, the kind and quality of religion turns out to be critical for the kind of social, ethical, and material systems developed in civilizations—the roles, relationships, institutions, rules, and expectations that guide us. And it is doubtful that the ethical norms for that religion can be gathered from science fiction.

For such reasons, one wide stream of the theological heritage is essentially reasserting continuity with the wisdom of previous ages and adapting it to today: sexuality, the formation of households and homes, the nurture of children, and the development of ways to aid those in need ought to take place in the covenanted relationships of a differentiated civil society that recognizes the reality of the basic orders of creation or spheres of life, and that we can know, with some degree of reliability, what some marks of such relationships are. Thus, some in the churches are seeking a deeper analysis of the concept of covenant as a moral theory for familial life in civil society, a theory that challenges the dominant notions of individualist self-expression on the one hand and the sovereign secular state on the other. In view of all the issues of sex and marriage, household and work, home and religion, corporations and schools, welfare and society, this question continues to haunt the churches' efforts: Can we construct a viable ethic for family life in a globalizing civil society, given the intellectual, economic, and psychosocial transformations at hand?

On the whole, the ecumenical Protestants do not oppose these transformations. In fact, many of them may well be rooted in attitudes and institutions that the Reformation and its implications engendered. Most Protestants do not want to be forced into becoming sectarians, hostile to culture, unable to perform marriages as a civil act, opposed to justice for women or minorities, or angry about the secular or pagan character of everything around them. Instead, they do want to live in, participate in, have a voice in, and shape things toward a more just and loving society. They simply do not believe that the present movement to make gay coupling equal to heterosexual marriage is likely to do that, nor do they believe that this is how God wants people to live.

On the whole, also, the answer is a prophetic one: love, indeed just love, is best grasped when linked to a basic appreciation of the way God created humanity for fidelity, fecundity, and family—a recognition that much is fallen—and neglected dimensions of our theological heritage of covenantal understanding may still be laden with valid, pluralistic, and dynamic possibilities more faithful and more graceful, and (thank God) more adequate to the deep and enduring needs of humanity than the alternatives. The alternatives are, to put it most sharply, false prophecy.

In one way, an unintended result of the churches' explorations is the discovery of how much influence theological nuances have had and may still have in this issue. It stands as a challenge to the churches and clergy, as well as to society in general, to understand these matters. It is not clear that contemporary religious leaders realize what an impact, and thus what an opportunity and a responsibility, they have in influencing souls and societies. Decisive, I believe, is a "prophetic" recovery and recasting of the covenantal tradition, linked to a fresh vision of how the family may find its place in a civil society where dual careers, a corporate economy, and a limited state in a global society are our likely future.

Notes

Portions of this essay have also appeared in my *Covenant and Commitments* (Louisville, KY: Westminster/John Knox, 1997).

1. See J. Gordon Melton, *The Churches Speak on Sex and Family Life* (Detroit: Gale Research, 1991), and idem, *The Churches Speak on Homosexuality* (Detroit: Gale Research, 1991); cf. Mary McClintock Fulkerson, "Church Documents on Human Sexuality and the Authority of Scripture," *Interpretation* 49, no. 1 (January 1995): 46–58.

2. Many of my views on these matters are more fully stated in my *Covenant and Commitments*, esp. chap. 1.

3. As far as I have been able to discover, every creation myth has a division of male and female linked with an ethic of order and fertility, but this is often among the gods. Humans stay home and honor their activities. The biblical story is distinctive in that it locates sexuality in creation and calls for humans to leave home and to create new institutions. Historically, there has been a major debate about this new community in regard to the priority of fidelity to the right order of things or of fecundity, or, as Aquinas wrote, of *fides* and *proles*, but some have argued that this third factor is central to the biblical record, and decisive for the formation of the nuclear family. See Otto A. Piper, *The Christian Interpretation of Sex* (New York: Harper, 1941).

4. Particular judgments or policies ought, I believe, to include a synthesis of the three basic modes of discourse, often called deontology, teleology, and ethology (or sometimes contextual). See my "The Trinity as Public Theology," in *Faith to Creed*, ed. M. Heim (Grand Rapids, MI: Eerdmans, 1991), pp. 162–97.

5. However, the City that welcomes all peoples and is planted for their healing is "adorned as a bride" (Rev. 21:2).

6. See, among the many treatises on this, Diogenes Allen, *Love: Christian Romance, Marriage, and Friendship* (Cambridge, MA: Cowley Publications, 1987).

7. See John T. Noonan, *Contraception* (Cambridge, MA: Harvard University Press, 1965), which is as yet unsurpassed as a general study of the institutions guiding mar-

riage in the early church, as well as of contraception specifically. Important information is also present in Kenneth Stevenson, *Nuptial Blessing: A Study of Christian Marriage Rites* (New York: Oxford University Press, 1983).

8. This view is not held by all Protestants equally. Some quite "conservative" views hold that a great deal can be known about God's creational intent by studying nature, and some quite "liberal" Protestants have almost identified creation with nature as understood in the Enlightenment or even in romanticism, and thus take whatever is found in nature as what God intended. We shall see later that some confusion in Protestant thought about nature, specifically in regard to homosexuality but also in regard to ecology and technology, is a source of contemporary debate.

9. The best treatment of this reorientation can be found in John Witte, Jr., "The Transformation of Marriage Law in the Lutheran Reformation," in *The Weightier Matters of the Law: Essays on Law and Religion*, ed. John Witte, Jr. and Frank S. Alexander (Atlanta: Scholars Press, 1988), pp. 57–97.

10. A very helpful treatment of these themes is Joseph L. Allen, *Love and Conflict: A Covenantal Model of Christian Ethics* (Nashville: Abingdon, 1984).

11. The term *compactum* signals a voluntary agreement, but it also includes the notion that the terms of the agreement were pre-given, and can be morally or legally voided if these terms are not met. See John Witte, Jr., "From Sacrament to Contract: The Legal Transformations of the Western Family," *Criterion* (Chicago: University of Chicago Divinity School, forthcoming). Later, a distinction between "covenant" and "contract" begins to suggest that "social contracts" are wholly constructed by human will, and voluntary, mutual actions between adults are exempt from theological-ethical evaluation. Similar ideas can be found in Rousseau, but became influential in ecumenical circles in regard to sexuality at the hands of the Quakers. See Alastair Heron, ed., *Towards a Quaker View of Sex* (London: Friends Home Service Committee, 1963); cf. P. Ramsey, "On Taking Sexual Responsibility Seriously Enough," in *Deeds and Rules in Christian Ethics* (New York: Scribners, 1967), pp. 11–20.

12. See, especially, the superb study by Edmund Leites, *The Puritan Conscience and Modern Sexuality* (New Haven: Yale University Press, 1986). It is fascinating that such an emphasis should be made in regard to sexuality in marriage simultaneously with the relative reduction of accent on the sacraments in worship. It is quite likely that this development parallels what Max Weber proposed with regard to economics—namely, the movement of the ascetic ethic from the monastery to the world of work. So, in this area, the "foretaste" of heaven is found as much in the disciplined ecstasies of the marriage bed as in the transubstantiated elements at the altar.

13. It is in protest against this loss and the Victorian denial of the religious significance of sensuality, as far as I can see, that prompts some today to press in the opposite direction, although some do so in the extreme. See, e.g., James B. Nelson and Sandra P. Longfellow, eds., *Sexuality and the Sacred* (Louisville: Westminster/John Knox, 1994).

14. E. Leites, "The Duty to Desire: Love Friendship, and Sexuality in Some Puritan Theories of Marriage," *Comparative Civilization Review* 3 (Fall 1979): 40–82. See also Mary S. Van Leeuwen et al., *After Eden* (Grand Rapids: Eerdmans, 1991) for what may be the best feminist treatment of many of these themes.

15. See E. S. Morgan, *The Puritan Family*, rev. ed. (New York: Harper, 1966); and the striking new study by Stephen Innes, *Creating the Commonwealth: The Economic Culture of Puritan New England* (New York: Norton, 1995).

16. Very few studies of this matter seem to exist, but these accents can be seen in the attitudes of the most "liberal" heirs of the Puritans when they met to discuss these

matters and were surveyed by Yoshio Fukuyama; see his "The Views of General Synod Delegates on Human Sexuality" (New York: United Church Board for Homeland Ministry, 1977, mimeographed).

17. See J. Gordon Melton, *The Churches Speak on Homosexuality*.

18. "Behind the Charge of Heresy," *Boston Globe,* 4 August 1996, sec. D, pp. 1, 3.

Sanctification, Homosexuality, and God's Triune Life

EUGENE F. ROGERS, JR.

While Christians have always debated "practical" issues like ordination of women, freeing of slaves, and marriage-like unions for gay and lesbian people,[1] they have also always treated embodiment as one of the "highest" concerns of their intellectual discourse, from the election of Israel to the incarnation of God and the resurrection of the dead. Put another way, theology has used one set of terms—creation, election, incarnation, resurrection—while ethically charged postmodern discourse uses another—embodiment, race, gender, orientation. Theologians such as Karl Barth tell us that ethics and high theology ought to be closely related,[2] and anthropologists of religion such as Clifford Geertz tell us similar things about ethos and worldview, or social and intellectual practices.[3] Yet only too rarely do Christian ethicists connect doctrines such as incarnation, election, and resurrection with race, gender, and orientation.[4] My constructive proposals attempt to *renegotiate* ethos and worldview in Christianity by reference to the central symbols that connect them—where ethos includes the practices of marriage (or lack thereof) for straight, gay, and lesbian people; worldview includes what Christians believe about the world, signally dogmatics ("a critical native model"[5]); and the central symbol is the body of Christ enacted in the sacraments. Marriage and the Eucharist (as well as baptism and monastic vows) tell Christians what bodies are for before God, or what they mean, by incorporating them into the body of Christ.

Along the wide spectrum of views about marriage for gay and lesbian couples, the extremes sometimes meet in claims that gay and lesbian marriages are irredeemable, on the far right because they are gay, on the far left because they are marriages. I claim the opposite: they can be a means of redemption. Moreover, they can be a means of anticipating God's catching human beings up into that wedding feast that God celebrates in the life of the Trinity, an elevation that the tradition has had the wisdom to call consummation. The question for the right is:

Given that gay and lesbian people are not going to go away, what shall the church *do* with them? The question for the left is: Given that gay and lesbian people are part of the church, how much shall it allow their bodies to *mean*? In the context of baptism, Eucharist, and (yes) monastic vows, the Spirit is now moving Christian communities to see marriage as the central symbol by which to test and renegotiate the fit of gay and lesbian bodies into the body of Christ.

Rowan Williams puts it this way:

> The whole story of creation, incarnation, and our incorporation into the fellowship of Christ's body tells us that God desires us, *as if we were God*, as if we were that unconditional response to God's giving that God's self makes in the life of the Trinity. . . . The life of the Christian community has as its rationale—if not invariably its practical reality—the task of teaching us this: so ordering our relations that human beings may see themselves as desired, as the occasion of joy.[6]

The question for both sides is then this: By what sort of sacramental practices can the church best teach gay and lesbian Christians to see themselves as occasions of joy, that God desires them as if they were God?[7] Marriage is peculiarly suited to teaching God's desire for human beings because it mirrors God's choosing of human beings for God's own. As Barth puts it, "In that the election of God is real, there is such a thing as love and marriage."[8] God's election of Israel, like marriage, involves a discipline of faithfulness in which God permits human beings to become what God sees. God's election of the mostly gentile church, like marriage for gay and lesbian couples, is (in Paul's metaphor) God's overturning of nature to graft wild olives onto a domestic tree—to include them, that is, in a structure (the law of the Spirit) that allows their selves, their souls and bodies, to mean much more than they would by nature, to be caught up into the very life and love by which God loves God.

Definitions and Disclaimers

A critic has complained that Williams's essay, just quoted, makes no "argument."[9] Williams seems to take the licitness of gay and lesbian relationships of certain sorts as given, and goes on from there. The critic thought the essay begged the question, and I thought it refreshed the debate, by not starting from the shared premises but by attempting to make its own premises attractive through disciplined elaboration. That is not a bad procedure in theology. It has been said of Karl Barth, perhaps the most important Protestant theologian since the Reformation (d. 1968), that he argued aesthetically, or by thick description: "He took the classical themes of communal Christian language molded by the Bible, tradition and constant usage in worship, practice, instruction and controversy, and he restated or redescribed them, rather than evolving arguments on their behalf."[10] Such a conceptual description does argue, implicitly; it argues from and to coherence. Even a theologian as famous for formal deduction as Thomas Aquinas can agree. Considering how theology properly mounts arguments, Thomas insists that no way lies open to persuade an opponent who begins from different premises, except to start from one's own and treat the opponent's generously as *solubilia argumenta*, difficulties to be overcome.[11]

The argument I offer is less the sort Christian theologians sometimes offer with definitions and entailments, givens and therefores, the sort a scholastic would have called an argument *ex necessitate*, or from necessity, although it is that in part. It is more an attempt to retell and renarrate bits of the Christian story so as to reveal the coherence of Christian thought with a practice of marriage broad enough to include gay and lesbian couples and leaving room for vowed celibates in community. Far from a lack of argument, that procedure mounts an argument of a different sort—one the scholastics called an argument *ex convenientia*, or from fittingness, and one Geertz would call thick description. It tests the hypothesis that gay and lesbian marriage can newly suit or befit the Christian tradition. I hope to identify fresh starting places for thinking about these matters, and treat traditional ones, liberal and conservative, constructively rather than polemically, as difficulties leading to a more adequate account, as Thomas uses objections and replies. I do not argue, that is, that Christianity could not exist otherwise, but that its existence in the way I describe does make better sense of central claims about God, the community of the faithful, and their relationship. It does them greater justice.

I ask such questions as these: What is the relation of the human body to the trinitarian life of God? To the incarnate body of God's Word? To the body of the church? To the body of Christ in the Eucharist? How does human procreation relate to divine creation? How does sex relate to grace? How does nature relate to redemption and consummation? What are gay people and celibates for? What does God want with sex, anyway?

The question of Christian marriage for lesbian and gay couples is political primarily in the sense that all theology is political: theology is always concerned with the question of life with God; life with God is a life in community, both with God and with other human beings; and politics is at best a reflection on what life in community ought to be. Talk of God's people, of God's kingdom or house, of a heavenly city, or a new Jerusalem is all talk of an ideal polity. So Thomas Aquinas characterizes life with God not only as "friendship," "homeland," and "community" but also as *"res publica,"* a commonwealth or republic, or, more literally, a political matter.[12]

Christian marriage for lesbian and gay couples is political secondarily in that marriage, too, is a community, a little polity, a domestic church, a way of life under God, one of the purposes of which is to build up that larger polity under God, the community of the faithful. So Bible and tradition describe God's choosing life with the community of Israel not only in terms of polity but also in terms of (sometimes adulterous) marriage, as they describe also the relationship of Christ and the church.

That is all miles away from the marriage politics that goes on in the Senate when politicians debate a "Defense of Marriage Act"—miles away in more ways than one, and by design. Yet a theological argument that churches should recognize gay and lesbian marriages now has political consequences of the ordinary sort in election campaigns, in legislative debates, and before the courts because religious citizens articulate positions controversial not only outside but also within their traditions.

Which traditions? I have quoted Barth, a Protestant, and Thomas, a Catholic, and spoken in Eastern Orthodox ways about sharing in God's triune life. In this my approach is ecumenically Protestant. Protestantism had its theological origin and reason for existence in a proposal about church teaching on the justification of the unrighteous.[13] Now that parties to ecumenical dialogue have experienced remarkable convergence on the very issue that divided them at the Reformation,[14] the only excuse for further Protestant proposals about church teaching (about married priests, ordained women, marriages for gay and lesbian couples) must be a return to their roots as prophetic or Pauline movements of the Spirit of unity, incomplete without magisterial or Petrine response from the rest of the church. The essay is Protestant precisely in that it does not stand alone; rather, it enjoys a characteristically Protestant obligation to take from and speak to the traditions that gave it rise. It finds itself citing Thomas Aquinas as the Catholic magisterium would not; but thus it comes inevitably into conversation with Catholics, saying: Can you not use Thomas this way? Similarly, it deploys Eastern Orthodox liturgy as the Orthodox would not, asking: Can you not use the liturgy this way?—as Protestantism too exists only from and for a community of the faithful larger than itself.

Creation, Procreation, and the Trinity

It has been argued that human beings are created in God's image in that as God creates, human beings procreate. Quite aside from the fact that it makes Jesus a deficient human being and separates celibacy from marriage, that argument makes creation necessary to God. The famous sermon is wrong that has God saying "I'm lonely. I'm gonna make me a world." Such views of creation ignore the Trinity. Even before creation, God was not lonely. Because God as Father, Son, and Holy Spirit is community already *in se*, God has no need of creation, and God's love for human beings is radically contingent.

> God has no need of us, He has no need of the world and heaven and earth at all. He is rich in Himself. He has fullness of life; all glory, all beauty, all goodness and holiness reside in Him. He is sufficient unto Himself. . . . The mystery of creation on the Christian interpretation is not primarily—as the fools think in their heart—the problem whether there is a *God* as the originator of the world . . . [but] whether it can really be the case that God wishes to be not only for Himself, . . . that *we* exist alongside and outside Him. . . . Creation is *grace*.[15]

Part of that grace is that God is vulnerable not necessarily, but by self-determination. God chooses to create; God chooses creaturely children. God woos Israel (Hos. 2:14), and Israel is allowed to ravish God (Song of Solomon 4:9a). In the love of Israel and the life of Jesus God becomes vulnerable by choice. God's need is God's *wish*. As Barth says, God is the One who loves in *freedom*. Yet God's chosen vulnerability is also not out of character for God; God is not deprived even of the blessings of mutual dependence, since the life of the Trinity is itself one of grace and gratitude, so that Jesus can truly give thanks to the Father before breaking bread. God's need is God's *wish;* God's wish is grace, and God's faithfulness to that wish, grace on grace. Created space and time, and thus our bodies, precisely as finite, are structures of mutual dependence by which we may experience grace and gratitude. In loving Israel, in the life of Jesus, in the practice of the Eucharist, called the Great Thanksgiving, God makes space and takes time for exchanges of mutual gift, for grace and gratitude.

The shock and wonder of God's self-determining love in creation has a better analogy, according to biblical metaphor, in the contingency of the love of one human being for another, than in procreation. The marriage covenant itself (human or divine) adds to love time and space for exchanges of mutual gift, with procreation or without. Passages that speak of Israel as God's bride are distinct from those that speak of Israel as God's child, and do not speak of procreation. Jesus and Paul both speak of marriage without mentioning children. That they do so because they expect the imminent end of the world only heightens the point that marriage has an integral, eschatological end in the grace and gratitude of the trinitarian life, apart from childbearing. God's extention of the covenant to the gentiles, just because it comes eschatalogically at the end of the world, grows by baptism, which is a rite of adoption, not procreation, and promises a future by resurrection, not childbirth. That is clear in Paul's metaphors too, where the gentiles do not grow naturally on the Jewish tree, but by ingrafting (Rom. 11). The whole pattern of adoption, ingrafting, and resurrection, which goes to the very heart of God's extension of the covenant to the gentiles, relativizes procreation, insisting that all human beings (that is, Jew and gentile) find fulfillment in sanctification—that is, in God. The mutual self-giving of the marriage covenant, divine or human, has an integral end not in multiplication, as such, but in the mutual self-giving of the Trinity—an end to which children may contribute.

Indeed, children constitute an extraordinary case of other people generally. Other people are our neighbors, who can help in sanctification, in making us better, and in consummation, in fulfilling our lives; if they do so, that too is grace. Children, like neighbors generally, can sanctify also by delight, a delight by which the Spirit catches up human beings into the love of the Father for the Son. Procreation can be grace, as creation is grace; and since procreation is also natural, it is a good of the species—though certainly not of every sex act and not necessarily, either, of every marriage. The inability of a human pair to procreate may be a misfortune, but not one that undermines the likeness of human beings to God. On the contrary, Christians lay more weight on God's *adoption* of them as children in baptism. Furthermore, since God is creator and human beings are creatures, the fulfillment of human community *cannot* be in more creaturely children; the fulfillment of human community is in sharing the trinitarian community of God.

Indeed, talk of children as a necessary goal of marriage risks idolatry. Here Eastern Orthodoxy's critique of western Christianity is telling. So Paul Evdokimov writes, "Both the preservation of the species and selfish sexual pleasure reduce the partner to a mere tool and destroy [human] dignity."[16] Related stories of children central to Judaism and Christianity insist that children are not to be taken for granted, but as gifts of grace. In the binding of Isaac, Abraham shows that God's fulfillment of the promise to make him a father of many nations does not, somehow, depend on his only child, a pattern that Christianity takes up and repeats in the story of the crucifixion of God's Son. At the crucial moment, Abraham trusts in God to fulfill the promise, not Isaac; for Christians it is Christ's resurrection, not their progeny, that guarantees them a future. So far from holding that children sanctify marriage, some Christian thinkers have even interpreted the remarks of Paul ignoring childbearing in marriage at 1 Cor. 7:25–40 and of Jesus positively discouraging it at Mark 13:17 and parallels as indicating that biological procreation not taken up into community with God simply carries forward the body of death.[17] Barth, who elsewhere disapproves of homosexuality, turns the tables when he comes to comment on the passage in Rom. 1 usually taken to connect homosexuality with idolatry, referring idolatry instead to child, family, and (assuming the reader is a heterosexual man) woman, putting them in the disreputable company of the Fatherland:

> Wherever the qualitative distinction between human beings and the final Omega is overlooked and misunderstood, that fetishism is bound to appear in which God is experienced in "birds and fourfooted things," and finally, or rather primarily, in "the likeness of the corruptible human being"—Personality, the Child, the Woman—and in the half-spiritual, half-material creations, exhibitions, and representation of the human being's creative ability—Family, Nation, State, Church, Fatherland.[18]

A nuptial sermon has had the audacity to admonish bride and groom that rings can signify not only faithful but also idolatrous commitment, so that wedding bands can make a cult of marriage much as the Israelites took rings of idolatry to make themselves a Golden Calf.[19] The goal of marriage is God, and community with God fulfills the human sexual nature for married and unmarried alike. For celibacy in community, like marriage, makes something before God precisely of the body.

Worried about the sort of idolatry that comes from too high a view of sex and marriage, a friend has complained that "all married couples need is to have a theologian telling them that they should not only expect great sex but *spiritually significant* sex, God help us."[20] A contrary view is that of the celibate Sebastian Moore: "The most dramatic, indeed comic, instance of cross-purposes between the Vatican and the married, is that the Vatican sees the problem as one of curbing desire, whereas the married know that the problem is to keep desire going, which means to keep it growing, which means deepening."[21] Both remarks are true. It is entirely beyond the power of human beings to render sex *spiritually* significant; that expectation would be idolatrous. It is entirely in character for *God*, however, to do just that; to deny it would be to despair of God's ability to make good on creation. More important is the deepening of desire that Moore talks about; in marriage, it has the opportunity to become the more reliable means of sanctification that eros may trick lovers into: acts of faith, hope, and charity. Christian life is an expansion, a straining forward (*epektasis*) into ever-greater love of God, which means that God is constantly expanding human desire for God even as God fulfills it.

True desire is ever greater.[22] Marriage is a sacrament because it gives desire time and space to stretch forward (another *epektasis*) into things that are *more* desirable. Marriage allows sex to mean *more*. "Decisions about sexual lifestyle . . . are about how much we want our bodily selves to mean, rather than what emotional needs we're meeting or what laws we're satisfying."[23] "Who devalues the body? Those for whom its gestures make no commitments, or those for whom they can make irrevocable commitments? Those who find freedom in casual nakedness, or those who reserve this most visible word for those to whom they have something extraordinary to say?"[24] "Marriage is a place where our waywardness begins to be healed and our fear of commitment overcome"[25]—that, and much more. The last remark comes from a manifesto denying gay and lesbian couples the right to marry, yet they too need that healing and overcoming of fear. No one has seriously claimed, so far as I know, that they are any less in need of sanctification than straight couples. Indeed marriage shares with celibacy the end of sanctifying the body,[26] of permitting it something *more* to be about, something *further* to mean, something *better* to desire, until finally it gets taken up into the life in which God loves God. In this process of desiring ever more, one incidentally or intentionally gives up—lets go of, gets rid of—the petty things that one used to want, and in that way the life of ever-greater desire is one of asceticism, an asceticism in which self-control serves self-abandonment. In this way, too, the end of marriage and monasticism is one. Life with others can bring the rewards of its difficulties—that is, it sanctifies, whether in the community of monks or the community of marriage (straight or gay), whether the shitty diapers one is committed to changing come from babies or AIDS patients. Sexual activity does not make sanctification any "easier" than celibacy does. As traditional marriage and childrearing are gifts of grace more than human achievements, and means of sanctification more than satisfaction, so too monogamous, committed gay and lesbian relationships are also gifts of grace, means of sanctification, upbuilding of the community of the people of God. They are means, bodily means, that God can use to catch human beings up into less and less conditioned acts of self-donation, finally into that unconditional response to God's self-donation that God's self gives in the Trinity.[27]

Someone might object that human beings are made in God's image as God wills and acts, rather than as God is *in se*. And God wills and acts to create. Therefore, human beings are in the image of God just as they procreate, after all. So Aquinas says that we are in the image of God as ones who have the power of our own reason and act, or free will.[28] And yet we are not in God's image, but depart from it, when we will evil. Procreation is therefore normative for sex, and parent-parent-child is a human vestige, or left-over image, of the Trinity.

On the contrary, Augustine considers the human being as in the image of the Trinity in terms of internal structures, in the capacities to will and act, not in their particular use, and certainly not in terms of their use for procreation. Indeed, Augustine does consider the image parent-parent-child for the Trinity, and rejects it.[29]

Furthermore, when Aquinas considers human beings in the image of God as having the power of their own acts, he could require procreation to complete that imitation of God only if he considered procreation a necessary good of every individual human being. But he does not, since celibacy does not impugn the image of God. (Indeed celibacy makes another creation precisely of the body.) Too easy, the critic will say: procreation is not required of celibates; it is only required (as in *Humanae Vitae*) that every sex act not be intentionally closed to procreation. (Gay and lesbian couples might invoke the principle of double effect to argue that the infertility of their unions is precisely not intentional, but a foreseen yet unintended side effect.) That critic would have the facts of nature, and the sense of the great majority of the Christian faithful against him: procreation is not, naturally or faithfully, the result of every sex act, and the proper use of human reason and will involves prudence about circumstances—without being closed to the possibility of children, even accidental ones. Well then, the critic will say, procreation is necessary only for couples. It is properly a good of marriage, so that as long as the marriage is open to children (but not necessarily every sex act of that marriage), then sex is licit.

But procreation is simply not a good that belongs to the couple as such, much less to every sex act. Rather, it belongs to the species. Procreation is a good of the species because the species is what procreation exists to promote. But if procreation is the good of the species, then not every human being must accomplish it (so celibacy is allowed), and not every sex act must accomplish it (so marriages of the postmenopausal or infertile, or arguably of gay and lesbian people, are licit), and not even every fertile couple need accomplish it; rather, the species as a whole must accomplish it. There need only be enough procreation to keep the species flourishing, and then procreation as the good of the species is fulfilled. And that need, fortunately or unfortunately, is in no danger of going unmet. Genesis 1:28 famously says "Be fruitful and multiply." It is not usually remembered that the command has an explicit end: "and fill the earth." The earth is now more or less full. Already in the fourth century, Chrysostom could write, "As for procreation, it is not required absolutely by marriage. . . . The proof of this lies in the numerous marriages that cannot have children. This is why the first reason of marriage is to order sexual life, especially now that the human race has filled the entire earth."[30] Speaking precisely of the good of the species leaves room for those considerations. Sex before God is for sanctification, for God's catching us up into God's triune life. Sex is for procreation to the extent that procreation promotes that end. The chief end of sex is not to make children of human beings, but to make children of God. And Christians best imitate God's relation to them as children not when they bear and beget them, but when they adopt them.

God's Acting Contrary to Nature (Rom. 11:24) and Homosexuality

God is said to act "contrary to nature," *para phusin,* in bringing the gentiles into the covenant with Israel, grafting wild branches onto a domestic olive tree (Rom. 11:24).[31] That shocking phrase, the same one Paul uses in Romans 1 to condemn homosexual behavior, governs the earlier passage theologically because it places nature in the service of salvation. It calls for a reconceptualization of "nature" in soteriological terms, in terms—that is, of God's freedom to complete what God began with human beings,[32] God's intent to elevate nature into the glory of the trinitarian communion. Better, it reminds us that in Rom. 1, as in Rom. 11, Paul is not talking about human beings *in general*; Paul is talking about human beings as Jews and gentiles, and therefore of the nature, and salvation, not of all human beings as a class but of all human beings as Jews and gentiles. In Rom. 1, acting contrary to nature characterizes idolatrous *gentiles*, and the great amazement that drives Paul's ministry is that God pours out the Spirit also on *those* people, an amazement Paul expresses in Rom. 11 by characterizing God's saving action as itself contrary to nature. It is more than a horticultural metaphor to express how God grafts gentiles regarded as wild, idolatrous, and unfruitful into the domestic trunk of Israel—close enough already, perhaps, to justify the grafting of another group sometimes regarded as promiscuous, idolatrous, and infertile into the domestic practices of marriage. It is also another of Paul's rhetorical sting operations.[33] It is a reversal of guilt by association. God becomes "guilty" of acting contrary to nature by choosing solidarity with the gentiles, whose identifying characteristic it is to act contrary to nature. "Nature" must become logically subsequent to soteriology, to God's concrete history with Jews and gentiles, which means also that we must reconceptualize nature not in terms of predetermined end, immanent to a general human nature, or *telos* (such as procreation), but in terms of a God-determined end, or eschaton,[34] such as the mutual blessing of God's own trinitarian life. In good Barthian fashion we learn about nature, such as it is, from what God does with it: if God appears to be capable of using sexual orientations too, both heterosexual and homosexual, just in their concrete, messy details, just in their complicated relations to the larger Christian community that they both upbuild and both betray, for God's saving purposes, then that is of a piece with God's surprising salvation of the gentiles. Like the claim that the Spirit of Christ is joining the gentiles to the tree in baptism, the claim that the same Spirit is building up the body of Christ by joining together gay and lesbian couples is a pneumatological one—a claim, that is, about what the Spirit is doing new in the church, one that will one day, if not soon, be empirically verifiable in the church's life.

In Galatians 3:28, Paul writes, "There is no longer Jew or Greek, there is no longer slave or free, there is no longer male and female; for all of you are one in Christ Jesus." The formula is to be taken as a warning. If the Jew/gentile distinction is read in the way of Paul's opponent, then there is no salvation for the gentiles as gentiles, but only as circumcised, as Jews. The salvation of almost all Christians, those who are not ethnically Jews and do not observe Torah, depends on taking this verse seriously. If Christians have endangered their salvation by ignoring the other members of the formula—if they took some 1900 years to overcome the pairs slave and free, male and female—that is no argument why they should continue to do so. Prohibiting gay marriages may put some Christians in the same danger of forfeiting their ingrafting into Israel—which is their very salvation—as maintaining the distinction Jew/gentile or slave/free: it disbelieves in that ingrafting. If Paul himself failed to see that consequence, he also warns explicitly that the ingrafting is precarious and subject to reversal (Rom. 11:21–22). Failing to accept faithful, monogamous gay and lesbian marriages puts gentile Christians in danger of their salvation. Marriage for gay and lesbian spouses depends upon the work of the Holy Spirit no less than baptism for the gentiles, and disbelief in either risks blasphemy against the Spirit.

A critic may hold that "male and female" is overcome only in a way that accords with "nature," or insist that while civil rights are due groups whose distinctions are natural (such as blacks and women), similar, "special" rights are not due to those whose distinctions are moral (such as thieves and homosexuals). "Differences of race are in accord with—not contrary to—our nature, and such differences do not provide justification for behavior otherwise unacceptable. . . . Certain discriminations are necessary within society; it is not too much to say that civilization itself depends on the making of such distinctions (between, finally, right and wrong)."[35]

But "nature" applies in Paul's vocabulary also to "Jew or Greek," and in that case, most important to him of all, it is overcome. "Jew or gentile" is for Paul both a natural and a moral distinction. The application shows how discrimination of the good, moral sort has in fact not rarely, but *usually* been called upon to justify a discrimination of the bad sort. Crucial to my response are cases in which the pairs Jew/Greek, male/female, and free/slave were all cited by their defenders as moral, not neutral, distinctions. Or better, in all cases there was a natural difference that led to a moral defect. So gentiles, women, and slaves were considered in the antique Jewish tradition to be *constitutionally* incapable of keeping the commandments, and especially at risk of moral fault.[36] That reasoning is structurally isomorphic with the current Vatican line on homosexuality—that it is a natural difference, innocent in itself, which nevertheless tends toward a moral defect.[37] Similarly, some Christian slaveholders during the positive defense of slavery in the 1850s and some recent Mormons have argued that the curse of Ham represents a moral fault that, like the Fall, gives the natural difference between blacks and whites a permanent moral distinction.[38] So slavery is a "divine institution . . . not to be removed until the curse pronounced on Ham shall have been removed from his descendants."[39] Or, more mildly, slaves, women, and homosexual persons have not, perhaps, a necessary subordination, but they do have a contingent vocation in the order of things: "The slave . . . is an actor on the broad theater of life—and as true merit depends not so much upon the part which is assigned, as upon the propriety and dignity with which it is sustained—so fidelity in this relation may hereafter be as conspicuously rewarded as fidelity in more exalted stations."[40]

As all are called to fidelity in their station according to pro-slavery Christians, of which the fidelity of slaves (to masters) is only a particular case, so all are called to chastity in their state of life according to certain Christians, of which the chastity of gay and lesbian Christians (in celibacy) is only a particular calling. "Christians who are homosexual are called, as all of us are, to chaste life."[41]

Indeed, the argument is so common that I think of it as "the standard argument." In some cases, it may be true that a natural distinction leads to a moral fault. But since versions and sections of this compound argument have been offered at various times about gentiles (by Jews), Jews (by Christians), women (by Aquinas), blacks (by Southern Presbyterians before the Civil War), and gay and lesbian people (by the Vatican in the 1980s),[42] prudence suggests that *the burden of proof should shift*. Since we have rejected its implications in all the other cases, we should ask for additional proof in the case of gay and lesbian people. Let me present the standard argument in its most comprehensive form.

1. In a feature of the standard argument least often appealed to in sophisticated versions, but accounting for much of its continuing power, decline or fall narratives in Scripture purportedly reveal that God has punished certain groups. God has punished the gentiles for their idolatry with the animal character of the ass, according to Genesis Rabbah on v. 22:5. God has punished the Jews for "rejecting" Christ. God has punished women on account of Eve's sin, according to Genesis 3:16. God has punished blacks as "Hamites," or descendants of Noah's son Ham, condemned to be "a slave of slaves" for uncovering his father's nakedness, according to Genesis 9:22–25. And God has punished performers of homosexual acts as a punishment on idolatrous gentiles so that they will die out, according to Romans 1:18–27.[43]

2. God's just punishment of the disfavored group for some narrated sin comes in the form of a natural disorder or weakness that is not yet itself a moral fault. Gentiles, Jews, women, blacks, or gays are not evil in themselves, but they are so constituted (or "oriented") that they are specially subject to temptation—in each case especially sexual temptation.[44]

3. As members of a naturally labile group, gentiles, Jews, women, blacks, or gays are more prone to violate natural law or commit moral fault, although they need not. Natural disorder (orientation) tends to moral fault (act).

4. Therefore, a religious objection to equality for gentiles, Jews, women, blacks, or gays in religion or society can claim not to be based on mere prejudice, but on the disfavored group's characteristic but freely chosen behavior, which *does* constitute a moral fault.

5. And specifically, sexual restrictions can therefore purport to *protect* both the religious and the labile group. Thus Jews might not marry gentiles; Christians might not marry Jews; blacks (until 1967 in Virginia) might not marry whites—or indeed, when slaves, legally marry each other. Such marriages, between males as between slaves, are naturally unstable and morally wrong.

6. Even should one charitably find the state of the disordered a subject of pity or apparent injustice, one can still hold that the duty of those so afflicted is to do the best they can with what they have. Thus it is the contingent vocation, if not the necessary nature, of gay people or women or slaves to have a special service, even if their condition is not their fault. It is true that calls to a particular vocation usually come not by visions or voices but by an accumulation of particular circumstances, so that being female may contribute to a vocation to motherhood or being gay to a vocation to celibacy. But to make those determinations in advance and across the board does not attend to particular circumstances, but levels them out.[45] Otherwise God would elect only the first born and not second sons, or only the fertile and not the barren, or only the righteous and not the sinful, or only the Jews and not the gentiles. As Barth was fond of quoting, *Latet periculum in generalibus*: danger lurks in generalities. In the standard argument, women are called to childrearing, blacks to service, gay and lesbian people to celibacy, in each case *as a*

group, whether the particulars to which God usually attends indicate that vocation or not.

The insistence on a general theory of vocation rather than particular cases of it can persist even when the author concedes generalization's apparent injustice. For example:

> The propriety of slavery, like that of the restraints and punishments of civil government, rests on the fact that man is depraved and fallen. Such is his character, that the rights of the whole, and the greatest welfare of the whole, may, in many cases, demand the subjection of one part of society to another, even as man's sinfulness demands the subjection of all to civil government. Slavery is, indeed but one form of the institution, *government.* . . . And this is the Scriptural account of the origin of slavery, as justly incurred by the sin and depravity of man.[46]

Despite a far different account of sin, and a far higher estimate of human dignity, one now hears, to similar effect, that universal homosexual celibacy is, indeed, but one form of the virtue chastity.

Not only do I propose that the standard argument has been unjustly used so often that the burden of proof must shift, but I also propose that God's providential order of salvation specifically *overturns* the standard argument. That is one meaning of God's acting *para phusin,* or against the standard. If God has not acted to overturn the standard argument on Jews and gentiles, then we gentile Christians are not saved after all. *We are not saved!* It is the wild branches that God grafts on according to Romans 11, the gentiles with whom Paul associated sexual license and on the hearts of whom the Spirit writes a new law, in this case, I argue, the law of marriage. As God grafts gentiles, the wild branches, onto the domestic covenant of God's household with Israel, structured by the Torah of the Spirit, so God grafts gay and lesbian couples (whom detractors also associate with sexual license) by a new movement of the Spirit onto the domestic, married covenants of straight women and men.

The Body's Grace?

Williams's essay bears the title, "The Body's Grace." In it he claims that grace, like some sexual love, works a change in a human being by causing her to reperceive herself as loved by Another. This passage introduces another we have seen before:

> Grace, for the Christian believer, is a transformation that depends in large part on knowing yourself to be seen in a certain way: as significant, as wanted.
>
> The whole story of creation, incarnation, and our incorporation into the fellowship of Christ's body tells us that God desires us, *as if we were God,* as if we were that unconditional response to God's giving that God's self makes in the life of the Trinity. We are created so that we may be caught up in this; so that we may grow into the wholehearted love of God by learning that God loves us as God loves God.
>
> The life of the Christian community has as its rationale—if not invariably its practical reality—the task of teaching us this: so ordering our relations that human beings may see themselves as desired, as occasions of joy.[47]

A critic might raise related objections to the concept of the body's grace—one about grace and one about the body:[48] (1) Despite the stirring trinitarian ring, the concept of the body's grace trades on too vague a concept of grace, reducing it to any kind of transforming, positive regard, of which God's grace becomes a mere example. (2) The concept of the body's grace psychologizes the body because a concept takes the body seriously as a body only if it takes account of real bodily differences.

A shorter answer to these objections has to do with how justice constructs bodies and grace. Bodies, as we have seen, are one of the ways in which Christians ought to take particulars seriously: God chose the Jews; the incarnation took place in a particular place and time; the sacraments locate Christ again in space and time; the priest represents Christ still another way in space and time; particular bodily things—this bread and this wine—do matter. And so, to sum up, it really does matter whether someone has a penis or a vagina. I don't mean to belittle this objection. There is more to the "insert tab A in slot B" argument than meets the ear of most revisionists. Christians believe other things that are just as closely tied to the body. The question is: *Which* bodily things ought Christians to believe? Are some bodily forms, like gay and lesbian relationships, irredeemable, or can God sanctify them? Which bodily forms we revere has a lot to do with what sort of society we are, what our external boundaries and internal organs are in the *social body*.[49] And here the question depends upon what vision of justice we want to uphold. Societies that distinguish sharply between men and women have justice; it is different from the justice that obtains in an individualist society. Justice among the baptized must be specified by the formula "In Christ there is no Jew or Greek, slave or free, male and female." The center of biblical embodiment is circumcision. The important thing about Jesus' birth in space and time was that his mother was Jewish, and so was he. God's covenant with the Jews is specific, and only by being grafted into it do gentiles have a leg to stand on. But one center of the bodily, circumcision, is relativized in that saying of Paul's by another center, the body of Christ. If the bodily distinction of circumcision is overcome, then gay/straight means nothing, especially if sexual license is the issue of concern about both gay and gentile Christians. Indeed, to the peril of the church, it was unbelieving Jews, not gay and lesbian people, whom Paul assimilated to Sodom and Gomorrah (Rom. 9:29). Jewish and Christian societies have constructed gentile and Jewish bodies according to better and worse notions of justice.[50] Paul overturns those patterns. Paul (at his best) causes bodies to be constructed, not according to human justice but according to God's justification, because he believes in a God who justifies *gentiles* and justifies them *uncircumcised*.

A longer answer to the question of the body's grace depends on the theological procedure of realistic analogy. According to the procedure of analogy, related realities generate related meanings.[51] So in the standard medieval example, dating to Aristotle, both food and urine can be "healthy" because food *contributes* to health and urine *indicates* health. The two relations are not the same, but they are real, and the notion of a healthy *person* stands in the center to give sense to all appropriate uses. The healthy person is the "primary analogate," the one who gives sense to the others, whom theologians call the secondary analogate. The theory of analogy offers a solution to the problem of human language about God generally. Take the statement "God is good." If the primary analogate of "good" is *human* goodness, then it is hard to see how the word can apply properly to God. Human goodness is so unreliable that applying it to God is equivocal, not appropriate. On the other hand, if *God's* goodness is the primary analogate, then "good" applies properly to God in the first place and to human beings only derivatively, deficiently, and secondarily.[52]

The procedure is often used to defend traditional language about God. For example, on this view it is not a good objection to "Father" language for God that human fathers are unfit to represent God. They are unfit. But that is not the way the analogy works. It is not relevant that we *learn* the word first from its application to human fathers. Its true, proper application is to God. God, not a human parent, is the father *par excellence*. Human beings ordained as "father"—that is, priests—are the derivative, deficient, and secondary analogates to the fatherhood of God. And that makes biological fathers only derivative, deficient, and *tertiary* analogates. It is the father in the story of the prodigal son who teaches priests and parents what true fatherhood is like, not they who specify what God is like.

But analogy also turns to nontraditional purposes. For example, the tradition has always held that God, though spoken of as Father, is nevertheless not biologically male. It follows that God's priests may also be "father," without being male.[53] Similarly, in the Middle Ages Jesus, though biologically male, became mother *par excellence*. Secondarily, Cistercian abbots, who were biologically male, were called mothers, too.[54] Does "the body's grace" respect or reverse the proper order of analogates?

The objection to a grace of the body, then, is this: it sounds as if it takes an all-too-general category, transformative, positive regard, as the primary analogate, of which God's grace is not the defining example, but a mere illustration, if the most impressive. To be theologically adequate, grace must be defined first of all as what God does, and the grace of the body related to that. But that is just what Williams does:

> [T]he body's grace itself only makes human sense if we have a language of grace in the first place; and that depends on having a language of creation and redemption. To be formed in our humanity by the loving delight of another is an experience whose contours we can identify most clearly and hopefully if we have also learned or are learning about being the object of the causeless, loving delight of God, being the object of God's love for God through incorporation into the community of God's Spirit and the taking-on of the identity of God's Child.[55]

The references to God's Spirit and Child are crucial. For if *God* defines what grace is, then grace is simply an impersonal name for the Holy Spirit. "The gift of the Holy Spirit is nothing but the Holy Spirit."[56] That Spirit is identified in the Christian community by the biblical stories about Jesus, since the Spirit is also the Spirit of Christ. Without saying so, Williams makes the word *grace* an analogy in the strict theological sense, where the grace of God supplies the primary analogate. The grace of the body only makes sense by reference to the grace of God identified in a community that tells certain stories of God's creation and redemption. Only thus can it emerge that the body is one of God's ways of catching human beings up in God's own life, and therefore a possible means, derivative and second or third hand, of grace. The body's grace, should it occur, is not a movement of the body up to God, but a movement of the Spirit down, so that human bodies will not be left out of salvation.

The word *body* also has to work analogously because Christian theology is committed to speaking in a number of ways about that central body, the body of Christ. The body of Christ is at once the body assumed by the Second Person of the Triune God, and thus God's body. The body of Christ was also a specifically identifiable, historical human body. The body of Christ is the church, and the body of Christ is the consecrated bread of the Eucharist. Christ's body, to sum up, names a place where God locates God's own self, a place where God has chosen to become vulnerable to human touch and taste and hurt, "God with us." Technically, Christians should say that the body of Christ is the primary analogate of the word *body* in their discourse, the use from which others derive their sense.

Salvation is itself bodily. It depends, for gentile Christians, upon the crucifixion of God's body, and it depends on their human bodies' getting taken up into God's body. For Christians, bodies are no more or less than a means by which God catches hold of and sanctifies human beings. In short, bodies are made to be saved. Union with God does not take place otherwise than by incorporating physical bodies into God's. What does that mean?

At the fraction, or breaking of the bread, of the Eucharist, the Trinity also breaks open to let human beings, through their bodies, into God's triune life. The broken bread is the broken body of Christ, which is the broken body of the triune God, the body by the breaking of which on the cross the Son was forsaken by the Father and the Trinity risked its unity, the Persons threatening to come apart. Better, for humanity's sake the Persons *promise* to come apart, their unity restored in the same way that human unity with them begins, in the Holy Spirit. As Paul writes, "If the Spirit of the One who raised Christ from the dead dwells in you, the One who raised Christ from the dead will give life to your mortal bodies also through the Spirit that dwells in you" (Rom. 8:11).[57] That is the body's grace *par excellence,* the transfiguration of the body by the indwelling of the Spirit who just is grace, the Spirit trinitarianly defined as the *Spirit* of the *One* who raised *Christ,* where Christ is defined in turn as the one who was crucified. The body's grace is first of all what identifies the Trinity by the crucifixion and reunites it in the resurrection. At the Eucharist, secondarily, the fraction breaks open the Trinity to let the body in. The Trinity is entered by the body of a believer through the broken body of the Lord, and the body of Lord is also broken to enter into the bodies of believers. This co-enveloping or interpenetration of bodies is itself the trinitarian life embodied, broken open, entered into, which could not take place with unembodied human beings.

Human bodies, like human reason, are not left out of the Spirit's work and love's communion, but taken up into it in the pattern of the assumption of flesh by the Logos. Even as older atonement theories talked about the flesh as bait and hook, so God can use eros as bait and hook for a life of commitment and care that takes eros up into agape. As Gregory of Nyssa writes, "Agape which is aroused is called eros."[58] Yet eros still belongs among what remains of God's plan not to leave human bodies out of consummation when we abstract bodies from their purpose to incorporate human beings into God's life. Sexual desire, especially as portrayed by such celibates as St. John of the Cross, prefigures the Eucharist, in which, for Christians, God desires to enter into human bodies and to be desired bodily by them. The Eucharist also begins to consummate their life in God, since in it they partake of the trinitarian communion—they pray to the Father, invoke the Spirit, and commune bodily (the only way they can?) with the Son. Eros, for Christians, ought to be a remainder concept left over from the Eucharist; sex, like the Eucharist, is a participation, analogous and derivative, in a marriage of sacrifice for others and therefore a thanksgiving for involving us in their involvements (among them children or care of the sick). Taken up into the Eucharistic community in a marriage that upbuilds it, eros returns home, performing its task of pointing to the trinitarian community when it issues in fruits of the Spirit that satisfy only as they sanctify. It does so particularly in a wedding centered on the Eucharist, since the kingdom of heaven is like a wedding feast;[59] in a wedding feast the Spirit catches the people up in its own proper work of witnessing, blessing, sanctifying, celebrating, and enjoying the love between the Father and the Son, using the people like the couple as a means to the ascesis of living with others. A wedding feast too emparables, enacts, and furthers the unity of God as it catches human beings up in the love by which God loves God, seducing them into agape for the other even after they leave the feast, a movement prepared by the Son's commitment to the Father—the Father to whom the Son draws near precisely by going out into the far country of God-forsakenness.

Thus gay and lesbian marriages can, like straight marriages, take bodies seriously in a handful of ways:

1. Since the true body, or the primary analogate of "body" in Christian discourse, is the body of Christ, any body is taken seriously that extends and deepens the Eucharistic entry into God's body. Marriage, gay or straight, receives its sacramental character not independently but from the welcoming of the one flesh, in soteriological ways a new body, into the eucharistic community.[60]

The male-female version of the one flesh can be especially apt for representing the union of Christ with his bride the church, but not everyone need represent this union in the same way. The analogy is flexible enough already that both celibates and the married can represent it. Gay and lesbian couples also need not threaten the aptness of the relation between Christ and the church, but can be taken up into it. As the Fatherhood of God is not male, so priests need not be male to be called "Father." Similarly, the frequent identification of the human race with the figure of Mary in Roman Catholic and Eastern Orthodox traditions can lead to taking the race as a whole as ontologically female, yet not everyone must be female for the typology to work.[61] Whether male or female, priests are (as human) brides to Christ's groom and (as ordained) father to the church's children. Religious discourse works in a much richer and subtler fashion than by supposing that one has to instantiate physically what one honors or even represents figurally. What matters is mirroring the election and fidelity of God to God's people; as Barth put it, again, "in that the election of God is real, there is such a thing as love and marriage." So, too, gay and lesbian Christians need have no quarrel with the special aptness of the Genesis account of male and female and their procreation as normative for the *species,* as long as not everyone has to instantiate it to be in God's image.

To say otherwise is to limit the freedom of God in an unbiblical manner. The first chapter of Matthew picks out several stories that lead up to Mary as the supreme example—she who represents the race as a whole—of departures from "normative" marriage and childbirth: the anomalous cases of the women named in the genealogy of Jesus, Tamar, Ruth, Rahab, and "the wife of Uriah," emphasizing the adultery of David with Bathsheba. In each case God proves capable, *mirabile dictu,* of using irregular sexual unions for God's own purposes, even the purpose of human redemption. "Taking the body seriously" must leave room for the way in which the Bible shows *God* taking the body seriously in the history of salvation. Many accounts of sexual relations outside of traditional marriage do not actually leave room for the scandals God delights in using to lead up to the incarnation. They tend to rule out a category of providence or divine freedom or the blowing of the Holy Spirit that could make any more of the virgin birth than a case of unwed motherhood.

2. Any body is taken seriously in which the eucharistic community is built up. Weddings, gay or straight, build up the eucharistic community by contributing the institutional stability of marriage and because weddings represent the trinitarian life. In a wedding, third parties guarantee, celebrate, witness, bless, testify to, and delight in the love of two. When Jesus says the kingdom of heaven is like a wedding feast, and theologians say that the role of the Spirit is to guarantee, celebrate, witness, bless, testify to, and delight in the love of the Father and the Son, they are speaking of the same reality. The Spirit incorporates the wedding guests into the public of love. It bears repeating that Augustine rejects the triad father, mother, child as an analogy for the Trinity, while the analogy of the Spirit to the guests at a wedding has implicit support in the parables of Jesus (Mt. 9:15, 22:2)—the second passage issuing a dire warning about those who do not celebrate the wedding, who refuse the Spirit's work.

3. Any body is taken seriously in which the Holy Spirit dwells so as to raise it from the dead. Anticipation of that resurrection is the bodily sanctification that marriage, as a form of ascetic practice, carries out. Note well, in the Christian view marriage is not for satisfaction, but for sanctification, of which satisfaction and enjoyment will be an inalienable part of its perfection. Marriage and monasticism have exactly the same end: the sanctification of the person by means of the body, by putting the body so in the power of others that one cannot escape their love and truth.[62] Human beings imitate God when they take time and make space for each other, as God takes time and space for Israel and in Jesus; in so doing they honor the body that exists over time and in space. Sartre notoriously opined that "hell is other people"; so is holiness. Indeed, in Eastern Orthodoxy the crowns placed over the heads of bride and groom are crowns of martyrdom. This leaves room for the fading of sexual urgency in marriage (gay or straight) and its being taken up into other forms of care for the partner and the community. So it is too that "in heaven they neither marry nor are given in marriage." The pas de deux

with which a romance may begin is taken up into the trinitarian circle: As the carol puts it,

Then up to heaven I did ascend,
Where now I dwell in sure substance
  On the right hand of God, that man
May come unto the general dance.[63]

4. Any body is taken seriously in which a human being begins to fulfill the chief end for which she or he was made, which, according to the first answer of the Westminster catechism, is to "glorify God and enjoy him forever." Sanctification and the Eucharist and wedding feasts certainly glorify God. Properly understood, they enjoy God, too. And if human beings were so created to enjoy God, then the joy of sex, under sanctifying circumstances, cannot be unfitting. Sexual attraction is explicitly or implicitly concerned with real bodies. Gay and lesbian people care about bodies—otherwise many of them would take the easier route and settle for those of the opposite sex. There is *something* right about insert-tab-A-in-slot-B—or there is something in having tabs and slots. What is it? And why is it wrong that God should give it to some with tabs to admire the tabs of others? Or, to be less crude, the chests and shoulders? Even Augustine was able to speculate about the placement of nipples on a man's chest: "They articulate the space of the chest, and they prove that beauty is a value in itself, not tied inevitably to utility in the human body."[64] Or better, the utility is for bodies made aware of grace, the utility of joy.

Williams puts it this way:

Same-sex love annoyingly poses the question of what the meaning of desire is—in itself, not considered as instrumental to some other process, such as the peopling of the world. We are brought up against the possibility not only of pain and humiliation without any clear payoff, but, just as worryingly, of nonfunctional joy—of joy, to put it less starkly, whose material "production" is an embodied person aware of grace.[65]

Just because a body is pleasing to me I become vulnerable, and God has made us so to be vulnerable in one another's bodily presence. The embodiment of God's creation is borne in upon me and will not leave me alone.[66] Neither monogamy nor celibacy cause these interventions of God through bodily forms of the neighbor to go away.[67]

Perhaps this is the point to mention that the phenomenon of gay and lesbian desire, contrary to popular belief, can do a good job of articulating what celibacy is for in the Christian tradition. For celibacy also raises the question of nonfunctional joy. Both Jesus and Paul speak of sexual desire and fulfillment without mentioning children. If sex is for *God,* then the task of celibacy is to bear witness to that fact *directly* and *immediately,* whereas the task of people in sanctifying sexual relationships of whatever orientation is to bear witness to that *indirectly* and *mediately.*

It is perhaps because of our need to keep that perspective clear before us [that the body's grace depends on the loving delight of God] that the community needs

some who are called beyond or aside from the ordinary patterns of sexual relation to put their identities direct into the hands of God in the single life. *This is
not an alternative to the discovery of the body's grace.* All those taking up the
single vocation . . . must know something about desiring and being desired
if their single vocation is not to be sterile and evasive. Their decision (as risky
as the commitment to sexual fidelity) is to see if they can find themselves, their
bodily selves, in a life dependent simply upon trust in the generous delight of
God.[68]

5. Any body is taken seriously that is *ruled* by the *Spirit*. The further objection
arises that if grace is properly to be described as "grace," it must occur in morally
licit circumstances. The Bible and the tradition determine morally licit circumstances, and therefore it begs the question to deploy a concept of grace against received traditional morality. The body's grace, says this objection, is antinomian.
But reliance on the Spirit rather than on concrete forms of the created order, or the
previously revealed order (such as that of circumcision), is not antinomian. On the
contrary, the Spirit's work is also and precisely that of fidelity, or of keeping faith
between the Father and the Son. Fidelity is a work proper to the Spirit, particularly "the Spirit of the One Who raised Christ Jesus from the dead," the *vinculum
caritatis,* the one who "restores" the bond between Father and Son and works
(much less successfully?) to restore unity also among human beings, even through
the witnesses of the wedding to restore unity in a couple.

The twentieth-century mystic Adrienne von Speyr suggests a name for the Spirit
bridging the gap that opens between spirit and letter and makes appeals to the
Spirit seem antinomian to western Christian ears. She calls the Spirit "the Rule,"
as in the Benedictine rule,[69] or, though she neglects to say so, the Torah—a structure that liberates us for sanctification. Similarly, Paul refers to the Spirit's law
(Rom. 8:1). The Spirit loves the law enough to write it on fleshy hearts (Heb.
8:10). To rely on the Spirit is the only way not only to keep but to *"delight* in the
law of the Lord" (Ps. 1:2), since it is proper to the Spirit to delight in the love of
the Father for the Son. Taken up into the delight of the Spirit in witnessing, vindi-
cating, celebrating, and furthering the fidelity of the Father and the Son, human
beings also, in the community the Spirit, gather, become free to witness, vindicate,
celebrate, and further analogous forms of covenant among themselves. There can
be no question of antinomianism where the Spirit is rightly invoked, since the
Spirit is the Rule of faith keeping.

Gay and lesbian relationships not only must exhibit the spiritual fruits of faith,
hope, and charity but must also exhibit them in sacramental form. Just as marriage gives form or rule to the sanctifying possibilities of heterosexual sex, so gay
and lesbian people need sacramental forms, or inspired rules. Perhaps Boswell's
ceremonies provide them, perhaps not.[70] In any case they are not celebrated in the
modern West. Gay and lesbian relationships must wait upon a churchly form—
call it sacramental if you think of marriage as a sacrament—to give their holiness
ecclesial shape, just as heterosexual relationships had to wait centuries for the
church to integrate them fully into its life with heterosexual marriage forms. Conservatives are right to complain about what you might call unformed love: we
must mine Scripture and tradition under the Spirit, who will rule new rules for us.

If we want to see the Rule enacted who is the Spirit, we need to look to the liturgy—especially liturgies that tell stories of lives ruled by the Spirit, or inspired by the Rule.

Sexuality as Narrated Providence in Eastern Orthodoxy

The liturgy teaches best of all that the lives of believers need inspiration by the Rule, or that nature needs reconceptualization as part of God's *oikonomia*. Consider this Orthodox prayer:

> O Lord our God, who didst grant unto us all those things necessary for salvation and didst bid us to love one another and to forgive each other our failings, bless and consecrate, kind Lord and lover of good, these thy servants who love each other with a love of the Spirit and have come into this thy holy church to be blessed and consecrated. . . . [B]estow . . . also on these, O Christ our God, . . . all those things needed for salvation and eternal life.[71]

Whatever this ceremony means, it manifests the economy of bringing *nature* to *salvation*. Similarly, in the Orthodox Order of Crowning, as the marriage proper is called, Jesus' presence at the marriage of Cana is ascribed to the "saving providence" of "the Lord our God."[72] In the order of second marriage, too, the appeal is to God's providence: "O Master, Lord our God, who showest pity upon all human beings, and whose providence is over all thy works."[73] In all those cases, the appeal to God's providence emerges from a catena of biblical and saintly examples, so that the economy of salvation of the couple before the congregation is incorporated into the economy of biblical salvation history. The Order of Betrothal is best, if few Orthodox would use it as I propose:

> For thou, O Lord, hast declared that a pledge should be given and confirmed in all things. By a ring was power given unto Joseph in Egypt; by a ring was Daniel glorified in the land of Babylon; by a ring was the uprightness of Tamar revealed [!]; by a ring did our heavenly Father show forth his bounty upon his Son; for he saith: Put a ring on his hand, and bring hither the fatted calf, and kill it, and eat, and make merry.[74]

Note well: It is the prodigal—one might by application say, the gay son—that receives the ring!

And the Order of Second Marriage is wittiest:

> O thou who knowest the frailty of human nature, in that thou art our Maker and Creator; who didst pardon Rahab the harlot, and accept the contrition of the Publican: remember not the sins of ignorance from our youth up. For if thou wilt consider iniquity, O Lord, Lord, who shall stand before thee? Or what flesh shall be justified in thy sight? For thou only art righteous, sinless, holy, plenteous in mercy, of great compassion, and repentest thee of the evils of human beings. Do thou, O Master, who hast brought together in wedlock thy servants, N. and N., unite them to one another in love: vouchsafe unto them the contrition of the Publican, the tears of the Harlot, the confession of the Thief; that, repenting with their whole heart, and doing thy commandments in peace and oneness of mind, they may be deemed worthy also of thy heavenly kingdom.[75]

If that can go for remarriage after divorce, how much more for almost any wedding now in our complicated society, where very few, straight or gay, save sex for marriage. What couple should *not* invoke the contrition of the Publican, the tears of the Harlot, the confession of the Thief, by the time they marry?

One might object that such narratives about God's providential rule are best understood as the way in which God acts through evil to bring about good rather than as establishing a pattern for behavioral norms. Those who put forward patterns for behavioral norms, on the other hand, tend not to take account of biblical stories in which God seems unconcerned with the ethics of the characters, or at least the editorial rescension records no moral judgment one way or the other. It would be hard to argue for divine disapproval of Tamar's subterfuge, for example; still less of Mary's bearing a child not begotten by Joseph. The "low estate" of the Magnificat refers not to barrenness, as usual, but to her apparently illegitimate pregnancy. The reason I turn to *liturgically worked* biblical texts is precisely to overcome the dichotomy between behavioral norms and providential action, between letter and spirit. In the liturgy the Spirit who rules is invoked and present. In the liturgy the church *does* take up biblical narratives and put them to moral use, integrating divine providence and behavioral norms, holding together spirit and letter. Thus the liturgies quoted neither overlook nor prettify Rahab the harlot, but invoke her for a particular purpose. In that way they serve as the proper model for the *integration* of behavioral norms and providential narratives. They invoke the latter to qualify and inculcate the former. Better, the liturgy casts the people *inside* the providential narratives as the context where alone their behavior can begin to make sense before God. It is in such a context that gay and lesbian couples must also place their lives, to make room for going on when they inevitably fail to measure up to their models and vows. It is that context that Eastern Orthodoxy calls, in a delightfully delicate word, the *economy* of salvation. It is the economy of salvation that allows the Holy Spirit to be itself a Rule or Law that gives life.

The pattern to be recovered from the liturgies is this: *everything* is given to human beings for use in God's economy of salvation, or less starkly, nothing is left out; and the economy of salvation is identified by incorporating the community into the biblical narratives. This pattern goes for *nature itself,* as we have seen, in that God conforms nature itself to the economy of salvation in grafting the gentiles onto the Jewish trunk. Not only that: the original nature, which Paul has God contravening for the salvation of the gentiles, is not so much natural in any general, metaphysical sense of the term, as covenantal. What is natural is that God should love the Jews especially. What is unnatural is that God should incorporate the gentiles into that love. The same reasoning might well go for straight and gay. What is natural is that God should love bearers of children, especially bearers of Jewish children: Abraham and Sarah. But God also incorporates into that love gentiles such as Zipporah and Ruth, the childless such as the eunuchs, and delights in irregular pregnancies, such as the ones Matthew singles out as leading to the birth of Jesus, for God's providential purposes.

Gay and lesbian unions can build up the church as well as straight marriages do, with or without children in both cases. Certainly lesbian and gay relationships can exhibit an egoism *à deux,* but they need not, any more than straight ones do. Still, marriage forms that include gay and lesbian couples would make clear that their unions too are from and for the larger community—indeed, if the kingdom of God is like a wedding feast, then it is thus that they represent the Trinity. That leads to my final offering—the charge for a wedding.[76]

Charge for a Wedding

Dearly beloved: We have come together in the presence of God to witness and bless the joining together of these God's human creatures, [N and N], in Holy Matrimony. Marriage signifies the mystery of the love that God bears to human beings, in that God desires, befriends, and keeps faith with us. That love is mysterious to us in that unlike us God *just is* love,[77] an interior community, never lonely, already rich. That love is open to us in that God desires, befriends, and keeps faith in God's very self, as these two desire, befriend, and keep faith with each other. And God's Spirit internally witnesses and blesses and keeps faith with the love in God[78] as today we externally witness and bless the love of these two human creatures in God's image. Today the celebration, blessing, and witnessing of this wedding catches us up into a parable of the inner love and life of God.[79]

In desire God says to us, "You have ravished my heart."[80] God declares of Israel, "I will allure her."[81] As Jacob worked twice seven years for Rachel;[82] as Ruth seduced Boaz upon the threshing floor;[83] as the soul of Jonathan was knit to the soul of David;[84] as these two of God's human creatures desire each other, so God desires us. Grace like desire transforms us by showing us to be perceived in a certain way: as significant, as desired.[85]

In the friendship of the best sort, says Aristotle, the friends make each other better.[86] As Naomi became to Ruth a teacher, and Ruth became to Naomi more than seven sons;[87] as Jonathan prepared David for kingship;[88] as these two befriend each other; so too God says, "No longer do I call you servants . . . but I have called you friends."[89] In friendship God does not merely condescend to be God with us, but God elevates us to be with God. Marriage's friendship too may elevate you so that your "love is patient and kind."[90]

In faith we grant time to desire's risk and friendship's work. Faith sustains the will to let ourselves be formed by the perceptions of another.[91] As Jonathan promised David that "the Lord shall be between you and me, between your posterity and mine forever";[92] as Ruth pledged to follow Naomi till death did them part;[93] so God, too, counts the cost of love for Israel and declares: "I will betroth you to me forever. . . . I will betroth you to me in faithfulness; and you shall know [who I am]."[94]

"Beloved, let us love one another; for love is of God, and whoever loves is born of God and knows God."[95] We are created—and we marry—so that the desire of a spouse, divine or human, may show us to ourselves as occasions of joy.[96] We are created—and we marry—so that the friendship of a spouse, divine or human, may make us worthy of that showing. We are created—and we marry—so that the faithfulness of a spouse, divine or human, may teach us who we are. We are created—and we marry—so that on this wedding day we may be caught up into those things, so that we may grow into the wholehearted love of God by seeing how God loves us as God loves God.[97]

Notes

For constructive comments and fruitful objections on earlier versions of this paper, I wish to thank the Department of Religious Studies at Yale University, especially Marilyn Adams, Gene Outka, David Kelsey, and Wayne Meeks; students and faculty at Duke Divinity School, especially Stanley Hauerwas; the Department of Religious Studies at the University of North Carolina at Greensboro, especially Henry Levinson, Ben Ramsey, and Derek Krueger; other writers in this volume, especially Saul Olyan, Kathryn Tanner, Keith Green, and David Novak; David Yeago; Robert Jenson; and anonymous reviewers for the National Endowment for the Humanities and the National Humanities Center. Thanks also to Rowan Williams for delivering me a copy of "The Body's Grace" before it was easily available in the United States. Errors remain my own.

1. For more detail on "marriage-like unions for gay and lesbian people" compatible with the views of this essay, see David McCarthy Matzko, "Homosexuality and the Practices of Marriage," *Modern Theology* 13 (1997): 391–97, and Rowan Williams, "The Body's Grace," 10th Michael Harding Memorial Address (pamphlet) (London: Institute for the Study of Christianity and Sexuality, 1989), now reprinted in (and cited from) Charles Hefling, ed., *Our Selves, Our Souls and Bodies: Sexuality and the Household of God* (Boston: Cowley Press, 1996), pp. 58–68. For a political argument that deals with religious views, see Andrew Sullivan, *Virtually Normal: An Argument About Homosexuality* (New York: Alfred A. Knopf, 1995).

2. "What is called ethics I regard as the doctrine of the command of God. Hence I do not think it right to treat it otherwise than as an integral part of dogmatics." Karl Barth, *Church Dogmatics,* 4 vols. in 13 bks., trans. G. W. Bromiley et al. (Edinburgh: T. & T. Clark, 1956–75), I/1, xvi.

3. "[R]eligious symbols, dramatized in rituals or related in myths, are felt somehow to sum up, for those for whom they are resonant, what is known about the way the world is, the quality of the emotional life it supports, and the way one ought to behave while in it." Clifford Geertz, "Ethos, World View, and the Analysis of Sacred Symbols," in his *The Interpretation of Cultures* (New York: Basic Books, 1973), p. 127.

4. Karl Barth is, as noted, an exception. For reflections on the general case of how issues of social ethics and dogmatic theology relate in Christian discourse, see Kathryn Tanner, *The Politics of God: Christian Theologies and Social Justice* (Minneapolis: Fortress Press, 1992).

5. Geertz, "Ethos," pp. 14, n. 1, 15, n. 2.

6. Williams, "The Body's Grace," 1989, p. 3, almost identical in Hefling, *Our Selves*, p. 59.

7. Even the Vatican now insists that there is such a thing as a constitutionally "homosexual person," made in the image of God. Congregation for the Doctrine of the Faith, "Letter to the Bishops of the Catholic Church on the Pastoral Care of Homosexual Persons," reprinted in *The Vatican and Homosexuality,* eds. Jeannine Gramick and Pat Furey (New York: Crossroad, 1988), pp. 1–10, passim. The best commentary

is Andrew Sullivan, "Alone Again, Naturally: The Catholic Church and the Homo-sexual," *New Republic,* 28 November 1994, pp. 47, 50, 52, 54–55.

8. Karl Barth, *Church Dogmatics,* III/1, 318. The comment refers in context only to heterosexual marriage.

9. Personal correspondence.

10. Hans W. Frei, "Eberhard Busch's Biography of Karl Barth," in Frei, *Types of Christian Theology,* eds. George Hunsinger and William C. Placher (New Haven and London: Yale University Press, 1992), pp. 147–63; here, p. 158.

11. Thomas Aquinas, *Summa Theologiae,* part 1, question 1, article 8. Hereafter cited as: *ST* 1.1.8.

12. *ST* 1–2.99.2 and 100.2, 5. In saying that life with God is a political matter, I am not recommending theocracy, but simply observing that the human participation in the divine life (II Peter 1:4) is described in political terms.

13. This thesis is defended in Robert W. Jenson and Eric Gritsch, *Lutheranism: The Theological Movement and Its Confessional Writings* (Philadelphia: Fortress, 1976).

14. See, for example, H. George Anderson, T. Austin Murphy, and Joseph A. Burgess, eds., *Justification by Faith: Lutherans and Catholics in Dialogue VII* (Minneapolis: Augsburg, 1985).

15. Karl Barth, *Dogmatics in Outline,* trans. G. T. Thompson (London: SCM, 1949), pp. 53–54, italics added and sentences transposed.

16. Paul Evdokimov, *The Sacrament of Love: The Nuptial Mystery in the Light of the Orthodox Tradition,* trans. Anthony Gythiel and Victoria Steadman (Crestwood, New York: St. Vladimir's Seminary Press, 1985), p. 43.

17. For a recent argument along those lines, with references to Maximus the Confessor and Gregory of Nyssa, see John D. Zizioulas, *Being as Communion: Studies in Personhood and the Church* (Crestwood, New York: St. Vladimir's Seminary Press, 1985), pp. 50–65.

18. Karl Barth, *The Epistle to the Romans,* 6th ed., trans. Edwyn C. Hoskyns (New York: Oxford, 1980), pp. 50–51, reading "human being" for *Mensch.*

19. Charles Hawes, unpublished typescript. Exod. 32:1–6 mentions earrings of both men and women; Gen. 35:4 and Judg. 8:24 connect them with idol worship.

20. Personal correspondence.

21. Sebastian Moore, "The Crisis of an Ethic Without Desire," in his *Jesus the Liberator of Desire* (New York: Crossroad, 1989), p. 104.

22. Cf. ibid., pp. 89–93.

23. Williams, "The Body's Grace," in Hefling, *Our Selves,* p. 64.

24. Robert W. Jenson, *Visible Words: The Interpretation and Practice of the Christian Sacraments* (Philadelphia: Fortress, 1978), pp. 24–25.

25. "The Homosexual Movement: A Response by the Ramsey Colloquium," *First Things* (March 1994): 15–20; here, p. 17.

26. This is the thesis of "Marriage and the Monastic State," in Evdokimov, *The Sacrament of Love,* pp. 65–84. For another call for holiness as the standard for committed, monogamous relationships, gay or straight, see Luke Timothy Johnson, "Debate and Discernment: Scripture and the Spirit," *Commonweal* (28 January 1994): 11–13.

27. Williams, "The Body's Grace," in Hefling, *Our Selves,* p. 59.

28. *ST,* prologue to 1–2.

29. Augustine, *De Trinitate,* bk. 12, chaps. 6–7, nos. 8–9.

30. Quoted in Evdokimov, *The Sacrament of Love,* p. 120, citing simply Chrysostom, *On Marriage.*

31. As I have learned from Richard Hays's article, "Relations Natural and Unnatural: A Response to John Boswell's Exegesis of Romans 1," *Journal of Religious Ethics* 14 (1986): 184–215, which uses it quite differently. For a reply to Hays, see Dale B. Martin, "Heterosexism and the Interpretation of Romans 1:18–32," *Biblical Interpretation* 3 (1995): 332–55.

32. A chapter title in Anselm's *Cur Deus homo.*

33. I owe the phrase, but not its application, to Richard Hays.

34. As I have learned from David Novak.

35. "The Homosexual Movement," p. 19.

36. Michael Satlow, "'Try To Be a Man': The Rabbinic Construction of Masculinity," *Harvard Theological Review* 89 (1996): 19–41.

37. "Although the particular inclination of the homosexual person is not a sin, it is a more or less strong tendency ordered toward an intrinsic moral evil; and thus the inclination itself must be seen as an objective disorder. Therefore special concern and pastoral attention should be directed toward those who have this condition, lest they be led to believe that the living out of this orientation in homosexual activity is a morally acceptable option. It is not." Congregation for the Doctrine of the Faith, "Pastoral Care of Homosexual Persons," no. 3, paragraph boundary elided.

38. See, for example, Robert Gottlieb and Peter Wiley, "The Priesthood and the Black," in *America's Saints* (New York: G. P. Putnam's Sons, 1984), pp. 177–86. See also authoritatively Bruce McConkie, *Mormon Doctrine,* 2d ed. (Salt Lake City, Utah: Bookcraft, 1966; reprint, 1979), s.v. "Negroes." This view was overturned by special revelation to Spencer Kimball in 1978.

39. Quoted from Brigham Young, in Gottlieb and Wiley, "The Priesthood and the Black," p. 178.

40. James Henley Thornwell, *The Rights and Duties of Masters: A Sermon* (Charleston, 1850), p. 44, cited in Robert M. Calhoun, *Evangelicals and Conservatives in the Early South, 1740–1861* (Columbia, SC: University of South Carolina Press, 1988), p. 163.

41. Congregation for the Doctrine of the Faith, "Pastoral Care of Homosexual Persons," nos. 3, 12.

42. For the cases of gentiles and women, see Satlow, cited above. For the case of Presbyterians (for example), see Earnest Trice Thompson, *Presbyterians in the South,* 3 vols., Presbyterian Historical Society Publication Series, no. 13 (Richmond: John Knox Press, 1963–73), 1: 1607–1861, especially the speeches indexed under Thornwell. See also Larry E. Tise, *Proslavery: A History of the Defense of Slavery in America, 1701–1840* (Athens, GA: University of Georgia Press, 1987). For the Vatican, see Congregation for the Doctrine of the Faith, "Pastoral Care of Homosexual Persons," esp. nos. 3, 6. Note that although antiquity lacked a modern-style race theory of slavery, slaves were still constitutionally incapable of keeping the law, so that a male Jew could give thanks that God had not "made" him a woman, a gentile, or a slave.

43. On the last, see most recently, Stanley K. Stowers, *A Rereading of Romans* (New Haven: Yale University Press, 1995).

44. On the purported lability of blacks, for example, see George M. Frederickson, *The Black Image in the White Mind: The Debate on Afro-American Character and Destiny 1817–1914* (New York: Harper and Row, 1971), pp. 250–54, 273–88.

45. For detail, see M. Basil Pennington, "Vocation Discernment and the Homosexual," in *A Challenge to Love: Gay and Lesbian Catholics in the Church,* ed. Robert Nugent, with an introduction by Bishop Walter F. Sullivan (New York: Crossroad, 1984), pp. 235–44.

46. Robert Lewis Dabney, quoted in Calhoun, *Evangelicals and Conservatives,* p. 186.

47. Williams, "The Body's Grace," 1989, p. 3, almost identical in Hefling, *Our Selves,* 59.

48. I have developed these objections from personal correspondence.

49. See Mary Douglas, *Purity and Danger* (London: Routledge, 1966), chaps. 2, 10. For a use of Douglas to address the homosexuality issue, see Jeffrey Stout, "Moral Abominations," chap. 7 in *Ethics After Babel: The Languages of Morals and Their Discontents* (Boston: Beacon Press, 1988), pp. 145–162. Most recently, see Dale B. Martin, *The Corinthian Body* (New Haven: Yale University Press, 1995).

50. See Howard Eilberg-Schwartz, ed., *People of the Body: Jews and Judaism from an Embodied Perspective* (Albany, NY: State University of New York Press, 1992).

51. To readers disturbed to see references to social construction in one paragraph and reality in the next, suffice it to say that Christian theologians have seen that debate before: it is realists versus nominalists all over again. For application, see John Boswell, "Revolutions, Universals, and Sexual Categories," in *Hidden From History: Reclaiming the Gay and Lesbian Past,* eds. Martin Duberman, Martha Vicinus, and George Chauncey (New York: New American Library, 1989), pp. 17–36.

52. E.g., *ST* 1.13.3, 5–6. For a recent defense, see Janet Martin Soskice, *Metaphor and Religious Language* (Oxford: Clarendon, 1985), esp. the final chapter.

53. For a defense of "Father" language for priests as not only compatible with but *requiring* the ordination of women, see Stanley Hauerwas, "Priesthood and Power: What It Means To Be a Father," (unpublished typescript).

54. Caroline Walker Bynum, "Jesus as Mother and Abbot as Mother: Some Themes in Twelfth-Century Cistercian Writing," in *Jesus as Mother: Studies in the Spirituality of the High Middle Ages* (Berkeley: University of California Press, 1982), pp. 110–69.

55. Williams, "The Body's Grace," in Hefling, *Our Selves,* p. 65.

56. Augustine *De Trinitate* 15.19.

57. I owe my attention to this verse to David Yeago.

58. Gregory of Nyssa, *Commentary on the Song of Songs,* homily 13, trans. Casimir McCambley (Brookline, MA: Hellenic College Press, 1987), p. 234; for commentary, see Evdokimov, *The Sacrament of Love,* p. 82.

59. E.g., Matt. 9:15, 22:2.

60. Note for sacrament-counters: This statement does not make marriage an *independent* sacrament, but one that depends upon the Eucharist.

61. Human beings are ontologically female by identification with Mary in Evdokimov, *The Sacrament of Love,* pp. 34–35. For an even more recent example, see Hans Urs von Balthasar, *Theo-drama,* vol. III (San Francisco: Ignatius, 1992), p. 287. For a critique of such notions, see Marilyn Chapin Massey, *Feminine Soul: The Fate of an Ideal* (Boston: Beacon, 1985).

62. Cf. Williams, "The Body's Grace," in Hefling, *Our Selves,* p. 62.

63. "Tomorrow Shall Be My Dancing Day," English traditional carol, in *The Shorter New Oxford Book of Carols,* eds. Hugh Keyte and Andrew Parrott (New York: Oxford, 1993), no. 76.

64. Gary Wills, *Under God* (New York: Simon and Schuster, 1990), p. 293, citing Augustine, *City of God,* 22.24.

65. Williams, "The Body's Grace," in Hefling, *Our Selves,* p. 66.

66. See Thomas E. Breidenthal, "Sanctifying Nearness," in Hefling, *Our Selves,* pp. 46–57.

67. Cf. Williams, "The Body's Grace," in Hefling, *Our Selves*, p. 65.

68. Ibid. Emphasis added.

69. Adrienne von Speyr, *The Word Becomes Flesh,* trans. Wiedenhoever and Dru (San Francisco: Ignatius, 1994).

70. John Boswell, *Same-Sex Unions in Premodern Europe* (New York: Villard Books, 1994).

71. "Grottaferrata gamma," B, 2, trans. in Boswell, *Same-Sex Unions,* p. 296.

72. *Service Book of the Holy Orthodox-Catholic Apostolic Church,* 6th rev. ed., trans. Isabel Florence Hapgood (Englewood, NJ: Antiochene Orthodox Christian Archdiocese of North America, 1983), p. 299.

73. Ibid., p. 304.

74. Ibid., pp. 292–93.

75. Ibid., p. 304.

76. In fact, I read it at a heterosexual wedding but wrote it with both that couple and these considerations in mind.

77. 1 John 4:8b.

78. Matt. 3:17, Mark 1:9–11, Luke 3:21–22, John 1:31–34.

79. Matt. 9:15, 22:2.

80. Song of Sol. 4:9a.

81. Hos. 2:14.

82. Gen. 29.

83. Ruth 3.

84. 1 Sam. 18:1.

85. Williams, "The Body's Grace," in Hefling, *Our Selves*, pp. 59, 65, near quotation.

86. Aristotle *Nichomachean Ethics*, bk. 9, chap. 12, 1172a11–14.

87. Ruth 2:2, 22; 3:1–4; 4:15.

88. 1 Sam. 18–23, esp. 23:17.

89. John 15:15.

90. 1 Cor. 13:4 ff.

91. Williams, "The Body's Grace," in Hefling, *Our Selves*, p. 62, near quotation.

92. I Sam. 20:42.

93. Ruth 1:16–17.

94. Hos. 2:19a, 20.

95. 1 John 4:7.

96. Williams, "The Body's Grace," in Hefling, *Our Selves*, p. 59, near quotation.

97. Ibid.

Response to Max Stackhouse
and Eugene Rogers

KATHRYN TANNER

Protestant Ethics

The essays by Stackhouse and Rogers exemplify the distinctive character of reasoning on moral matters in the mainline Protestant churches.[1] Moral reasoning is fully embedded in a theological context. Theological claims with a bearing on the character of human moral agency—claims, for example, about the order of human affairs that God created, the nature of covenant, the character of sanctification, and the relation between nature and grace—are the primary focus of the two essays. These theological interests set the terms for evaluating the moral status of homosexual relationships, for determining, more specifically, whether the moral standing of homosexual relations warrants their official sanction by marriage rites in Protestant churches.

The theological character of the ethical reasoning present in both papers reflects the fact that moral inquiry in Protestantism does not easily form a separate discipline of intellectual activity independent of theology, the way it may in Roman Catholicism, where moral questions are closely associated with questions of canon law and with the practical needs of the clergy for direction in administering the sacrament of penance. For a great part of its history, Protestant ethics is found completely integrated with systematic theology or is simply part and parcel of the theological treatment of particular Christian doctrines of primary significance to Protestants—for example, justification and sanctification. Theological concerns established the distinctiveness of Protestantism—for example, a concern for justification by faith alone or worries about idolatrous claims for church practices—and therefore those distinctively Protestant theological claims often fueled ethical discussion. Protestant ethics becomes just a way of summing up what it means to live in light of a God who forgives and turns human life around in a completely gracious and free manner.

The fundamentally theological character of Protestant ethics is a consequence, moreover, of the fact that clearly defined institutional bodies with authority on moral matters are not often found in Protestant churches. Protestant reflection on moral matters hasn't the luxury of starting from the established moral teachings of the faith, as these have been promulgated, say, by the magisterium or authorized teaching authorities of the church (as they are in Roman Catholicism). Theological reasoning is not, then, primarily concerned with what properly follows from those established teachings or with an after-the-fact assessment of them by argumentative means. Instead, the Protestant ethicist is always in the position of having first to produce moral judgments by argumentative means. Those moral judgments are always the result of theological argumentation for which, in keeping with the Protestant emphasis on individual conscience, each Christian assumes responsibility. The only thing that authorizes those conclusions, then, is the strength of the arguments that a theologian provides in support of them; the institutional standing of the persons who affirm them does not supply in itself an independent reason for agreeing with them.

Finally, the theological character of its reasoning is a distinguishing mark of Protestant ethics in that its arguments are specifically theological or theological in a strong sense. They are specifically theological, or theological in a strong sense, in that they do not trade on what any experienced or rational person might find plausible, as the natural law arguments commonly found in Roman Catholicism do. While Protestants often affirm the existence of natural law, their ideas about the strongly corrupting effects of sin make them less sanguine about the general accessibility of that law to ungraced reason. Specifically Christian sources of moral insight—primarily the Bible as that place where revelation in Jesus Christ becomes known to us in a normative fashion—therefore figure centrally in Protestant moral reasoning.

Where, as in the essays by Stackhouse and Rogers, such appeals to the Bible for moral direction are not fundamentalist, they involve appeal to concepts and principles that are biblically based—for example, ideas about covenant and the meaning of God's grace. There is no effort to make a direct application of specific biblical passages to modern times, by drawing parallels between the circumstances discussed in the Bible and our own. Instead, one establishes the significance of the Bible for ethical judgments about current affairs by way of more general theological notions and principles that are thought to be true to what the Bible reveals about God, the world, and the human beings in it.[2] Thus, Stackhouse finds in the first few chapters of Genesis a biblically based structure for sexual relations in norms of fidelity, fecundity and family; this "order of creation" for sexual relations forms one of the general theological principles behind his reservations about the morality of homosexual relationships. Similarly in Rogers's case, the idea that God in Christ works graciously in a fashion contrary to nature, an idea which Rogers ties to certain Pauline texts, is a major strand in his advocacy of church-sanctioned gay marriage.

In short, unlike the Roman Catholic employment of natural law arguments in ethics, Protestant ethics is theological in that biblically based theological concepts and principles, which only Christians are initially likely to give credence to, form the linchpin of the arguments.

The absence of clear moral teachings with the institutional backing of Protestantism as a whole, and the theological character of Protestant ethics that goes along with it, make sense of both negative and positive sides of Protestant ethics. On the positive side, they suggest, in the first place, the flexibility of Protestant ethics. Without the restraints of authoritative church teaching, Protestant ethics can adjust to changing situations and to new sources of information—ones, for example, that suggest the need for alterations in the way in which the general theological claims being employed in Protestant ethics are interpreted or applied. Thus, Stackhouse is interested in the way developments in Protestant views of marriage as a covenantal relationship adapt theological ideas to the needs of modern times. The absence in Protestantism of clear institutional direction of theological inquiry generally—Protestant churches have few institutional channels with which to exercise authority over their theologians on any matters, moral or otherwise—means that Protestant theologians such as Rogers can avail themselves rather freely of theological notions that are historically typical of more than Protestantism. His work is quite ecumenical, taking inspiration, for example, as much from Thomas Aquinas as Karl Barth, and expressing interest in Eastern Orthodox sacramentology. Without having to answer in any narrow way to the theological concerns of any particular church tradition, a Protestant ethicist such as Rogers can work very creatively, bringing together and rethinking in the process a variety of theological notions characteristic of the whole history of Christian thought.

Also on the positive side are the capacities of Protestant ethics for self-criticism and change. The diversity of ethical judgment in Protestantism, which is the likely result of independent lines of theological argumentation by different individuals, is a constantly available resource for further controversy and self-questioning. Any agreement about moral matters among Protestants remains, moreover, susceptible to revision by new arguments since the primary authorization for what is agreed upon lies in the quality of the arguments that support it.

On the negative side, the lack of any clear moral teachings distinctive of Protestantism as a whole may suggest that conclusions about moral matters are not matters decided by one's Protestant commitments. Protestants often seem willing consequently to let their ethical judgments be determined simply by principles current in the wider society—for example, the propriety of women's ordination following from the equal rights of women in modern society. Certainly the ease with which Stackhouse and Rogers come to opposite conclusions about the propriety of church-sanctioned gay marriage might give one pause; perhaps it is not reasonable to think that Protestant commitments give a definite shape to ethical judgments, and one should look elsewhere for direction—for example, to the society at large.

The lack of institutional authorization for moral claims can, moreover, lead, not to an increased focus on theologically principled judgment, but to completely ad hoc, unintegrated lines of argument that seem designed to make up for the lack of institutional religious authority for moral claims by appealing to anything and everything that particular audiences might find plausible at the time. Dependent for their authority on whatever their listening public will find persuasive, Protestant moral judgments often seem, in short, to be at the mercy of the diverse perspectives of their audience. The arguments to be found in the documents on sexual ethics produced by Protestant churches have, more often than not, just this sort of purely occasional and scattershot quality to them.

To their credit, the essays of Stackhouse and Rogers represent the general shape of Protestant theological ethics at its best. Each intends to be adaptable and self-critical, while theologically principled in judgments on moral matters. Each believes that theology matters; Christian commitments should make a difference in how one judges the proper character of human relationships.

What Makes a Good Theological Argument in Protestant Ethics

In keeping with the strongly theological character of Protestant ethics, the way Stackhouse and Rogers proceed to make ethical judgments suggests good argument on such matters is primarily a matter of theological "fit." While both are concerned that their conclusions about gay marriage fit in some sense with the experience and beliefs of contemporary people whether Christian or not, the initial claim for the plausibility of those conclusions is based on how well they fit with basic theological notions and principles. Stackhouse argues that gay marriage fits poorly with respect for the structures and norms of the order of creation discussed in Genesis and with the covenant model for heterosexual family life peculiar to Protestantism. Rogers argues that the inclusion of gay men and lesbians in marriage rites fits well with the idea of a sanctified life in God as the ultimate end of marriage and with the free grace of God, which God displays by working contrary to those natural distinctions (between Jew and Gentile, male and female, slave and free) that might otherwise seem to bar the way to inclusion in the divine life.

Protestant judgments about how one should live out one's sexuality clearly change with the times, but both Stackhouse and Rogers are concerned that theological concerns remain in the ascendancy in such judgments. For neither of them, for example, is it proper for the trends of the times to eclipse the force of theological reasoning in Protestant judgments about the propriety of gay marriage. Stackhouse expresses this concern with reference to the willingness of the prophets to condemn the distortion and loss of fidelity to what God demands of us; he posits "the classic [Protestant] tradition," an apparent prior consensus in moral and theological judgment, as a benchmark for the assessment of licit and illicit adaptation to new circumstances, with the clear implication that approval of gay marriage is such an illicit modification. "The classic tradition" has the resources to meet the needs of the time and in that way adapt to them, but it is not proper to repudiate that heritage in the sort of clear violation of basic principles that Stackhouse believes the approbation of gay marriage represents.

Rogers makes no strong claims about any prior theological and ethical consensus—*the* tradition or heritage—that his judgments must remain true to, but he clearly argues on the same grounds as Stackhouse by trying to show that gay marriage is fully compatible with—and therefore no grievous violation of—theological notions and principles that put heterosexual marriage in its deepest religious light. Those basic theological notions and principles have not been so radically modified to permit a fit with gay marriage that they lose all continuity with the meaning they have when used to support the religious sanctioning of heterosexual relations in marriage rites.

Who Has the Better Argument

Rogers and Stackhouse argue past one another to a great extent in that they seem to operate with very different theological interpretations of Christian marriage rites. Rogers views marriage within a context of sanctifying grace; marriage is understood in light of our ultimate end of being incorporated within the divine life of the Trinity. For Stackhouse marriage is proper to the "order of creation" of family life, a particular sphere of human relations with definite connections to others in civil society, in which we are called by God to enjoy our God-given capacities as embodied creatures in a disciplined fashion that both restrains sin and approximates God's directives for holy living. While instituting a religiously significant way of living, the relation of marriage to one's ultimate redemption is not at issue for Stackhouse; the Christian character of daily life in civil society is.

The argument between them turns, then, on fundamentally different theological viewpoints about the relations between nature and grace, creation and salvation. This becomes clear, for example, in cases where the two papers seem to address each other directly. Thus, Rogers can suggest that Stackhouse's refusal to sanction gay marriages is a denial of God's free grace, that such a distinction between gay and heterosexual relations is theologically parallel to the distinctions between Jew and Gentile, free and slave, male and female, that the New Testament says are no bar to God's unexpectedly inclusive work of redemption in Christ. If gay and straight make the kind of difference Stackhouse thinks they do, then Stackhouse's own claim to be redeemed in Christ against nature—that is, against the natural standing of Jews in God's eyes—is also jeopardized. But of course Stackhouse does not have to—and in fact does not—buy into Rogers's account of what is at stake theologically in church-sanctioned marriage: marriage does not have, for Stackhouse, this close a connection with questions about the character of God's grace in Christ. The argument between them is not, then, so much about how to understand homosexuality and about how well or ill that understanding fits with particular theological notions or principles; it is at bottom an argument about which theological principles and notions are appropriate for understanding marriage, an argument that leads directly into wider theological issues about how to understand nature and creation in relation to grace and redemption. Determining who has the better argument about the propriety of homosexual marriage would ultimately turn on determining who has the better understanding of the latter more fundamental theological issues.

"Better" here is not, however, a finally resolvable issue because from a Christian point of view there is nothing radically objectionable about either; these are just two different theological perspectives with long and illustrious pedigrees in the history of Christian thought. (Which is not to say that one might not be able to supply good theological reasons for preferring one over the other; every theologian has to make an informed choice of that sort if these theological perspectives are not compatible with one another. I, for various reasons too complicated to go into now, favor Rogers's basic theological outlook.) One might try to suggest that Stackhouse's theological perspective is more appropriate for a specifically Protestant theological ethics, since the ideas he works with—"order of creation," "covenant"—are more identifiably Protestant that Rogers's. It would be unusual, in other words, for a Roman Catholic ethicist to make those ideas central when considering the propriety of gay marriage. The flexibility of Protestant theology clearly permits, however, Rogers's theological preoccupations; and the ideas about the relation between creation and redemption that his arguments trade on have as much a Protestant heritage as they do a Roman Catholic or Eastern Orthodox one—for example, in the work of Karl Barth, one of the premier Protestant theologians of the twentieth century.

The very existence of arguments such as Rogers's in favor of gay marriage does, however, directly contradict one of the major ways Stackhouse defends his position. On the basis of affirmations of gay marriage that show Protestant ethics at its worst (failings to which, as we have said, Protestant ethics is generally prone, whatever side it is on), Stackhouse strongly suggests that those who favor gay marriage simply cannot be arguing theologically but must be rejecting the relevance of religious traditions in favor of purely nonreligious understandings of social matters. Theological arguments in favor of gay marriage, such as those of Rogers, suggest that there is less theological consensus on this issue than Stackhouse is willing to admit. Or, that if there is a factual consensus—who can deny that for most of church history gay marriages have not been condoned?—it is susceptible to rather stringent theological criticism. The fact of agreement here does not prove that good theological arguments sustain it, any more than the condoning of slavery or the forbidding of women's ordination for most of the church's history needs to.

Despite their differences in specific theological starting points, the general shape of Rogers's argument also contradicts the way that Stackhouse's rhetoric aligns gay sex with the unrestrained desires that covenant and the structures and norms of orders of creation are designed to discipline. If there are theological reasons, like those Rogers supplies, for supporting gay marriage, advocates of it no longer seem to personify the sheer insistence of personal need and impulse in human life; they no longer seem to be proposing, as Stackhouse suggests, that "what feels right should be right" or seem unwilling to recognize that sexuality is subject to sinful distortions. For all their theological differences, Rogers, as much as Stackhouse, thinks of sexuality in terms of its possible contribution to the individual's religious edification and the community's upbuilding; the propriety of sexual relations, gay or straight, is assessed by him in those terms.

If direct comparison between their arguments is difficult, one can still ask who has the better argument on its own terms. That is, one can investigate the degree to which either draws proper consequences from the theological principles with which he works. On this score, Rogers, to my mind, clearly makes the better case; unlike Stackhouse, Rogers's conclusions about gay marriage seem to follow consistently from his own premises.

Despite Stackhouse's disapproval of gay marriage, the theological principles he works with easily suggest that gay relationships are the moral equals of heterosexual ones to the extent that both uphold norms of fidelity, fecundity, and community. It is only when those norms are so narrowly defined as to be inseparable from heterosexual relations that they exclude the moral equivalence of homosexual ones. For example, homosexual partnership could not meet the norm of fecundity were that norm to be identified with sexual relations that are sufficient in and of themselves, at least in principle, of producing children. Only when defined that narrowly would such a norm rule out the propriety of sanctifying homosexual unions entered into with the intention of raising children—say, by means of artificial insemination (a technological innovation about which Stackhouse in principle has no theological reservations). Defining the norms so narrowly that only heterosexual relations fit them is simply question begging. It also suggests a kind of biblical literalism that is incompatible with the use of biblically based theological concepts and principles when interpreting the Bible's directives for today. If a structure of sexual relations is part of the Genesis account, then certainly male-female relations are what is being talked about. But aren't the norms at issue more general than what a simple identification of them with heterosexuality suggests? *Why* is it that homosexual relations cannot be marked by fidelity and restraints on personal impulse? Why is it that they cannot be personally edifying for the individual Christian and a force, like stable heterosexual families, for an ordered civil society? They seem of themselves fully capable of being what heterosexual families are at their best; the major obstacle seems to be the very lack of institutional support for gay fidelity, fecundity, and family that Stackhouse encourages by his repudiation of gay marriage.

Moreover, Stackhouse does not seem to take fully seriously the narrowly defined principles he uses to exclude the propriety of gay marriage: he does not apply those principles in the same way to gay and straight relationships. Stackhouse does make clear that if homosexual partnerships are not the ideal, neither are some straight relationships—for example, those entered into by straight couples unwilling or unable to procreate. Perhaps, as Stackhouse argues elsewhere, homosexual relations are to be suspected of narcissism, as one might presume—unless sexual differences are the only ones that matter—straight relations might be where the bond between persons seems based on similarities of background or need. The impression of fairness here—that Stackhouse applies the same standards to both straight and gay and is prophetically courageous in calling out deviations from the ideal wherever they occur—is undercut, however, by a very obvious point. Straight people, even when they clearly deviate in these ways from the ideal, are able, at least in Protestant churches, to have their relationships officially sanctioned by the church in marriage rites. Gay people—even when they intend to start families and contribute thereby to the stability of a well-ordered civil society, even when they make commitments to one another in hope for the future of the human community, even when bound by ties of fidelity and unselfish in their concern for the well-being of their partners and children—never are.

Stackhouse seems lulled into argumentative complacency by the fact of continuity between his own position against gay marriage and Protestant practice so far. How strong an argument need one make for a position that seems so obviously continuous with past and present practices of the churches? The prophetic witness, which Stackhouse hopes to be true to, is, however, a call to self-criticism as much as it is a call to return to an established norm from which the church is in danger of straying. The Protestant principle, as many Protestant theologians have insisted, is a principle of constant criticism. As the prophets teach, one thing for which religious practices are always to be criticized is a lack of justice. Although the issue of gay marriage may not seem the best example, questions about the standing of gay people in church and society are always at their roots questions about discrimination and oppression. Will one's gifts as a pastor and preacher be allowed to flourish for the upbuilding of the community? Or will the vocation for which one seems so well suited be denied one for no other reason than one's active engagement in sexual relations with a member of the same sex? Must one sustain the hardships of loneliness and broken ties of intimacy that come when one's partner, whom one cannot marry, is deported by the state as an illegal alien? Must one's person and relationships always be judged of less moral worth than others, and therefore be the constant object of negative moral scrutiny, whatever their character, no matter how faithful, loving, and self-disciplined in classic Protestant terms? In my judgment, any Protestant ethicist whose complacency about the propriety of established church practices is not seriously ruffled here by worries about the perpetration of injustice hardly has a good claim to be a faithful proponent of a prophetic witness. If for no other reason than out of concern for the suffering of gay people, one must be sure that longstanding church practices that exclude them from marriage and ministry have only the very best theological arguments on their side. No Protestant ethicist that I know of has satisfactorily met the obligation. Arguments that are question begging and self-contradictory simply will not do.

Notes

1. See James Gustafson, *Protestant and Roman Catholic Ethics* (Chicago: University of Chicago Press, 1978).

2. Ibid., pp. 28–29.

AFRICAN-AMERICAN CHURCHES

Introduction: Three Perspectives on Gays in African-American Ecclesiology and Religious Thought

LEWIS R. GORDON

W. E. B. Du Bois, the dean of African-American scholarship, made a valuable contribution to the study of humankind in 1903, when he counseled his fellow researchers and curious-minded folk to be wary of problematizing the people they study instead of studying the people's problems.[1] We need not here rehearse the many violations of this counsel throughout our century. Du Bois also reminded us in the same text, with perhaps an eye for irony, that the trope through which this admonition was conditioned—the infamous problem of the color line—would be fortified and take on new dimensions in spite of his warning's signaling his hope to be contradicted. The color line has received many commentaries, and it continues to transform and meet the challenge of each generation as it increasingly becomes clear that the color line stands also as a metaphor for our age. Our age is marked, after all, by two dominating motifs that, at the century's end, seem to gain more relevance as their significance continues to be denied by many of us who, perhaps, find responsibility for effecting social transformation too daunting a demand on any age. These motifs are identity and liberation—in other words, questions of who we are and what we should be doing to realize a world in which our identities need not be our liabilities. The color line addresses the identity question, and in that regard, it extends into the realm of excluded humanity. It cries out for social transformation, making liberation its intimate ally: liberation *from* forces that militate against identity recognition; liberation *toward* a world in which difference is not a problem but a celebration, where the problem becomes the failure to appreciate such possibilities.

Could not this difference, this manifestation of the color line, include recognition of the claustrophobic dimensions of heterosexual normativity? How would, or should, African-American ecclesiology be developed in light of such recognition?

The three authors in this section explore these issues in a dialectical exchange of African-American Christian and liberal responses, whose critical synthesis, if we will, is a philosophical reflection on whether a higher thesis is possible. This dialectical dimension is indeed ironic since none of the authors is a dialectical theorist by any stretch of the imagination. The understanding drawn out by each one's case, however, warrants this conclusion by virtue of the dialogical aspirations of these dimensions of contemporary liberal discourse.

But where are African-American homosexuals and lesbians in this dialogue? The identity question forges itself in contemporary theory by virtue of the complexity of gay identity. On the banal level, gay identity is often reduced to gay acts, where the gay person is collapsed into a phobogenic object of uncontrolled genital desire. Homophobia is, after all, precipitated by a theme of anonymity: for the homophobe, the homosexual or the lesbian desires *all members of his or her sex* in general, which makes each member uniquely a target of homoerotic or lesbian desire. This theme overdetermines gay desire into constant, uncontrollable desire, which erases the humanity of the gay person and leaves his or her sexuality as a mark of dysfunctional sex. There is always the "deed."

The arguments that follow explore the deed, or perhaps better the deeds, of gay realization and recognition in an African-American context, and they ask to what extent the overdetermining features of racial oppression have occluded the specificity and consequent humanity of African-American gay Christians. The African-American gay Christian finds him or herself in a complex relation to the many communities to which he or she belongs. The relation is perhaps mar¹ ᵉd by paradox and a healthy realization that human perfection is, in the end, an ideal: whether Christian, gay, American, or African descended, each constellation has its set of limitations that make criteria for membership, in the end, always contingent.

It is membership that animates the concerns of Cheryl J. Sanders in her essay "Sexual Orientation and Human Rights Discourse in the African-American Churches." I will not rehearse the many facets of her argument, since Professor Sanders articulates her position well enough and Professor Hart provides a commentary in his essay. Membership shall be my prime concern here. Sanders's argument is that membership in Christian churches carries with it a presumption of the validity of biblical authority, and biblical authority militates against gay normativity. Moreover, African-American communities suffer from disintegrated family structures—where normal family structures are monogamous, heterosexual households modeled after the bourgeois nuclear family—which call for a struggle against values that will contribute to further deterioration. She argues that most African-American churches' mission is the cultivation of healthy families of faith, which puts advocacy of gay lifestyles—lifestyles that do not foster the nuclear heterosexual family—in opposition to that mission. For the sake of a black family plagued by many social evils, then, Sanders advises a membership policy of existence without advocacy for African-American gay Christians, a policy in sync with the Clinton administration's "don't ask, don't tell" policy for the military.

We may wonder, however, why black families should follow models of bourgeois families when bourgeois families are not antiquated features of basic human relations. Were not ancient northeast African, Semitic, and Mediterranean families, upon which biblical filial values are based, extended families whose models of normality were often very different from bourgeois families'? In her essay, Sanders addresses at least the appeal to extended filial relations by arguing that the root from which these relations spring is the monogamous heterosexual nuclear family. There have, however, been many families premised upon fidelity and heterosexuality but not monogamy. Think, for instance, of traditional African families south and north of the Sahara. That African cultural formations have contributed to African-American cultural practices suggests that the hegemony of monogamy should be considered primarily as a limited Christian position at best.[2] But since Sanders presumes Christian validity, the consideration of whether homosexual and lesbian lifestyles are antipathetic to monogamy is raised. There are monogamous homosexuals and lesbians, and there are those with multiple sex partners. In other words, homosexuals and lesbians are no *more* nor *less* monogamous than, in the least, unmarried heterosexuals. How "married" homosexuals and lesbians would behave is beside the point here, since the United States is a nation in which divorce is permitted. Thus, since failed efforts at monogamy do not for Sanders necessitate elimination of heterosexual hegemony, why should it necessitate rejection of homosexual and lesbian relationships?

An odd feature of membership discussions is that they seem to parallel discussions of antiblack racism. As black families were considered deviant and therefore beyond the pale of normal American membership, so, too, is gay lifestyle. Similarly, as African Americans are often associated with music—nature speaking subliminally, perhaps, through human sites of reduced reason—so, too, is the narrative on gays in African-American churches almost always associated with the gospel choir, the keyboards, and other aspects of the arts. It is as if the androgynous Dionysus—god of wine, women, and tragedy—manifested himself in the art of African-American gospel performance. The gospel chorus is, in other words, a space in which gay (or often effeminate heterosexual) men and heterosexual women commune with God.

Why gay or gay-seeming men?

These essays do not explore the homoerotics of Christian aesthetics and the African polyrhythmic syncretizations that may have led to the near impossibility of *heterosexual* aesthetic presentation: the enthusiasm embodied in black gospel performance is such that it is almost impossible for males to perform that enthusiasm heterosexually. Demanding what African Americans call "getting the spirit," the art form calls for women and men who are willing to let God, in a word, *enter* them. Given the norms of heterosexual masculinity in the United States, such an openness of the self challenges the comfort zones of a structurally homophobic society.[3]

Another question is thus raised: the discourse on black gays, in at least the three succeeding essays, is almost exclusively about the erotics, identity, and recognition of males; the lesbian has been, for the most part, a hidden point of African-American gay iconography.[4] Yet there are African-American churches that have been led by women whose public persona is supposedly nonsexual—that is, unavailable to the allure of males. These women are almost always in traditional male ministrial roles, and nearly never in the festive moment of the choir. Sanders hints at the interests of this group when she discusses the lesbian dimension of "womanism," the term coined by Alice Walker to describe a woman-of-color agenda of being in communion with (and often therefore loving) other women of color. Although womanism may have taken a theological path that centers the experiences of women of color as a liberatory theoepistemology, Sanders suggests that the project may speak to a minority group within black churches, a group whose existential reality was tapped into by the lesbian dimension of the ascription. I do not see how that identification among those women of color is a problematic theoretical move. What is problematic, and is implied by Sanders's discussion, is that the womanist claim as *the* position of women of color is an inaccurate if not simply methodologically flawed position: not all black women are lesbians. Perhaps it should articulate itself as a standpoint theory out of the lesbian of color's experience. Sanders's position of silence, however, suggests at best an abstract mentioning of the lesbian dimension of womanism, which poses an obstacle to its articulation: how could one articulate an actual position of a lesbian of color when one should not ask or tell whether a womanist is a gay woman of color? On this matter, the ecclesial space is encouraged to be a silent one.

Victor Anderson is critical of these silent spaces in his "Deadly Silence: Reflections on Homosexuality and Human Rights," and it is perhaps not accidental that his narrative begins with a tale of the church and the gospel choir. Through a series of events precipitated by an absence of a public sphere for gay congregants to be openly accepted as *gay* congregants, tragic outcomes of alienation, despair, and death emerge. Anderson attributes this absent sphere to a silence on gay issues that militates against gay being: to be openly gay in most African-American churches is, that is, to be a problem. Criteria for membership are often offensive to gay being—demands of atonement and renunciation, which foster increased silence. Anderson advocates a liberal theory of social justice, premised upon natural rights, for gay congregants, where churches are compelled to realize that they need to restructure their positions to meet the dictates of political society. Whatever their religion's demands may be, Anderson argues that the overriding consideration of a liberal society is that they could practice their religion freely so long as they do not violate the laws of the land.[5]

A startling feature of Anderson's analysis is its resolute stand on the age-old tension between civil and political society in the modern state. He advances a natural rights position, which suggests that he is not a legal positivist. Yet his appeal to the natural rights of a human being presents a position that exceeds Christian specificity. Christianity in principle demands compassion, love, and respect for all, but its history, like that of all universalisms, falls prey to the specifics of those who constitute members of the supposedly inclusive "all."[6] The matter of membership now makes a turn to a discourse that dominates nearly all discussions of gay identity: whether gay lifestyles are "natural." In recent theories of culture, the notion of the natural has been questioned through an array of social and post-structural critiques. In an antiquated and medieval Christian universe, the natural meant simply a creation of God, but since God is attributed with creating everything—by virtue of omnipotence, omnipresence, omniscience, and benevolence—a theodicy of the unnatural emerged: sin, we are often reminded, is a feature of humanity's freedom; freedom is often abused in spite of its origins as an act of grace.[7] That theological discussions of homosexuality have focused on homosexuality as sin has locked gays in the world of the unnatural. It is no wonder that a discourse on the naturalness of being gay—that is, not having *chosen* being gay but having been *born* gay—has dominated gay resistance to the charge of violating nature. The defense is, however, a "Catch 22," for in denying that there is something intrinsically wrong with being gay, one need also assert that one would choose to be gay if one were to have the choice. It is an existential positioning of a simple ethical challenge: is not part of loving oneself the willingness to choose, eternally, to be oneself?

William Hart taps into this question of nature in his essay, "Sexual Orientation and the Language of Higher Law." He is concerned that discussions on gays usually lead to notions of nature versus culture, the natural versus the constructed. For Hart, human beings are natural existents; consequently, there is nothing unnatural about things they produce, especially culture. In that regard, there is nothing unnatural about gays, and appeals to their naturalness obscure discussion of how to relate to them in community. Although he does not spell out the theodicean dimensions of this position—of comporting God, the omnipotent source of the natural, with the biblical rejection of certain dimensions of God's creations' deeds—Hart criticizes Sanders and Anderson for appealing to notions of higher nature in their assessments of gay advocacy in the church. Sanders rejects it on the basis of the supposedly natural and higher injunctions of heterosexual hegemony; Anderson supports it on the basis of supposedly natural and higher injunctions of political society. Hart's move is what is called these days a *deconstructive* move, where he asks us to go beyond the language of the high and the low in our emancipatory projects. I wonder, however, whether a religious intervention could any longer be made when the high has been decentered.

Black churches have faced many challenges. Historical narratives of these churches as emancipatory institutions are equally matched by narratives of them as oppressive, conservative mediators between black and white communities.[8] In truth, there is not a single narrative that captures the prescriptive force of these churches beyond their sociological role of providing spaces for membership, belonging, community. In other words, they fulfill the same basic functions that all religious institutions provide their members by simply being available to them. Black churches have, however, unique cultural resources for African Americans in particular, and Americans in general, that lead to cultural hybridizations that constantly raise questions of alternatives. In the end, we discover that African-American churches are also *American* churches, and in that regard, they have the same strengths and weaknesses as other American institutions. Making them better places of worship contributes to making American society a better place. The reality is that some houses of worship are more amenable to such projects than others. Everyone has stories of compassion and hate, as I shall now, in closing, relate.

Some years ago I visited a cousin whose kidneys no longer functioned after his three-year struggle with AIDS. My cousin sat up, alert, looking ahead as the dying do. I have seen that look too often; it is similar to airline passengers on standby. He wiped away a tear that was trickling down his cheek.

"Black men got it bad in this town," he said.

Just then, a nurse opened the door. She knelt, her hand carefully protected by latex gloves, and shoved a tray of food along the floor into the room. The door gently closed behind her.

My cousin didn't make a fuss. His eyes, holding onto his dignity as best he could, said a lot. He looked at the tray. For him, feeling sorry for himself required resentment, which he refused to feel. I decided to change the subject. I climbed onto his bed, held him in my arms, and brought up the driving lessons I gave him over a decade before, the mishaps we endured as he struggled on more than one occasion to obtain his driver's license, and his membership in the world of licensed drivers.

"I only have six weeks," he declared. "Six weeks."

Six weeks later, there he lay. The funeral home was so packed that another wing was opened. Nearly all of the family and many friends were there. I gave the eulogy, but there were others who spoke spontaneously. A friend spoke, mentioning how much he loved my cousin and how he wished he had had the opportunity to say goodbye. Unlike my cousin, who died in the company of family, his friend died alone and was not accepted, even in death, by his mother.

My cousin was a private fellow who, although not a bisexual man in the closet, did not feel that his sex life was any one's affair but his own. Why do I relate my last experiences with him? I relate them because I am concerned by the argument, espoused by Anderson, that an injustice is done to a gay person if any gay advocacy is not included in his or her eulogy. I do not know what it means to eulogize someone as gay, black, female, or working class outside of, say, its relevance to a political life focused on alleviating the suffering of gay, black, female, or working-class people. Most eulogies are, in the end, family affairs—where family could be anything from one's biological relations to one's closest friends to members of one's most devoted communities to one's lovers—which means that they will carry ethical dimensions of their own.

Churches, like all institutions, function according to who counts as one of their own. The three portraits of these struggles over advocacy's relation to membership are far from exhaustive. It is hoped, however, that the lively debate stimulated by these three religious thinkers will have an impact on the public debate about communities of love, where, perhaps, less time will be wasted as so many continue to seek membership in beloved, albeit imperfect, communities.

Notes

1. See W. E. B. Du Bois, foreword to *The Souls of Black Folk*, with a new introduction by Randall Kenan (New York: Signet/Penguin, 1995).

2. The history of the Mormons, of course, not withstanding.

3. For discussion, see Lewis R. Gordon, "Can Men Worship? Reflections on Male Bodies in Bad Faith and a Theology of Authenticity," in *Men's Bodies, Men's Gods: Male Identities in a (Post-) Christian Culture*, ed. Björn Krondorfer (New York and London: New York University Press, 1996), pp. 235–50.

4. See Audre Lorde's open letter to Mary Daly in *Sister Outsider: Essays and Speeches*, with an introduction by Nancy K. Bereano (Freedom, CA: The Crossing Press, 1983).

5. Anderson was not able to develop his position here, but for such a treatment of his position on African-American religious thought's relation to American political society, see his *Beyond Ontological Blackness: An Essay on African American Religious and Cultural Criticisms* (New York: Continuum, 1995), and for a critical discussion of this work, see Lewis R. Gordon, "Pan-Africanism, Womanism, and Postmodernism: Three Dimensions of Recent African American Religious Thought," *Religious Ethics* (forthcoming).

6. See Tzvetan Todorov, *The Conquest of America: The Question of the Other*, trans. Richard Howard (New York: Harper Perennial, 1984).

7. The classical statement on theodicy and sin is St. Augustine's *The City of God*, trans. Marcus Dods, with an introduction by Thomas Merton (New York: Modern Library, 1950). For a contemporary, poststructural discussion of St. Augustine's position as also embedded in language itself, see Katherine Rudolph's "This Body of My Dreams: Augustine and Descartes on the Body of Language," (Ph.D. diss., The Johns Hopkins University, Humanities Institute, 1996).

8. For discussion, see Lewis R. Gordon, "God in an Antiblack World," pt. 4 of *Bad Faith and Antiblack Racism* (Atlantic Highlands NJ: Humanities Press, 1995).

Sexual Orientation and Human Rights Discourse in the African-American Churches

CHERYL J. SANDERS

I will begin by addressing in very broad strokes the history and tradition of the African-American religious community with respect to same-sex orientation, preference, and conduct. What follows is an outline of a moral stance that argues for strong prescriptive advocacy of covenanted monogamous heterosexual unions in light of the ongoing disintegration of family and parenting structures in the African-American community. I will conclude by noting some key implications of this particular moral stance for African-American participation in the formulation of law and public policy regarding legal protection from discrimination on the basis of same-sex domestic partnerships.

My own assessment of the history and tradition of the African-American churches with respect to this issue in "broad strokes" is so broad that it merits only one stroke—that these churches have generally frowned upon homosexuality on the ground of Scripture. However, since the time of their inception during the late eighteenth century, the African-American churches have contributed significantly to the various liberation struggles undertaken by black people in a white racist society, including also the nineteenth-century abolitionist movement and the twentieth-century civil rights movement. While the sexual conduct of gays and lesbians has not been endorsed by most of the African-American religious community, the quest for human dignity and civil rights has been viewed as all-inclusive. Analogous to this position is the treatment of women in the African-American churches; while there remains a strong resistance to accepting the full equality of women in the church, especially in leadership roles requiring ordination, few have argued against the right of women to equal treatment and access in the public sphere. In view of the fact that gays and lesbians have participated in the life of these churches at all levels, perhaps most visibly in music ministries, the general ecclesial stance of black churches can perhaps best be described as acceptance without advocacy. In their recent sociological study of the black church, C. Eric

Lincoln and Lawrence H. Mamiya address the church's involvement in civil rights and the ordination of women, but do not give any attention to human sexuality as an issue of concern.[1] The fact that they fail to address the issue at all in their otherwise comprehensive survey of black clergy can be regarded as a reflection of a widespread reluctance to draw attention to these concerns.

There are some noteworthy exceptions to this trend among black clergy. The Reverend Jesse Jackson, a civil rights activist and Baptist clergyman, made a televised statement a few years ago affirming the rights and dignity of gays and lesbians in response to a viewer's question as posed by talk show host Arsenio Hall. The late Dr. James S. Tinney was an advocate for gay and lesbian issues in the Pentecostal churches. He taught journalism at Howard University, edited *Spirit*, a journal of black Pentecostal studies, and was the founding pastor of Faith Temple, a Pentecostal congregation in Washington, D.C., that welcomed gay and lesbian members. In 1977 he published an analysis of the ecclesiological and theological implications of homosexual practice among Pentecostals entitled "Homosexuality as a Pentecostal Phenomenon."[2] He died of AIDS in 1986. Curiously, Tinney's work has been virtually ignored by contemporary black scholars who have assumed a liberal posture with respect to same-sex orientation and practice in the context of religion. Generally speaking, it seems now to be the rule and not the exception for contemporary black religious scholars to align heterosexism with racism and sexism as sins of oppression in their published works. Even so, I have not observed in the growing body of literature in the study of black religion much forthright advocacy of gay and lesbian issues beyond the act of naming the sins of homophobia and heterosexism and seldom, if ever, any detailed analysis of the theological and ethical dimensions of the problem.

My own moral stance with regard to same-sex orientation, preference, and conduct reflects the ambivalence of the black church, but is ultimately grounded in my commitment to the holiness tradition. I am an ordained minister in the Church of God (Anderson, Indiana), an interracial religious body whose black congregations constitute an estimated 25 percent of the total number of churches in the United States. The General Assembly, the church's highest decision-making body of ministers, passed a resolution in 1979 articulating the church's opposition to homosexuality based upon a commitment to "biblical holiness," "high regard to scriptural injunctions against homosexuality," the conviction that "homosexuality is sin," and firm opposition to the "licensing, ordination, or approving of persons in leadership actively involved in this life-style."[3] Although I was not present and did not vote, I am in agreement with this position.

First, my commitment to biblical holiness is grounded in the view that the Bible presents holistic models and mandates for holiness as the integration of three distinct areas of spiritual accountability: individual morality, proper worship, and social justice. This view is informed by John Gammie's comprehensive study of holiness in the Old Testament: "for the different groups of religious persons within Israel—prophets, priests and sages—the kind of cleanness required by holiness varied. For the prophets it was a cleanness of social justice, for the priests a cleanness of proper ritual and maintenance of separation, for the sages it was a cleanness of inner integrity and individual moral acts."[4] As Christians, and especially as leaders of faith communities, we are called to practice lifestyles that are consistent with our communities' highest moral standards for personal piety, ecclesial authenticity, and prophetic social response.

Second, I do hold in "high regard" the several scriptural injunctions against homosexuality, and recognize that the Bible is very consistent in its witness against homosexual practice as sin. However, I am neither enlightened nor persuaded by most of the sources I have consulted that purport to offer critical exegesis and modern interpretations of Scripture on this issue. On the contrary, I have been profoundly disappointed to discover the extent to which both liberal and conservative interpreters engage in what I would call proof-texting to support their claims on behalf of same-sex conduct. In my opinion, proof-texting always means what others do with the Bible to support views we don't affirm. Among liberals I detect a tendency to negate the relevance of each and every biblical text on the grounds of cultural specificity or other contextual limitations. On the other hand, conservative interpreters sometimes cite Scriptures referring to same-sex practices without fully examining what God requires of Christians today in light of what God required in ancient times.

One recent work in biblical ethics I have found helpful is *The Moral Vision of the New Testament* by Richard Hays. Hays's text begins with a broad but compelling survey of the ethics of the New Testament as articulated in the Epistles, the Gospels, and the book of Revelation. He discerns therein three major themes or, to use his terminology, focal images: community, cross, and new creation. He uses these concepts to construct a hermeneutical or interpretive strategy for addressing several contemporary ethical dilemmas from the vantage point of biblical ethics. In the chapter on homosexuality, Hays claims that the few biblical texts that address homosexual behavior "are unambiguously and unremittingly negative in their judgment."5 The texts cited are Genesis 19 (the story of Sodom and Gomorrah); Leviticus 18:22 and 20:13 (prohibitions against male same-sex intercourse in the Holiness Code); I Corinthians 6:9–11, I Timothy 1:10, Acts 15:28–29 (lists including homosexuals among persons who do things unacceptable to God); and Romans 1:18–32 ("the only passage in the New Testament that explains the condemnation of homosexual behavior in an explicitly theological context"). Hays notes that the Genesis story is irrelevant to the topic: "the gang-rape scenario exemplifies the wickedness of the city, but there is nothing in the passage pertinent to a judgment about the morality of consensual homosexual intercourse." He adds, however, that the "clearest statement about the sin of Sodom" is found in Ezekiel 16:49—namely, the failure of the affluent to aid the poor.6 Although the question of homosexual behavior is not directly addressed in the Gospels, there and throughout the rest of the Bible it is affirmed repeatedly that "God has made man and woman for one another and that our sexual desires rightly find fulfillment within heterosexual marriage."7

Regarding the ordination of homosexuals, Hays argues that it is arbitrary to single out homosexuality as a special sin that precludes ordination, and goes on to conclude that "a person of homosexual orientation seeking to live a life of disciplined abstinence would clearly be an appropriate candidate for ordination."8 He frames his entire discussion of homosexuality and the Bible in terms of the story of his friendship with a college friend who, while dying from AIDS, engaged Hays in a biblical and theological dialogue on homosexuality. Hays presents this chapter of the book as an act of keeping covenant—that is, the completion and publication of an exchange of ideas between friends.

No reference is made to the black church per se in Hays's discussion of homosexuality, but it would have been illuminating had he attempted to show how the three focal images—community, cross, and new creation—can be brought to bear on the treatment of homosexuals in the black church. Such an illustration is provided in the chapter on abortion, where Hays shows how the gospel is embodied in the witness of a black church and pastor whose opposition to abortion entails making provision for teenage girls and their babies in terms of the three focal images: community (assuming responsibility for the teenager), cross (enduring shame and making sacrifices in the interest of the child), and new creation (administering grace and hope through the sacrament of baptism).[9] Indeed, there are numerous black churches and pastors who administer pastoral care and support to persons living with AIDS, and who conduct funerals and memorial services for persons who have died from AIDS with words of comfort and hope rather than guilt and condemnation.

While I remain opposed to the licensing, ordination, or approving of persons in leadership "actively involved in this lifestyle," I also believe that whatever inquiry is made into sexual conduct ought to be equally applied to all, regardless of sexual orientation or marital status. My impression is that married heterosexual clergy probably commit most of the sexual misconduct that occurs in the churches. It does seem unfair for a church to deny ordination to a homosexual while readily ordaining a heterosexual womanizer, for example. Outward conformity to socially acceptable sexual convention does not necessarily signify adherence to the church's sexual norms. The much maligned policy developed by the Clinton administration in relation to gays and lesbians in the military, "don't ask, don't tell," perhaps is an accurate description of what actually occurs when decisions concerning ordination and pastoral appointments are made in a church where same-sex conduct is not advocated, but sexual conduct in general is not necessarily subjected to careful scrutiny.

As a pastor of a local church, my policy is not to seek out and condemn gays and lesbians, but rather to advocate and encourage heterosexual monogamy as the optimal structure for family life both inside and outside the church. Each weekday morning our church extends hospitality to a diverse mix of poor people, largely from the streets and homeless shelters of Washington, including gays, lesbians, cross-dressers, and heterosexuals whose lifestyles are not in harmony with our commitment to holiness. Some participants are HIV-positive or have AIDS, but they receive no special treatment beyond the compassion extended to anyone with a disease or disability. We occasionally offer HIV testing and counseling in our sanctuary. We do not use sexual orientation, preference, or conduct as criteria for admission to our services. However, any person who desires to become actively involved as a member of our church "in good standing," especially in a leadership capacity, is expected to conform to the church's moral teachings with respect to sexual conduct. It remains important for me as a pastor to find ways to welcome, affirm, and include persons who visit our church but who may not conform to our moral norms, to treat them as persons worthy of dignity and respect whether I approve of their sexual conduct or not.

In 1989 I wrote an article for the *Journal of Feminist Studies in Religion* that served as the centerpiece for a roundtable discussion by womanist scholars. In that piece I raised questions concerning the suitability of the term "womanist" as a label for Christian theological and ethical works, in view of the fact that Alice Walker originally coined the term as an alternative to "black lesbian." I expressed my own ambivalence about the womanist concept, not because of any disagreement with what Walker intended by it but, rather, based upon my own pastoral concern for advocating heterosexual monogamy within the African-American community. That article elicited angry responses from the womanist scholars who participated in the roundtable, and also from others who did not, but who have felt it necessary to condemn my views.[10] I remain ambivalent about the suitability of the womanist nomenclature for my own academic work, but in 1995 I published an anthology of womanist theological scholarship, *Living the Intersection: Womanism and Afrocentrism in Theology*. I am unwilling to embrace too tightly any label or identity that compromises my personal and pastoral witness on behalf of marriage and dual parenting partnership as structures that promote the survival and wholeness of men, women, and children in the African-American community and beyond. In other words, my endorsement of the ends of womanist thought and action is governed by my adherence to sexual norms associated with evangelical Christianity.

In my opinion, the strongest rational argument that can be offered against same-sex orientation, preference, and conduct—without specific reference to Scripture or revelation—flows from the observation that in the African-American community in particular, and also in society at large, the ethic and practice of sexual freedom have seriously undermined the stability of families and their parenting structures during the past three decades. This is not to suggest that gays and lesbians are to blame for the demise of the black family; rather, it is to state that if nobody is willing to support and encourage the formation of covenanted heterosexual monogamous units where the emotional, educational, and economic needs of children and adults can be fulfilled, then the rampant antisocial behavior of adolescents and young adults that has terrorized our neighborhoods and schools will certainly increase. There are many voices in the black community that would celebrate the strengths of the extended family as a support for all our children, but I would argue that if everybody rejects the institution of marriage, so that nobody ever marries anybody, then the extended family will ultimately collapse. Our basic notions of kinship—father, mother, grandmother, grandfather, brother, sister, aunt, uncle, cousin—all presuppose some form of marital relationship in the family tree. In fact, heterosexual marriage is the trunk of the family tree.

It seems obvious that one key to reversing the demise of the black family is to model and advocate an ethic of fidelity that is binding both for sexual partners and for parents and children. I agree with Don Browning that advocacy of homosexuality, bisexuality, and the "softening and blurring of the boundaries of sexual activity would offer little benefit to other basic human needs . . . [and] would certainly exacerbate the already deteriorated condition of the basic environment provided today for the raising of children."[11] I disagree with feminist theologian Mary E. Hunt that an ethic of "sexual integrity" only requires doing the best we can to "love well," and enables us to substitute mutuality, consent, and pleasure for concerns about orientation, identity, and preference.[12] My own concept of sexual integrity envisions the activity of "loving well" in a relationship of mutuality, consent, and sensual pleasure, but roots this activity in an eternal covenant with the Creator of male and female, a confession of the gospel of Jesus Christ as a word of reconciliation and redemption, a lifelong commitment to one's spouse in light of the teachings of Jesus, and an obligation to ensure that our sexual choices do not subvert our best efforts to encourage our children to become mature and responsible adults. Marriage means forfeiting our rights to sexual freedom in exclusive pursuit of sexual and personal fulfillment in relation to one similarly committed partner of the opposite sex. In this regard, my thinking is more in harmony with the thought of ethicist Lisa Sowle Cahill, who has argued that the "relationality of sex is fulfilled most perfectly in the parenthood of spouses, situated within an intergenerational family network which opens out onto and participates in the common good of the community as a whole."[13]

The advocacy of covenanted heterosexual relationships in the African-American churches and community bears several important implications with respect to African-American participation in the formulation of law and public policy regarding legal protection from discrimination on the basis of same-sex domestic partnerships. Notwithstanding the important role religious language and networking played in Marion Barry's successful bid to regain the office of mayor of Washington, D.C., in November 1995, on a platform of redemption and recovery after being convicted and incarcerated for illegal drug use in the company of a woman with whom he had an extramarital affair, there are occasional clashes between conservative black religious leaders and liberal politicians over human rights issues. Several black ministers have been active participants in public debates about domestic partnership legislation and the repeal of sodomy laws; most seemed to oppose these initiatives on the ground of scriptural injunctions against homosexual practices. In public discussions the black churches sometimes get blamed for contributing to the HIV-AIDS problem, but at the same time are criticized for promoting abstinence and counseling against the various sexual practices that put persons most at risk. At present, the most pressing concern facing the city of Washington in the era of welfare reform is the reduction of social services to the poor while middle class taxpayers and businesses flee to the suburbs. The vast majority of children in that city live with one parent or with neither parent, and the prevailing ethos seems to endorse the sexual freedom of adolescents and adults who will not or cannot provide for the needs of the children produced as a direct consequence of their sexual choices. Although most churches accept single parents and their children without condemnation, as they ought, in my view the churches represent the last bastion of advocacy and support for marriage and dual parenting in the community. Even if the black churches' objections to liberal public policies regarding same-sex partnerships resound as a "voice crying in the wilderness" of libertine sexual ethics, their ongoing role as enablers of stable, nurturing families makes a significant contribution to public life.

Notes

1. C. Eric Lincoln and Lawrence H. Mamiya, *The Black Church in the African American Experience* (Durham, NC: Duke University Press, 1990).

2. James S. Tinney, "Homosexuality as a Pentecostal Phenomenon," *Spirit* 1, no. 2 (1977): 45–59.

3. "Stand Against Homosexuality," June 1979 General Assembly Resolution, *Annual Reports 1982*, Executive Council, Church of God (Anderson, IN), pp. 29–30.

4. John G. Gammie, *Holiness in Israel* (Minneapolis: Augsburg Fortress, 1989), pp. 195–96.

5. Richard B. Hays, *The Moral Vision of the New Testament* (San Francisco: Harper San Francisco, 1996), p. 381.

6. Ibid.

7. Ibid., p. 390.

8. Ibid., p. 403.

9. Ibid., pp. 459–60.

10. See Kelly Brown Douglas, *The Black Christ* (Maryknoll, NY: Orbis Press, 1994), and Gayraud S. Wilmore and James H. Cone, *Black Theology: A Documentary History,* vol. 2 (Maryknoll, NY: Orbis Press, 1992).

11. Don S. Browning, *Religious Ethics and Pastoral Care* (Philadelphia: Fortress Press, 1983), p. 94.

12. Mary E. Hunt, "Sexual Integrity," *Waterwheel* 7, no. 3 (Fall 1994): 2.

13. Lisa Sowle Cahill, *Women and Sexuality* (Mahwah, NJ: Paulist Press, 1992), p. 78.

Deadly Silence: Reflections on Homosexuality and Human Rights

VICTOR ANDERSON

The black homosexual is hard-pressed to gain audience among his heterosexual brothers; even if he is more talented, he is inhibited by his silence or his admissions. This is what the race has depended on in being able to erase homosexuality from our recorded history. The "chosen" history. But these sacred constructions of silence are futile exercises in denial. We will not go away with our issues of sexuality. We are coming home.

—Essex Hemphill, *Brother to Brother*

I

About twenty years ago, when I was a young minister in Chicago, I befriended one of my Sunday school students. Because of the sensitive nature of the case and the secrecy under which he lived, I will simply refer to him by the letter S. S was a very bright, creative, and popular teenager. He had excellent grades and was active in our church as the director of the youth choir. He was also black and gay. In the early seventies, not many of us knew anything about the word *gay*. However, in the idiom of his times and community, S was a sissy. In the black churches, sissy is a euphemism for "faggot." Only a few of us knew S's secret. His popularity and active participation in the church led him to conceal his sexual identity from his family, friends, and church.

I had known S's terrible secret. I talked with him, and he would talk with me about his feelings and fears. They were expressed more as anxieties or worries than as declarations. One was expected to read between the lines. If one were "in the life," one was expected to recognize who was gay either by some magic of sexual intuition or by an a priori understanding of the codes and signs uttered in quiet conversation or overt actions such as how one talked, walked, or twirled one's wrist. I must admit that I first approached S when I saw our church organist, a well-aged black gay man, constantly pursuing and playing around with young boys like him in the church. When they would not yield to his temptations, I also saw the organist ruin the reputations of those boys and their relationships with their girlfriends and friends with his vicious gossip. He was indiscriminate. He simply liked boys, whether straight or gay. But his cruelties were mainly targeted toward boys whom he thought were gay. S had become a target of his seductions, rage, and eventual scandal, just as I had seen other boys become his victims, and just as I myself was one of his victims when I was a teen.

I had not talked to S for a while. As a youth minister, I busied myself studying the Bible, attending prayer meetings and fellowship, and was busy with church stuff. I began to hear from S's friends and parents that he was becoming withdrawn and that his grades were declining. He had only to complete the spring quarter of high school to graduate. However, on a spring day in April, only a couple of months before his scheduled graduation, I received a phone call that has haunted me to this day. S was found dead in the basement of his home. He was 16 years old and dead from a self-inflicted bullet to his head. As the youth worker and his Sunday School teacher, I was asked to say a few words at his funeral. I could only say that graduation day had come for S. These were my words as I looked at the organist as he played for the funeral. I asked myself how many more boys like S would have to encounter him and how many would not healthily survive his seductions. Of the many reasons that may have contributed to S's death (peer pressure, his popularity in a heterosexual black mainstream, and his lack of mentors), I have always suspected that S's inability to come to terms with being black and gay led him into a silence that ended with a gunshot.

This was my first encounter with the violent, deadly consequences of homosexual silence in the black community. I know now that S's death was not a single, isolated case.[1] Behind the doors of many black homes are countless persons living in sexual secrecy, shame, silence, and violence. As a number of social scientists have noted, scientifically measuring homosexuality among any population is difficult. However, this is a particularly difficult problem among African Americans, who are usually excluded from major statistical research studies on sexuality.[2] Most researchers on homosexuality agree that there is a dire need to develop research models for the study of sexual behavior and preferences among African Americans.[3] However, available resources are mostly anecdotal, journalistic, and literary. In this regard, Essex Hemphill, who contributed much to the development of black gay literature in the United States, suggests that the silence that eventually led to S's suicide is a deeply entrenched fact of black gay and lesbian life. Referring to Joseph Beams's *In the Life: A Gay Anthology*, Hemphill says, "If I had read a book like *In the Life* when I was fifteen or sixteen, there might have been one less mask for me to put aside later in life."[4] He continues: "There would have been one less mask for me to create when long ago it became apparent that what I was or what I was becoming— in spite of myself—could be ridiculed, harassed, and even murdered with impunity. . . . Come out at your own risk was the prevailing code for boys like myself who knew we were different, but we didn't dare challenge the prescribed norms regarding sexuality for fear of the consequences we would suffer."[5]

It has been some twenty years since S's death. And the climate of pervasive silence that once characterized homosexuality in the United States has been challenged by the revolutionary impulses of the gay liberation, gay pride, and gay civil rights movements of the seventies and eighties.[6] These movements made the civil rights of homosexuals public discourse. Like so many other minority Americans, African-American gays and lesbians are the beneficiaries of these movements, which broke open secret hiding places, turned the shame of homosexuality to pride, and helped create in our various communities openness toward gays and lesbians in the United States. However, a number of writers remind us that for too many African-American gays and lesbians today, it is still not safe to come out of the sexual closets in their homes, jobs, neighborhoods, and churches. I think that there are a number of factors that contribute to this silence, factors that too often characterize the lives of black gays and lesbians. I want to focus on two factors: the cult of black masculinity and religious homophobia.

II

In *Beyond Ontological Blackness: An Essay on African American Religious and Cultural Criticism* (1995), I offered a critique of a racial, moral discourse that I described as the "Cult of Black Masculinity." My critique was based on a retrieval of the Latin root of *virtue. Virtue* is derived from Latin *virtus*, meaning "maleness," "worth," "valor." Sometimes *virtus* is translated as "manliness." I criticized what I saw as a pervasive preoccupation of black intellectuals with the classical, heroic virtues of courage, manliness, strength, self-determination, and racial loyalty in their attempts to establish normative requirements for authentic race consciousness and criteria for the moral valuation of one's membership in the black community. I metaphorically described these preoccupations as a "cult of black masculinity." That is, I sought to expose the ways that black cultural studies (literary criticism, art, history, philosophy, and religion) have defined and evaluated representations of black life in terms of classical masculine virtues.

The virtues stipulated in the cult of black masculinity inscribe on black moral consciousness a hierarchy of virtues that favors race loyalty and the good of the race over one's loyalties to gender or sexual goods. It favors an unmitigated commitment to race over the claims that one's sexual desires, preferences, and orientation make on one's communal choices. When African-American identities are defined morally in terms of the cult of black masculinity, blackness becomes "a totality that takes narrative formations that emphasize the heroic capacities of African Americans to transcend individuality and personality in the name of black communal survival."7 I also proposed that cultic devotion to these moral virtues often "conceals, subjugates, and calls into question African Americans' interests in fulfilled individuality."8

The virtues of black masculinity circumscribe African Americans' gender and sexual interests and provide an overarching depiction of black moral consciousness. The virtues of masculinity exhibit a universality that transcends the particularities of black women's commitments to each other when they are threatened by domestic abuse and violence, and encounter sexual harassment by black men. And they trump the preferences of black gays and lesbians for sexual association and the fulfillment of their desires for same-sex unions. In the cult of black masculinity, the "race man or woman" becomes the moral hero of the community. He or she is strong, self-determined, conscientious, and uncompromising in his or her commitment to the good of the race in all of her or his endeavors. The ritualized practices of the cult are also played out in a hierarchical evaluation of the vocational choices that blacks make.

Devoted to the virtues of manliness that led them to the professional fields of higher education, law, medicine, politics, and ministry (whether males or females), these members of the metaphorical "talented tenth" are counted among the best of the race when their endeavors are rationalized and justified as signs of their personal struggles for and commitments to racial uplift. Moreover, while highly valued throughout this century, blacks in the arts and entertainment fields continue to form today, as they did in the early decades of this century, a subculture of black life (the celebrity class). Yet, in black expressive culture, moral valuations of this celebrity class also continue to be accessed by the cultic virtues of black masculinity. That is, figures such as Michael Jackson, Tina Turner, Michael Jordan, and Tiger Woods, to name a few, are usually celebrated in and by the major organs of the black media for their race loyalties—that is, insofar as they are role models of authentic, black moral consciousness.

If our intellectuals, politicians, ministers, and lawyers are gays and lesbians— and many are—their sexual identities too often remain of secondary importance in their public discourses, owing to the often discriminatory and alienating experiences that homophobia creates. However, the sites of the arts and entertainment are the context of sexual toleration. They are the normative places where the rhetorical affirmation that "we have always had gays and lesbians in the black community" prevails. Moreover, black presses, magazines, and electronic journals tend to select black heroes of the month from among the black professional and celebrity classes and the criteria remain the morals of black masculinity. I contend that the silence among these classes of black teachers, politicians, physicians, lawyers, ministers, and many in the arts and entertainment about the legitimacy, value, alienation, and sufferings of black gays and lesbians in the black community is a negative consequence of homophobia in the black community and its rationalization in this moral discourse. Therefore, those in publicly responsible positions who can provide leadership to the black community in understanding, appreciating, and advocating the legitimate presence of black gays and lesbians in the community and their civil rights are themselves muted by personal, economic, and status privileges that their conformity to the cult black masculinity confers and with which society (black and dominant) rewards them.

Only recently has the history of homosexuality been developed as a genuine contribution to black cultural studies. Hemphill recalls searching the public library for an understanding of his own internal black sexual presence in the great Negro novels, the legacy of the black intelligentsia on black consciousness from Du Bois and Garvey to Larry Neal and Amira Baraka (the so-called new black aesthetic school). He searched for a place in the literature where he enters as a legitimate black subject. He writes: "What was there for me to read in 1969 was in no way affirming of the sexual identity germinating within me. The material regarding homosexuality considered it to be an illness or an affliction, and at worst, a sin against God and nature. . . . The books made no reference to black men that I can recall, nor were there black case studies for me to examine, and in a few pictures of men identified as homosexual, not one was black."[9] The literature celebrated racial genius—its loves, struggles, and forms of resistance. However, "nothing in those books said that men could truly love one another. Nothing said that masturbation would be comforting. Nothing celebrated the genius and creativity of homosexual men or even suggested that such men could lead ordinary lives. Nothing encouraged me to love black men—I had to learn that on my own," says Hemphill.[10]

Given the ways that the virtues of black masculinity have informed black moral consciousness, the very idea that black homosexuals can and ought to love and fulfill their desires for same-sex intimacy and unions constitutes a moral emasculation of themselves in the black community. They become moral perverts, except in the countercultural world of the clubs, in alternative restaurants, and in the secrecy of their homes and apartments, where they look for and sometimes find one another. Their presence is all too often greeted with suspicion, rejection, rage, and violence. In a recent book, *One More River to Cross: Black and Gay in America*, Keith Boykin, a black gay novelist, writer, and activist, argues that the deadly silence created by homophobia in the black community and rationalized under the rhetoric of black masculinity influences black society at every level.[11] He describes the rejection by the planning committee of the Bud Bilikin Parade of a black gay and lesbian group in Chicago known as "The Ad Hoc Committee of Proud Black Lesbians and Gays."[12] The parade is a historic event that marks the end of the summer and the beginning of the school year in the African-American community. The Ad Hoc Committee's application to march in the parade was rejected on the grounds that the limitations of time, space, and manpower restricted the number of groups that would be allowed to march.

The committee filed a second application, this time under the name "Diverse Black Role Models." The application was approved by the Bilikin Parade's planning committee. Spokespersons for the black gays and lesbians spoke publicly about their contingent in the parade. However, opposition to their marching flooded Chicago black radio stations and the *Chicago Defender*, a major newspaper serving the Chicago black community and the primary sponsor of the Bilikin Parade. Opponents charged the group with "ruining" the parade because it was a family event. Others expressed fears that black drag queens would be marching down Martin Luther King Jr. Drive. Still others expressed suspicion that the black gays and lesbians must be part of a white conspiracy to "divide the black community." According to Boykin, when the committee threatened to sue the *Defender*, it was granted permission to march in the parade. In this incident, Derrick Bell's judgment seems to be confirmed (even with respect to the black community) that litigation appears to be the only recourse African Americans have for securing justice.[13]

Boykin finds the cult of black masculinity behind much of the homophobic antagonism toward black gays and lesbians. He writes: "Many ordinary black men, like their counterparts in the Black Power intelligentsia, have expressed concern about homosexuality because of its effects on black manhood. Not thinking to challenge the stereotype, they know that the black man is supposed to be strong and believe that the homosexual man is inherently weak."[14] Boykin also suggests that black women "suspect male homosexuality everywhere. They see this not so much as a manhood problem but as a numbers problem."[15] That is, they are concerned that with the diminishing availability of suitable black men as potential mates, owing to the large number incarcerated, drug dependent, or unemployed; those men who are gay contribute to their lost opportunities for forming suitable black partnerships, marriages, and families. Boykin rightly notes that this expression may not necessarily represent homophobia, "but it does encourage some black gay men to lie about their sexual orientation so they can try to fulfill an unwritten obligation to black women."[16]

In a roundtable discussion on womanist theology, Cheryl Sanders explicitly ties this sentiment about black gay men and the morals of black masculinity to black lesbians in her critique of womanist theology.[17] Sanders criticizes those black women theologians who affirm Alice Walker's vision of womanism, which includes the legitimacy of sexual love of black women for each other. She argues: "In my view there is a fundamental discrepancy between the womanist criteria that would affirm and/or advocate homosexual practice, and the ethical norms the black church might employ to promote the survival and wholeness of black families."[18] Sanders sees black homosexuals (gay men and lesbians) as departing from the moral consciousness that values the health, well-being, empowerment, and survival of the black family. In other words, they are regarded as morally degenerative influences on the black community. She therefore argues that "there is a need for the black churches to promote a positive sexual ethic within the black community as one means of responding to the growing normalization of the single-parent family, and the attendant increase in poverty, welfare dependency, and a host of other problems."[19] To be fair to Sanders, however, she does not attribute these kinds of social problems to the presence of black gays and lesbians. Nevertheless, she thinks that affirming their sexual practices constitutes a moral contradiction of the received moral values that ground the ethical norms of the black church and the black community. And those norms are explicated in the cult of black masculinity.

Although Boykin reports a great litany of discriminatory practices against black gays and lesbians throughout black cultural spheres, including the arts, entertainment, politics, and religion,[20] neither Boykin nor I are interested in discrediting those black institutions and organizations that have been genuine sites for promoting the social, political, and moral well-being of the black community. Rather, our interest is in showing the ways that homophobia in such black institutions and organizations contributes to the deadly silence of black gays and lesbians, whose motives and practices too often exclude them from the well-being of the community. In their attempts toward sexual self-fulfillment, black gays and lesbians are often dismissed by opponents as detractors from the real interests of the black community. For others, they are regarded as aliens, freaks, and a source of death in the black community. And regrettably for too many others, their demise is viewed as no great loss to the survival of the black community.

III

Among the many cultural institutions and organizations responsible for the moral well-being of the black community and despite claims to the contrary, black churches remain a major institution that promotes forms of homophobia that keep black gays and lesbians silent and make them particular objects of the community's disdain and violence. In his recent book, *Race Rules: Navigating the Color Line*, Michael Eric Dyson paints a picture of the black church and its relation to sexuality that greatly distorts the experiences of black gays and lesbians in the churches. Dyson exhibits a confidence in the black churches that, I suggest, many black gays and lesbians have good reason to question. He believes that the black churches are basically oriented toward liberating, prophetic, and avant-garde practices. In all civil rights issues, he argues that they are impressive exemplars of social justice when compared to white institutions.

However, in their attitudes toward sexuality, Dyson offers a genealogy that traces their lack of moral leadership to white sexual distortions that the black churches inherited from the homophobic practices of slavery. Consequently, the black churches are complicit in white Manichean sexual theologies in which the body is regarded as evil and the soul worthy of salvation. By contrast, Dyson argues that in black religious discourse, the black body is exonerated in ecstatic and ejaculatory forms of worship, preaching, and enthusiasm for social justice. However, Dyson recognizes that the black churches have not developed a sexual theology, much less a theology of homoerotica or homosexuality, that is compatible with its erotic qualities in worship. Rather, the white sexual theologies of the black churches, Dyson thinks, are at odds with the sexual interests and loves of their members.

Dyson traces the homophobic practices of the black churches to their conceptual dependence on white theology. Therefore, in their legitimate attempts to resist "myths of super black sexuality," in which black sexual appetites were regarded by the slaveholding society as unquenchable,[21] Dyson argues that blacks bought into "the split between mind and body that leads them to confusion about a black Christian theology of incarnation."[22] He sees this dualism at work in the interplay between the black pulpit, the black preacher's railings against homosexuality, Sunday after Sunday, and his or her use of gay members to play music and sing songs that will set the stage for his or her delivery and his or her hortatory ejaculations.[23]

Dyson suggests that in this ritualized, erotic moment a certain irony occurs. The preacher renders his gay members complicit in acts of self-hatred, while the musical performances of gay members negate the gay-bashing sermon just preached.[24] According to Dyson, the black churches' sexual theologies suggest a fundamental contradiction between their liberationist orientations toward social justice and their refusal to "unlock the oppressive closet for gays and lesbians."[25] He also extends these contradictions to homosexual members themselves, who participate in acts of self-hatred in their denials and secrecy while they affirm the homophobia of their churches. Dyson's point is that all of these homophobic practices can be seen as consequences of blacks' endorsements of a white ideology of heterosexism that is rationalized under a body/soul dualism.

If the black churches are to be faithful to their essential nature as liberating, prophetic institutions that are fundamentally motivated toward social justice, according to Dyson, the churches must develop a black theology of sexuality and homoeroticism. He also calls for black gays and lesbians to come out of their sexual closets, where "they can leave behind as well the destructive, erotic habits that threaten their lives."[26] He asks the black churches to affirm healthy unions between gay and lesbian adults.[27] And he asks the black churches to make certain their solidarity with the "despised members of our society." The despised in this case are not the homeless, prostitutes, or crackheads, but black gays and lesbians. "Black Christians, who have been despised and oppressed for much of our existence," Dyson argues, "should be wary of extending that oppression to our lesbian sisters and gay brothers."[28] He calls for the black churches to be centers of sexual healing: to be at the forefront of sexual justice, just as they have been at the forefront of "every major social, political, and moral movement in black culture."[29]

Dyson's essay is an impressive attempt on the part of an African-American intellectual to articulate a morally responsible critique of black sexuality, and it takes seriously and treats substantively the sexual repression of black gays and lesbians. However, his genealogy, I think, distorts more than it explains about homophobia in the black churches. Dyson's suggestion that the homophobic activities of the black churches can be understood or explained in reference to African Americans' acquiring a self-hating theological body/soul dualism is far too constricting for an adequate critique of homophobia in the black religious community. Homophobia is not reducible to the particular accidents and discursive practices of any one cultural group. It certainly is not the unique characteristic of European thought and culture. According to recent social psychology findings, it appears to be a cultural phenomenon not only in modern mass societies but also in many traditional societies, including African traditional societies. Homophobia is so culturally pervasive that one is tempted to regard it as a "natural" human condition.[30] However, it is a mistake to regard it as a natural attitude among all human beings. Rather, it develops in complex matrices of cultural experience that are experiential, social, and political. Therefore, homophobia cannot be reduced to any one matrix.[31] For the many ways that people feel repulsed by others and develop prejudices toward others are not explainable simply in terms of their psychophysiological reactions to others' strangeness or to irrational fears and anxieties about others. Such psychophysiological signs of homophobia are related to social taboos, associations, and cultural conditions that cultivate both negative and positive effects throughout the culture.[32]

My talk of homophobia in terms of negative and positive cultural practices is a logical judgment and not a moral judgment. Negatively, homophobic practices may be maintained for the purpose of "deterring" forms of human association, sexual and social, that some in the community fear are threats to the moral cohesion of the culture. Positively, homophobic practices may "ensure" the cultivation of moral behavior through socialization in proper sexual practices that the culture deems worthy of propagation. The point is that homophobia ought not to be explained away simply by appealing to a genealogy of its European transmission. Such an explanation, it seems to me, doesn't give much credence to the argument that African-American cultural practices are not only reactive to the deformation of black culture in chattel slavery. They are also the effects of blacks' own initiatives in developing and guiding their moral universe. Therefore, Dyson's analysis of homophobia in the black church treats it as a reactive consequence of whites' actions on black cultural life and not a consequence of the black churches' proactive intentions to establish African-American cultural practices that are as likely as European cultural activities to produce in the black community homophobic activities, self-hating practices, and antigay discourses. This recognition that homophobia in the black community is a consequence of African Americans' reactive and proactive moral intentions toward cultural generativity goes a long way toward providing a more complex moral critique of black homophobia than does Dyson's genealogical reduction.

I think that it is an important aspect of moral maturity to recognize friends from enemies. In this regard, I also think that Dyson lands on the right side of the black churches' contestations over homosexuality. He is right to insist that black churches have good moral reasons for resisting the destructive powers of homophobia. However, these moral reasons do not negate the fundamental (negative and positive) human anxieties and cultural motives that are inscribed in the sociological description of homophobia. And black gays and lesbians cannot trust that black religious resources can do for them what black moral consciousness cannot—namely, eradicate homophobia from the African-American community. Therefore, I do not share Dyson's confidence in the goodness of the black churches. I suspect that he asks the black churches to deliver more than they can. And black gays and lesbians have good reason to maintain a guarded trust in the churches. For too many black gays and lesbians, the black churches are not safe havens of rest.

Boykin describes an incident that occurred at the funeral of a black gay man. The incident took place at a black church. He reports that Vaughn died of AIDS in the summer of 1995. While he was sick in the hospital, his mother was kind and respectful of his relationship with his friend, David. However, when Vaughn died, David recalls that her attitude changed drastically toward him. "She resisted David's effort to find a minister to perform the funeral service and instead insisted on her own minister. She also rejected Vaughn's wish that David sing at the funeral."[33] At Vaughn's funeral, David was confronted by a black preacher who took advantage of the occasion to evangelize the contingency of the black gay men present. He offered them the good news that if they repent of their sins, they could escape the fate of their beloved friend, Vaughn, whom the minister said was "on his way to Hell."[34]

When my own brother, Barry, died from AIDS-related complications, I recall that no word was spoken that told those present about his sickness; no mention was made of his delightful, wonderful, playful, and talented life; no mention was made of his loves. Like S, whom I introduced at the beginning of this essay, my brother also died in silence. The black church was not there to receive him in his life; it only received his dead body in the end. I have written this essay in memory of Essex Hemphill, writer, poet, and advocate. He labored to break through the deadly silence that characterizes the unfulfilled lives of too many black gays and lesbians in the United States. He died on November 4, 1995, at the University of Pennsylvania Hospital, from AIDS-related complications. Like the many black gays now gone home, he "was eulogized in a church ceremony that minimized his homosexuality and his contribution to the black lesbian and gay community," says Boykin.[35] Boykin concludes that "as they prepare to go to their final resting place, many black [gays] cannot find peace in the churches."[36]

I need not recount the litany of abuses of black gays and lesbians carried out by the black churches. And I am not interested in rehearsing the many ways that black gays and lesbians inflict personal injury on each other in the churches. The pain runs deep, and the memories last long. However, I do not believe that because some black churches express an openness toward black gays and lesbians, the black churches and the black community overall are more accepting of them than other mainstream communities.[37] That many black gays and lesbians are members of church choirs, church musicians, soloists, and ushers, that their gifts are used and exploited by their churches and their communities, ought not to be confused with genuine acceptance and love.

In black churches and among black church leaders discussing homosexuality, I have heard such statements as "God calls Christians to love the sinner and hate the sin, to have solidarity with the despised, and to embrace the alien." However, these statements only disclose the reality that it is black gays and lesbians who are signified by these images. They have no good reasons for accepting or celebrating such images, for it is they who are regarded in such statements as the despised, the aliens outside the community, and the sinners in need of the black churches' love and acceptance. It is they whom the black churches call to turn away from sexual sins and wretchedness. And it is they who are called to a life of sexual self-denial. However, the idea that Christians can love the sinner and hate the sin is internally contradictory when the sin in this case is homosexual sex. Homosexual sex is how gays and lesbians love each other, fulfill their sense of sexual union, and practice sexual intimacy. To require them to forsake sex for Christian fellowship is a trade-off that I think is less than gracious. That one may be committed to a life of celibacy is a matter of one's personal calling; it ought not to be a requirement for one's inclusion in black religious faith. In light of Dyson's argument, such a norm only perpetuates the soul/body dualism that he criticizes. And from the perspective of Christian love ethics, this norm is not morally consistent with an unconditional love of the other. In my judgment, it is a sexual conviction that is unworthy of a Christian's assent.

IV

I do not want to leave the impression that the religious lives of African-American people are without the possibility of transcendence from the destructive powers of homophobia and the malicious forms of alienation they create among black gays and lesbians. However, transcendence is more likely to come from black religious leaders' and church members' commitments to the human rights of black gays and lesbians than from appeals to the distinctive, internal sexual theologies of their churches. That is, their respect for and commitment to black gays and lesbians may be helped by their theologies of redemptive love and grace. And the theological languages of the black churches may be compatible with the humanistic rationality that supports the languages of natural, human goods and rights. However, the respect and commitment that black gays and lesbians require of black church members and religious leaders do not require theological justifications—although they are welcomed.

Black religious leaders and church members participate in many communities of moral discourse, where they come in contact with, know, and associate with black gays and lesbians. They are their teachers, lawyers, ministers, musicians, bus drivers, bankers, funeral home directors, siblings, uncles, and aunts. Some are also parents. My point is that black gays and lesbians are not a degenerative presence in the black community, they contribute to the flourishing of the black community. Moreover, the basic human needs, desires, and goods that they seek to fulfill do not differ from those of the black heterosexual mainstream. Therefore, advocating their needs, desires, and goods does not require theological justification any more than one requires theological justification to support the basic human needs and goods of black heterosexuals. In African Americans' contestations over homosexuality, I think that it is more morally relevant that black religious leaders and churches support the goods that gays and lesbians seek to fulfill, not because God requires it or requires that they love them but because what is at stake is nothing less than respecting the needs and natural rights of black human beings (gay, lesbian, straight, or bisexual).

I derive my theory of natural goods and natural rights from the new natural law theory of John Finnis, Germain Grisez, Joseph Boyle, and others.[38] For these moral theorists, what counts as possible candidates for a system of natural human goods and rights does not require that we first place our moral judgments under prior metaphysical or theoretical constraints. Therefore, our moral judgments need not be based on scientific theories about how the world of nature is ordered, into which we then fit our moral practices. To be sure, we can benefit from the use of the social and natural sciences to inform us about the probable effects that our moral actions are likely to have on each other and on our environment. And social, scientific, and biological theories of sexuality may have great importance for our understanding homosexuality among blacks and homophobia in the black community. However, appealing to scientific data to justify our moral judgments about the legitimacy of homosexuality is not necessary.

Moreover, the new natural law moral theory does not require particular religious beliefs about creation, its orders, and its ultimate ends to adequately delineate a system of natural goods and natural rights. If this were the case, it is unlikely that we would get very far in establishing public consent on the legitimacy of homosexuality, for we are likely to have little agreement on whose account of creation, its ordering, and its ultimate ends is theologically correct. Rather, a system of natural goods and natural rights can be agreed upon in public discourse if it is based on human reflections on basic human needs and goods. Natural needs and goods constitute human beings as a species. However, they are not only categorical, they are also moral goods. Human beings can freely elect them as goods worthy of themselves and worthy of fulfilling.

Candidates for natural goods are usually understood in two ways: categorical goods and reflexive goods. Categorical goods are basic human needs that every human being requires and that are not dependent on human preferences or personal choice. Such goods are biological life, knowledge, work, and leisure. These basic goods are balanced by reflexive goods that all need and desire and may consciously elect for themselves, if they think about what makes for a satisfying sense of personal wholeness. It is in this sense that they are reflexive. Such goods are fellowship (peace with others), mental peace (inner peace of mind), truth (harmony between one's convictions and one's choices), and spiritual peace (peace with any "other than human others" that unifies one's life and world).

One must be careful not to equate these basic human needs and goods with the common goods of liberty and justice. These common goods establish the rights of all if any is to pursue and fulfill the basic human goods. The liberty of each to pursue what is necessary for sustaining his or her physical life gives rise to the public interest in health and safety, just as the liberty to satisfy the need of knowledge, without which one is neither able to keep one's life from danger nor know what is publicly required of one's citizenship, gives rise to public interest in education. Public interest in fair employment is based on one's liberty to procure work and labor, which is necessary for maintaining those material goods required for sustaining one's life.

If we regard persons as having a fundamental liberty to pursue every peaceful means of forming a common life with others, then justice requires that persons are at liberty to move or locate in a neighborhood of their choosing without any undue threat to their well-being. Moreover, persons are at liberty to pursue those goods (material, filial, and affilial) that will support their mental health, for the satisfaction of this subjective good is necessary if persons are to perform their legitimate roles as citizens without any privation of rationality. And justice requires that persons be at liberty to pursue the harmony of their choices and convictions in relation to their consciences without fear of harm, undue incarceration, and intimidation if they are to participate in genuine public debate without falsifying their beliefs and preferences. Finally, each is at liberty to worship and believe as each wills about the ultimate unity of life and the world, but justice requires that none is at liberty to violate the religious liberty of others. The basic categorical and reflexive goods are the conditions on which public interest in health and safety, education, and fair access to markets and labor are negotiated. Moreover, it is as persons attempt to fulfill their reflexive or subjective needs that each citizen has a right to associate freely, establish families, unions, and societies for mutual support, create open and free environments where members can act with respect to their consciences, and congregate for the advancement of their spiritual needs without fear of undue interference, coercion, or intimidation.

I have turned to the new natural law theory as a rationalization for my assertion that African Americans' support of black gays and lesbians as citizens of a democratic society does not require that one justify one's support on the findings of the social sciences or the demands of religious beliefs. Rather, the recognition that black gays and lesbians are human beings with rightful claims to the fulfillment of their bodily, mental, and spiritual integrity is a sufficient basis for advocating their protection from bodily harm, threat to life, gay bashing, and sexual harassment. They are human beings who possess a natural right to associate, establish friendships, companionship, and families. These human liberties are not nullified just because these human beings happen to be people oriented in their love, affections, and filial and affillial bonds to members of the same sex. The recognition that black gays and lesbians are human beings possessing a natural right to secure adequate means of labor, I suggest, is an adequate basis for grounding the commitments of black religious leaders to support their litigations for fair opportunities in employment, health insurance, pensions, and social security.

The recognition of the humanity of black gays and lesbians and their right to associate freely is a sufficient basis for advocating their liberty to travel and live in residential areas free from harassment, overinflated rents, muggings, and verbal humiliation when they walk streets either alone or with their lovers and friends. These liberties are not special interests peculiar to gays and lesbians. They are basic human liberties.

I recognize that for many members of the black churches and national religious leaders, advocating these human goods and natural rights on behalf of gays and lesbians creates conflicts of interest. These conflicts emerge from their loyalties to the established sexual teachings of their churches and their loyalties toward the advancement of basic human rights. And for many, trying to reconcile their moral commitments to the human rights of gays and lesbians with the sexual moralities of their churches requires a balancing act that is difficult to sustain. The story that Boykin tells about Vaughn's funeral may reveal such a conflict in the actions of Vaughn's mother, whose expressed friendliness toward David was only an expression of her commitment to her dying son. With his death, she was compelled to enact a set of practices and dispositions that then reflected her loyalty to her black church and its homophobic sexual teachings.

However, black church leaders and members (straight, gay, and lesbian) live in many communities of moral discourse—the church is only one. Not all of their judgments and practices are justified by theological reasons. In some contexts, jurisprudential reasoning overrides theological and religious commitments. For instance, if one's religion requires a human blood sacrifice, the legality of murder takes precedence over the ritual claims of the believer, and the believer is required to find a substitute sacrifice (in conformity to the law) for completing the ritual. And if one's religion justifies and encourages sexual exchanges between adults and children, statutory rape laws provide a sufficient basis for setting aside any theological rationality for the legitimacy of such a practice. Black religious leaders and church members participate in a public where they daily encounter gays and lesbians with genuine claims to liberty and justice. However, if they are to engage public life with all of its pluralities in a morally responsible manner and with some measure of civility, then the particularity of their sexual theologies must be balanced, negotiated, and perhaps even set aside if they are also to respect and support the legitimate claims that gays and lesbians have to the fulfillment of their basic human rights.

V

To conclude, I recognize that the claims that I have made for homosexuality and human rights and their relation to black religious discourse are highly contestable.

I also recognize that I have negatively construed the ways that the black churches and black religious leadership relate to black gays and lesbians. However, even if my criticisms are strong, I do not think them unwarranted. Nevertheless, as I examine the attitudes and practices of the black churches and black religious leaders toward gays and lesbians, there are a few models of transcendence on which black gays and lesbians can ground their hope of overcoming the deadly silence that has characterized too much of their living and dying.

There are a few havens of rest where black gays and lesbians are greeted as signs of divine grace and not objects of divine judgment. There are some religious safe places where they can find peace of mind and spirit, can celebrate their same-sex loves and sexual fulfillment without resorting to self-hating denigration of themselves as despised persons, aliens, and sinners in need of love and the religious believer's missionary commitment, without forsaking the good of same-sex intimacy for the "right hand of Christian fellowship." A few safe places exist for black gays and lesbians. And that gives me hope that the black churches and black religious leaders can transcend the parochialism of their received sexual theologies. I hope that out of genuine moral commitment to human rights, they can embrace the human interests of black gays and lesbians even if such moral commitments perpetually test their religious loyalties to the sexual moralities of their churches.

It is appropriate to conclude these words in my own voice. However, I remain mindful of the deadly silence that characterizes too many of the lives and deaths of black gays and lesbians, some falling to AIDS, others to suicide, others to gay bashing: S, Barry F. Anderson, Vaughn, Eric Jordan, Joseph Beams, Marlon Riggs, Essex Hemphill, and many others. I grant the last word to Hemphill: "I speak for thousands, perhaps hundreds of thousands of men [and women] who live and die in the shadows of secrets, unable to speak of the love that helps them endure and contribute to the race. . . . We will not go away with our issues of sexuality. We are coming home."[39]

Notes

1. Paul Gibson, "Gay Male and Female Youth Suicide," in *Death by Denial: Studies in Suicide in the Gay and Lesbian Teenager*, ed. Gary Remafedi (Boston: Alyson Publishing, 1994), pp. 36–38; also Susan Cochran and Vickie Mays, "Depression and Distress Among Homosexually Active African American Men and Women," *American Journal of Psychiatry* 151 (1994): 524–29.

2. Rupert A. Francis, Frederick A. Ernst, Jessy G. Devieux, and Joyce Perkins, "Race and Sexuality in the U.S: Sexuality and Sexual Preference in the African American Population," in *The Psychology of Sexual Orientation, Behavior, and Identity: A Handbook*, eds. Diamant and McAnulty (Westport, CT: Greenwood, 1995), p. 384.

3. Ibid., p. 392.

4. Hemphill, *Brother to Brother*, p. xv.

5. Ibid.

6. Martin Duberman, Martha Vincinus, and George Chauncey Jr., ed., *Hidden From History: Reclaiming the Gay & Lesbian Past* (New York: Meridian Books, 1990), pp. 1–2; Roger E. Biery, *Understanding Homosexuality: The Pride and the Prejudice* (Austin, TX: Edward-William Publishing, 1990), pp. 254–62.

7. Victor Anderson, *Beyond Ontological Blackness: An Essay in African American Religious and Cultural Criticism* (New York: Continuum, 1995), p. 15.

8. Ibid.

9. Hemphill, *Brother to Brother,* p. xv.

10. Ibid., p. xvi.

11. Keith Boykin, *One More River to Cross: Black and Gay in America* (Boston: Alyson, 1996), p. 170.

12. Ibid., pp. 176–77.

13. Derrick Bell, *And We are Not Saved: The Elusive Quest for Racial Justice* (New York: Basic Books, 1987), p. 255.

14. Boykin, *One More River to Cross,* p. 170.

15. Ibid., p. 171.

16. Ibid.

17. Womanist Theology is a theological project being developed by black women theologians and Christian moralists who, inspired by Alice Walker's poetic trope, use black women's literary, artistic, religious, and other cultural resources to critique critically a trimodal form of alienation that they characterize as racism, sexism, and classism, which they argue fundamentally defines black women's lives. Positively, they seek to support and advance the agency of black women whose lives are characterized morally by struggle and resistance. See Katie Cannon, *Black Womanist Ethics* (Atlanta: Scholars Press, 1988); Jacquelyn Grant, *White Women's Christ and Black Women's Jesus* (Atlanta: Scholars Press, 1989); and Delores Williams, *Sisters in the Wilderness: Womanist God-Talk* (Maryknoll, NY: Orbis Press, 1993); see also my discussion of womanist theology in *Beyond Ontological Blackness,* pp. 104–117.

18. Cheryl J. Sanders, "Roundtable Discussion: Christian Ethics and Theology in Womanist Perspective," *Journal of Feminist Studies in Religion* 5 (1989): 90.

19. Ibid.

20. Boykin, *One More River to Cross,* pp. 155–211.

21. Michael Dyson, *Race Rules: Negotiating the Color Line* (Reading, MA: Addison-Wesley, 1996), p. 84.

22. Ibid., p. 87.

23. Ibid., p. 104.

24. Ibid., p. 105.

25. Ibid.

26. Ibid., p. 106.

27. Ibid.

28. Ibid., p. 107.

29. Ibid., p. 108.

30. Gregory M. Hereck, "Beyond 'Homophobia': A Social Psychological Perspective on Attitudes Toward Lesbians and Gay Men," *Journal of Homosexuality* 10, nos. 1–2 (Fall 1984): 3.

31. Ibid., pp. 7–8.

32. John Wayne Plasek and Janicemarie Allard, "Misconceptions of Homophobia," *Journal of Homosexuality* 10, nos. 1–2 (Fall 1984): 23–27.

33. Boykin, *One More River to Cross,* p. 123.

34. Ibid., p. 124.

35. Ibid., p. 125.

36. Ibid.

37. Alvin F. Poussaint, "An Honest Look at Black Gays and Lesbians," *Ebony,* September 1990, pp. 124–31; Frederick Ernst et al., "Condemnation of Homosexuality in

the Black Community: A Gender Specific Phenomenon?" *Archives of Sexual Behavior* 20, no. 6 (1991): 579–85.

38. Advocates of the new natural law morality are mostly but not exclusively Catholic moral philosophers and professors of jurisprudence who seek to further the requirements of the Stoic morality. The principal representatives of the school are John Finnis, Germain Grisez, and Joseph Boyle. They are staunch defenders of American liberal democracy. What separates these thinkers from classical natural law theorists are two of the most radical claims to emerge in recent moral philosophy. They agree with Immanuel Kant and John Rawls that the belief in God is not a necessary foundation for either ethics or morality. Hence, one can do ethics and live a morally virtuous life without appealing to religion as the ultimate basis. But this is a strange claim for Catholic theorists to make. They also hold that neither ethics nor morality depend on "theoretical knowledge" for first principles. And this is a strange claim for natural law theorists to make. New natural law theorists acknowledge that theoretical knowledge can be an aid to ethics. But they argue that such knowledge is not necessary for grounding the first principles of practical reason. New natural law theorists propose that the first principles of practical reason are derived from our capacity to grasp or discover the "basic motives," the reasons persons "do what they do" or "act as they act." For the new natural law theorists, first principles of practical reasoning must answer the question, "Why did you do that?" in such a way that there is no further reducible motive to explain the action.

First principles are the sole, ultimate, primal, and last ends of all human motivations for action. All other motives of human action are justified only in relation to these basic goods. For example, new natural law theorists do not consider either the ethical values or the beliefs we hold about God as properly basic. Meaning and value are derived from reflection on our natural dispositions toward human fulfillment both categorically and reflexively. Ethically, no principles such as "perfect happiness," "dignity," and "self-respect" are properly basic (first principles). This is because they are themselves derived from and have their meanings based on the primacy of the seven basic goods, particularly the four reflexive goods. See John Finnis, *Fundamentals of Ethics* (Washington: Georgetown University Press, 1993), pp. 37–53; Germain Grisez and Joseph Boyle Jr., *Life and Death with Liberty and Justice* (Notre Dame: University of Notre Dame Press, 1979), pp. 21–58, 336–80; Germain Grisez and Russell Shaw, *Fulfillment in Christ: A Summary of Christian Principles* (Notre Dame: University of Notre Dame Press, 1991), pp. 54–56.

39. Hemphill, *Brother to Brother,* p. xxix.

Sexual Orientation and the Language of Higher Law

WILLIAM D. HART

What are "we" trying to do when we use the language of "natural" or "higher" law? Why are claims about sexual orientation especially likely to be articulated in such language? These questions circumscribe my effort to make sense of natural law as a common vocabulary for both advocates and opponents of same-sex relationships. My voyage into these troubled waters is anchored by Victor Anderson's advocacy and Cheryl Sanders's opposition. My purpose is not to navigate a safe and neutral middle passage, but to chart my own position by clearly fixing theirs.

Cheryl Sanders argues strongly and prescriptively for "covenanted monogamous heterosexual unions in light of the ongoing disintegration of family and parenting structures in the African-American community." Thus, she draws a strong connection between heterosexual monogamy, stable family life, and quality parenting. It is precisely this nesting of issues that I will challenge, but only after a fuller account of her position. Sanders's position is in accord with the General Assembly of the Church of God, which "passed a resolution in 1979 articulating the church's opposition to homosexuality based upon a commitment to 'biblical holiness,' 'high regard to scriptural injunctions against homosexuality,' the conviction that 'homosexuality is sin,' and firm opposition to the 'licensing, ordination, or approving of persons in leadership activity involved in this life-style.'" In support of her argument, Sanders cites Richard Hays's *The Moral Vision of the New Testament* (1996). This book is a thoughtful argument against homosexuality on textual grounds. It will not persuade many; I am not persuaded. But it will persuade those like Sanders, whose hermeneutical circle begins with "conservative" presuppositions about biblical authority and ends with conservative conclusions. Thus, critical exegesis that purports to show a fundamental "undecidability" with respect to the Bible's treatment of same-sex relationships does not persuade Sanders. On her view, scriptural injunctions against homosexuality are clear, but she is no "grand inquisitor." Sanders advocates a "don't ask, don't tell" policy with respect to same-sex relationships. Every upstanding member of her church, however, "especially in a leadership capacity, is expected to conform to the church's moral teachings with respect to sexual conduct."

In pursuing her argument, Sanders draws an analogy between "the African-American church's" positions on women and gays and lesbians. The problem with this analogy is readily apparent—lesbians are a subset of the class women. Clearly what she must have intended was an analogy between gays and lesbians, on the one hand and heterosexual women, on the other. But even here the analogy is muddled because it is not clear that lesbians are treated unequally for reasons of sexuality rather than gender. (The fact that lesbianism ultimately is an "unanalyzable" bundle of sexuality and gender is not relevant at this point.) A better analogy is the status of women and gays, which brings into stark relief the relative volatility of gender vs. sexual orientation.

Sanders's chief claim centers around what she calls the "ethic of sexual freedom." Without any effort to analyze the complexity of the notion of sexual freedom, she implies that same-sex relationships, which exemplify such freedom, are a threat, perhaps the major threat, to stable families and healthy parenting structures. At times, Sanders's argument is one non sequitur after another. Note the following:

> In my opinion, the strongest rational argument that can be offered against same-sex orientation, preference and conduct—without specific reference to Scripture or revelation—flows from the observation that in the African-American community in particular, and also in society at large, the ethic and practice of sexual freedom have seriously undermined the stability of families and their parenting structures during the past three decades. This is not to suggest that gays and lesbians are to blame for the demise of the black family; rather it is to state that if nobody is willing to support and encourage the formation of covenanted heterosexual monogamous units where the emotional, educational, and economic needs of children and adults can be fulfilled, then the rampant antisocial behavior of adolescents and young adults that has terrorized our neighborhoods and schools will certainly increase.

Sanders wants to make a rational argument that does not depend on theological assumptions: the notion of revealed truth. Here I should mention the editorial constraints under which Sanders wrote. The editors of this volume asked all participants to address the following question: "What moral stance do you believe your religious community ought to take on this issue [same-sex orientation] at this time? Do you believe that these moral arguments (1) are, and (2) ought to be arguments that are persuasive independent of issues of revelation?" Sanders's argument may *merely* reflect the limitations of these questions; to the extent that it does, she and the reader should discount my response as they deem appropriate. They would be advised to regard "Sanders" as a character constructed by Cheryl Sanders (under a particular set of editorial constraints) who represents a common point of view on the issue of same-sex orientation. In any event, my argument assumes that Sanders's answer to the editors' questions is yes. Again, if this assumption is incorrect, then my argument bears less on Sanders than it does on the questions themselves. My disagreement with Sanders, as will become evident, has a lot to do with her rhetorical strategy, a strategy that leans heavily on the notion of abstract neutrality, which is inherent in the editors' questions. It is that strategy that I shall criticize. I do not believe that rationality, understood as abstract neutrality, is a good way of making moral arguments. In my view, Sanders need not accept these assumptions to make a rational argument. Rationality does not mean "without presuppositions," religious or otherwise. Arguments from divine revelation are no less rational than any other argument; furthermore, whether rational arguments *of any kind* are persuasive or not may have everything to do with what might best be described as revelation.[1] At some point, we hit bedrock and our spade is turned. Our ability to give reasons is exhausted; all we can say is "this is how I live." It is on the level of these subrational, "primitive" forms of behavior that important ethical issues such as same-sex orientation must be addressed.

Sanders (and whether this refers to Sanders the author or Sanders the character is a question that I have already concluded cannot be decided) finds a candidate for her argument in what she takes to be a set of facts—namely, the cause-and-effect relationship between sexual freedom and the erosion of family and parenting structures. Apparently this is an empirical claim that "flows" from her observations. Sanders presents as an uncontroversial fact what, on the contrary, is an object of intense disagreement. Whether sexual freedom causes family and parenting breakdown is an open and unsettled question; much, if not everything, depends on how one construes sexual freedom. This reveals a structural irritant that the reader constantly encounters in Sanders's argument; she slides, unselfconsciously no doubt, between her purported desire to make a "rational," empirically based argument and a tendency to make bold assertions without supporting evidence. For example, does the evidence really show the breakdown that she alludes to? If it does, can one really establish a cause-and-effect relationship between such breakdown and the "ethic and practice of sexual freedom?" What would she regard as evidence anyway?

And what does she mean by sexual freedom? The abolition of antisodomy laws? Greater tolerance for the public "display" of same-sex relationships? The extension of social welfare benefits to same-sex couples on college campuses and in a small slice of the corporate world? What is the relationship between these developments and family and parenting breakdown? Sanders does not say. She persists in making what under one description is simply a bad argument but under another description, a shrewd argument. To put this more directly, Sanders implicitly affirms what she explicitly denies: "that gays and lesbians are to blame for the demise of the black family." The shrewd nature of this argument is apparent when, immediately after making the previous observation, Sanders solemnly cites the consequences of the failure "to support and encourage the formation of covenanted *heterosexual* monogamous units." How exactly do same-sex unions produce the emotional, economic, and educational problems that she enumerates, much less the antisocial behavior and terror? The answer is implicit in her definition of the problem: same-sex relationships are neither heterosexual nor monogamous. Heterosexuals can marry, homosexuals cannot. Without marriage, "our basic notions of kinship—father, mother, grandmother, grandfather, brother, sister, aunt, uncle, cousin" would collapse. This claim is not as bizarre as it is inflated. Granted, our notions of kinship do presuppose some form of "marriage." But does it presuppose what Sanders apparently thinks that it does—that is, heterosexuality and monogamy? I think that the arguments for monogamy are strong, especially under the constraints imposed by the bourgeois or nuclear family,[2] but what does this have to do with heterosexuality? This is a tough question, but it is not made easier by assuming that one has definitively or persuasively answered the question by simply posing it. The question, "Is homosexuality inherently non-monogamous?" cannot be answered without "foregrounding" the conditions under which the choice of homosexuality is made. What we surely cannot do, but what Sanders does, is to confuse monogamy, which means one spouse, with sexual fidelity. As we all know, not everyone with one spouse is faithful and not everyone with multiple spouses or no spouse at all is unfaithful. The issue of sexual freedom and responsibility is much more complicated than being married or not married; but, again, I do not deny the importance of some form of marriage for the well-being of children.[3]

Some of Sanders's claims are troubling, as, for example, when she attributes her ambivalence toward the concept of womanist not to its status as a synonym for black lesbian but to her "pastoral concern for advocating heterosexual monogamy within the African-American community." Does she really believe they are unrelated? Is she really ignorant of the constitutive role of this relationship for her ambivalence? What else could possibly account for it? Sanders's claim borders on the incomprehensible, which is precisely how I characterize her claim that "the black churches sometimes get blamed for contributing to the HIV-AIDS problem, but at the same time are criticized for promoting abstinence and counseling against the various sexual practices that put persons most at risk." Here, if I may use a cliché, Sanders gilds the lily. Black churches are criticized not for preaching against unsafe sex, but for preaching against homosexuality, which they construct as unsafe and sinful. Here Sanders ignores what any knowledgeable person knows: HIV-AIDS, among other modalities, is a sexually transmitted disease, not a specifically same-sex transmitted disease. Surely she is aware of the predominantly heterosexual mode of transmission in Africa? Would she construct African heterosexuality as unsafe, sinful, and destructive of the African family? Ideas of this sort, more than any others, show the after-the-fact character of Sanders's argument; she marshals the arguments that she does only to give added weight to a position she already holds, which she holds on other grounds. Homosexuality is sin. Every other argument is mere supplement, an attempt to indulge (or "backdoor") those readers who reject her basic presupposition. If you can't get them to buy your basic moral claim that homosexuality is sin, then give them a secondary moral argument that homosexuality destroys black families! Here, more than any place else, do I find Sanders's rhetorical strategy troubling and her particular way of addressing the editors' questions problematic. If my tone is polemical, it is not because I think that Sanders's views are unreasonable. We may have good reason to believe wrong or even despicable things—things that we later look on with embarrassment. (This shows why being wrong, which I clearly think Sanders is, and being blameworthy are not necessarily the same thing.) My tone, therefore, is designed to expose a rhetorical strategy, which includes the pretense of rational neutrality, that gets in the way of honest and effective dialogue. Again, how much of this can be blamed on Sanders, as opposed to the limitations of the editors' questions, is an open question. Whatever the case, Sanders's argument would be stronger if she owned up to the explicitly theological presuppositions that ground her ethical and moral reflections. That is to say, her answer to the editors' questions should have been no. That would be an honorable (and perhaps blameless) position, however wrong, from my perspective, her views on same-sex orientation are and however vicious their consequences.

If Sanders describes her views as "don't ask, don't tell," then Anderson describes "the violent, deadly consequences of homosexual silence in the black community." My views are much closer to Anderson's than to Sanders's; it is especially important, then, that I clearly fix Anderson's views as I chart my own position. I shall focus, therefore, on three issues that Anderson addresses: black masculinity, the black church, and human rights. The last issue provides a bridge to concluding reflections on the irremediable character of natural and higher law language in discussions of sexual orientation.

Anderson defines the "cult of black masculinity" as "a pervasive preoccupation of black intellectuals with the classical, heroic virtues of courage, manliness, strength, self-determination, and racial loyalty." Let me say at the outset that I am not quite sure what Anderson means by "classical." Are his classical virtues those of Homeric Greece or is he referring to a specifically African-American tradition of heroic virtue, in which case his allusions to self-determination and racial loyalty make sense? Assuming that he must mean the latter, the virtues he describes define racial membership and the "order of rank" within the race. Obviously, these virtues are constructed as sex- and gender-specific; women and femininity, by definition, occupy a lower order of rank. So too do homosexuals, whose status is always read through sex and gender identity: Gays behave like women (subjecting themselves to male sexual subordination) and lesbians behave like "misbegotten" men (because like men they desire women sexually). Homosexuals as a class are lower in the order of rank and their status in the race is more precarious. The cult of masculinity still awaits its Bertrand Russell—someone who will do for masculinity what he did for Christianity (however "flatfooted" his effort) when he wrote "Why I am not a Christian." We still await the essay "Why I am not a Man"; whoever writes this essay, however, must be nimble of foot and know how to dance. One thing is certain: he cannot write such an essay under Anderson's assumptions. When he speaks of conflicts of loyalty over racial and gender-and-sexual goods, he adopts a serial, additive, liberal pluralist, multicultural notion of identity. Destroying the cult of black masculinity, among other things, demands that we reject constructions of race and sex-and-gender as discrete identities between which we can choose. This isn't to say that there are not people demanding that we make these choices; rather, it is a call to change the subject by rejecting the choice as necessary or even possible. What we certainly cannot do is articulate our opposition to that notion of identity in their language.

Anderson's analysis would be stronger if he said something about the always already gendered character of racial identity and the racializing of gender. I do not believe that the notion of a "cult of black masculinity" can, otherwise, be properly understood. From nineteenth- and early twentieth-century descriptions of black people as the "feminine race" to the infamous "Moynihan Report," with its thesis on the matriarchal structure of the black family, black racial identity has predominantly been gendered female. In the former case, black men are constructed as lacking the manly virtues of courage, strength, and aggressiveness; in the latter case, they are construed as effeminate because they do not conform to the bourgeois ideal of breadwinner and head of household. Thus, there is a devious and deviant inversion of masculine and feminine identity in a group otherwise gendered female. Black masculinity, then, is a complex assertion of gender prerogatives under the constraints of racial and gender hierarchy (themselves interpenetrating) and enforced, again in a complex way, by "compulsory heterosexuality." We can better understand the cult of black masculinity (why it is so tenacious and hyperbolic) and attack it more effectively when we understand the complex conditions of its production. This goes part of the way in explaining the counterconstruction of black identity, within the "cult of black masculinity," as normatively *male,* ingroup subordination as distinctively *female*, and racial deviance as prototypically *homosexual.*

Anderson's critique of the black church as a major promoter of homophobia is surprisingly mild, given his assessment of the ravages of black masculinity. The black church is a profoundly ambivalent and contradictory site. No site is as important in the production of heterosexist ideology, few as important in their potential store of antiheterosexist resources. This ambivalence and ambiguity may explain Anderson's mood. Anderson's critique is a running commentary on the views of Michael Eric Dyson, a kind of point counterpoint. Dyson paints a romantic-heroic portrait of the black church to which Anderson objects. Dyson makes an argument that is thoroughly idealist where, on the level of form, "the musical performances of gay members negate the gay bashing sermon just preached." Anderson passes over this claim in editorial silence, concealing what I would imagine is a sardonic smile. Dyson makes a ludicrous argument about the Manichean and Cartesian[4] derivations of black church homophobia, and Anderson demurs. There is something especially distasteful about Dyson's desire (attributable no doubt to his narrow black nationalism) to construct the human-all-too-human failures and foibles of black people as a "white thing." Thankfully, Anderson speaks to that point. Surprisingly, Anderson does not take Dyson to task for his hyperbolic reading of the black church as "liberationist." Dyson's account of the black church is liberal racial apologetics at its worst. What Dyson calls the black church's social justice orientation has always been the tail that occasionally (and always sluggishly) wags the dog. On the issue of homosexuality in particular, public, "prophetic" care and concern is merely the tip of an iceberg of silence, lethargy, and contempt.

It is not surprising given this state of affairs that Anderson rejects the absolutism of theological rationality, proposing instead multiple centers, sources, and modes of ethical reflection. Each of these ethical rationalities (or languages) has the power to "trump"; none has the power to trump absolutely, but the language of "higher law" comes close. It is in this context that I place Anderson's allusions to "human needs" and "natural rights." Recognition of these needs and rights, according to Anderson, is a sufficient basis for protecting the lives and bodily integrity of gays and lesbians, ensuring their access to adequate means of labor, freedom of movement, and psychological goods such as basic human respect. Cruelty and humiliation exemplify what it means not to respect the basic humanity of gays and lesbians.

Anderson's position is indebted, he says, to the new natural law theories of John Finnis, Germain Grisez, Joseph Boyle, and others. Presumably, they do not derive their views of natural law from Aristotelian or Christian teleologies; nor do they depend on scientific notions of nature, especially those that regard nature as a "closed," mechanistic, causal continuum. On Anderson's view, science may help us better understand homosexuality, but it cannot determine our normative judgments. Nor can particular religious beliefs about the orders and ends of creation determine our judgments; again, here as with science, religious beliefs are not privileged, but they may be a factor in our judgments. In the end, Anderson's is a democratic vision, where agreement is forged through public discourse. One need not be seduced by illusions of "distortion-free communication" or forget Marx's critique of the formal character of liberal democracy[5] to see the virtues of Anderson's position. When he argues that "a system of natural goods and natural rights can be agreed upon in public discourse," I do not construe "public discourse" in liberal or ideal terms.

In explicating his account, Anderson establishes a "hierarchy of goods." Natural goods are basic and include an internal hierarchy of "categorical" or primary and "reflexive" or secondary goods. Categorical goods refer to the bodily aspects of the self and reflexive goods to spiritual dimensions. Both presuppose "common goods of liberty and justice." Common goods, therefore, are fundamentally political goods. They are political in a foundational or higher way in the same way that constitutional law is higher than statutory law in the American political system. The very possibility of fulfilling basic human, natural goods depends on the common political goods of liberty and justice.

Anderson cites the new natural law theorists, but his language (indeed all human rights language) owes a great deal to Lockean notions of higher law, reformulated by Jefferson and radicalized by the French Revolution, where they were called the "Rights of Man." This is not to suggest, of course, that there aren't other genealogies, or that Anderson's account cannot supplement this one. But human rights, on this view, is a bourgeois humanist notion. Revolutionary in its time as a critique of the arbitrary and absolutist power of church and state, it is still revolutionary, as the events in Tiananmen Square demonstrate. We may owe our knowledge of the limitations of this liberal idea to Marx, but that has not prevented human rights from being a powerful weapon against the tyranny of actually existing socialist regimes. Only in the "downbeat and Alexandrian culture"[6] of the West, with its terminally, "pyrrhonically" skeptical, pseudosophisticated savants, are human rights construed *solely* as metaphysical—a dangerous humanist illusion. Like these skeptics, I do not think that metaphysical accounts of human rights are persuasive; that is to say, those predicated, in most cases, on Aristotelian and/or Christian notions of natural law. Human rights are what *ought* to be the case in all societies and what *is* the case, however precarious, in some societies. This does not mean that the notion of human rights is an empty formalism, an abstract moral "ought" with no real prospects of becoming a concrete ethical "is." Human rights are a historically contingent practice and task; they have no foundation other than our imagination. They are actual only so far as we are willing to fight for them, human rights being something for which we are willing to live or die. Their universality is a project; there are no guarantees. To say that human rights are not underwritten by God, necessity, or the nature of things is only to say, again, that they are a human project. Higher law, in short, is a "language game"[7] and those who play this game (the vast majority of us) know what higher law means because they (we) know how it is used. Yes, words refer to other words in an endless play of "signification" and nothing can bring that process to an end, but everyone who knows how to play the game called higher law knows that the language of human rights trumps other claims. This is not grounded or justified; it is how we live, the condition for the possibility and actuality of what we do ground and justify. The fact that we are always already living is what makes us ethical subjects in the first place.[8]

Wittgenstein's notion of a language game suggests an important difference between the way Sanders and Anderson use the common vocabulary of natural and higher law. For Sanders, the game of sexual orientation is structured by the laws of nature, which is reminiscent of Thomas Aquinas, perhaps the most influential of all natural law thinkers. When her crypto-Thomistic notion of natural law is put into Aquinas's own words, it sounds like this:

> It is evident that all things partake in some way in the eternal law, in so far as, namely, from its being imprinted on them, they derive their respective inclinations to their proper acts and ends. . . . This participation of the eternal law, in the rational creature is called natural law. . . .
>
> [T]here is in man an inclination to things that pertain to him more specifically, according to that nature which he has in common with other animals; and in virtue of this inclination, those things are said to belong to the natural law, which *nature has taught to all animals*, such as sexual intercourse. . . .
>
> By human nature we may mean either that which is proper to man, and in this sense all sins, as being against reason, are also against nature . . . or we may mean that nature which is common to man and other animals, and in this sense, certain special sins are said to be against nature: e.g. contrary to sexual intercourse, which is natural to all animals, is unisexual lust, which has received the special name of the unnatural crime.[9]

These passages are long, but well worth quoting. Lisa Sowle Cahill puts the following gloss on Aquinas's view: "On this scale, sins which respect the procreative structure of the [sexual] act are deemed less grievous than those which violate or preclude it, so that contraception, masturbation, homosexuality and bestiality would all be worse than adultery, fornication, incest and rape."[10] I doubt that Sanders would adhere strictly to Aquinas's view; nevertheless, her view depends on this sort of reasoning. Anderson, on the view I am attributing to him, rejects *this* notion of natural law and regards the language of higher law as a game. To say it is a game is not to say that it is unimportant or trivial; on the contrary, the stakes in this game are very high, as high as they can get. In the game of higher law, as in many others, there are winners and losers. It would be a mistake, however, to think that we can simply stop playing, that this is a game we should be done with. When we stop playing the game, the game doesn't stop and the prospects of us losing only increase.

The stakes are high because our sexual orientation isn't something we have, it's what we do, how and where we live. The language of social construction is a poor substitute for the language of the natural; you simply can't do in the game of construction what you can do in the game of nature. That is why claims for the constructed nature of sexual orientation go hand in hand and often slide into natural-scientific claims. The way out of this slipsliding is to recognize the language of social construction as quite natural, as always already natural. The only interesting question pertains to the relative malleability of various aspects of our nature. Only those who have been seduced by the "modern world-picture" think they are making a distinction between nature and something else when they distinguish between what (relatively speaking) we can change and what we can't, between relative mutability and immutability. They are further seduced when they construct those aspects of our nature that resist change as primary and normative and the changeable aspects as secondary. On the flip-side are those who view regularities as social constructs, impositions of fixed identities on fluidity, multiplicity, non-identity, difference. I think that both perspectives are miscast. On the view recommended here, the language of social construction is simply the natural under another description; again, it is the way we refer (should refer) to those aspects of our nature that are more easily changed. From my perspective, sexual orientation *isn't* a "social construct," if by construct one means unnatural or easy to change. On the contrary, sexual orientation is one aspect of our nature that is least malleable and most difficult to change. What follows from this? That sexual orientation is fundamental to our identity, its soul, secret truth, and destiny? Not at all. All that need follow is that in constructing our identity, some aspects of our nature are less malleable than others. This doesn't make them truer, more natural, prototypically natural; it simply makes them more difficult to deal with.

I take very seriously Judith Butler's question, "What [is the] best way to trouble the gender categories that support gender hierarchy and compulsory heterosexuality?"[11] But I reject her answer, disagreeing essentially about what should be done with the ethical-political power of the "natural." Where Butler reaccents the natural as a discursive artifact, a social construct, I do just the opposite. For me, discourse and construction are other ways of talking about our nature. What's at stake here? Both of us are clearly unhappy with the language of the natural as we find it; but again, I do not construe nature (thus accepting the modern view) as determinism, biological or otherwise. Nor do I construe construction, change, and difference as antonyms for nature. Where Butler sees the language of nature as something that we had "best get rid of" or at least imprison forever in scare quotation marks, I view the natural as too valuable a tool not to use, too effective a weapon to concede to the "enemy."

The power of the tool nature becomes even clearer when we consider the aporias (dialectical deadends) of discourse. Butler's claims for discourse seem inflated. What does she mean by discourse anyway? How does she use the word? How Foucauldian is it? This is no call for a bloodless, analytic treatment of the word *discourse;* however, Butler's use of the word and its implications do command our attention. Foucault always delimits discourse: madness, medicine, penology, sexuality. He attends to their "conditions of emergence," which are always circumscribed in his account by Europe, the West, the ancient Mediterranean world. In contrast, Butler speaks of the discursive construction of sexuality and gender hierarchy by the "discourse of gender" without reference to any delimitations. Is the discourse of gender modern, premodern, or postmodern? Or does it cut across such temporally oriented and periodic constraints? Is the discourse of gender universal? How can a discourse be universal without feeding surreptitiously, parasitically, on humanist notions of the universally human? Notions of the universally human are not nearly as abhorrent to me as they are to Butler. Like her, I think such notions are dangerous, but I also think they are unavoidable.[12] If the discourse of gender is not universal, then how does she account for the wide generality, if not universality, of compulsory heterosexuality? Granted, the intensity of the compulsion may have interesting regional variations, but does she doubt the near universality of the heterosexual regime? Let me be clear about the purpose of these questions. I do not want to undermine (nor do I think I have) Butler's efforts to expose and delegitimize the regime of gender hierarchy and compulsory heterosexuality; her goal is my goal. What I have tried to do is show why we can do more in the game of "nature" than we can in the game of "construction."

Whether we repress the natural through the languages of discourse or social construction really doesn't matter; the natural will always return. It will do so because nature is a more powerful and intuitively persuasive way of talking about regularities (not the universally necessary) in human affairs. On my view, the natural can be reconfigured, it can't be set aside. Consequently, I think that notions of sexual orientation (whether we have one, many, or none) will always be articulated in the language of the natural, the lawful, and the higher. These notions will always stand in the shadow of God, under the authority of science, on the inscrutable ground of fate, or otherwise be haunted by spirits we have never imagined.

Notes

1. Both arguments for and against same-sex relationships are warranted. Both are rational, which only shows the limits of rationality. It shows just how weak a term of approbation or disapprobation rationality is. The truly interesting question is the inexplicable persuasiveness (the qualitative leap) that accounts for why we find one argument persuasive and not the other. It is because of this bedrock—the things that we do and for which we can give no account, that we can reason at all; these inexplicable things are the conditions for the possibility of rationality itself.

2. Of course, there is nothing necessary about the bourgeois family. Furthermore, the world is teeming with societies in which polygamy and strong parenting go hand in hand.

3. We all know good parents who have terrible children and terrible parents whose

children are good. We also know of unhealthy, dysfunctional two-parent families and healthy, highly functional single-parent families. That there are such exceptions on either side only proves the rule. We can talk about norms without thinking that deviations (we may have to amend our language) from the norm are abnormal or bad. If we can't do this, then we cannot talk about what is best for most people most of the time while simultaneously recognizing that it may not be best for some people some of the time, maybe most of the time.

4. *Manichean* is a fairly conventional term referring to a radically dualistic perspective: good and evil, light and dark, spirit and matter. This idea derives from the Manichees, a religious group, of Persian origin, which was widely influential in the Roman world of the third and fourth centuries. *Cartesian* refers to the philosophy of Rene Descartes (*Meditations* and *Discourse on Method*), especially his mind-body dualism, where subjectivity, the real self, that which is highest and noblest in man, is identified with the thinking *I*.

5. See Karl Marx, "On the Jewish Question," in *The Marx-Engels Reader*, 2d ed., ed. Robert Tucker (New York: W. W. Norton, 1978) for a classic and controversial version of this critique.

6. I get this formulation, which I adopt for a similar but different purpose, from Roberto Unger, *Social Theory* (New York: Cambridge University Press, 1987), p. 223.

7. This term is associated with the philosopher Ludwig Wittgenstein, who defines a language game as a "primitive language" where language and actions are part of a complex weave. The meaning of words is defined by their use, their place in a particular "game." Human rights is a particular kind of game, differing significantly from other games such as guessing riddles or making a joke. Each of these games is a tool in the toolbox of language, but they do different things: we regard them differently, give them different weight, feel ourselves obligated to different degrees or not at all, and so on. See Wittgenstein's *Philosophical Investigations*, 3d ed., trans. G. E. M. Anscombe (New York: Macmillan, 1953).

8. Michael Weston, *Kierkegaard and Modern Continental Philosophy* (London: Routledge, 1994), pp. 121, 125, 127, 133.

9. Thomas Aquinas, *Basic Writings of Saint Thomas Aquinas*, vols. 1 and 2, ed. Anton C. Pegis (New York: Random House, 1945), pp. 750, 775–76.

10. Lisa Sowle Cahill, *Women and Sexuality* (Notre Dame, IN: Saint Mary's College, 1992), pp. 9–10.

11. Judith Butler, *Gender Trouble: Feminism and the Subversion of Identity* (New York: Routledge, 1990), p. viii.

12. I have never found "totalizing" arguments against humanism persuasive. Most antihumanist arguments of which I am aware presuppose the very essentialism they criticize. They speak of humanism as if it had an essence. Or they hold humanism to standards of purity that those of us whose "hands are dirty," and necessarily so, find amusing. Humanism, like any other form of evaluation, is dangerous. That is hardly an argument against it.

Part Two

TWO LEGAL PERSPECTIVES

Sexual and Religious Pluralism

ANDREW KOPPELMAN

The contending claims in this volume may be roughly taxonomized into two competing moral visions. According to one, sex can be morally worthy precisely and only because of its place in procreation. Even the marriages of infertile heterosexual couples take their meaning from the fact that they form a union of the procreative kind, and their bodily union therefore has procreative significance. From this perspective, the movement for same-sex marriage is a misguided attempt to deny fundamental moral distinctions.[1]

According to the other moral vision, sex is valuable, either in itself or because it draws us toward friendship of a singular degree and kind. This bringing together of persons has intrinsic worth, whether or not it leads to childbearing or childrearing. On this account, sexuality is linked to the flourishing of the next generation only to the extent that it is one of a number of factors that can bond adults together into stable familial units in which children are likely to thrive. It is not necessary or even important that the children be the biological product of the adults' sex acts. From this perspective, it is the devaluation of same-sex intimacy that is immoral because it reflects arbitrary and irrational discrimination.[2]

Today, both visions are reflected, at least to some extent, in the law. The view that homosexual conduct is intrinsically wrong often receives official sanction. Homosexual acts are still illegal in nearly half the states.[3] Although they have been on the books for a long time, these laws are not mere anachronisms; that they manifest an official line is most obvious in regulations of recent provenance in certain states that require public schools to teach that homosexual conduct is unacceptable.[4] (It is also manifest in the behavior of certain public school officials, who sometimes openly ridicule gay students and tolerate harassment and even violence against them.[5]) Gay people are sometimes officially discriminated against in public employment, notably in education, positions requiring security clearances, and the military.[6] Homosexuality is treated by some states' divorce courts as a per se reason for denying a parent custody or visitation rights.[7] And, of course, same-sex couples are denied the right to marry.

But the other vision is gaining ground. A bare majority of the states have gotten rid of their sodomy laws. There have been efforts to reform school curricula in order to make them positively accepting of homosexual conduct.[8] Official discrimination against gay people has become far less frequent than it once was, to the point that the United States military no longer admits that that is what it is doing.[9] Discrimination against gays is illegal in a growing number of jurisdictions,[10] and those laws are sometimes enforced with astonishing zeal.[11] And family law has become less discriminatory against gay couples than it was, in some places offering them a status that approaches that of married heterosexual couples.[12]

Because both visions are reflected, to a certain extent, in the law, both sides feel stigmatized and marginalized. Consider the recent debate between Kenneth Karst, a prominent proponent of gay rights legislation, and Richard Duncan and Gary Young, two opponents of such legislation, about the social significance of Colorado's Amendment Two, eventually invalidated by the U.S. Supreme Court,[13] which nullified local ordinances prohibiting discrimination against gay people. Karst argues that the amendment stigmatized gays by "formally declaring the separation of a group of people from the community of citizens who are worthy of governmental protection against discrimination."[14] By constitutionalizing the right "to discriminate against citizens on the basis of their sexual orientation,"[15] the citizens of Colorado "pronounce[d] an official anathema on homosexual orientation."[16] The amendment, Karst concludes, was an official "permission-to-hate."[17]

Duncan and Young respond that the amendment's effect "is exactly the opposite of what Karst asserts. It is gay rights legislation that stigmatizes, marginalizes, and fences out identifiable groups of individuals, and Amendment Two serves to remove this stigma and its associated harms and restores government to a position of benign neutrality."[18] The purpose and effect of laws that protect gays from discrimination, Duncan and Young contend, is to destroy "the ability of traditional believers to govern their businesses in accordance with their most profound and deeply held principles and beliefs."[19] The religious beliefs of those who wish not to do business with practicing homosexuals are declared "homophobic, wrong, and immoral," and the believers themselves are forced "to choose between [their] deeply held (and widely shared) ethical beliefs and the right to participate in the economic life of the community."[20] The amendment, Duncan and Young conclude, merely restores the state to a position of neutrality, in which citizens may do business or not with anyone they choose.

For those who aspire to a society in which no group is unnecessarily stigmatized and marginalized,[21] this debate may present a problem with no solution. In this essay, however, I want to explore one possible resolution. The basic idea is drawn from the disestablishment of religion, in which none of the contending factions has been officially handed the victory palm, and instead the stakes of politics have been lowered. The proposal is that here, too, no faction's views are to be adopted by the state. Rather, the state would remain neutral about the moral status of homosexuality.

I remain undecided about whether I endorse this solution. This essay is tentative and exploratory. I have argued in the past and remain impressed by the arguments to the effect that the state should aggressively combat the stigmatization of homosexuality.[22] Nonetheless, I think that "disestablishment"[23] deserves more discussion than it has received. This essay is an attempt to begin that discussion.

In the first, longer part of the essay, I shall attempt to explain why a "disestablishment" solution is attractive. I will consider three arguments for neutrality about sexual morality. The first is that neutrality fosters *civil peace*. The second is that neutrality *avoids religious sectarianism*. The third, which is a reconceptualization of the second, is that neutrality *respects the plurality of reasonable views*. In the second part of the essay, I shall offer some preliminary reflections on what neutrality would mean in practice.

Why "Disestablishment"?

Civil Peace

The first and most obvious attraction of neutrality is that it promotes civil peace, which is a good thing both in itself and as a means to other valued political goals. Neutrality toward competing sexual moralities has the same advantage that, as Douglas Laycock has observed, the principle of government neutrality toward religion has: unlike the alternatives, it is not in principle impossible that everyone could agree to it.

> If we could all agree on the principle of government neutrality toward religion, we could all abandon our efforts to influence government on religious matters, and devote all that energy to religious practice and proselytizing in the private sector. Conflict over government's role in religion could, in theory, end. But if we interpret the Religion Clauses to mean that government may promote the religious views of the dominant religious faction so long as it refrains from coercion, we ensure perpetual battles for dominance, perpetual battles to control or influence the government's religious message. That interpretation abandons in principle the goal of eliminating conflict over the government's role in religion.[24]

Only a solution in which government remains neutral about the cultural status of homosexuality has any hope of eliminating political conflict over this issue.

Not only is civil peace a good thing in itself, but the warring factions may have other goals that are thwarted by the ongoing struggle over sexual morality. Large political stakes may turn on the amelioration of the culture war over homosexuality. For example, many on both sides of the homosexuality debate are uncomfortable with the prospect of a regime in which the corporate colossi that wield increasing power over Americans' daily lives are able to operate unconstrained by government regulation. The groups most inclined to resist corporate power, the neosocialist left and the religious right, will probably never be able to resist that power effectively until they are able to work together, at least for limited purposes.[25] Large elements of both sides, therefore, have good reasons to want a truce, if terms acceptable to both can be devised.[26]

Nonsectarianism

The second reason for a "disestablishment" solution is nonsectarianism. An official position concerning the status of homosexual conduct, it is sometimes argued, impermissibly creates an official government line on a matter of religious conscience. Although this argument reflects a sound intuition, it will not work without modification. In this section, I will explore what I take to be the strongest form of the argument. In the next, I will offer the modification.

The argument is strongest when brought to bear against the longstanding official condemnation of homosexuality, which, as Chief Justice Warren Burger observed while *defending* that official position, "is firmly rooted in Judaeo-Christian moral and ethical standards."[27] A major reason why homosexuality is stigmatized is because many Americans are Christians or Jews who interpret the Bible as forbidding homosexual conduct.[28]

Biblical morality as a justification for a law is problematic in the United States because the Supreme Court has held that, to be constitutional, a law must "have a secular legislative purpose."[29] Kent Greenawalt has explained why religious arguments are not a proper basis for state action.

> A liberal society . . . has no business dictating matters of religious belief and worship to its citizens. It cannot forbid or require forms of belief, it cannot preclude acts of worship that cause no secular harm, it cannot restrict expression about what constitutes religious truth. One needs only a modest extension of these uncontroversial principles to conclude that a liberal society should not rely on religious grounds to prohibit activities that either cause no secular harm or do not cause enough secular harm to warrant their prohibition.[30]

This does not mean that a law is invalid if it was enacted with religious motives;[31] that would mean, as Michael McConnell has argued, "that those whose understandings of justice are derived from religious sources are second-class citizens, forbidden to work for their principles in the public sphere."[32] It does, however, mean that those with moral objections to homosexual conduct have an obligation to translate those objections into secular terms.[33] At a minimum, the law ought to be *translatable* into such terms, even if its proponents do not actually do the translating.[34] "The absence of a strong secular justification for the categorization is the best evidence that the program favors religion over nonreligion, or one religion over another."[35]

Efforts to translate religious objections to homosexual conduct into secular terms have been, at least as of this writing, a conspicuous failure. Consider the argument that homosexual sex is morally defective because it is radically separate from procreation. Homosexual acts, it is sometimes argued, "close the sexual act to the gift of life."[36] The obvious response to this argument is that it cannot explain why the intercourse of sterile heterosexual couples is regarded as worthy rather than impermissible. This objection can be answered, but only by relying on premises that are deeply unsuitable for legislation in the United States. It is not possible to sustain a moral distinction between infertile heterosexual couples and homosexual couples, and thus to support legal discriminations between the two, except by relying on sectarian beliefs.[37]

The difficulty can be illustrated by considering David Novak's claim, in his essay in this volume, that homosexual unions cannot fall within the definition of a family because "by design these unions preclude procreation."[38] First, this is less clear than in the case of heterosexual couples who contracept. It is sometimes the case that a homosexual couple resembles many infertile heterosexual couples, wishing that their union could produce a child but knowing that it cannot. Novak does address the sterile-couples objection, but after setting aside the case of persons who are unaware of their sterility, notes that those who know they are sterile are "usually persons who are clearly beyond the age of childbearing."[39] In this way, he avoids discussing what should be the hardest case for him: a young couple, both of whom know that one of them is infertile. Of sterile couples and homosexual couples he writes, "in a homosexual union *ipso facto* sterility is intended, which is not the case in a heterosexual union. Unlike a homosexual union, it is not meant to be a substitute for a normal heterosexual union."[40] This depends on what is meant by a "normal" heterosexual union. If that means a procreative union, and one member of the couple is fully capable of procreating (with a different partner), then that person has chosen this marriage as a substitute for a "normal" heterosexual union. Is it immoral for that person to enter into that marriage? Novak does not appear to think so. What can justify drawing the line in this way?

One of the few writers who has offered a coherent justification for this distinction is James Hanigan.[41] Hanigan acknowledges that homosexual partners can become intimate friends. "But their oneness is and remains the oneness of friends to which unity sexual activity is not essential and is often a distraction. If sex is, in fact, essential to their friendship, the moral value of the friendship is called into question, for it brings into doubt the unconditional nature of their being for one another as friends."[42] Why is this not equally true of heterosexual couples? Why doesn't Hanigan regard *their* intercourse as an inessential distraction? "The unity of friends has features of unity and difference, but that difference is not sexual and so it is not in their sexual relationship that they manifest this unity and difference."[43] The specifically sexual difference of even the infertile married couple, it appears, gives their sexual union a value that the homosexual couple cannot attain. What is this value? "The unity ritualized and enacted in sexual behavior is a two-in-one flesh unity, a unity that has its created basis in the physical and biological complementarity of male and female. There are various ways human beings can imitate, or play at imaging this unity, but apart from the actual basis in reality of male and female sexual union, these ways are only pretense or imaginative simulations of the real thing."[44]

Everything here seems to turn on the "created basis" of the unity. From this perspective, as Paul Baumann has explained, heterosexual complementarity is taken to be a sign of God's creative design. "If we affirm a faith in a personal God who intends a purpose for us and whose creation evinces a design intelligible to reason as well as disclosed by revelation, it is only logical that we see that design manifest in the act that makes us."[45] Even a childless heterosexual marriage reflects this design, as it "remains a sign and symbol of humanity's foundational acts."[46]

Unless one posits a Creator whose intentions can be read off the sexual organs, however, the biological complementariness of the sexes contains, in itself, no moral implications whatsoever. To assert the contrary is to commit the well-known naturalistic fallacy, the mistake of deducing conclusions about what ought to be from premises that state only what is the case. Moreover, even if one believes for some reason that nonprocreative sex is intrinsically wrong, there remains the troubling case of the infertile heterosexual couple. Philo, a Judaeo-Platonist philosopher of the early Christian period, condemned as "unnatural" not only homosexuality and masturbation but also celibacy and failure to divorce a barren wife.[47] "Those who woo women who have been shown to be barren with other husbands are simply mounting them in the manner of pigs or goats and should be listed among the impious as enemies of God."[48] It is true that that complementariness means that heterosexual intercourse *typically* can realize a project, procreation, which homosexual intercourse cannot realize. But as soon as one extends one's approval to heterosexual intercourse that cannot be procreative, such as that of an infertile heterosexual couple, this distinction loses its salience.[49] One can still insist, as Hanigan does, that only heterosexual marriage can serve as "a symbolic sign of Christ's unity with his church,"[50] but here one has left philosophy behind and is entirely in the realm of dogmatic theology. There is, of course, no way to disprove the claim that sexuality is a sacrament that symbolizes the wholeness of the created order, but there is no way to demonstrate this claim, either. (And, of course, one may accept the claim without drawing any negative inference about homosexual conduct per se.)

This view of homosexuality is not a necessary consequence of monotheism, of course. It is at least equally consistent with (at least) the Judaeo-Christian tradition to consider it impious for one to presume knowledge of God's intentions in creating the universe: "Where wast thou when I laid the foundations of the earth? declare, if thou hast understanding."[51] Monotheism does not necessarily entail a belief in natural teleology. There is no reason in principle why one cannot believe in God without also believing that He is a kind of cosmic Kilroy, Who feels impelled to leave His initials carved on every tree. On the other hand, abandoning teleology does place great demands on religious faith. Without natural teleology, faith must stand on its own bottom, rather than leaning on comforting hints drawn from observed phenomena. And this is, perhaps, why ateleological accounts are resisted so fiercely. Faith is hard.

This kind of argument will not do as a basis for legislation in a nonsectarian state. Peter L. Berger observes that the most fundamental polarity that divides the world's religions is that between the typically Western "experience of the divine as the personal God who speaks to man,"[52] a being who is no part of the cosmos but stands outside it as its creator, and the typically Eastern conception of the divine that "does not confront man from the outside but is to be sought within himself as the divine ground of his own being and of the cosmos."[53] The idea of nature as the product of a divine artificer, such that any deviation from the ordinary tendencies of that order places one fundamentally out of harmony with the divine, makes sense from the Western, not the Eastern, perspective. A law that is enacted on this basis is predicated on the implicit denial of half the world's understanding of God. (It is noteworthy that Buddhism regards homosexuality with no particular opprobrium.)[54]

In sum, state neutrality on the homosexuality question may be an instance of neutrality on religious questions in general. An official line on the moral permissibility of homosexual conduct may be objectionable for the same reasons one might object to an official line on the moral permissibility of eating pork. In both cases, the state is taking a position on what seems to be essentially a religious question.

The antisectarian argument for neutrality has a crucial weakness, however. It depends on proving a negative: that there is no secular justification for an official line on homosexuality. Many are unpersuaded that this is so. When a federal law restricting Medicaid funding for abortions was challenged on the basis that "it incorporates into law the doctrines of the Roman Catholic Church concerning the sinfulness of abortion and the time at which life commences," the Supreme Court responded that the statute "is as much a reflection of 'traditionalist' values towards abortion, as it is an embodiment of the views of any particular religion."[55] One may similarly argue that state condemnation of homosexuality merely reflects the traditionalist view that homosexual conduct is worthless and harmful, a view that stands on its own bottom without depending on any particular religious doctrine.

This kind of response threatens to vitiate the secular purpose requirement altogether: a state could argue, for instance, that a statute prohibiting the teaching of the theory of evolution in the public schools reflects "traditionalist" values toward the origins of the human race. A claim of impermissible purpose is usually a claim that the justifications for a law that the state is offering are too implausible to be believed. Brian Barry has argued that, because "the moral condemnation of acts that are not harmful to others makes sense only against a background of religious belief," the common condemnation of homosexual conduct is intelligible only as "a sort of religious hangover."[56] Still, the causal connection with religion is less clear than it is in the case of the anti-evolution law. Barry concedes that "we find people in contemporary societies who are prepared to say that . . . homosexual acts between consenting adults are wrong, even though they are not willing to invoke any tenet of religion to back up their claim."[57]

Pluralism

There may, however, be a way of reconceptualizing the antisectarian argument that avoids this difficulty. Instead of saying that the homosexuality debate *is* a religious one, it may be more helpful and accurate to say that the debate is sufficiently *like* a religious debate that the kind of principled political approach we use for religious disagreements recommends itself here. The argument then would present itself, not as an application of the Establishment Clause of the First Amendment, but as a moral argument that resembles a First Amendment argument.

Even if it is stipulated that there are coherent, secular reasons for disapproving of homosexual conduct, there are equally coherent and attractive views that approve of that conduct. From the fact of reasonable disagreement, John Rawls and his followers have argued, it is possible to infer a moral imperative to respect the reasonable beliefs of others. The basic idea, as Stephen Macedo has expressed it, is that "the most basic political rights and institutions should be justified in terms of reasons and arguments that can be shared with reasonable people whose religious and other ultimate commitments differ."[58]

With both religion and sexual orientation, the citizenry is deeply divided about what is truly good and valuable. Many Catholics believe that they are members of the one true church; some Protestants think (and many more used to think) that the pope is the Antichrist. I am persuaded that many of the same-sex couples I know have achieved the precise kind of human good that I am pursuing in my own, heterosexual marriage, and that the good I am pursuing is not the only good that sex can realize; others think that all sexual acts outside heterosexual marriage are per se morally worthless and even pernicious. Both disagreements point up the difficulty of resolving disputes about the human good (which is why some liberal political theorists, such as John Rawls, Ronald Dworkin, Bruce Ackerman, and Robert Nozick, have wanted to leave such questions out of political theory altogether).[59]

American law is not neutral about the value of religion. On the contrary, religion holds a privileged place in the American regime. The state respects religion, even favors it with tax and other special exemptions. But "religion" is defined, for public purposes, so abstractly that most theological controversies are simply bracketed. The state thus takes a stance sufficiently lacking in specificity (without being vacuous of content) that citizens of widely varying religious convictions can endorse it. Whatever one's substantive religious belief, one could perhaps agree with Finnis that "if there is a transcendent origin of the universal order-of-things and of human freedom and reason, then one's life and actions are in fundamental disorder if they are not brought, as best one can, into some sort of harmony with whatever can be known or surmised about that transcendent other and its lasting order."[60] And this may be the best justification available for the special treatment accorded to religion—defined very abstractly—under the First Amendment of the U.S. Constitution.[61]

A similarly abstract endorsement of the good of sexuality may be the most principled position for the state to take in our present culture war. In constitutional law, the question of whether homosexual sex is protected by the right to privacy is generally understood to be bound up with the debate over the level of abstraction at which to define a fundamental right. That debate is relevant here.

Robert Bork has criticized the entire American privacy doctrine on the ground that the Court's choice of the level at which to define the protected liberty was necessarily arbitrary. In the germinal privacy case, *Griswold* v. *Connecticut*,[62] which struck down a law prohibiting married couples (among others) from using contraceptives, the Supreme Court certainly did not adopt the very broad principle that "government may not interfere with any acts done in private," but it is hard to explain why the principle should be defined narrowly, as "government may not prohibit the use of contraceptives by married couples."

Why does the principle extend only to married couples? Why, out of all forms of sexual behavior, only to the use of contraceptives? Why, out of all forms of behavior, only to sex? . . .

To put the matter another way, if a neutral judge must demonstrate why principle *X* applies to cases *A* and *B* but not to case *C* . . . , he must, by the same token, also explain why the principle is defined as *X* rather than *X minus*, which would cover *A* but not cases *B* and *C*, or as *X plus*, which would cover all cases, *A*, *B*, and *C*.[63]

Some constitutional interpreters have argued that the solution is to define rights as broadly as possible,[64] while others have relied on tradition to try to restrict their scope.[65] The latter strategy has elicited the persuasive rejoinder that tradition is too indeterminate for the task.[66] The way the United States deals with religious disagreement suggests another approach.

The problem of religious toleration is itself a "levels of abstraction" problem. Few people any longer will endorse the position of Fielding's Mr. Thwackum, who denounced the "absurd errors and damnable deceptions" of "all the enemies to the true Church" and declared, "nor is religion manifold, because there are various sects and heresies in the world. When I mention religion I mean the Christian religion; and not only the Christian religion, but the Protestant religion; and not only the Protestant religion, but the Church of England."[67] Today, we think about religious liberty more abstractly than that, and a kind of parity among religions, at least for political purposes, has been admitted and even made judicially enforceable. Government is forbidden to "aid, foster, or promote one religion or religious theory against another or even against the militant opposite."[68]

At least part of the reason why Mr. Thwackum's position has lost out is that many people now think that the good of religion is realized, albeit imperfectly, in denominations that are not their own. Many are also less sure than their ancestors were that their religion is the true and only way. Increasingly, the same can be said about our differences concerning sexual ethics. And so it becomes possible to agree on a state policy that, while not neutral with respect to *all* sexual practices—the state may continue to treat long-term unions differently from other sexual relationships—no longer discriminates between same-sex and opposite-sex relationships.

Why should the good of sexuality be defined at just this level of abstraction? I'm not sure that there's a better answer than the fact that, as increasing numbers of citizens understand, gay people have a respectable claim to moral parity. Proponents of gay rights are frequently challenged to explain why their position does not also require equality for pedophiles, sadists, practitioners of incest, and necrophiliacs. The distinction need not be drawn from high theory; it is enough to notice that none of these sexual practices has become the basis of a worldwide liberation movement whose moral claims persuade increasing numbers of citizens, legislatures, and courts.[69] (If some want to argue that these other practices are as good as the ones that are now valued and honored, they must make their case, as gay people have done.)

Most of us can, I hope, agree that a lasting commitment with another person, which is somehow connected with the bodily intimacy that our sexual faculties make possible, is a good thing, perhaps even one of the best things in life. Even if we disagree about whether homosexual intimacy instantiates this good, perhaps we can agree that the claims gay people have made that their intimacy realizes something valuable is at least as colorable as the claims of members of unconventional religions that their religious activity realizes something valuable. The Supreme Court's declaration in *Bowers* v. *Hardwick* that "[n]o connection between family, marriage, or procreation on the one hand and homosexual activity on the other has been demonstrated"[70] reveals an obtuseness reminiscent of Mr. Thwackum. The similarities between these two issues suggest a similar solution in each case: the state can recognize, promote, and protect the pursuit of the good in question, but should define that good at a sufficiently high level of abstraction as to be neutral between the competing factions. The state should not try to decide which faction is right. This means an end to discrimination against same-sex couples; it also, however, means that the state should not denounce religious doctrines that condemn homosexual conduct. The state should endorse neither the idea that gay people are perverts nor the idea that proponents of traditional sexual morality are bigots.

What Would It Look Like?

What would it mean in practice for the government to be neutral with respect to sexual orientation issues? This question is explored in detail in Michael McConnell's essay in this volume. I will not attempt to duplicate his thorough survey, but will offer some reflections about the difficulties of answering this question, and a few reactions to his answers.

With respect to indoctrination (on behalf of either faction) in the public schools, Gay Pride days, and the like, it is clear how the law would be modified because it is clear that the disputed policies depend on the state's taking a position on the morality of homosexual conduct per se. Without the state's taking such a position, the policy could not exist. Professor McConnell does not appear to disagree with Andrew Sullivan's argument that the public schools ought to teach the salient facts about homosexuality in those classes that deal with sexuality issues, without any evaluative overlay whatsoever.[71] McConnell's observations about the difficulty of maintaining neutrality in the public school curriculum are well taken. Nonetheless, it is not impossible to teach these facts fairly, any more than it is impossible to teach the facts about topics as controversial as evolution or abortion. Presumably, McConnell does not mean to suggest that disestablishment of religion means that we must reconcile ourselves to "the result that American children are dreadfully ignorant about their own religious traditions, as well as those of others."[72] I don't think that "disestablishment" with respect to sexual orientation means that we must reconcile ourselves to ignorance about homosexuality, either. The option of excluding discussion of homosexuality from the curriculum is neither neutral nor acceptable, for the same reasons that excluding, say, Darwin's theory of evolution from the curriculum is unacceptable: religious disagreement is not a good reason to withhold relevant information from students. Unless the state gets out of the education business altogether, turning that task over to private enterprise via vouchers or some similar school choice plan—and this *would* be a solution to our problem[73]—it must take a position on what the basic elements of an education are. Any educated person ought to know the basic facts about sex, and the incidence of homosexual conduct is one of those basic facts. Those facts by themselves dictate no particular moral evaluation of homosexuality: many who have no dispute about the facts still disagree vehemently about homosexuality's moral status. Schools should not be neutral about whether their students know anything about these matters.

In the case of school curricula that praise or condemn homosexuality, it is clear just what role the forbidden moral evaluation of homosexuality is doing in the formulation of the policy. We know that, absent that evaluation, the policy would be different. It is harder to say what a "disestablishment" solution would look like with antidiscrimination law or same-sex marriage because reasonable people disagree about the role that moral evaluation plays in the formulation of the policies we have now. Professor McConnell is correct when he observes that "few laws are based solely on moral disapproval."[74]

The difficulty may be made clearer by considering an analogous problem in antidiscrimination law. When courts monitor governmental decision making for illicit discriminatory motivation, David Strauss has observed, they must ask, "suppose the adverse effects of the challenged government decision fell on whites instead of blacks, or on men instead of women. Would the decision have been different?"[75] This standard, Strauss observes, threatens to dissolve into speculative or meaningless questions, such as "Would abortion be outlawed if men could get pregnant?"

A similar problem arises under the Establishment Clause. The "secular purpose" inquiry is somewhat less speculative than that required by the prohibition of racial discrimination, since the question is not the counterfactual one of whether, if a motivation had not been present, the state would have behaved differently, but rather the logical one of whether a conclusion follows even if a certain premise is denied. The difficulty remains, however. Reasonable people can sometimes disagree about whether the secular justification for a law is plausible, or rather is merely an excuse for sectarian legislation.[76]

It is likewise uncertain whether many state policies would be the same or different if the state were forbidden to consider any particular moral evaluation of homosexuality in its formulation of policy. "It is often the case," Kent Greenawalt observes, "that someone who is confident that arguments in combination are strong enough to yield a conclusion will not bother to decide whether the conclusion could survive elimination of one or more of the supporting arguments."[77] Would discrimination against gay people be prohibited if government were neutral about the morality of homosexual conduct? Is a negative judgment about such conduct the reason why some states *don't* protect homosexuals from discrimination? Is an affirming judgment the reason why other states do? If both judgments are excluded from decision making, what does the balance of remaining policy considerations dictate? These are hard questions.

The argument that antidiscrimination protection of gay people stigmatizes traditional moral views is a familiar one. As noted at the beginning, proponents of traditional sexual mores who think that homosexual conduct is per se immoral often complain that they are stigmatized by antidiscrimination laws that protect gay people. As Justice Scalia recently observed, such ordinances are intended by at least some of their supporters to achieve "not merely a grudging social toleration, but full social acceptance, of homosexuality."[78] Elsewhere I have agreed with Scalia's view, arguing that cultural transformation of this sort is a legitimate goal of antidiscrimination law.[79] For present purposes, of course, I must abjure that goal. But as Professor McConnell observes, state neutrality on sexual ethics does not necessarily exclude antidiscrimination protection of gay people, any more than the disestablishment of religion necessarily excludes antidiscrimination protection of religious minorities. "Disestablishment" does demand an easily available exemption for those who think that homosexual conduct is intrinsically immoral, but such exemptions may be defensible even without "disestablishment." The Civil Rights Act of 1964's moral condemnation of racism did not preclude exemptions for very small businesses.

Finally, in family law, most of the reforms would work to the benefit of gay people. The state would no longer discriminate against homosexual parents in granting custody or visitation rights. Same-sex couples would receive, at a minimum, some legal recognition.

Marriage is the issue with respect to which it is hardest to carve out a neutral position. It is misleading, although not precisely wrong, to say that gay people want government to "adjust the definition of a public institution to conform with the doctrines or desires of a minority."[80] The claim is rather that the present institution's contours can be defended only by relying on the forbidden view that heterosexual sex is morally superior to homosexual sex. To pursue the "disestablishment" analogy, gay people's claim is like the objection non-Orthodox Jews raise to Israel's laws that refuse to recognize their marriages unless they are performed by Orthodox rabbis.[81] In a sense, the Establishment Clause itself is a command that government adjust the definition of a public institution to conform with the doctrines or desires of a minority.

It is sometimes argued that "domestic partnerships," in which same-sex couples would receive limited legal recognition and some of the tangible benefits of marriage, would produce neutrality. However, even if those partnerships were to provide same-sex couples with *all* the tangible benefits that married couples receive, they still would presuppose that the partnerships of same-sex couples are a different, evidently inferior kind of thing from heterosexual marriage. Imagine if, after *Loving* v. *Virginia*,[82] which invalidated laws against interracial marriage, the Southern states had proposed domestic partnerships of this sort for interracial couples. The insulting connotations seem no less clear here. This looks like a regime of noncoercive establishment. It is not neutrality.

This is not to say, of course, that gay people should resist domestic partnership legislation. Such legislation may be the closest thing to equality that's politically feasible today. The best shouldn't be the enemy of the merely less bad. But the principled objection should be kept in sight. Domestic partnership may be better than what we have now, but it isn't neutral.

One answer to this objection is to say, as the Hungarian Constitutional Court did a few years ago, that the institution of marriage is somehow *sui generis*, and can be deemed inherently heterosexual without in any way stigmatizing same-sex relationships as inferior. The court thus rejected the claim that it was sex discrimination to confine marriage to the union of a man and a woman. But the court went on to hold that, to the extent that the state recognized and protected the partnerships of unmarried couples, there was no constitutional justification for discriminating against couples of the same sex. This reasoning seems to imply that any discrimination between same-sex couples and opposite-sex couples in distributing benefits *other* than marriage licenses is impermissibly discriminatory.[83] Whether the Constitutional Court's reasoning is deemed persuasive for present purposes will depend on whether you believe that the cordoning off of a "separate but equal" status for same-sex couples can avoid, at least in the context of American culture, being stigmatizing.

A second approach has been suggested by Ben Cayetano, the governor of Hawaii: simply remove the word marriage from all state documents and replace it with domestic partnerships that would be equally available to *all* couples, whether of the same or different sexes. "Marriage has a religious and a legal aspect," he said shortly before he was elected. "The state should leave the sanctioning of marriage to the religious organizations. The state should consider establishing domestic partnerships setting forth the legal rights and obligations of people who choose to enter into personal relationships, regardless of their sexual orientation. These rights and obligations include such matters as passing on assets on to partners, health plan coverage—rights and privileges which heterosexuals take for granted."[84] The trouble with this solution is that the institution of state-sanctioned marriage has real secular value. It recognizes and helps to maintain the stability of one of the most important forms of private association, one on which the well-being of adults and children alike depends. An institution that important cannot simply be reconstructed from scratch.[85]

These considerations are the reason why it is less obvious to me than it is to McConnell that "[t]he true 'disestablishment' policy is to eliminate marriage as a public institution: to leave all decisions about marriage to private contract."[86] "Disestablishment" does not mean that the state must be neutral with respect to sexuality or household arrangements. It means only that the state must be neutral with respect to the moral status of homosexuality. If preference for heterosexuality is the only reason for excluding homosexual couples from the existing institution of marriage, then that exclusion should end.

It is for this reason that I offer the suggestion that the best "disestablishment" approach *might* be for the state to issue marriage licenses to same-sex and opposite-sex couples alike. This, of course, invites the objection that the state is taking a controversial position here, too: it is declaring that same-sex couples are the moral equivalent of opposite-sex couples. This objection, though, seems equally applicable to the present state practice of permitting, for example, remarriage after divorce. Why is this not deemed an official repudiation of, for example, the Catholic Church's line on the indissolubility of marriage? As Charles Curran observes elsewhere in this volume, "[t]he civil law not only allows divorce but it also provides civil recognition and benefits to divorced and remarried people. Catholic leaders are not engaging in any activities to change the present divorce law." If the state has succeeded in desacralizing civil marriage in that context, perhaps it can in this one, too. Indeed, the problem may solve itself: many religious people will experience little confusion about the state's powers of sanctification once a practice as odious to them as same-sex marriage gets civil recognition.

Conclusion

As I stated earlier, this essay's ambition was to place the neutrality option on the table, not necessarily to endorse it. Prejudice against gay people is an ugly and pernicious thing, and it is pervasive in our society. It ought to be combatted. State neutrality toward it is toleration of evil. Nonetheless, neutrality has its attractions. I do not doubt that my cause is just, but I also recognize the costs of continued battle.

Notes

I have benefited from conversations with Michael McConnell during the writing of this piece. I am also grateful to Richard Duncan, Douglas Laycock, and Brian Leiter for helpful comments on an earlier draft.

1. See, e.g., Germain Grisez, *The Way of Lord Jesus: Living a Christian Life* (Quincy, IL: Franciscan Press, 1993), 2: 633–80; John M. Finnis, "Law, Morality, and 'Sexual Orientation'," *Notre Dame Law Review* 69 (1994): 1049–76; "The Homosexual Movement: A Response by the Ramsey Colloquium," *First Things* (March 1994): 15–20.

2. See generally Andrew Sullivan, *Virtually Normal: An Argument About Homosexuality* (New York: Knopf, 1995); Richard Mohr, *A More Perfect Union: Why Straight America Must Stand Up for Gay Rights* (Boston: Beacon, 1994); David A. J. Richards, *Sex, Drugs, Death, and the Law: An Essay on Human Rights and Overcriminalization* (Totowa: Rowman and Littlefield, 1982), pp. 29–83.

3. See William B. Rubenstein, *Cases and Materials on Sexual Orientation and the Law*, 2d ed. (St. Paul: West, 1997), pp. 147–48.

4. Official regulations on the subject also sometimes either prohibit the viewpoint that homosexuality is acceptable or totally ban the topic from the curriculum. See Nancy Tenney, "The Constitutional Imperative of Reality in Public School Curricula: Untruths About Homosexuality as a Violation of the First Amendment," *Brooklyn Law Review* 60 (1995): 1599–1651.

5. See *Nabozny v Podlesny*, 92 F3d 446 (7th Cir 1996); Donna Dennis and Ruth Harlow, "Gay Youth and the Right to Education," *Yale Law & Policy Review* 4 (1986): 446–78.

6. See generally Rubenstein, *Cases and Materials on Sexual Orientation*, pp. 507–666.

7. See ibid., pp. 810.

8. Thus, for example, the multicultural curriculum developed for use in public schools in New York City declared that first-grade classes "should include references to lesbians/gay people in all curricular areas," and to provide children with "actual experiences via creative play, books, visitors, etc. in order for them to view lesbians/gays as real people to be respected and appreciated." Board of Education of the City of New York, *Children of the Rainbow: First Grade* (1991), p. 372, quoted in Richard F. Duncan, "Who Wants to Stop the Church: Homosexual Rights Legislation, Public Policy, and Religious Freedom," *Notre Dame Law Review* 69 (1994): 414, n. 78.

9. See Andrew Koppelman, "Gaze in the Military: A Response to Professor Woodruff," *U.M.K.C. Law Review* 64 (1995): 188–93.

10. Ordinances or policies prohibiting discrimination on the basis of sexual orientation now "cover fully one-fifth of the American population." See James W. Button, Barbara A. Rienzo, and Kenneth D. Wald, "Where Local Laws Prohibit Discrimination Based on Sexual Orientation," *Public Management* (April 1995): 9.

11. For example, in one well-publicized case, two women who refused to share their apartment with a lesbian who had answered their advertisement were ordered to pay $3,300 in damages, plus attorney's fees. The decision was reversed on appeal. See Katherine Dalton, "Privacy and the 'Lesbian Roommate' Case," *Wall Street Journal*, 20 July 1992.

12. See generally Rubenstein, *Cases and Materials on Sexual Orientation*, pp. 687–800.

13. See *Romer v Evans*, 116 S.Ct. 1620 (1996).

14. Kenneth L. Karst, *Law's Promise, Law's Expression: Visions of Power in the Politics of Race, Gender, and Religion* (New Haven: Yale University Press, 1993), p. 185.

15. Ibid., p. 184.

16. Ibid., p. 185.

17. Ibid., p. 186.

18. Richard F. Duncan and Gary L. Young, "Homosexual Rights and Citizen Initiatives: Is Constitutionalism Unconstitutional?" *Notre Dame Journal of Law, Ethics and Public Policy* 9 (1995): 126.

19. Ibid., p. 127.

20. Ibid., p. 128.

21. For a defense of this aspiration, see Andrew Koppelman, *Antidiscrimination Law and Social Equality* (New Haven: Yale University Press, 1996), pp. 57–76.

22. See ibid., pp. 146–76.

23. In his essay in this volume, Michael McConnell uses "disestablishment," in lower case and in quotation marks, to refer to the proposed sexual orientation analogue of the Establishment Clause. I find this usage helpful, and adopt it in this essay.

24. Douglas Laycock, "Religious Liberty as Liberty," *Journal of Contemporary Legal Issues* 7 (1996): 322.

25. Norman Mailer's observations about the 1996 presidential candidacy of Pat Buchanan, which briefly threatened to deprive Senator Robert Dole of the Republican nomination, are astute and noteworthy:

In the military sense—and where was any pleasure to be found in a campaign analysis without a military analogy?—Buchanan had anchored his right flank on pro-life. Abortion, he had made clear, could never be acceptable. His right-wing credentials impeccable, therefore, Buchanan was free to move as far as he wished to the left, the economic left; the Corporation could now be attacked from the left *and* the right. A crucial difference. No political force would ever prevail against the Corporation if it could move forward on only one flank or the other; it would soon be opposed by the other wing brought along quickly to join ranks with the center (exactly what happened in the election crusades against Goldwater in '64 and McGovern in '72). The Corporation, monarch of the center, could be deposed only if both ends attacked in combination. Left-conservatism! For forty-five years, it had been no more than an oxymoron. Now, with Buchanan, there was a gleam of possibility, call it no more than a wink, but the possibility was there.

Norman Mailer, "Searching for Deliverance," *Esquire*, August 1996, 57. See also Garry Wills, *Under God: Religion and American Politics* (New York: Simon and Schuster, 1990), pp. 97–114.

26. It must be acknowledged that the abortion issue is an even deeper source of division between these two factions, and that with respect to that issue, a compromise that is minimally acceptable to all sides may not be possible even in principle.

27. *Bowers v Hardwick,* 478 U.S. 186, 196 (1996) (Burger, C.J., concurring).

28. In his contribution to the present volume, Max Stackhouse recognizes the centrality of religious views to the homosexuality debate. "It is unlikely that we can grasp the profound bases of reservation about homosexuality in our society if we do not understand that this reservation is rooted in a fundamental theological conception about the nature of human identity under God and of how human life therefore ought to be lived in society." Max L. Stackhouse, "The Prophetic Stand of the Ecumenical Churches on Homosexuality," p. 125.

29. *Lemon v Kurtzman,* 403 U.S. 602, 612 (1971).

30. Kent Greenawalt, *Religious Convictions and Political Choice* (New York: Oxford University Press, 1988), pp. 90–91.

31. "Although neither a State nor the Federal Government can constitutionally 'pass laws which aid one religion, aid all religions, or prefer one religion over another,' it does not follow that a statute violates the Establishment Clause because it 'happens to coincide or harmonize with the tenets of some or all religions.' That the Judaeo-Christian religions oppose stealing does not mean that a State or the Federal Government may not, consistent with the Establishment Clause, enact laws prohibiting larceny." *Harris v McRae,* 448 U.S. 297, 319 (1980), citations omitted.

32. Michael W. McConnell, "Religious Freedom at a Crossroads," *University of Chicago Law Review* 59 (1992): 144.

33. Cf. *Epperson v Arkansas,* 393 U.S. 97, 107 (1968) ("No suggestion has been made that Arkansas' law [prohibiting the teaching of evolution in public schools] may be justified by considerations of state policy other than the religious views of some of its citizens.").

34. John Rawls, the preeminent proponent of the idea that religious and other comprehensive views of the meaning of life ought not to drive political decision making, has come to a similar view. See his *Political Liberalism* (New York: Columbia University Press, paperback ed. 1996), pp. li–lii.

35. McConnell, "Religious Freedom at a Crossroads," p. 144.

36. *Catechism of the Catholic Church* (Vatican City: Liberia Editrice Vaticana, 1994), no. 2357.

37. My argument here has affinities with that of David Richards, "Sexual Preference as a Suspect (Religious) Classification: An Alternative Perspective on the Unconstitutionality of Anti-Lesbian/Gay Initiatives," *Ohio State Law Journal* 55 (1994): 491–553, but focuses more tightly than Richards does on the specific sectarian premises that underlie legislation that discriminates against gay people.

38. David Novak, "Religious Communities, Secular Society, and Sexuality," p. 15. Novak, to be sure, is not attempting to justify secular law, but the difficulties in his argument are likely to be replicated in any secular analogue.

39. Ibid., p. 21.

40. Ibid., p. 22.

41. In the present volume, Hanigan defends confining marriage to heterosexuals because "children or the possibility of children account for the state's interest in marriage." James P. Hanigan, "Sexual Orientation and Human Rights," p. 76. This ig-

nores the fact that many same-sex couples are very capably raising children. See Charlotte J. Patterson, "Children of Lesbian and Gay Parents," *Child Development* 63 (1992): 1025–42; *Baehr v Miike,* 1996 Westlaw 694235, 1996 Haw. App. Lexis 138 (Haw. Cir Ct., 1st Cir, 3 December 1996). The evidence does not support Novak's claim that "new citizens are best produced, cared for, and raised to responsible adulthood in a home founded on a permanently intended heterosexual union." Novak, "Religious Communities, Secular Society, and Sexuality," p. 16.

42. James P. Hanigan, *Homosexuality: The Test Case for Christian Sexual Ethics* (New York: Paulist Press, 1988), p. 100.

43. Ibid.

44. Ibid., p. 102.

45. Paul Baumann, "An Incarnational Ethic: Listening to One Another," *Commonweal,* 28 January 1994, p. 19.

46. Ibid.

47. See John Boswell, *Christianity, Social Tolerance, and Homosexuality: Gay People in Western Europe from the Beginning of the Christian Era to the Fourteenth Century* (Chicago: University of Chicago Press, 1980), p. 148.

48. Philo, trans. and quoted in ibid., p. 155.

49. I elaborate this argument in "Is Marriage Inherently Heterosexual?" *American Journal of Jurisprudence* 42 (forthcoming 1998), which critiques the arguments against homosexual conduct that have been offered by Aquinas, Germain Grisez, and John Finnis.

50. Hanigan, *Homosexuality: The Test Case for Christian Sexual Ethics,* p. 96.

51. Job 38:4, King James version.

52. Peter L. Berger, *The Heretical Imperative: Contemporary Possibilities of Religious Affirmation* (Garden City, NY: Anchor, 1980), p. 145.

53. Ibid., p. 147.

54. See Jose Ignacio Cabezon, "Homosexuality and Buddhism," in *Homosexuality and World Religions,* ed. Arlene Swidler (Valley Forge: Trinity Press International, 1993), pp. 81–101.

55. *Harris v McRae,* 448 U.S. 297, 319 (1980).

56. Brian Barry, "How Not to Defend Liberal Institutions," in *Liberalism and the Good,* eds. R. Bruce Douglass, Gerald R. Mara, and Henry S. Richardson (New York: Routledge, 1990), p. 46.

57. Ibid.

58. Stephen Macedo, "Liberal Civic Education and Religious Fundamentalism: The Case of God v John Rawls?" *Ethics* 105 (1995): 475. See generally Rawls, *Political Liberalism,* p. 44 and passim.

59. See John Rawls, *A Theory of Justice* (Cambridge: Harvard University Press, 1971), p. 19; Ronald Dworkin, *A Matter of Principle* (Cambridge: Harvard University Press, 1985), p. 191; Bruce Ackerman, *Social Justice in the Liberal State* (New Haven: Yale University Press, 1980), p. 11; Robert Nozick, *Anarchy, State, and Utopia* (New York: Basic Books, 1974), p. 312.

60. Finnis, *Natural Law and Natural Rights* (Oxford: Clarendon Press, 1980), pp. 89–90.

61. I thus am sympathetic to John Garvey's claim that the First Amendment protects religion because it regards it as a good thing. See John H. Garvey, "An Anti-Liberal Argument for Religious Freedom," *Journal of Contemporary Legal Issues* 7 (1996): 275–91. I differ from Garvey in defining religion more broadly than he does, to include the rejection of belief. The Court has consistently rejected the position, es-

poused by Justice Scalia, that government endorsement of religion is impermissibly "sectarian" only when it specifies "details upon which men and women who believe in a benevolent, omnipotent Creator and Ruler of the world are known to differ (for example, the divinity of Christ.)" *Lee v Weisman,* 505 U.S. 577, 641 (1992) (Scalia, J., dissenting). If religion is defined at *that* level of abstraction, it excludes not only atheism and agnosticism but also Buddhism and Hinduism. This is merely a different incarnation of Mr. Thwackum. The more attractive view is that the state should not endorse any particular religious doctrine, but only the idea that "it is, at any rate, peculiarly important to have thought reasonably and (where possible) correctly about these questions of the origins of cosmic order and of human freedom and reason—whatever the answer to those questions turns out to be, and even if the answers have to be agnostic or negative." Finnis, *Natural Law and Natural Rights,* p. 89.

62. *Griswold v Connecticut,* 381 U.S. 479 (1965).

63. Robert Bork, "Neutral Principles and Some First Amendment Problems," *Indiana Law Journal* 47 (1971): 7.

64. See Bruce Ackerman, "Liberating Abstraction," *University of Chicago Law Review* 59 (1992): 317–48.

65. See *Michael H. v Gerald D.,* 491 U.S. 110, 127 n. 6 (1989) (opinion of Scalia, J., joined by Rehnquist, C.J.); Robert Bork, *The Tempting of America* (New York: Free Press, 1989), p. 150.

66. See Laurence H. Tribe and Michael C. Dorf, *On Reading the Constitution* (Cambridge: Harvard University Press, 1991), pp. 97–117.

67. Henry Fielding, *The History of Tom Jones, A Foundling* (New York: Modern Library, 1940), p. 82.

68. *Epperson v Arkansas,* 393 U.S. 97, 104 (1968).

69. For an overview of the international movement, see Aart Hendriks, Rob Tielman, and Evert van der Veen, *The Third Pink Book: A Global View of Lesbian and Gay Liberation and Oppression* (Buffalo: Prometheus, 1993). On worldwide legal developments, see James D. Wilets, "International Human Rights Law and Sexual Orientation," *Hastings International and Comparative Law Review* 18 (1994): 1–120. See also Robert Wintemute's very capable survey of human law in three leading jurisdictions, *Sexual Orientation and Human Rights: The United States Constitution, the European Convention and the Canadian Charter* (Oxford: Clarendon Press, 1995).

70. *Bowers v Hardwick,* 478 U.S. 186, 191 (1986).

71. It seems obvious to me that Sullivan's view would exclude the examples of gay rights propaganda that McConnell quotes.

72. McConnell, "What Would It Mean," p. 245.

73. This was pointed out to me by Rick Duncan.

74. McConnell, "What Would It Mean," p. 238.

75. David Strauss, "Discriminatory Intent and the Taming of *Brown,*" *University of Chicago Law Review* 56 (1989): 957.

76. Compare, for example, the majority and dissenting opinions in the Supreme Court cases that invalidated the mandatory posting of the ten commandments in the public schools, or a law requiring equal time for scientific creationism in any class that taught Darwin's theory of evolution. See *Stone v Graham,* 449 U.S. 39 (1980) (ten commandments); *Edwards v Aguillard,* 482 U.S. 578 (1987) (creationism).

77. Greenawalt, *Religious Convictions and Political Choice,* p. 37.

78. *Romer v Evans,* 116 S.Ct. 1620, 1634 (1996) (Scalia, J., dissenting).

79. See Koppelman, *Antidiscrimination Law and Social Equality,* pp. 141–76.

80. McConnell, "What Would It Mean," p. 249.

81. See Martin Edelman, *Courts, Politics, and Culture in Israel* (Charlottesville: University Press of Virginia, 1994), pp. 61–63.

82. *Loving v Virginia,* 388 U.S. 1 (1967).

83. Hungarian Constitutional Court, Decision No. 14/1995 (III.13.) AB Resolution, 7 March 1995.

84. Quoted in *Honolulu Star Bulletin*, 5 July 1994, sec. A, p. 3. Cayetano repeated this view after the election: "Marriage is a matter for churches and not for government." Quoted in *Honolulu Weekly*, 7 December 1994, p. 7.

85. This objection was pressed upon me forcefully and persuasively in conversation by Jean Bethke Elshtain. See also Jean Bethke Elshtain, "Against Gay Marriage: Accepting Limits," *Commonweal*, 22 November 1991, pp. 685–86. Including gay people in that institution does not, however, seem likely to alter the institution's basic character. Homosexuals are a variegated lot, and that subset who extol polymorphous perversity does not overlap much with the subset who would marry if the option were available. Same-sex couples do not in fact differ all that much, in terms of promiscuity or stability, from opposite-sex couples. See Andrew Koppelman, "Three Arguments for Gay Rights," *Michigan Law Review* 95 (1997): 1663–66.

86. McConnell, "What Would It Mean," p. 250.

What Would It Mean to Have a "First Amendment" for Sexual Orientation?

MICHAEL W. MCCONNELL

As the essays in this volume confirm, reasonable thinkers from a wide spectrum of belief systems and communities of conscience disagree about the morality and legality of homosexual acts. The disagreements are deep and seemingly irreconcilable. If the gay rights position is correct, then the teachings of a number of venerable and beloved religious and philosophical traditions—and maybe the Bible itself—must be rejected as bigoted and ignorant. If these teachings are correct, however, then the gay rights movement is committed to the defense of immorality.

Rather than ask what is the right answer to the normative moral issues surrounding homosexuality, I intend to ask whether there is a way to get along in the face of these differences. Our constitutional tradition of religious pluralism offers a possible point of departure. Both religion and sexuality are central aspects of personal identity; opinions and practices with regard to sexuality and religion are not easily changed; both sexuality and religion involve opinion as well as conduct; both involve choice and something deeper than choice; both have public and private dimensions. Do these similarities suggest that our society could achieve a workable and mutually satisfactory peace about homosexuality, by using devices similar to those used to bring about peace in the face of religious difference? What can our experience with religious disagreement and conflict teach us about how to handle the gay rights controversy peacefully, with respect for the conscientious convictions of people on different sides of the question?

Our peaceful solution to religious difference was to refuse to decide the truth, falsehood, or merit of the contending religious views *as a collectivity*, but at the same time not to contest or disparage the legitimacy of private answers to those questions. Freedom of religion did not mean public agnosticism, but public abstinence from taking a position. It was not based on the epistemological proposition that religious truth is unknowable (let alone prejudiced or superstitious), but on the institutional proposition that "the Civil Magistrate is [not] a competent Judge of Religious truth."[1] Our forebears recognized that religious warfare is caused not by differences in opinion over matters of religion but by the attempt to resolve those questions at a public level.

The most striking feature of our religious settlement is the adoption of two constitutional proscriptions, which—though in the service of a single objective—look in opposite directions, toward opposite threats. The free exercise principle singles out religion for special protection against governmental hostility or interference. The disestablishment principle prevents the government from using its power to promote, advocate, or endorse any particular religious position. These principles balance the interests of people of competing, and indeed antithetical, views and thus achieve a kind of neutrality. Religious adherents receive protection for their practices, and secularists are assured that the government will not promote religion.

I am not suggesting that the Religion Clauses of the First Amendment actually apply to the gay rights controversy. The First Amendment singles out religion. There is no "free exercise" clause for sexuality of any sort, and the government is not prohibited from establishing an orthodoxy regarding sexuality (at least not by the Religion Clauses). This essay is not an exercise in constitutional interpretation, but in analogy: what would the world look like if there were a "first amendment" for sexual orientation?[2]

Application of "free exercise" and "disestablishment" principles to the controversy over homosexuality is more complicated than it may appear at first glance. But the starting point is to extend respect to both sides in the conflict of opinion— to treat both the view that homosexuality is a healthy and normal manifestation of human sexuality and the view that homosexuality is unnatural and immoral as conscientious positions, worthy of respect, much as we treat both atheism and faith as worthy of respect. By "respect," I do not mean agreement. I mean instead the civil toleration we extend to fellow citizens and fellow human beings even when we disagree with them. We should recognize that the civil magistrate is no more competent a judge of the truth about human sexuality than about religion. Under this approach, the state should impose no penalty on practices associated with or compelled by any of the various views of homosexuality, and should refrain from using its power to favor, promote, or advance one position over the other. The difference between a "gay rights" position and a "first amendment" approach is that the former adopts as its governing principle the idea that homosexuality is normal, natural, and morally unobjectionable, while the latter takes the view that the moral issue is not for the government to decide.

Neither of the contending sides in our public debate about homosexuality is likely to welcome this approach. In this debate, both sides have one important thing in common: both wish to wield the power and prestige of the state to support their moral position. Gay rights advocates want to use the state to teach that opposition to homosexuality is a species of bigotry, and to inflict penalties on those who "discriminate." They are likely to welcome the protections of "free exercise" but to resist the constraints of "disestablishment." Advocates of traditional sexual morality want to maintain a certain official stigma to discourage homoerotic behavior and bolster monogamous heterosexual marriage. They are likely to oppose application of both "free exercise" and "disestablishment" principles to behavior that, they believe, warrants public disapproval. The "first amendment" parallel is therefore unlikely to appeal to either of these contending forces. At the foundation of our settlement of the religion question is the idea that the government will stay out of the controversy among sects. That would not sit well with either gay rights advocates or their opponents.

But for some Americans, who find the political posturing of both sides in the debate excessive and distasteful, a "first amendment" solution may offer an attractive resolution. Their instincts on this matter are not necessarily merely muddled middle-of-the-roadism. Rather, Americans of this persuasion are offended by the *public* nature of controversy and discussion about an aspect of human life that is properly *private*. Both gay rights and traditionalist activists try to raise the public profile of this issue. For many, this is the problem. Their impulse is to live and let live. They have no sympathy for public policies that inflict stigma or injury on homosexuals, nor do they appreciate being forced to condone behavior that they neither understand nor approve. They are not troubled by—and may even welcome—homosexuals as co-workers, neighbors, and friends; but they do not wish their children to be taught that traditional morality is a reflection of bigotry and prejudice. For such people, the great attraction of a "first amendment" solution is that it removes the issue from the public domain.

My suggestion finds some common ground with the position espoused ' y Andrew Sullivan in his book *Virtually Normal*.[3] Sullivan argues, in essence, for elimination of all discrimination against homosexuals or homosexual conduct at the public level (including military service and matrimony), while leaving private persons and groups free to decide for themselves whether to discriminate in such fields as employment or housing. In broad outlines, this resembles the "first amendment" solution of differentiating between a neutral or secular state and a religiously pluralistic private sphere. But Sullivan neglects to discuss much of the "establishment" dimension of modern gay rights issues, and his discussion of some "free exercise" questions is too simple. I will therefore use his proposals as the basis for discussion, while disagreeing with some of his specific conclusions.

Our Religious Settlement: Privacy, Neutrality, Rights, and Virtue

The jurisprudence of the Religion Clauses (and especially the Establishment Clause) has tended to waver between two general ideas. The first is based on the public-private distinction, often called the "wall of separation" between church and state. Religious exercise (meaning both the formation of religious judgments without hindrance from the state and the ability to act in accordance with those convictions) is properly "a private matter for the individual, the family, and the institutions of private choice."[4] The government should not interfere with this private domain of the exercise of religion unless there are powerful *public* reasons for doing so—reasons unrelated to the truth or falsity, approval or disapproval, of the religion itself. Beyond that, the government should have as little involvement— "entanglement"—with religion as possible.

The second approach is based on neutrality between religion and its nonreligious counterparts, and among religions. The government may not favor religion over nonreligion, or vice versa. If it extends benefits to a wide range of institutions or activities on the basis of secular and objective criteria, religious institutions and activities may be included among the class of beneficiaries.[5] But they may not be singled out for special favors. By the same token, if government singles out religion (or any particular religion) for special burdens, or discriminates against religion, this violates the Free Exercise Clause.[6] Under this approach, religious individuals and institutions participate in public life, but strictly on neutral terms.[7]

These two general approaches can be understood as two devices for achieving the purpose of protecting religious freedom and pluralism. One device is *privatization*: by committing religion-sensitive issues and activities to the private realm, we eliminate the need for public agreement and allow everyone to go his or her own way. The other device is *equal access*: we allow the competing groups to participate in the public sphere on equal terms. Most of the modern controversies over church and state take the form of disagreement over which of these two devices should be used. In the area of education, for example, should religious education be treated as an entirely *private* matter, and denied public assistance, or should all forms of schooling receive equal access to public educational resources? For the most part, equal access norms have prevailed only when it is clear that private persons—rather than the government—are responsible for any religious messages, and where free speech principles are implicated as well. Thus far, the suggestion that religious institutions are entitled to full and equal participation in public programs, outside of cases involving free speech, has fallen on deaf ears. Moreover, even where equal access norms have been adopted, the Court has been insistent that the government undertake efforts, such as disclaimers, to dissociate itself from the religious speech that takes place.[8]

The gay rights analogy to privatization would insist that all activities directly related to the formation of opinion about homosexuality be confined to private institutions, where there should be no interference with either beliefs (orientation) or conduct. The gay rights analogy to equal access would insist that pro-homosexual opinion be given equal treatment within the public domain whenever it is clear that the various views being expressed are attributable to private persons, but to be careful not to convey the impression that the government is expressing a view.

In addition to this doctrinal split between privatization and equal access, another way to think about cases involving religion is according to the perceived purposes of the Religion Clauses, which often cut in different directions from the doctrinal approaches. Historically, three positions have been in contention. The first is a rights-based claim that religious exercise is a preferred freedom, entitled to "trump" at least some countervailing public policies. Madison argued for religious liberty on the ground that religion, being a "duty towards the Creator," is "precedent both in order of time and degree of obligation, to the claims of Civil Society."[9] Under this view, religious exercise is protected whether or not it is deemed beneficial to the public good. Second is the civic republican view that virtue is necessary to republican government and religion is conducive to virtue.

As Washington put it, religion is an "indispensable support" to republican government, and the "firmest prop[] of the duties of men and citizens."[10] This did not
mean that government should actively promote or coerce religion. Proponents of
this view were persuaded that active governmental assistance and involvement
would eviscerate the power of religion, whose force comes from the voluntary attraction of the spirit. The way to make religion strong is to make it free, just as the
way to make the economy strong is to make it free. Tocqueville reported that
members of every denomination agreed that religion was powerful in America precisely because of the separation of church and state.[11] The third is a secularist argument, to which I will return below.

The rights-based argument for religious freedom is most common, and may appear to be the strongest. But private freedom is limited by the public interest and
the rights of others. Jefferson was willing to protect religious freedom because "it
does me no injury for my neighbor to say there are twenty gods, or no god. It neither picks my pocket nor breaks my leg."[12] This means that any particular assertion of religious freedom will hinge on highly contested arguments about the impact on others. In practice, most free exercise of religion claims are rejected
because the countervailing governmental interests almost always appear strong.
Free exercise doctrine appears strong, but in reality is weak.[13]

What are the gay rights parallels to these positions? Under the rights-based
view, private sexual activity and orientation are entitled to protection because
they are central to the individual's identity, and it violates a proper understanding of human rights to interfere. But any individual case will depend on the
assessment by legislatures, school boards, military officials, judges, and others
about whether the exercise of homosexual liberties will have a deleterious impact
on school children, marriage, military morale, health, or other public policy interests. Simple moral disapproval of homosexuality would no longer suffice as
a justification for coercive legislation, but few laws are based solely on moral
disapproval.

Under the virtue-centered view, the purpose of extending rights, including the
right to marry, to homosexuals is to promote public virtue by encouraging gay
people to express their sexuality in monogamous and responsible ways. A recent
article by gay rights advocate Gabriel Rotello makes the argument:

> What kinds of rewards might encourage gay men to adopt a culture of sexual re-
> straint and responsibility, one in which they will be likely to reduce their contact
> rate and be as safe as possible within relationships? It seems likely that they are
> the same rewards that influence most people: a culture that grants status to those
> who exercise restraint and responsibility, and by implication withholds status
> from those who don't.[14]

According to this view, the promiscuous and detached sexual behavior that seems
typical of much gay culture (especially among male homosexuals) is attributable,
at least in part, to social mores that stigmatize all homosexual conduct, responsible as well as irresponsible, as immoral. If society were more discriminating—
approving of monogamous and caring homosexual relationships and disapproving

of promiscuous and detached relationships—this would contribute to the reform and domestication of homosexual life, just as a similar set of social mores tends to promote heterosexual responsibility and discourage heterosexual promiscuity. Or so the argument goes. It seems to me that this is emerging as the stronger of the arguments for gay rights, especially for gay marriage.

There is a third historic ground for supporting religious freedom: that religion is a divisive, irrational, and powerful force that can best be tamed and controlled by a policy of privatization and tolerance. I will call this the "secularist" position. Legal scholars of this stripe often warn of the dangerous and undemocratic tendencies of religion, in the course of advocating an expansive interpretation of disestablishment and a minimalist interpretation of free exercise.[15] Jefferson predicted that, with the advent of religious freedom, revealed religion would pass away in America and be replaced with rational religion.[16] Advocates of emancipation in France predicted that it would lead to the ultimate conversion and assimilation of the Jews.[17] Much of the rhetoric of groups such as Americans United for Separation of Church and State is animated by fear and distaste for active religiosity. The ACLU has been dubbed by its detractors the "Anti-Christian Litigation Union." Such charges may be unfair, but it cannot be denied that many religious Americans view separationist efforts in this light.

There is no direct parallel to the secularist position in the gay rights debate. I think it is safe to say that no one advocates gay rights in the hope or expectation that they will reduce the incidence of homosexuality. But from one gay point of view, the virtue-centered argument for gay rights presents precisely this threat. Rotello has described as "pervasive" among the gay community the "belief that those who are living at the most extreme fringes of gay sexual life are somehow the most liberated and the most gay," and has pointed out that many "gay and lesbian radicals" criticize legalization of same-sex marriage on the ground that it would "inherently undermine a major goal of gay liberation, which is to validate all kinds of relationships and all forms of sexual expression and experimentation."[18] If official recognition of gay rights—and especially gay marriage—has the intent and effect of promoting fidelity, monogamy, and responsibility, this can be seen as the equivalent of conversion and assimilation.

In the face of these tensions and disagreements over the meaning and purpose of the Religion Clauses, there can be no easy or confident transmutation of these principles into a formula for solving controversies over homosexuality. Nonetheless, pursuit of the analogy may help us to move beyond the usual dichotomous debate and focus more constructively on ways of getting along.

Applying the First Amendment Analogy to Controversies Over Homosexuality

Let us consider the implications of a "first amendment" approach to the following issues: antisodomy laws, equal protection, military service, public Gay Pride celebrations, public school curriculum, public school gay rights clubs, gay marriage, and private discrimination.

Antisodomy Laws

Perhaps the most important Supreme Court decision regarding homosexuality was *Bowers* v. *Hardwick*,[19] in which the Court, by a narrow 5–4 majority, upheld the constitutionality of laws imposing criminal punishments for engaging in the act of homosexual sodomy. It seems to me that, under a "first amendment" approach, the proper answer to this question is easy and obvious: states that adopt this approach would have to repeal antisodomy laws. The only justification offered for the laws was the longstanding moral condemnation of homosexuality. While that is sufficient for purposes of the Due Process Clause, as the Court held, it would not survive application of a "first amendment" for sexual orientation, which rules out laws based on a moral judgment regarding homosexuality.

To be sure, for many decades it was thought that the Free Exercise Clause protects only "belief" and not "conduct." "Laws are made for the government of actions," the Supreme Court opined in 1879, "and while they cannot interfere with mere religious belief and opinions, they may with practices."[20] This would be parallel to the view, which is sometimes espoused, that the state must not punish homosexual "orientation" but may punish or proscribe homosexual acts. But the "belief-action" distinction was a manifest distortion of the text and purpose of the First Amendment. "Exercise" surely refers to conduct, and not just belief, and the Supreme Court has long since repudiated the belief-action distinction, at least in its strong form. If it means anything at all, a "first amendment" for sexual orientation must include the right to practice one's sexuality, at least insofar as contrary laws are based solely on disapproval of homosexuality. Presumably, the state could impose regulations on particular sexual practices, if supported by sufficiently strong governmental purposes, such as the protection of the public health. But a blanket ban on sodomy would be contrary to the core of the "free exercise" principle.

Equal Protection of the Laws

An almost equally obvious implication of a "free exercise" principle for sexual orientation would be to require the state to protect individuals of all sexual orientations from private violence, without discrimination, and to provide "recourse to the courts if there is not equal protection of heterosexuals and homosexuals in law enforcement."[21] Indeed, I think this is the case even under current constitutional law, but the presence of a "free exercise" principle might justify extraordinary efforts to combat antigay violence, much as the principle of free exercise of religion provides support for laws imposing special penalties on those who vandalize religious buildings or disrupt religious services. In light of evidence of increasing levels of antigay violence, even homicide,[22] this is far from a trivial matter. Private violence and threats of violence probably are more responsible than any aspect of public policy for the second-class status most homosexuals perceive in our society. Homosexuals should be able to appear together openly in public places without the fear of being assaulted.

Commitment of adequate resources to the protection of gay people is not predicated on any particular view of the morality of homosexuality, but on the essential governmental responsibility to protect all persons from private violence, no matter who they are or what we make think of them. It is important to divorce the principle of equal protection from rhetoric about "homophobia" and "bigotry," lest it be thought that provision of equal protection is a sign of moral approbation of homosexuality (a controversial proposition in our society) rather than the non-negotiable responsibility of government under the social contract, which should be recognized and supported by those who disapprove of homosexuality no less than those who approve.

Military Service

It seems obvious to many supporters of gay rights that exclusion of openly gay men and women from military service is indefensible. Andrew Sullivan describes the military ban as "by far the most egregious example of public discrimination in the Western democracies."[23] Examination of the "free exercise" analogy, however, suggests that the homosexual ban (at least in its recent "don't ask, don't tell" incarnation) is symptomatic not so much of antihomosexual bias as of a military culture that places a high value on conformity and of a judicial system that declines to impose civil libertarian norms on the military. If "free exercise" rights were extended to sexual orientation on the same basis as free exercise rights for religion, this would provide cold comfort for advocates of gay people in the military.

To be sure, no one may be excluded from the armed forces merely on the basis of his or her religious status. The same would be true of sexual orientation. That principle might be sufficient to overturn past policies, which excluded homosexuals on the basis of orientation without regard to whether they were celibate or active, flagrant or discreet, off-base or on-base. But even when fundamental religious freedoms are involved, the military enjoys wide discretion to limit conduct that it deems injurious to morale or otherwise inconsistent with the military mission. The leading case is *Goldman v. Weinberger*.[24] In *Goldman*, the Court upheld military uniform dress regulations that, in effect, prohibited military personnel from wearing the Jewish skullcap, or yarmulke, while indoors.[25] Religiously distinctive items of apparel were permitted only if they were not "visible" (for example, undergarments) or, with permission of the base commander, worn only in designated living quarters. As a formal matter, this did not exclude Jews[26] from the military. But it prevented them from practicing their religion openly. And for those Jewish men who could not, in good conscience, refrain from wearing the yarmulke, it was a de facto Jewish exclusion.

From a civilian standpoint, the exclusion of yarmulke wearers seems almost bizarre. There is no reason to suppose that yarmulke wearers are any less effective as soldiers. Indeed, the valiant record of the Israeli army makes such a supposition seem laughable. Supporters of homosexuals in the military find that exclusion almost equally irrational. Experience shows that homosexuals have made good, indeed exemplary, soldiers. Nonetheless, the yarmulke ban was sustained. And so, in all likelihood, would the ban on openly homosexual behavior.

The Court's reasons for sustaining the yarmulke ban are suggestive. Military service, according to the Court, requires "the subordination of personal preferences and identities in favor of the overall group mission." Much of the symbolic importance of visible signs of religious faith, like yarmulkes, arises from the public proclamation of religious identity. This is especially true for a religious minority with a history of persecution; yet it is this very public proclamation of difference that is offensive to the military ideal of "uniformity." The diversity and autonomy that lie at the heart of our liberal pluralistic way of life is at odds with the military commitment to "instinctive obedience, unity, commitment, and esprit de corps." The military does not want its soldiers to identify themselves conspicuously with any identity group smaller than the nation and the military service. Moreover, as a constitutional matter, the Court explained that judicial review of military regulations, while not "entirely nugatory" (note the adverb), is "far more deferential than constitutional review of similar laws or regulations designed for civilian society." In evaluating the impact of challenged conduct on military morale and preparedness, the courts "must give great deference to the professional judgment of military authorities."[27] It is permissible for soldiers to wear religious symbols under their clothing, where they cannot be seen, or in the privacy of their living quarters, but not in the open, where they might generate feelings of sectarian division rather than military unity.

Of course, there is nothing "neutral" about the military's policy of uniformity. The dictates of uniformity could be satisfied as easily by a requirement that soldiers always wear headgear as by a requirement that they never do so. If we were a majority Jewish nation, that might well be the policy. It is not coincidental that the default position—no visible religious items of apparel—is congruent with majority (Protestant or secularist) norms. But this nonneutrality is inherent in the norm of uniformity. Inevitably, in contexts where uniformity is necessary, the majority norm will prevail over the minority. This does not necessarily reflect bias, prejudice, or even insensitivity.

The "don't ask, don't tell" policy, at least in its general outline,[28] is born of the same philosophy of military unity that forbids Jewish military personnel from wearing yarmulkes. Of course, the dangers arising from open display of religious identity are different from those arising from open display of homosexual orientation. In the one case, the danger is sectarian division; in the other, the danger is sexual attraction and repulsion, jealousy and fear. Indeed, if there is a difference, the ban on open display of homosexual inclination is more rational than the ban on open display of religious identity because of the privacy interests of heterosexual soldiers in the cramped and intimate circumstances of military service. In either case, military authorities can make a nonfrivolous claim that open displays of religious identity or of homosexual orientation have an effect on military unity and morale, and this essentially empirical judgment will receive deference from the courts. Even if we adopted a "free exercise" clause for sexual orientation, the ban on open homosexuality in the military would remain essentially a policy question, to be resolved on military grounds.

Goldman may have been wrongly decided. I have always thought so.[29] Congress apparently thought so too, at least as a matter of military policy. Shortly after the decision, Congress passed legislation designed to permit the wearing of yarmulkes and other unobtrusive religious apparel.[30] But it is significant that even Justice Brennan, in dissent, would have allowed the military to ban religious items of apparel that are not "unobtrusive" and "neat and conservative."[31] Even Brennan thus accepted the general idea that the military interest in morale legitimates restrictions on displays of religious identity; he just disagreed about where to draw the line. What would be the sexual parallel to the standard of "unobtrusive, neat, and conservative"? One possibility is "discreet." That is not much different from "don't ask, don't tell."

This raises the question: Why does the principle of free exercise (whether of religion or of sexual orientation) provide so little protection in the military context? I think it is because the principal device for protecting religious freedom—privatization—is largely inapplicable to these military questions.[32] The genius of separation between church and state is that it enables the state to stay out of religious questions. In the military, it cannot. When religious observance is dependent on military organization, there is no "neutral" stance: to provide opportunities for religious observance favors religion (and favors those religions whose observance the military chooses to recognize) and to refrain from providing such opportunities inhibits religion. Indeed, the problem of the public-private line in the military context goes even deeper than that. The private aspects of the soldiers' lives are few. Even their clothing is dictated by the state. The uniform regulations can be seen as an unconscious imitation of the "wall of separation" model—but the private side of the wall turns out to consist of invisible objects and conduct in designated living quarters. The public, secular side of the wall turns out to encompass most of the military life.

A neutral course would be all the more difficult in light of the likely consequences of requiring aggressive, undercivilized men of military age to live in close quarters with men known to be gay. In order to avoid violence and insult against gay soldiers, the military would have to undertake a massive effort to educate and discipline the troops to accept the homosexuals in their midst. This would almost certainly have to go beyond inculcation of the bare civil toleration that is sufficient for public peace in the civilian world, to promotion of the full acceptance of the moral legitimacy of homosexuality. This would commit the military to the very "cures or re-educations" and "political imposition of tolerance" that Sullivan elsewhere deplores,[33] and which "first amendment" principles reject. There is no neutrality in the military.

Public Gay Pride Celebrations

On the "disestablishment" side of the "first amendment" balance, governments would almost certainly have to abandon some forms of public endorsement of one view (or the other) in the debate over homosexuality. In the context of religion, the Establishment Clause and the Free Speech Clause combine to ensure that *private* religious speech is constitutionally protected (even on government property), but that the government must scrupulously refrain from even the appearance of endorsement of religious messages. In the leading case, *Capitol Square Review and Advisory Board* v. *Pinette*,[34] private citizens sought to erect a cross in a public square, where a variety of groups had been permitted to engage in expression, including the erection of symbols, in the past.[35] The city refused permission, citing its "interest in avoiding official endorsement of Christianity," which was especially strong because of the proximity of the cross to the seat of government. Seven of the nine justices overruled that decision, holding that private religious speech is constitutionally protected (an application of the equal access principle). But a majority of the Court insisted that religious speech may be permitted on public property only if it is clear from the context that the government is not endorsing the religious message.

If a "first amendment" principle is extended to sexual orientation, it will be clear (as it is under current law) that private speakers are entitled to use the streets, sidewalks, parks, and other public property for speech advocating their views on homosexuality. Examples would be the Gay Pride parades that are common in American cities on the anniversary of the Stonewall riots. But unlike now, it will be necessary for governmental bodies to refrain from endorsing such celebrations. If the government is to remain neutral with respect to sexual orientation, cities and states may no more proclaim official Gay Pride days or weeks than they may proclaim Good Friday a holiday. (Of course, the same would be true of antihomosexual symbols or proclamations, if any exist.)

Much of the Establishment Clause litigation involving public religious symbols has involved Christmas. In one controversial decision, the Court narrowly upheld the constitutionality of a municipal nativity display,[36] and the Court has never questioned the legality of the designation of Christmas as a national holiday. But the rationale for these decisions is that Christmas is a holiday with secular as well as religious meaning, and that it is permissible for government bodies to employ the religious symbols of the occasion so long as they are part of a wider display that includes nonreligious elements and does not emphasize the religious. This suggests that some symbols of gay pride could be employed by the government, but only in a context that vitiates any serious danger of an endorsement of the message.

This would be a major change from current law and practice.

Public School Curriculum

Public school curriculum would also be affected by adoption of a "first amendment" approach to sexual orientation. Such a principle would preclude inculcation by public schools of traditional views of sexual morality, but it would also preclude inculcation of positive teachings about homosexuality—and indeed, of sexuality in general.

The general formula for public school treatment of religion is that schools may teach "about religion" but may not "teach religion." This means that the schools can teach objective facts about the impact of religious belief on culture and history, and can include information about the teachings of various religions during as part of appropriate courses in social studies or comparative religion. In practice, as numerous studies of public school textbooks have discovered, public schools typically ignore the subject of religion, even when it is pedagogically relevant.[37] In part this may be attributable to ignorance or prejudice, and in part it may be due to the desire to avoid controversy. But in large part, this is the predictable (even if unfortunate) consequence of the happy decision to privatize the teaching of religion. The idea that government-run schools may teach "about religion" in an objective and neutral way may sound attractive in the abstract, but it is extraordinarily difficult in practice. Let me give a few examples of problems that arise. First, even the facts "about" religion are often matters of dispute. How can the schools teach what "Jews" believe about *kashruth*, or what Christians believe about the trinity, when these are points of disagreement among them? Second, the discussion of religion in exclusively "external" terms may convey a message of exoticism that is disorienting to children accustomed to thinking in "internal" terms. Third, the "facts" about religion are often not value neutral. Should the truth "about religion" be presented "warts and all"? How much emphasis should be placed on the Spanish Inquisition? And who decides on which "warts" to expose to public gaze? Should religious figures be given the sort of hero status that is accorded many figures in history? If so, which ones? Fourth, the allocation of time and attention may convey messages about the relative importance of various religious traditions; but there is no "neutral" basis for the allocation decision. It is no wonder that, faced with unanswerable questions like these, the public schools have tended to leave most teaching about religion to the children's families—with the result that American children are dreadfully ignorant about their own religious traditions, as well as those of others.

The public schools would face an even more severe problem if a "first amendment" principle were adopted for sexual orientation. To be sure, all educated persons need to know the basic facts about sexuality. But the predominant purpose of sex education courses, and especially of AIDS awareness programs, is to mold behavior rather than to acquaint students with facts. Adoption of a "first amendment" approach would render sex education of this sort difficult if not impossible.

Andrew Sullivan has made a similar suggestion, arguing for "inclusion of the facts about homosexuality in the curriculum of every government-funded school, in terms no more and no less clear than those applied to heterosexuality (though almost certainly with far less emphasis, because of homosexuality's relative rareness when compared with heterosexuality)."[38] By limiting his proposed teaching to "facts," Sullivan appears to be employing a distinction similar to that between "teaching about" and "teaching" religion: facts, not advocacy. Presumably Sullivan's standard would exclude curricula with the explicit intention of "fostering positive attitudes" toward various manifestations of sexuality, in the terms of one prominent curriculum.[39] To the extent that curricula are designed to teach children moral attitudes about homosexuality—either accepting or disapproving—this would fall outside the legitimate function of the public school. Clearly, Sullivan's formulation would preclude adoption of a teen curriculum prepared by the Hetrick-Martin Institute, which includes the following passage: "For oral sex, use no lubricant on the outside of the condom. For vaginal or anal intercourse, put a lot of water-soluble lubricant . . . on the outside of the condom. For anal intercourse, lube up the receptive partner's anus (asshole) as well. . . . Do it! (Have fun!")."[40] It is no more appropriate for public schools to exhort students to engage in sex acts than to engage in prayer. Maybe less.

A more interesting question is what Sullivan means by the "facts" about homosexuality. Consider this passage from a pamphlet designed for distribution in high school: "Homophobia is the irrational and unnecessary fear of Gay people based solely on their sexual orientation and sometimes on their personal behaviors. It often results from ignorance about homosexuality and Gay people. As we said before, Gay people comprise about 10-15% of the population."[41] Are these "facts"? Could they be taught in a public schools? Are only "facts" favorable to homosexuality to be presented? Who decides? How much attention should homosexuality be given? Who decides? Which of these are matters of community judgment?

I suspect that, if the "first amendment" principle were adopted, the effect would be the opposite of Sullivan's wish: That less, rather than more, information about homosexuality—and heterosexuality as well—would be presented in public schools. Education of the youth of America about sexual practices and sexual morality would be consigned largely to their families, much as education about religion is consigned to their families, and for essentially the same reason: that the civil magistrate is not a competent judge of the truth of these matters.

This would require a major change in current practice and law. Sex education curriculum is often directive rather than informational, and there are currently no serious limits regarding its offensive or propagandistic character. In a recent case, the federal Court of Appeals for the First Circuit dismissed all constitutional objections to a public school AIDS awareness program, presented to fifteen-year-olds, in which (according to the court's own description) the instructor:

> 1) told the students that they were going to have a "group sexual experience, with audience participation"; 2) used profane, lewd, and lascivious language to describe body parts and excretory functions; 3) advocated and approved oral sex, masturbation, homosexual activity, and condom use during promiscuous premarital sex; 4) simulated masturbation; 5) characterized the loose pants worn by one minor as "erection wear"; 6) referred to being in "deep sh—" after anal sex; 7) had a male minor lick an oversized condom with her, after which she had a female minor pull it over the male minor's entire head and blow it up; 8) encouraged a male minor to display his "orgasm face" with her for the camera; 9) informed a male minor that he was not having enough orgasms; 10) closely inspected a minor and told him he had a "nice butt"; and 11) made eighteen references to orgasms, six references to male genitals, and eight references to female genitals.[42]

This is a real case, involving real people, in a typical suburban school district. It shows how far we are from any genuine protection for dissenters from the new orthodoxy.

There is a contradiction at the heart of modern progressive ideas about sexuality and sex education. On the one hand, it is thought that sexual behavior is a private matter, with which the state may not legitimately interfere. On the other hand, it is thought that education in sexual behavior is a public matter, and that children should be instructed in proper attitudes to take toward it. But if it is not acceptable to leave instruction in sexual practices and sexual morality to families and private institutions, there is no possibility of a neutral public stance. If there must be sex education in government schools (beyond presentation of "the facts"), the only fair alternatives are (1) some kind of parental choice among a diverse set of offerings, or (2) that the teaching reflect the moral judgment of the community, whatever that may be. There is no reason, in principle, to favor a "nonjudgmental" curriculum, which in practice espouses the pro–gay rights position, unless that is, in fact, the moral stance of the community. Such teachings may be garbed in the rhetoric of tolerance, but they are not tolerant toward all views. They have the inevitable effect (and no doubt the purpose) of stigmatizing traditional beliefs as ignorant, bigoted, or (what is worst of all to the normal teenager) uncool.

Gay Clubs in Public School

One of the most contentious church-state issues of the 1980s was whether voluntary Bible and prayer clubs could meet on the premises of public high schools. School boards generally resisted, and several courts of appeals held that it would violate the Establishment Clause to allow such clubs to meet, largely because meetings of this sort would constitute a governmental "endorsement" of religion. Congress intervened by passage of the Equal Access Act, which requires schools that permit any noncurriculum-related student clubs to provide equal access to all student-initiated clubs without discrimination on the basis of the "religious, political, philosophical, or other content of the speech at such meetings."[43] The statute was upheld by the Supreme Court, and now high school religious clubs flourish all over the country.

The premise of the Equal Access Act was that allowing extracurricular clubs to meet does not constitute an official endorsement. As the Supreme Court stated:

> [T]here is a crucial difference between government speech endorsing religion, which the Establishment Clause forbids, and private speech endorsing religion, which the Free Speech and Free Exercise Clauses protect. We think that secondary school students are mature enough and are likely to understand that a school does not endorse or support student speech that it merely permits on a nondiscriminatory basis. (*Board of Education of Westside Community Schools v. Mergens*, 496 U.S. 226 [1990])

Note that the right of religious students to meet was not predicated on any official judgment, by court, school board, or legislature, that religious meetings are worthwhile or on any suggestion that the attempt to exclude religious meetings was based on prejudice or hostility. Equal access was seen as a neutral solution, by which public schools would avoid making contentious value judgments of this sort.

The act was invoked recently in support of the right of a student group called the Gay/Straight Alliance to meet at a Utah high school. Elements of the community, where moral opinions against homosexuality run strong, perceived the meetings as school "sponsorship" or "endorsement" of a lifestyle repugnant to many parents and to the community. They succeeded in inducing first the school board, and then the legislature, to eliminate the entire extracurricular program at Utah's high schools. This made the Equal Access act inapplicable, since the Act applies only when the school allows at least one noncurriculum-related club to meet.

These actions, in turn, were roundly denounced by other elements in the community as an example of bigotry and intolerance. One prominent civil libertarian called them "ignorant," "sick," and "mean-spirited."[44]

These controversies illustrate how difficult the line between public and private can be. During the height of the equal access controversy, one scholar wrote an article entitled "When Separate Is Equal: Why Organized Religious Exercises, Unlike Chess, Do Not Belong in the Public Schools."[45] Her arguments were strikingly similar to the arguments of Utahns who think that sexually oriented clubs, unlike chess, do not belong in the public schools. The same civil liberties organizations that were so outraged by the legislature's action in Utah had argued in litigation in Washington State that a religious group should not be allowed because this would "endorse" religion.[46] This is precisely what the Utah parents thought about the gay rights club. And after the federal court in the Washington litigation had concluded that the Equal Access Act applied and was constitutional, the civil liberties groups argued that the entire extracurricular program of the State of Washington should be eliminated rather than allow the religious club to meet. That is what they did in Utah. It is remarkable how different issues of endorsement look when you are on the other side.

From the perspective of the "first amendment" approach, both sides in the Utah controversy got it wrong. Under the equal access principle, the student group was plainly entitled to meet. To eliminate the extracurricular program of the schools was pedagogically indefensible, whatever one may think of gay rights. On the other hand, supporters of the student group should not have framed the issue as one of "prejudice" or "bigotry." Whether homosexuality is moral or proper is a contested matter, about which citizens are entitled to disagree. The point should have been that, whether the Gay/Straight Alliance was right or wrong, all student-initiated groups have an equal right to meet, and that it is dangerous to allow government officials to pick and choose what groups they think would promote the public good. The same power that allows the schools to exclude the Gay/Straight Alliance today could exclude the Bible club tomorrow. And did.

By casting this as a dispute over "prejudice," the students' supporters actually weakened their case. Those who think that homosexuality is immoral could never, in good conscience, agree to allow the Gay/Straight Alliance meetings if the reason for allowing the meetings is that antihomosexual opinion is bigoted or prejudiced. The only peaceful way to resolve this issue—the only way to resolve the issue without requiring one or the other side to repudiate its conscientious convictions—is to declare that the school board is not a competent judge of the truth of these matters, and to leave the citizens (including students) free to take positions on their own.

Same-Sex Marriage

The call for same-sex marriage is at the forefront of the gay rights movement. Sullivan calls present marriage laws "the most public affront possible to [homosexuals'] public equality" and extension of marriage rights to homosexual couples the "centerpiece" of reform.[47] As a "free exercise" claim, however, the argument is weak. The most closely analogous case is *Reynolds v. United States*,[48] in which a Mormon unsuccessfully asserted the right to marry multiple wives, in accordance with the dictates of his religion. The Supreme Court unanimously rejected the claim. More interestingly (since many of us believe the *Reynolds* case was wrongly decided), even if Reynolds had won, a victory would not suggest that the state is required to change the contours of its marriage laws. Reynolds did not claim the benefits or recognition of the legal state of "marriage" for his polygamous relationships. His sole claim was that the state could not prosecute him for living with multiple "wives," in light of the religious injunction to do so. He asked only that the government leave him and his wives alone.

In other words, Reynolds unsuccessfully sought what homosexuals already have:[49] the right to live with the person(s) of their choice, as if married, without hindrance from the state. It is hard to imagine a plausible "free exercise" claim that would be analogous to the claim for same-sex marriage. It is one thing to say that the government may not interfere with a religious (or sexual) practice in the privacy of the home, and quite a different thing to say that the government must adjust the definition of a public institution to conform with the doctrines or desires of a minority. Free exercise protects the right of religious communities and their members to perform marriage ceremonies as they wish; even today, many gay couples are married in religious ceremonies by cooperative clergy. But free exercise does not dictate how the state should define "marriage" in its public aspect.

The essential weakness in the "equal access" claim for same-sex marriage is that, contrary to the rhetoric, homosexual couples are not being discriminated against. Most combinations of human beings are ineligible for matrimony. Groups of more than two cannot "marry," as George Reynolds found out. No one suggests that good friends lacking an intimate relationship should be permitted to "marry." Two widows living together cannot "marry." Rather, heterosexual couples are singled out, among all the various groups and combinations of human beings, for the special benefit and privilege of marriage. This, presumably, is because the function of begetting and raising children requires a long-term commitment, deserving of public support and approbation, and because of the special value to children of having both a female and a male parent.[50] That judgment does not rest on a condemnation of gay sexuality, but on the social function of families.

Andrew Sullivan asserts that "[a]s a classic public institution, [marriage] should be available to any two citizens."[51] Why only two? Is it not arbitrary to exclude groups of consenting persons, of whatever number, from the benefit of marriage, once we have cast aside its traditional form? But I doubt that Sullivan really means this. Most groups of "two citizens" utterly lack the sort of relationship that bears resemblance to marriage. The argument must be that homosexual couples (unlike most other combinations of "two citizens") are sufficiently similar to heterosexual couples—sharing in the same goods of love and commitment, reinforced by a similar bond of sexual intimacy—that they should be treated the same way by the law. The two types of relationship may well be analogous in those respects. But homosexuals do not have all the characteristics of heterosexual couples, including the one most salient for social policy as it has been traditionally conceived: the ability to procreate and raise children. It casts no moral aspersions on homosexuality to say that homosexual couples—like most other combinations of "two citizens"—lack the essential quality on which the justification for special benefits to marriage has traditionally rested.

Obviously, this child-centered view of marriage is not the only possible view. Some contend that the most central value of marriage has to do with the relationship of the spouses: their emotional, financial, spiritual, and sexual union. Some question the truth of the claim that children are best raised in a family with a male and a female parent figure. If society adopts alternative understandings of these matters, then, in all likelihood, marriage will be extended to others. But as long as society, through its legislatures, courts, and popular opinion, continues to take a traditional child-centered view of the purpose of marriage, that is not likely to happen.

The claim for gay marriage is really more a "disestablishment" than a "free exercise" claim: It asserts that a certain privilege is extended to heterosexual couples for no reason other than preference for heterosexuality. I do not think that is true; it seems to me that opinions about child rearing are logically independent of moral approval or disapproval of any particular form of sexual behavior. But even if it is true, the argument does not lead to the conclusion that marriage should be extended to same-sex unions. That would not solve the "establishment" problem, but only broaden the "establishment" to give favored status to two "churches."

The true "disestablishment" policy is to eliminate marriage as a public institution: to leave all decisions about marriage to private contract.[52] Individuals and groups would be free to celebrate and recognize "marriages" in accordance with their own convictions (just as people are free to form "churches") and the state would play no role, other than the enforcement of contractual commitments. There are legitimate objections to the privatization of marriage, however, and as long as the government defines the institution of marriage and reserves it, for public reasons, to particular classes of relationship, the argument that it should be extended to gay unions cannot be based on a claim of "neutrality." Limitation of marriage to heterosexual unions necessarily implies that homosexual unions lack the qualities for which marriage is legally recognized and favored, while extending marriage to homosexual unions would necessarily imply that homosexual unions have those socially favored qualities. There is no neutral course.

To my mind, the more persuasive argument for same-sex marriage is not based on rights or equality,[53] but on moral social policy, and as such should be addressed to the electorate rather than to the courts. The argument centers not on the child-bearing aspect of marriage (which has arguably been most salient from a traditional perspective) but on what Bill Eskridge has called "the civilizing functions of marriage."[54] A combination of social ostracism for homosexuality (without distinguishing between its forms) and a lack of any social affirmation of stable, monogamous gay relations has contributed to a gay sexual culture in which multiple partners, sex with strangers, and relationships of fleeting duration are all too common. According to one authority, only one-quarter of male homosexuals involved in a relationship are faithful to their partners, only 40 percent of all homosexuals have had a relationship that lasts more than a year, only 10 percent have had relationships lasting more than three years, and 60 percent of male homosexuals have sex with strangers.[55] I do not vouch for the accuracy of these numbers; there have been no reliable statistical studies of the subject. Andrew Sullivan states that "many lesbian and gay male relationships are virtual textbooks of monogamous commitment."[56] Perhaps so. Still, it is widely reported, even in sources sympathetic to gay rights, that rates of promiscuity among male homosexuals significantly exceed those of heterosexuals.[57] Gay rights advocate Gabriel Rotello writes:

> Unprotected sex is good old-fashioned sex, without inhibitions and restraints, which to many people is the whole point. In addition, sexual intimacy is a way of connecting with other gay men, a way of creating community, a source of psychological meaning. In a gay world in which sex provides the sense of meaning and community that marriage and children provide for others, a world in which many influential forces continue to extol sexual freedom and pleasure as its highest values, the surprising thing is not how much unsafe sex is occurring but how little.[58]

It is argued, with some plausibility, that by offering the social affirmation of marriage to homosexual couples who bind themselves to a long-term monogamous relationship, society would aid in the "construction of a gay culture that validates sexual moderation."[59]

It is not obvious that the availability of marriage would do much to affect this. Perhaps only those already predisposed to monogamy would marry. Perhaps the propensity to promiscuity (whatever its magnitude) is as impervious to social pressure as homosexual inclination itself is said to be. Nor can anyone predict what the wider social consequences of so untested a change would be. No jurisdiction in the history of the world has formally recognized same-sex unions as equivalent to marriage. This suggests caution. Moreover, marriage itself is an increasingly fragile institution in our society. Demands for gay rights and same-sex marriage are often coupled with attacks on the supposedly "patriarchal" and "oppressive" nature of marriage itself. This suggests double caution. Nonetheless, traditionalists should seriously consider the possibility that, on their own terms, gay marriage would be a step forward—a paradoxically conservative reform that would publicly reaffirm the values of faithfulness and monogamy, while subordinating the more contentious moral question of homosexuality per se. From a traditionalist perspective, the recognition of gay marriage might be a second-best solution: far preferable to the view that society should be neutral toward all sexual choices, or actively hostile toward traditional marriage. In any event, these virtue-centered arguments suggest a more fruitful line of discussion than the sterile and ultimately semantic dispute about whether same-sex unions have all the necessary characteristics of a "marriage."

Private Discrimination

Andrew Sullivan departs from the large majority of his gay rights allies in opposing laws against discrimination against gays in the private market—employment, housing, and the like. He offers a number of reasons for this position, but ultimately it follows from his classical liberal commitment to state neutrality and the public-private distinction. Sullivan explains:

> For many people in Western societies, and most others, the sexual and emotional entanglement of two people of the same gender is a moral enormity. They find such behavior abhorrent, even threatening; and while, in a liberal society, they may be content to leave such people alone, they draw the line at being told they cannot avoid their company in the workplace or in renting housing to them. Antidiscrimination statutes that force them to do so are an affront to these people, and a flagrant violation, from their point of view, of the moral neutrality of the liberal state.[60]

At bottom, the problem is that antidiscrimination statutes label antihomosexual feeling as "discrimination"—akin to racism. The law thus "contains an approval of homosexual behavior."[61] This is confirmed by the rhetoric of most supporters of such laws. In a recent speech supporting federal legislation protecting gays and lesbians against employment discrimination, President Clinton described it as part of his "ongoing fight against bigotry and intolerance."[62]

If antidiscrimination laws are based on this "anti-bigotry" rationale, they conflict with the "first amendment" position, which insists that the government not take a moral position for or against homosexuality. Sullivan thus appears right to oppose such laws. But the parallel to religion suggests that this is not the only way to understand the public–private distinction, or the social meaning of antidiscrimination laws. To be sure, if we focus simply on the First Amendment, Sullivan's position would be perfectly parallel. The First Amendment applies only to state action and leaves private actors free to discriminate on the basis of religion at will. But since 1964, federal law (Title VII of the Civil Rights Act of 1964) has forbidden private employers to discriminate on the basis of religion, and since 1970, private employers have even been required to "accommodate" the religious needs of their employees (so long as the burden this entails on the employer is not "undue"). It is difficult to square this with formal First Amendment logic, since it would seem to promote religion by eliminating one of the naturally occurring disincentives to religious practice (namely, the hostile reaction of private persons) and even to shift a portion of the cost of religious practice from the adherent to the employer. It seems to transgress the classical liberal public-private distinction.

The Supreme Court has never satisfactorily explained why this intervention into the private sphere on behalf of religion is consistent with the Establishment Clause. Justice O'Connor has come the closest to offering an explanation. She recognizes that Title VII cannot be justified under the usual religious accommodation doctrine, since it does not lift a government-imposed burden on the practice of religion. But she justifies it on the ground that it is part of a general "anti-discrimination statute" outlawing employment discrimination based on race, color, religion, sex, or national origin. Thus, she concludes that it has the valid secular purpose of "assuring employment opportunity to all groups in our pluralistic society."[63] This is a logical application of the equal access principle. Since the benefits of antidiscrimination law apply to so many other categories, it is permissible to extend it to religion.

But it is necessary for her theory that she not look too closely at the law. Contrary to the justice's statement, Title VII does *not* protect "all groups in our pluralistic society" from job discrimination. It does not protect members of political parties, people who are physically unattractive or obnoxious, members of private societies, adherents of unpopular moral codes, or—most interestingly, for present purposes—homosexuals. Indeed, religion is the only system of belief that is protected. And the accommodation requirements go beyond what is applicable even to race, color, sex, and national origin. Under her theory, what justifies this special treatment? Despite this lack of doctrinal justification, however, the religious nondiscrimination provisions of Title VII are supported by virtually the entire spectrum of organizations committed to fostering First Amendment freedoms, from liberal secular separationists to advocates of the religious right, and are deemed uncontroversial by the academy.

The question is why. The classical liberal version of the public–private distinction cannot provide the answer. I would suggest that a different version of the public-private distinction is at work, resulting from the civil rights era and deeply embedded in modern legal and popular conceptions. Under this conception, some aspects of the market, though privately owned and controlled, are seen as "public" for certain purposes, including application of nondiscrimination norms. Thus, just as the government is seen as overstepping the proper bounds of its authority when it makes religious judgments, so is General Motors. If General Motors decides to promote Christianity by dismissing all non-Christian employees, and the employees run to the state for protection, how will the conflict be perceived? The classical liberal would say that the government should mind its own business, and leave the decision to private forces. This means General Motors wins. Most ordinary Americans today will say that it is General Motors that should "mind its own business" and leave the decision about what religion to follow to the individual. That means the employee wins. The modern view retains key features of the old classical liberal view: it is not based on who is ultimately right in his or her religious judgment, but on drawing the line between private and collective judgments. The difference is that the modern view conceptualizes at least some parts of the economic marketplace as a collective judgment and treats "private" as meaning the individual. I think this explains why, though opinion polls suggest continuing widespread moral disapproval of homosexuality and even more widespread opposition to gay marriage, there is far more support for extending antidiscrimination laws to homosexuals.[64]

It is not my place to argue whether such a view is right or wrong. I might well join Sullivan and the few remaining classical liberals, if it were my choice. But I think it is an established social fact that modern legal culture has shifted from classical to modern liberalism, and unless we are willing to take the classical liberal view to its logical conclusion (striking down Title VII protection for religion), that view cannot provide an adequate justification for resisting antidiscrimination laws for homosexuals.

The key to understanding modern public opinion is to see that many ordinary Americans do not perceive laws against discrimination on the basis of sexual orientation as weapons in the culture war. Rather, they are seen as reflections of the boundaries between the private world, in which moral, religious, and sexual decisions are properly made, and the public world. One does not have to think homosexuality is moral to believe that employers have no business interfering in the private lives of their employees.[65]

This suggests that the legitimacy of antidiscrimination laws, under the "first amendment approach," depends on their actual and stated purpose. If enacted as part of a program of "cultural transformation," as some advocates have suggested,[66] or to seize the mantle of official policy for the view that "homophobic" opinions are bigoted and immoral, as President Clinton's words indicate, antidiscrimination laws violate the core of the "first amendment" principle. They use the power of the government to brand one view about the morality of homosexuality as orthodox and to stigmatize and punish the other view. Anyone committed to a "first amendment" for sexual orientation should oppose such laws, if that is their stated or actual purpose. On the other hand, if the laws are enacted for what Rick Hills calls "institutional" reasons[67]—that disapprobation of aberrant sexual practices ought to be expressed by means other than the economic power of employers over workers—then "first amendment" principles would not necessarily be offended. (If it seems odd that the same legislation might be constitutional if enacted for one reason and unconstitutional if enacted for another, this is the logical outcome of the "secular purpose" requirement under the Establishment Clause.[68])

In light of the rhetoric of supporters of antidiscrimination legislation, it seems unlikely that the law can be squared with "first amendment" principles. But if advocates cast the laws carefully, this is not impossible. First, they must be cautious about their explanations of the rationale for the law. Second, the law should contain language disavowing any intention to speak to the underlying moral question. Several state antidiscrimination statutes already contain provisions declaring that the laws are not intended to endorse or condone homosexuality.[69] Third, these provisions should not be part of the general civil rights laws, which cover forms of discrimination widely recognized in our society as reprehensible. If sexual orientation is placed in the same category with racist or sexist action, it inevitably communicates the message that moral disapproval of homosexuality is of the same ilk. The laws should be cast as limitations on the power of the employer, landlord, or other economic actor to refuse to deal on the basis of moral objections to the individual's sexual orientation. The legislative history should make clear that the reason for the law is not that moral objections to sexual orientation are wrong or irrational, but simply that it is the judgment of the American people that such judgments should be irrelevant to employment.

But what of Sullivan's excellent point that antidiscrimination laws would be a "flagrant violation" of the rights of employers or landlords to refuse to contract or associate with those whom they view as engaging in immorality? This concern can be addressed by providing an easy and respectable exception for those who wish to refuse to contract or associate on the basis of a conscientious (religious or non-religious) belief in the immorality of homosexuality. The precise contours of such an exception could vary. It need not cover large bureaucratic organizations (like General Motors), which are not moral actors and whose moral sensibilities therefore are of no real concern. But it must cover proprietorships, closely held corporations, and other smaller units of economic organization in which the business is genuinely part of the identity and expression of the owner(s). It is not sufficient to exempt religious institutions, as if they were the only ones in America entitled to hold and act upon moral convictions. Without such exceptions, the antidiscrimination law would be sheer partisanship; forcing dissenters to comply with a controversial moral judgment that they cannot conscientiously support.

This is not to say that the "first amendment" approach compels such legislation (as noted, the First Amendment does not apply to the private marketplace), or even that it would be good public policy. Antidiscrimination laws impose large costs on society, in the form of legal bills, litigation, increased friction, false claims, and decreased economic liberty. Before embarking on new legislation, it would be useful to know how much discrimination against homosexuals actually exists in corporate America. According to Sullivan, in jurisdictions that already have antidiscrimination statutes, there have been only a handful of cases.[70] As a group, homosexuals do not seem to suffer the usual incidences of economic discrimination; indeed, they are above average in education and income. Most of the large and elite institutions of America (which include the economically most powerful) have already been converted to gay rights. If antidiscrimination laws are not actually necessary, this suggests that they may be desired largely as a symbolic measure: to convey government support for the notion that the refusal to associate or contract with homosexuals is bigoted and immoral. That, however, is an argument against the laws, not in their favor.

To be sure, some supporters of gay rights laws may not be willing to make these concessions. They may oppose any authoritative statement that makes it appear that the government is equally concerned about the rights of "homophobes" and homosexuals—between "prejudice" and "equality," according to their view. This is the mirror image of gay rights opponents who will resist any suggestion that the nation be neutral between "immorality" and "morality." But if advocates of gay rights are seriously concerned about the real effects of discrimination, as opposed to wishing to use the government to score ideological victories over their opponents, they could cast antidiscrimination laws in such a way as to obviate the legitimate objections of those who disagree with them on the underlying moral question. If they do not, it will be apparent that their real purpose is not to achieve a balanced "free exercise" and "disestablishment" position for sexual orientation, but to impose their beliefs through the power of the state.

Postscript

As I cast my eye over the preceding thoughts, I am struck by the indeterminacy of many of the arguments. As with many church–state issues, reasonable people employing roughly the same "tests" can come to remarkably different conclusions, and some of the results appear to be uneasy compromises rather than logical inferences. Whether that is a defect in my powers of reasoning or is inherent in the project, I leave to others to decide. It is the general attitude that a "first amendment" approach fosters that is most important, rather than the details of policy.

One reaction to my attempt to work out the "free exercise" and "disestablishment" analogies may be that the analogies are unpersuasive. One of the reasons our religious settlement has worked as well as it has is that there exist in this country a multiplicity of religious sects and denominations, each one jealous of the rest. For reasons set forth by Madison and others, this is more conducive to a stable solution respecting the rights of all than a bipolar division into two antagonistic camps would be. Unfortunately, the culture wars over sexual orientation are mostly bipolar. A second reason to doubt the analogy is that the two contending views—that homosexuality is immoral and that the opinion that homosexuality is immoral is immoral—are mutually exclusive in a way that different religious views are not (necessarily). Many (maybe most) religious adherents believe that other religions, while perhaps inferior to their own, contain some glimmer of the truth, and that the conscientious pursuit of the divine is a good and honorable thing even if the particular expression is in some sense defective. There is no such mutuality in the dispute over homosexual morality. Opponents of gay rights do not believe that homosexual unions are a good and honorable thing; and advocates of gay rights consider the conscientious conviction that homosexuality is immoral a species of prejudice and bigotry. A skeptic is entitled to ask whether a "first amendment" approach could possibly succeed under these conditions.

Maybe a "first amendment" approach is too ambitious. If so, there is a more modest alternative: tolerance. By "tolerance," I mean a regime in which the government supports the moral position of one side or the other, but refrains from using the coercive power of the state to force dissenters to conform. If traditionalists were to prevail, the government would promote the view that heterosexual monogamy is right and that other expressions of sexuality are not—but it would not coerce or humiliate the homosexuals in our midst. It would look the other way whenever it can, and protect all citizens in their basic civil rights (including protection from private violence). On the other hand, if gay rights proponents were to prevail, the government would act on the assumption that homosexuality is natural and normal. It would teach that position in government schools, and extend the benefits of marriage and antidiscrimination protection to gay people. But it would refrain from the cruder forms of propaganda and thought control, and would allow dissenters to express and act upon contrary convictions.

The alternative, I think, is culture war. That would not be a happy thing for this country. Public arguments about sexuality, like public arguments about religion, seem to bring out the worst in people. Advocates lose their sense of balance and moderation. Self-righteousness abounds. Excessive attention is paid to the perceived sins of others—supposed sins of the body on one side and supposed sins of intolerance on the other. Advocates on both sides are all too ready to seize the weapons of state power to stigmatize their foes and to inculcate their chosen positions in the children of the next generation. A "first amendment" solution would disarm both.

Partisans on neither side are likely to accept this solution, or anything like it, if they think they will ultimately prevail in the political and cultural struggle. So who are the possible constituents of a "first amendment" resolution? Those who fear a total victory of their foes more than they savor a total victory for themselves, those who think a total victory for either side would come at too high a cost in freedom for the losers, and those who prefer our public life to focus on issues more appropriate to the competence of civil government.

Notes

The author wishes to thank Richard Duncan, John Garvey, Richard Hills, Terry Kogan, Andrew Koppelman, Douglas Laycock, Martha Nussbaum, and Lynn Wardle for helpful comments on an earlier draft.

1. James Madison, "Memorial and Remonstrance Against Religious Assessments," ¶ 5 (1785).

2. To emphasize this point, I will use the terms First Amendment, Free Exercise, and Establishment (capitalized, without quotation marks) to refer to the actual constitutional provisions, and the same terms, lower case and with quotation marks, to refer to the sexual orientation analogues.

3. Andrew Sullivan, *Virtually Normal: An Argument About Homosexuality* (New York: Vintage Books, 1995).

4. *Lemon v Kurtzman,* 403 US 602, 625 (1971).

5. See *Rosenberger v Rector and Visitors of the University of Virginia,* 115 S. Ct. 2510 (1995).

6. See *Church of the Lukumi Babalu Aye v City of Hialeah,* 113 S. Ct. 2217 (1993).

7. There are, of course, other approaches to church–state issues. One historically important approach is the tolerant establishment, in which a religion is granted official approval and benefits, but dissenters are accorded full civil rights and freedom to exercise their faith without hindrance. See Michael W. McConnell, "Establishment and Toleration in Edmund Burke's 'Constitution of Freedom,'" *Supreme Court Review* (1995): 393. If applied by analogy to the gay rights controversy, this approach would accord official approval in school curriculum and other public pronouncements to traditional morality, but homosexuals would be protected in their civil rights and not persecuted or punished for their private acts. This would resemble the position described by Andrew Sullivan as "conservative." See Sullivan, *Virtually Normal,* pp. 94–132.

8. See *Rosenberger v Rector,* 115 S. Ct. 2523 ("the University has taken pains to disassociate itself from the private [religious] speech involved in this case"); *Capitol Square Review & Advisory Bd. v Pinette,* 115 S. Ct. 2440, 2452–54 (1995) (O'Connor, J., concurring).

9. James Madison, "Memorial and Remonstrance Against Religious Assessments," ¶ 1 (1785).

10. George Washington, Farewell Address (1796).

11. Alexis de Tocqueville, *Democracy in America,* ed. J. P. Mayer (Garden City, NY: Anchor Books 1969), p. 295.

12. Thomas Jefferson, *Notes on the State of Virginia,* (1787), ed. William Peden (Chapel Hill: University of North Carolina, 1955), p. 159.

13. This was true even before *Employment Division v Smith,* 494 US 872 (1990), which eliminated all free exercise protection from formally neutral laws.

14. See Gabriel Rotello, "Creating a New Gay Culture: Balancing Fidelity and Freedom," *The Nation,* 21 April 1997, p. 11. Andrew Sullivan falls into this camp.

15. See, e.g., Stephen Gey, "Why Is Religion Special? Reconsidering the Accommodation of Religion under the Religion Clauses of the First Amendment," *University of*

Pittsburgh Law Review 52 (1990): 75, 79; Suzanna Sherry, "Enlightening the Religion Clauses," *Journal of Contemporary Legal Issues* 7 (1996): 473, 477–78.

16. Thomas Jefferson to Dr. Benjamin Waterhouse, 22 June 1822, *The Works of Thomas Jefferson*, ed. P. Ford (New York: G.P. Putnam's Sons, 1905), 12: 241, 243; Thomas Jefferson to James Smith, 3 December 1822, *The Life and Selected Writings of Thomas Jefferson*, eds. A. Koch & W. Peden (New York: Modern Library, 1944), p. 703.

17. See Arthur Hertzberg, *The French Enlightenment and the Jews* (New York: Columbia University Press, 1968).

18. Rotello, "Creating a New Gay Culture," pp. 14, 16.

19. *Bowers v Hardwick*, 478 US 186 (1986).

20. *Reynolds v United States*, 98 US 145, 166 (1879).

21. Sullivan, *Virtually Normal*, p. 171.

22. See Gary D. Comstock, *Violence Against Lesbians and Gay Men* (New York: Columbia University Press, 1991); for more recent evidence, see Sue Anne Pressley, "Gays Fear Texas Slaying Reflects Trend," *Washington Post*, 31 January 1996, sec. A, p. 1. It is possible these statistics have been exaggerated, but the principle does not depend on the size of the phenomenon.

23. Sullivan, *Virtually Normal*, p. 173.

24. *Goldman v Weinberger*, 475 US 503 (1986).

25. The regulation provided that "[h]eadgear will not be worn . . . [w]hile indoors except by armed security police in the performance of their duties." AFR 35–10, ¶1–6.h(2)(f) (1980). There was a narrow exception for headgear worn during religious services.

26. Many Jewish men do not interpret their religious obligations as requiring the wearing of yarmulkes. The discussion in text applies only to those who do.

27. *Goldman v Weinberger*, 475 US 507–10 (1986).

28. Many of the details of the "don't ask, don't tell" regulations strike me as irrational and even as counterproductive. I take no position on whether any specific detail is defensible. For purposes of this essay, I am addressing only the general notion that homosexuals should be allowed to serve in the military without inquiry into their private affairs, so long as their sexual preferences remain discreet.

29. As Assistant to the Solicitor General, I was principal author of the government's Brief in Opposition to the Petition for Certiorari in *Goldman*, which urged that the Court not accept the case for review. That brief relied, in large part, on the fact that Congress and the executive were engaged in a systematic review of uniform regulations and their impact on religious practice. After the Supreme Court granted certiorari, I did not choose to work on the merits brief defending the regulation.

30. 10 US Cong. §774.

31. *Goldman v Weinberger*, 475 US 519–20 (1986).

32. Nor is the alternative device, equal access, of much significance in this context, since there are no areas of personal freedom on which religious exercise can base a claim of equal treatment.

33. Sullivan, *Virtually Normal*, p. 171.

34. *Capitol Square Review & Advisory Bd. v Pinette*, 115 S. Ct. 2440 (1995).

35. The group seeking to erect the cross was the Ku Klux Klan, but the Court treated the display as if it were an ordinary religious display.

36. *Lynch v Donnelly*, 465 US 668 (1984).

37. See O. L. Davis, Jr. et al., *Looking at History: A Review of Major U.S. History Textbooks* (Washington, DC: People for the American Way, 1987), pp. 3–4, 11;

Charles C. Haynes, *A Teacher's Guide: Religious Freedom in America* (Silver Springs, MD: Americans United Research Foundation, 1986), p. 6; Paul C. Vitz, *Religion and Traditional Values in Public School Textbooks: An Empirical Study* (Washington, DC: National Institute of Education, 1985), pp. 3–7; "Educators Urge Turn to Studies About Religion," *New York Times*, 2 July 1987, sec. A, p. 16 (report of the Association for Supervision and Curriculum Development).

38. Sullivan, *Virtually Normal*, p. 172.

39. This is taken from the heading of a section of *Children of the Rainbow—First Grade*, quoted in Midge Decter, "Homosexuality and the Schools," *Commentary* (March 1993): 19.

40. Quoted in ibid., p. 25.

41. Sexual Minority Youth Assistance League, *What Does It Mean If I Am Attracted To Another Man?* (Washington, DC: Sexual Minority Youth Assistance League, n.d.).

42. *Brown v Hot, Sexy and Safer Productions, Inc.*, 68 F3d 525, 529 (1st Cir 1995).

43. 20 US Cong. § 4071.

44. Edwin Firmage, "Address to the Utah State Coalition for Human Rights" (Salt Lake City, 2 March 1996, unpublished document obtained from author).

45. Ruti Teitel, "When Separate Is Equal: Why Organized Religious Exercises, Unlike Chess, Do Not Belong in the Public Schools," *Northwestern University Law Review* 81 (1986): 175.

46. See briefs for the American Civil Liberties Union and the American Jewish Congress, as *amici curiae*, in *Garnett v Renton School District*, 987 F2d 641 (9th Cir), cert. denied, 114 S. Ct. 72 (1993).

47. Sullivan, *Virtually Normal*, pp. 178–79.

48. *Reynolds v United States*, 98 US 145 (1879).

49. This assumes that antisodomy laws are either unconstitutional or unenforced.

50. It is true that heterosexual couples can marry even if they do not intend to have children or are biologically incapable of doing so. Exclusion of these couples from marriage would not be practical without great invasion of privacy, and in many instances (especially among older persons) the couples perform the role of parents and grandparents in a substitutionary fashion.

51. Sullivan, *Virtually Normal*, p. 179.

52. See David Boaz, "Privatize Marriage: A Simple Solution to the Gay-Marriage Debate," *Slate*, 24 April 1997, p. 16.

53. Most rights-based arguments for same-sex marriage are not based on the rights of homosexuals at all, but on the claim that the denial of same-sex marriage is a form of gender discrimination, just as antimiscegenation laws are form of racial discrimination. See *Baehr v Levin*, 852 P2d 44 (Haw. 1993). The problem with the argument is that gender discrimination has to do with laws that treat one sex as inferior to the other. The rationale for forbidding a man to marry a man is not that men are inferior to women, or vice versa, but that the resulting relationship does not fulfill the social function of a marriage. It has nothing to do with whether the two sexes are equal.

54. William Eskridge, *The Case for Same-Sex Marriage* (New York: Free Press, 1996), p. 17.

55. Thomas E. Schmidt, *Straight & Narrow: Compassion and Clarity in the Homosexuality Debate* (Downers Grove, IL: Inter-Varsity, 1995), p. 127.

56. Sullivan, *Virtually Normal*, p. 183.

57. Andrew Koppelman, *Antidiscrimination Law and Social Equality* (New Haven:

Yale University Press, 1996), pp. 173–74 n. 97: 29 percent of gay men form stable relationships; David P. McWhirter and Andrew M. Mattison, *The Male Couple* (Englewood Cliffs, NJ: Prentice-Hall, 1984), pp. 252–59: only 7 out of 172 male couples in the sample had monogamous sexual relationships.

58. Rotello, "Creating a New Gay Culture," p. 12.

59. Ibid., p. 14.

60. Sullivan, *Virtually Normal,* p. 161.

61. Ibid.

62. Peter Baker, "Clinton to Push to Outlaw Anti-Gay Bias," *Washington Post,* 25 April 1997, sec. A, p. 21.

63. *Estate of Thornton v Caldor, Inc.,* 472 US 703, 712 (1985) (O'Connor, J., concurring).

64. For citations to polling data, see Roderick M. Hills, Jr., "You Say You Want A Revolution? The Case Against The Transformation Of Culture Through Antidiscrimination Laws," *Michigan Law Review* 95 (1997): 1701, 1736–37 nn. 70–71.

65. For an elegant statement of this position, see Hills, "You Say You Want A Revolution?" pp. 1728–40.

66. Koppelman, *Antidiscrimination Law and Social Equality,* p. 5.

67. Hills, "You Say You Want A Revolution?" p. 1728.

68. See *Wallace v Jaffree,* 472 US 71, 75–76 (1985) (O'Connor, J., concurring).

69. See "Developments in the Law—Employment Discrimination," *Harvard Law Review* 109 (1996): 1568, 1628–29.

70. Sullivan, *Virtually Normal,* p. 157.

Sexual orientation & human
rights in American religious
discourse